Strategies for Teaching Students with Mild to Severe Mental Retardation

Edited by Robert A. Gable
Old Dominion University
and Steven F. Warren
George Peabody College of Vanderbilt University

Jessica Kingsley Publishers
London and Philadelphia

First published in the United Kingdom as *Advances in Mental Retardation and Developmental Disabilities Vol 5* in 1993

First published in paperback in the United Kingdom in 1993 by
Jessica Kingsley Publishers Ltd
116 Pentonville Road
London N1 9JB

Copyright © 1993 Jessica Kingsley Publishers Ltd

British Library Cataloguing in Publication Data

Strategies for Teaching Students with
Mild to Severe Mental Retardation. - New
ed
  I. Gable, Robert A.
  II. Warren, Steven, F.
  371.92

ISBN 1 85302 174 1

Printed and Bound in Great Britain by
Cromwell Press Ltd., Melksham, Wiltshire

Strategies for Teaching Students
with Mild to Severe Mental Retardation

DEDICATION

This book is dedicated to the memory of Tom Haring. Tom made major contributions to our knowledge of how to teach social and communication skills and, perhaps most importantly, how to nurture meaningful friendships between children and adolescents with disabilities and their peers. His tragic death has deprived us of countless other contributions that were sure to come. Tom's blend of keen intellect, scientific rigor, and deeply held values remain a model for all of us. His courage, warm smile, and ever-present sense of humour live on in our memories.

January 18, 1993

CONTENTS

SECTION II
STRATEGIES FOR TEACHING STUDENTS WITH MORE
SEVERE LEVELS OF MENTAL RETARDATION

LIST OF CONTRIBUTORS

Rose M. Allinder

Special Education
and Communication Disorders
University of Nebraska
Lincoln NE

Donald M. Baer

Human Development
and Family Life
University of Kansas
Lawrence KS

Linda M. Bambara

College of Education
Lehigh University
Bethlehem PA

Janis Chadsey-Rusch

Department of Special Education
University of Illinois
Champaign IL

Lana Collet-Klingenberg

Department of Special Education
University of Illinois
Champaign IL

Alan R. Frank

Division of Curriculum
and Instruction
University of Iowa
Iowa City IA

Lynn S. Fuchs

Department of Special Education
George Peabody College
of Vanderbilt University
Nashville TN

Robert A. Gable

Department of Child Study
and Special Education
Old Dominion University
Norfolk VA

James W. Halle

Department of Special Education
University of Illinois
Champaign IL

Thomas G. Haring

Graduate School of Education
University of California
Santa Barbara CA

Jo M. Hendrickson

Division of Curriculum
and Instruction
University of Iowa
Iowa City IA

Lori Korinek

Department of Special Education
College of William and Mary
Williamsburg VA

John Wills Lloyd

Curry School of Education
University of Virginia
Charlottesville VA

Margo A. Mastropieri

Department of Educational Studies
Purdue University
West Lafayette IN

Edward A. Polloway

School of Education
and Human Development
Lynchburg College
Lynchburg VA

Joe Reichle

Department of Educational
Psychology
University of Minnesota
Minneapolis MN

Thomas E. Scruggs

Department of Educational Studies
Purdue University
West Lafayette IN

Jeff Sigafoos

Department of Educational
Psychology
University of Minnesota
Minneapolis MN

Elizabeth Talbott

Curry School of Education
University of Virginia
Charlottesville VA

Melody Tankersley

Curry School of Education
University of Virginia
Charlottesville VA

Stanley C. Trent

Curry School of Education
University of Virginia
Charlottesville VA

Steven F. Warren

Department of Special Education
George Peabody College
of Vanderbilt University
Nashville TN

THE ENDURING VALUE OF INSTRUCTIONAL RESEARCH

Robert A. Gable and Steven F. Warren

The field of special education has evolved in extraordinary ways over the past three decades due to the dedicated efforts of thousands of persons. Together, these efforts have led to significant advances in societal attitudes, laws, regulations, educational practices, services, and opportunities in many countries. Instructional practices have evolved too, although the changes have perhaps been less dramatic than the settings and contexts in which they have come to be utilized (e.g., regular classrooms, competitive employment situations, homes, restaurants, leisure activities, early intervention programs).

Despite these changes, the potential effectiveness of special education efforts obviously remain dependent on the development and dissemination of highly effective instructional practices. It is evident that the most enlightened social and educational policy is no substitute for effective instructional methods and procedures. It is the purpose of this book to revisit the enduring topic of effective instruction for students with mild to severe mental retardation.

The critical need for an increased amount of high quality instructional research relevant to the needs of both typical and atypical students was succinctly put by Slavin:

> The reason education goes from fad to fad rather than making the steady generational progress characteristic of, for example, medicine or agriculture

is that in education practice so often outruns (or ignores) the evidence supporting it. We see a crisis and mandate solutions on a massive scale long before the data are in. (Slavin, 1986, p.170)

The potential role of behavioral science – particularly in the identification and provision of educational curriculum and instruction – has been largely ignored by legislators, administrators, and practitioners. Carnine (1991) contends that this inattention is linked to the absence of even a rudimentary scientific outlook by these individuals. He has argued that educational reform is failing in the United States primarily because the solutions being proposed are based on strongly held beliefs and good intentions, rather than on tested educational methods.

Like Carnine, Meyer (1991) too has noted the distressingly low impact that research has had on instructional (and other) practices. However, in reviewing the gap between research and practice for children and adults with severe disabilities, Meyer places a substantial share of the responsibility squarely in the lap of the research community. She argues that, among other things, many applied researchers tend to be limited by inherent restrictions of the methodologies they choose (e.g., single subject design approaches), by their own definitions of disability, and by their remoteness from the real world for which their interventions and procedures are intended. Like Carnine, Meyer acknowledges that the gap between research and practice is at least partly a reflection of the certain values and constraints emanating from policymakers and practitioners. But the thrust of her argument, and that of others who have examined the discrepancy between research and practice (e.g., Baumeister, 1981; Skrtic, 1986), is that as the relevance and credibility of the research increases, so too will its likely impact.

The research community has often been quite open in identifying the limitations of their efforts, at least among themselves. For example, the limited generalization and maintenance of treatment results often achieved in instructional research within various domains (e.g., language, motor skills instructions, employment skills, social skills, reading, etc.) has been widely critiqued, dissected, and analyzed (e.g., Horn, 1991; Kaiser, Yoder, & Keetz, 1991; Westling & Floyd, 1990). Less attention has been focused on the scarcity of quality research conducted on many instructional problems. For instance, in a recent review of intervention research with individuals with profound multiple disabilities, Reid, Phillips, and Green (1991) discovered only 39 published articles over a 40-year time span (an average of less than one per year). Horn (1991), in a review of motor skill intervention research, discovered only 28 studies with appropriate experimental controls published over a 20-year period. Perhaps more surprisingly, Mathes and Fuchs (1991) found only 8 'high quality' studies (out of 125 studies initially identified) in the literature on peer tutoring of reading skills, an area with a supposedly rich and extensive research base. Indeed, the research basis in special education remains so limited that we do not yet have sufficient data bases on most issues to conduct meaningful meta-analyses of the results (Sindelar & Wilson, 1984).

There are many explanations for the relatively limited amount of instructional (and other) research conducted to date in both special and general education settings. One compelling reason is that too little funding is provided for such research. The United States spends considerably more on educational research than any other country in the world. However, despite the so-called crisis facing public education in the United States, only $145 million was spent by the U.S. Department of Education on Research and Development activities in 1989. In contrast, Research and Development activities by the National Institutes of Health accounted for $7.1 billion, and accounted for $4.2 billion by the National Aeronautics and Space Administration. Altogether, the U. S. government spent $62 billion on Research and Development activities in 1989. Only two-tenths of one percent of this amount went to education and one-tenth of one percent went to special education. Fuchs and Fuchs (1990) summed up the impact of this nonexistent funding base combined with other hindrances on special education research as follows:

> It is the difficulty of doing school-based research, together with inadequate funding and traditional notions of what educational research should and should not be, that keeps many talented researchers from getting involved with practitioners to make schools more effective. As a result, there are small, and sometimes nonexistent, databases associated with many pressing practical problems. This, in turn, often prevents researchers from offering tried-and-true solutions, thereby proving themselves as worthy to teachers as medical researchers are perceived by their physician colleagues. (Fuchs and Fuchs, 1991, pp.105–106)

To summarize just a few of the basic problems that beset the instructional research enterprise in special (and general) education at this point: (1) Its results and efforts are unappreciated or ignored by administrators, teachers, legislators and the public at large; (2) In most cases it has yet to achieve results of sufficient magnitude, credibility, and validity to convince even some critics within the field of its value; and finally, (3) Little high quality research has actually been conducted and only a small amount of resources have been expended on it. In short, governments don't fund it, the public doesn't pay attention to it, and much of what does exist isn't very good anyway! The obvious question becomes – So now what?

It is our opinion that, despite the disheartening view that we have presented, all is not lost; far from it. It is clear that over the long haul significantly more money needs to be invested in educational research, that the quality, sophistication and relevance of the research itself must improve, and that those responsible for the curriculum and instructional methods used in our schools need to start paying attention to the knowledge being generated by the research community. In the meantime, we contend that important progress is being made on a variety of instructional problems by many dedicated, creative, resourceful applied researchers who are steadily developing and refining reasonable instructional methods and approaches targeted at some of the most intractable problems imaginable. We offer the contents of this book as evidence of this assertion. Within its pages the reader will find compelling examples of just the type of sophisticated research that will lead to increasingly effective practice in the field.

In recruiting authors and organizing this volume, our goal was to select a representative sample of what essentially are evolving 'best practices' of the field in each selected area represented. In every case, the authors have approached the topic under consideration from both an empirical research perspective, and a practical, field-oriented viewpoint. Thus, the reader will find a substantial amount of instructional research discussed, but will also find that an effort has been made to couch this work in the real world contexts in which persons with disabilities must learn and prosper.

PLAN FOR THE BOOK

The book is divided into two parts, each with four 'content' chapters followed by a commentary presented by a leading researcher (or researchers). Part I addresses strategies for teaching students with mild disabilities and Part II addresses strategies and issues related to students with more severe levels of mental retardation.

Part I begins with a chapter by Hendrickson and Frank (Chapter 2), in which they underscore the importance of student engagement in academic success. They provide a wealth of information on small group and tutorial instruction, detailing strategies that have been shown to positively influence the outcome of instruction. A series of guidelines for instituting many of the practices is included.

In Chapter 3, Fuchs and Allinder explore the tremendous surge in computer applications in special and remedial education. They discuss the burgeoning use of that technology as either a direct or an indirect teaching tool for carrying out daily instruction. Drawing from their own research and that of their colleagues, Fuchs and Allinder provide various examples of ways to conduct computer-assisted and computer-managed instruction.

The subject of social skills is addressed by Korinek and Polloway. In Chapter 4, they analyze the accumulated research on social skills training, discuss popular curricular programs, and describe ways to facilitate the acquisition of prosocial skills. Also, they provide important coverage of the thorny issue of maintenance and generalization of social skills of students with mild disabilities.

In Chapter 5, Lloyd, Talbott, Tankersley, and Trent discuss the use of cognitive-behavioral techniques to improve classroom performance of students with mild retardation. Lloyd and his colleagues discuss procedures that have been applied successfully – singly and in combination – to student self-regulation of classroom behavior. Student performance that relates to academics as well as the critical subjects of arithmetic, reading, and writing are covered.

In the final chapter of this part, Scruggs and Mastropieri summarize, comment on the content and lend their own perspective to best practices for teaching students with mild mental retardation. Their commentary is especially useful because it incorporates discussion of their own research in the area of academic instruction of students with mild disabilities.

Part II begins with a review by Haring of the research basis of instructional procedures used to promote social interaction and integration of students with severe disabilities. Haring notes at the outset of his paper that understanding and shaping social interaction ought to be fundamental to education, but unfortunately isn't. His chapter then goes on to cover current issues and research in the areas of assessing social interaction skills, development of targets for intervention, and evaluation of programs that seek to influence social interactions and friendship relationships. He notes, in conclusion, that interventions that act directly to increase the participation of individuals with severe disabilities in cohesive social networks (vs. isolated, one-shot social exchanges) are both most critical and most lacking at present.

In Chapter 8, Bambara and Warren revisit an 'old' technology, the use of massed teaching trials in instruction. They note that massed trial instruction has received something of a bad rap in some quarters in recent years as attention has turned toward more 'naturalistic', embedded' and distributed trial teaching approaches. However, Bambara and Warren caution against 'throwing the baby out with the bathwater'. They review a number of appropriate applications of massed trial training. They also offer recommendations for how to avoid certain troublesome pitfalls long associated with this type of instruction.

Effective communication is of critical importance to the development of all children, but particularly those with severe disabilities. Without an effective communication system, they risk spending their entire lives in highly dependent and often highly segregated contexts. Thus, the final two chapters of Section II are devoted to methods of enhancing communication skills development. In Chapter 9, Sigafoos and Reichle focus on a particularly difficult problem for many individuals with severe disabilities – spontaneously communicating their needs and wants. They provide a comprehensive review of what is currently known about teaching spontaneous communication repertoires to these individuals from a stimulus-control learning perspective.

Halle, Chadsey-Rusch and Collet-Klingenberg take a different approach to communication instruction in Chapter 10. Like Sigafoos and Reichle, they draw heavily from the behaviorally-based, stimulus-control learning literature in their approach to communication instruction with children who have severe levels of mental retardation. However, the bulk of their chapter elaborates on two relatively new and promising general approaches that can be used in combination or independently to teach generalized communication. These are general-case instruction and interactive routines.

In the final chapter in this volume, Baer offers a lucid commentary on the four chapters in Part II. In a variety of insightful ways, and with his trademark logic and wit, he ties the research presented by these authors directly to a set of policy and procedural issues effecting the education and lives of children with severe disabilities.

CONCLUSION

There is an enduring value and quality to good instructional research. It provides the basis, the building blocks, for the field to bootstrap its way to ever increasing effectiveness. High quality research leads to further research, and to further refinements until a method or procedure is both maximally efficacious and appropriate for use in the 'real world'. In time this should lead to changes in practice that are based on an empirical science rather than simply the best guesses of commercially oriented curriculum developers. Ultimately, systematic, meaningful, problem-oriented research can become the force that drives educational reform, not merely an irrelevant afterthought. Indeed, Keogh has noted:

> It is clear that major changes are needed in the delivery of services to problem learners, and that these services need to be the responsibility of regular as well as special educators. It is also clear that teachers are the central players in bringing about change in practice. It follows, then, that our greatest and most pressing challenge in the reform effort is to determine how to improve the quality of instruction at the classroom level. This is a formidable challenge that requires both creativity and hard work. It also forces us to examine the realities of linking policy and practice (Keogh, 1990, p.190).

In succeeding chapters, the latest instructional research is encapsulated by well respected researchers, teacher educators, and practioners. Together, their work offers the reader strategies that have direct application in the classroom and beyond. For this reason, we believe the contents of this book represent one response to the challenge Keogh has put before us.

REFERENCES

Baumeister, A. A. (1981). Mental retardation policy and research: The unfulfilled promise. *American Journal of Mental Deficiency, 85*, 445–456.

Carnine, D. (1991). *Reforming educational leaders: The role of science.* Unpublished manuscript. University of Oregon, Eugene, OR.

Fuchs, D., & Fuchs, L. (1990). Making educational research more important. *Exceptional Children, 57*, 102–107.

Horn, E. M. (1991). Basic motor skills instruction for children with neuromotor delays: A critical review. *The Journal of Special Education, 25*, 168–197.

Kaiser, A., Yoder, P., & Keetz, A. (1992). Evaluating milieu teaching. In S. Warren & J. Reichle (Eds.), *Causes and effects in communication and language intervention.* (pp.9–47) Baltimore, MD: Paul H. Brookes Publishing Co.

Keogh, B. K. (1990). Narrowing the gap between policy and practice. *Exceptional Children, 57*, 186–190.

Mathes, P. G., & Fuchs, L. (1991). *Peer-mediated reading instruction in special education: A critical review.* Unpublished manuscript. Vanderbilt University, Nashville, TN.

Meyer, L. H. (1991). Advocacy, research, and typical practices. In L. H. Meyer, C. A. Peck & L. Brown (Eds.), *Critical issues in the lives of people with severe disabilities* (pp.629–649). Baltimore, MD: Paul H. Brookes Publishing Co.

Reid, D. H., Phillips, J. F., & Green, C. W. (1991). Teaching persons with profound multiple handicaps: A review of the effects of behavioral research. *Journal of Applied Behavior Analysis, 24*, 319–336.

Sindelar, P. T., & Wilson, R. J. (1984). The potential effects of meta-analysis on special education practice. *The Journal of Special Education, 18*, 81–92.

Skrtic, T. M. (1986). The crisis in special education knowledge: A perspective on perspective. *Focus on Exceptional Children, 18* (7), 1–16.

Slavin, R. E. (1986). The Napa evaluation of Madeline Hunter's ITIP: Lessons learned. *The Elementary School Journal, 87* (2), 165–171.

Westling, D. L., & Floyd, J. (1990). Generalization of community skills: How much training is necessary? *The Journal of Special Education, 23*, 386–406.

PART I

STRATEGIES FOR TEACHING
STUDENTS WITH MILD DISABILITIES

ENGAGEMENT AND PERFORMANCE FEEDBACK:
ENHANCING THE CLASSROOM ACHIEVEMENT OF STUDENTS WITH MILD MENTAL DISABILITIES

Jo M. Hendrickson and Alan R. Frank

INTRODUCTION

The decade of the 1990s will witness, in classrooms serving students with mild mental retardation, the implementation of a group of instructional methods often referred to as *effective teaching practices* or *direct instruction*, if we heed the literature published in this area over the past 15 years. This research base, comprised largely of studies conducted in regular education classrooms, has produced several consistent findings concerning the relation between teacher behavior and student achievement. Support in the special education literature for the effectiveness of these teaching practices with students labelled mildly mentally retarded (e.g., Delquadri, Greenwood, Whorton, Carta, & Hall, 1986; Englert, 1983, 1984; Sindelar, Espin, Smith, & Harriman, 1990) is growing. The purpose of this chapter is to describe ways special education teachers may implement these effective teaching practices in two areas: (a) teacher-directed group instruction and (b) small group and independent work; and to describe how formative evaluation can be used to measure the effectiveness of instruction in these contexts.

One of the consistent research findings concerning instructional organization in general is that classroom teachers who maintain a high level of content coverage produce greater academic gains than teachers who do not (Brophy, 1979; Carnine, 1981). Teachers obtain greater student achievement when they provide practice activities that produce student responding of 80 per cent or higher accuracy (Brophy & Evertson, 1977; Rosenshine, 1983; Stevens & Rosenshine, 1981). The immediacy of teacher feedback during practice activities is also very important (Brophy & Evertson, 1977; Rosenshine, 1980; Stallings & Kaskowitz, 1974), with rapid feedback accelerating learning. When correct student responses are obtained, teachers should reinforce students for their answers. If an error occurs, teachers should indicate the nature of the error and provide time for students to practice the correct/appropriate response. Teachers need to be adept at providing cues and/or prompts to facilitate learning of students who have responded incorrectly; indeed, partial cuing may be preferable to supplying the correct answer or calling on other students (Stevens & Rosenshine, 1981).

Research in regular classroom settings also has determined that effective teachers conduct individual lessons with notable differences from lessons taught by less effective teachers. At the beginning of a lesson, effective teachers communicate rules and expectations regarding behavior (Anderson, Evertson, & Emmer, 1980; Brophy, 1983). They focus attention on the concept to be learned by expressing the objective of the lesson or by linking the lesson to previous lessons or experiences (Berliner & Rosenshine, 1976; Brophy, 1983; Duffy, 1983). Closely associated with this procedure is the use of advance organizers – visual and/or oral cues that assist students in proceeding with a task while keeping a definite purpose in mind (Darch & Gersten, 1986).

After setting the stage for the lesson, effective teachers model the specific strategies/skills to be learned by the students and provide several varied examples of the concepts being taught. Effective teachers are those who precue or prompt student responses by focusing attention on the relevant features of the strategy or concept in order to maintain high levels of student accuracy in responding (Stevens & Rosenshine, 1981). An example of precueing a student response is, 'Do "pants" and "trousers" mean the same thing – are they synonyms?'In this example, precueing involved presenting the student with a question, then indicating that the nature of the question was related to synonyms.

Effective teachers carefully supervise student practice of the strategy, skill, or concept and require active responding. During the lesson, or series of lessons, effective teachers provide students with the opportunity to overlearn strategies, skills, or concepts through repeated practice of the learned responses (Carnine & Silbert, 1979; Hall, Delquadri, Greenwood, & Thurston, 1982; Stevens & Rosenshine, 1981). In this phase of the lesson, effective teachers provide corrective drill immediately following errors (Carnine & Silbert, 1979). Finally, students are provided with firm-up exercises (e.g., five consecutive correct trials) at the end of the lesson (Carnine & Silbert, 1979). A post organizer, or brief review of the objective and content of the lesson, ties the day's work together.

Two major themes are apparent in the execution of effective teaching practices: (a) *successfully engaged time* (referred to as *academic learning time* by Fisher et al., 1978) and (b) *performance feedback*. *Successfully engaged time* refers to the time students actually participate in instructional activities related to their individual educational needs. *Performance feedback* refers to the quantity, quality, and timing of feedback students receive. Methods that teachers use to inform students of the quality or correctness of their responses during instructional activities can vary significantly, yet still be effective. The remainder of this chapter presents strategies for increasing student engagement and performance feedback during teacher-directed group instruction, small group and independent work.

TEACHER-DIRECTED GROUP INSTRUCTION

Teacher-directed group instruction refers to teaching/learning activities primarily led by the teacher and aimed at meeting a limited number of instructional objectives. Within this section, planning and designing lessons (lesson format), creating an engaging environment, teacher questioning strategies, control of student errors, choral responding, and progress monitoring (formative evaluation) are discussed.

Lesson Format

Carnine, Silbert, and Kameenui (1990) recommend that different lesson formats for teaching be used, depending upon the student's stage of learning (see Smith, 1989, for discussion of stages of learning). Hallmarks of the 'introductory lesson' format that they recommend are the presentation of one new skill or concept and careful teacher guidance as students respond to questions. In an introductory lesson format, the teacher plans to model the new skill (e.g., telling time to the hour) or concept (e.g., the equality rule in mathematics), given that the students are able to imitate. After students have imitated the model(s) provided by the teacher, they are asked to respond in unison with a decreasing amount of antecedent support or teacher guidance (see section on choral responding). It is critical that the teacher does not deviate from the objective and keeps in mind the preskills (i.e., prerequisites) necessary for students to succeed in the introductory lesson. Consider the teacher who tries to teach rote counting from one to ten simultaneously with point counting one to ten objects. Pupils in this situation will be learning to say number names in sequence and to point to objects in a set while counting. These two skills may represent two different objectives, require different prerequisite skills, and need to be taught sequentially, rather than simultaneously (Frank, 1989). An example of an introductory lesson format is presented in Table 1.

Table 1: Introductory Lesson Format
for Teaching Time Telling to the Hour

Teacher	*Student*	
Place the clock in front of students. Point to the hour hand and say, 'The hour hand is pointing to the 5. Now you tell me what number the hour hand is pointing to'.	5	(Group)
Signal for a group response. Repeat the modeling procedure if any incorrect student responses are given.	5	(Group)
Move the hour hand to 8. Point to the hour hand and say 'The hour hand is pointing to the 8. Now tell me what number the hour hand is pointing to'.	8	(Group)
When group responding is firm, call on individual students for a response. 'What number is the hour hand pointing to, Marcy?'.	3	(Individual)

Note: After each correct response the teacher provides a praise statement such as, 'Yes, that's right! Good, the hour hand is pointing to the 3.'

Following the introductory lesson, Carnine et al. (1990) recommend that teachers prepare a 'practice lesson' format. The teacher uses a practice lesson format to plan for students to ultimately respond to questions with little or no teacher guidance. Students also may need to learn to discriminate between situations in which similar skills are used. The latter teaching activity actually may be considered a form of planned generalization training. Two types of discrimination activities generally are presented in the practice lesson format. For example, during the practice lesson, the student may be required to (a) determine whether or not a label matches a sample of a member of a set and (b) label independently different members of the set. Table 2 illustrates a practice lesson containing both types of discrimination activities. For the practice lesson format, the teacher must plan to withdraw antecedent support at a rate that keeps errors to a minimum. She will want to teach those discriminations which are most functional and most supportive of later learning and life applications.

Table 2: Practice Lesson Format for Teaching Time Telling

Matching sample to label Teacher	Students
Tell students you are going to point to a clock face and ask about its numbers. 'Listen (pointing to the 2), is this a 2?' Signal for a response (e.g. lower hand).	'Yes.'
'Listen (pointing to the 7), is this a 2?' Signal for a response.	'No.'
'Listen (pointing to the 12), is this a 12?' Signal for a response.	'Yes.'
'Listen (pointing to the 6), is this a 12?' Signal for a response.	'No.'
Continue in this manner until students have responded correctly in unison and individually on several trials. When errors occur, model the correct response.	
Place a clock in front of the students. Say, 'I will touch a number, and you tell me what its name is. Listen, when I point to this number (3), you say, *3*. When I point to this number (8), you say *8* '.	
'Your turn, what is this number (point to the 4)?'	'4.'
'What is this number (point to the 1)?'	'1.'
Continue until each hour has been practiced several times, first with the group responding and then with individual turns. When errors occur, model the correct response and repeat the question.	

Note: After each correct response, the teacher provides a praise statement such as, 'Yes, that's right! Good, that is 5'.

Creating an Engaging Environment

An important first step in conducting teacher-directed lessons is to form small groups of students who have similar skills (Carnine et al., 1990) and similar learning needs. The physical characteristics of the small group setting are important. Children should be seated in a semi-circle (with their backs to the remainder of the students) facing the teacher who is positioned to see past the small group in order to monitor the rest of the class (Carnine et al., 1990). Students who have the most difficulty in learning should be seated directly in front of the teacher. In addition students with behavioral or attentional difficulties may benefit by sitting on an end of the semi-circle, in close proximity to the teacher. Teacher explanations or demonstrations should be brief and concise (Silbert, Carnine, & Stein, 1990).

The pace of instruction should be brisk, although not rushed. Rapid pacing requires that the teacher be very familiar with the content of the lesson and this method of presentation. In addition, materials should be organized so that they can be quickly located and distributed.

Asking Questions

Teachers use questions for many purposes. A single question may provide information ranging from the level of a student's attention to identification of a precise reading difficulty. Questions can be employed directly to promote acquisition, mastery, and generalization of academic skills, language and social-affective development, self-help and community living skills as well as (pre)vocational skills. Questioning strategies may function as (a) diagnostic tools, (b) instructional tactics, and (c) feedback mechanisms for students and teachers (Stowitschek, Stowitschek, Hendrickson, & Day, 1984).

In spite of the rich potential of question use by teachers, many of the purposes of questioning are not attained by the classroom teacher because of a number of errors teachers commonly make when questioning students. Research from the direct instruction literature indicates that effective teachers ask more questions to assess student understanding than less effective teachers. Joyce and Weil (1986) cite research which substantiates certain features of effective questioning. They note that questions which check student understanding are those which require specific answers or ask for an explanation of how answers were found. They further point out that effective questions are those which do not digress from the academic objective of the lesson.

Fisher et al. (1980) note that effective teachers initiate the majority of classroom questions, not the students. Asking questions which (a) are within a student's reach a high percentage of the time and (b) are convergent as opposed to divergent in nature is associated with effective direct instruction (Rosenshine, 1983). Finally, as noted previously, effective teachers are better at providing feedback than noneffective teachers. Effective teachers immediately notice and immediately correct student errors. Questioning strategies may be very useful for supplying feedback to students yet do not relieve them of the necessity of answering (see response-dependent questions). The same question can function as praise and stimulate reflection and self-assessment of the student's problem-solving strategy (e.g., 'Wow! How did you figure out that answer?').

Table 3: General Guidelines for Questioning Students

---

1. Have a specific objective in mind for each question asked. Base the next statement or question on whether or not you achieved this objective.

2. Ask one question at a time.

3. State questions as clearly and concisely as possible.

4. Wait for a response. Allow students enough time to formulate their answers. The amount of wait time will depend to some extent on the difficulty and complexity of the question.

5. Praise correct responses. Give feedback (verbal or nonverbal) on all responses, particularly during the acquisition stage of learning.

6. Avoid random questioning.

7. Avoid rephrasing questions as a matter of course. Rephrase questions as part of your plan for promoting generalization or when the student's response indicates the question was confusing or misinterpreted.

8. Avoid repeating questions. Establish attention and then ask the question.

9. Never rely exclusively on questions requiring only a yes or no answer.

10. Do not limit instructional objectives to recall and memory questions if the aim of a lesson is problem-solving and higher-order thinking.

11. Use age appropriate language.

12. Make the objective of the question clear to the student.

13. Keep questions specific, relevant, and directly related to the goal of instruction.

14. Evaluate your questions and their effectiveness in achieving your objective for the student.

There are other common errors teachers make when using questions. For example, often the intended purpose of a given who, what, when, where, how, or why question is never realized because teachers do not wait a sufficient time before asking the second question (Stowitschek et al., 1984). Many teachers supply the answer or call on another student before the first child has an opportunity to respond. In fact, students learn that if they wait long enough the teacher will say the answer or move on to someone else. On the other hand, frequently questions are repeated or reworded so often that it is impossible to determine if the objective of the original question has been met.

Table 3 provides general guidelines for teacher use when questioning students. The remainder of this section presents three specific questioning strategies which teachers may employ for a variety of purposes.

The basic question-answer sequence. The simplest and most frequently used question-answer sequence can be described temporally and structurally as a teacher-student-teacher interaction in which the teacher question (antecedent event) is followed by a correct student response (answer), and terminates with an appropriate teacher consequence behavior (feedback). The majority of all basic questioning sequences begin with a wh-question. The function of most wh-questions during a direct instruction lesson is different from its function outside of the classroom. For example, when an effective teacher asks, 'What time is it?' the question is likely to be related to a specific objective (e.g., The student will state orally the correct time in hours and minutes 9 out of 10 times when asked to do so during the school day for 5 consecutive days). When mom or dad ask, 'What time is it?' they may be prompting the child to hurry, inquiring about the time, or using the question for another function.

When a student responds incorrectly in the basic question-answer sequence, the teacher must (a) interpret the error diagnostically and (b) determine the type of feedback to provide based on the error analysis. An appropriate form of teacher feedback for an incorrect response might range from simply restating the question verbatim to providing a model of the entire question-answer sequence and prompting the student to respond correctly upon a second presentation of the stimulus question.

Lead questions. Teachers should select questions that challenge students (e.g., in difficulty or in the rapidity with which they are expected to respond). To increase the probability that the student will respond correctly/appropriately in a given situation, teachers can set the stage for a specific question by employing lead questions. Lead questions have two primary functions – to focus the student's attention on the topic or experience to be discussed and/or to introduce new knowledge and concepts. Thus, if a teacher wants to increase the likelihood that the question, 'What time is it?' will be answered correctly, she might prepare the student by asking lead questions such as 'What numeral is the big hand pointing to?' In introducing a new concept related to time (e.g., seconds) the teacher might ask the following lead questions; 'How many hands are on the clock?' 'What does the big hand tell us?' 'What does the middle-sized hand tell us?'

Student answers to the basic question-answer sequence and lead questions may be verbal, nonverbal, or both. If lead questions do not produce the desired response, the teacher may formulate other questions to cue/prompt the student or to restrict the response alternatives available to the student.

Response-dependent questions. Response-dependent questions are question types which have been sequenced to gain a certain kind of response from the student. A variety of question types usually are arranged in order beginning with those that request a complete answer with little or no prompting to questions which provide considerable support and perhaps target only one aspect of the original question (Stowitschek et al., 1984). That is, in response to errors by the student, the teacher asks a series of questions each of which contains more cues and further restricts the possible answers a student might give (Hendrickson & Stowitschek, 1980). If the student answers question 1 incorrectly, the teacher presents question 2. If question 2 is answered incorrectly, the teacher asks question 3. Ultimately, the final question also includes the expected answer. By employing a response-dependent questioning sequence, the teacher can ascertain the level of support a given student requires to answer correctly. Progress can be measured in terms of movement from highly supportive questions to questions which provide few or no cues.

To illustrate a response-dependent questioning sequence, consider the following series of questions: an open question (OQ), a multiple choice question (MC), a restricted alternative question (RA), a yes or no question (YN) and a complete model question (CM). Assume that each question is answered incorrectly or that no response was given within 5 seconds.

OC: What did Mr. Way do on Monday?

MC: Did Mr. Way go to work, steal the car, or rob the bank?

RA: Mr. Way did *not* go to work or steal the car. What did Mr. Way do?

YN: Did Mr. Way rob the bank?

CM: Mr. Way robbed the bank. Now you tell me, what did Mr. Way do?

In many situations, the teacher may wish to employ only two or three questions in her sequence. During group instruction, teachers can modify their question types to match student characteristics and achievement level. For example, a low performing student initially may be asked the above question within a yes-no format while a higher achieving student would be asked to respond to the open question. Response-dependent question sequences may be applied progressing from no support to full support or in the opposite direction.

Until recently, teacher questions have been assessed in terms of the kinds of questions asked (e.g., higher- or lower-order questions) rather than in terms of the function of those questions in helping students master educational objectives. Ultimately, the type of question a teacher asks may not be nearly so critical as the manner in which the teacher applies the question. Stowitschek and his colleagues (1984) cite research which indicates that response-dependent questioning improves the performance of both handicapped and gifted learners and that such sequences have value as diagnostic tools in pinpointing student errors in a precise manner. Over two decades ago, Gall (1970) concluded that instead of trying to teach by using several categories of questions, the teacher should (a) define the educational objective and (b) delineate questions and questioning sequences to meet the objective. This advice appears to be timely and applicable to today's classrooms for students with mild mental disabilities.

Controlling Rate of Errors

Wolery, Bailey, and Sugai (1988) have provided four reasons why teachers should strive to keep student response errors to a minimum. First, students learn more when errorless learning procedures are used. Second, these procedures also tend to promote positive social interactions between students and teachers since students respond correctly most of the time and consequently receive more teacher reinforcement. Third, research suggests that errorless learning procedures are associated with fewer disruptive and aggressive behaviors in students. Finally, research indicates that students, in fact, learn little by making errors.

Teachers may use a number of methods to control error rate when working with students and using a direct instruction approach. Time delay or wait time procedures can be employed to create a nearly errorless learning environment in which control of student responding is transferred from a teacher's prompts to naturally occurring stimuli (Lee, O'Shea, & Dykes, 1987; Schuster & Griffen, 1990). The teacher guides students through a task or chain of skills by first asking a question (or giving a direction), then immediately supplying the student with the correct response and requiring the student to repeat the modelled answer. After several trials of this type in which 0 seconds separate the question and response, the teacher begins to wait longer (e.g., 1–5 seconds) after asking a question (or giving a direction) before supplying the correct response. The time delay is increased gradually up to 5 or more seconds. For example, teaching a student to correctly label objects as red in response to the question, 'What color is this?' could be accomplished with a time delay procedure. During a direct instruction lesson, the teacher asks the question, 'What color is this (pointing to an object on the table)?' and immediately provides the correct response 'red.' After several trials of this type with 0 seconds of wait time, the teacher begins waiting 1 second after asking the question to give the student an opportunity to respond before the model is provided. After 1 second, the correct answer is given if no response has been made by the student. After several correct responses by the student, the teacher increases the wait time to 2 seconds and so on.

Time delay procedures also can be used in conjunction with teaching students to perform skill chains. To illustrate the use of increased wait time in teaching students skill chains, consider the task of making popcorn. The first step in the teaching procedure is to complete a task analysis of making popcorn. Such a task analysis might result in the sequence of steps shown in Table 4.

In the beginning stage of teaching, the teacher tells the student he is going to make popcorn, then says the first step, 'Get the electric popper from the

Table 4: Task Analysis for Making Popcorn

Step 1.   Get electric popper from cupboard.

Step 2.   Get popcorn and oil from cupboard.

Step 3.   Measure popcorn and put it into popper.

Step 4.   Measure oil and put it into popper.

Step 5.   Put lid on popper.

Step 6.   Plug popper into wall outlet.

Step 7.   When popping is finished, unplug popper.

Step 8.   Put popcorn into a bowl.

---

cupboard.' Immediately after giving this direction (0 second time delay), the teacher gets the popper from the cupboard. All eight steps are modelled in this manner. After a few trials involving a 0 second wait time, the teacher begins delaying the prompting procedure by 1, 2, and more seconds.

Students may vary in terms of the prompt they need in order to respond correctly, with the range of prompts including verbal prompts, gestural prompts, full or partial models, partial physical assists, and full physical guidance. The teacher can begin by using the least intrusive prompt, a verbal direction, to obtain a correct response from the student after the time delay. In this example, the prompt following the command, 'Get the electric popper from the cupboard' might be, '(student's name), get the popper'. If this does not result in a correct response, the teacher may move to a more supportive prompt (e.g., a gesture or model). In this example, the prompt following the command, 'Get the electric popper from the cupboard' might be '(student's name), watch me (the teacher models getting the popper)'. If necessary, the teacher may need to use a partial or full physical prompt to guide the student through the response. For example, following the command, 'Get the electric popper from the cupboard', the teacher might take the student's arm and escort him to the cupboard, guide his hand to the door, then guide his hand to the popper. During subsequent training sessions, the teacher uses the most supportive prompt necessary in order to obtain a correct response. (See *Evaluating Student Progress* in this section for a method of charting student progress.)

Choral Responding

Opportunities for individual students within an instructional group to respond can be increased significantly per unit of time if choral responding (CR) is used, a process which produces greater learning gains than calling upon students individually (Sindelar, Bursuck, & Halle, 1986). CR not only provides students with more opportunities to respond, but, when carried out properly, commands the attention of each member of the group.

According to Heward, Courson, and Narayan (1989), CR is best used in instructional activities that meet the following criteria: (a) responses required are brief, (b) only one correct response is possible, (c) instruction is presented at a lively pace with very little time between each question and response, and (d) a maximum of 5 to 10 minutes is allotted per session. An example of a situation in which the use of CR is appropriate would be one in which students are learning sound/symbol correspondences; each response is short and for most letters only one response is acceptable. Thus, if the teacher individually

Table 5: Instructional Activities Suitable for Choral Responding

---

Math

      Rote counting (e.g., from 1–10)
      Skip counting by multiples such as fives and tens
      Saying months of the year in sequential order

Reading/Language Arts

      Reading sight words on flash cards
      Reading short sentences
      Naming punctuation at end of sentences

Social Studies

      Naming towns, cities, roads, rivers, and other locations on a map
      Saying dates to match historical events or important community
        events
      Naming persons to match accomplishments

Science

      Identifying household products with dangerous chemicals
      Naming planets in the solar system
      Reading technical terms

Prevocational Skills

      Reading phrases from a job application
      Saying complete words abbreviated in *Help Wanted* advertis-
        ments
      Reading warning and safety signs

Health/Life Management Skills

      Identifying healthy and unhealthy foods
      Naming the steps in a personal hygiene task
      Identifying safe and unsafe games/play activities

---

presented letters on a chart, the group of students would make the sound of each letter as the teacher pointed to the letter. Additional examples of instructional activities that meet the criteria for using CR are presented in Table 5.

Heward et al. (1989) recommend that the following procedures be used in implementing CR during small group instruction. First, students need to understand the kind of response they will be required to make. Therefore, each session is begun with an explanation and a demonstration of the correct response. To continue with the example of sound/letter correspondences, the teacher would begin by explaining to the students that they will practice saying the sound of each letter on the chart. She would give this direction, 'Listen, when I point to the letter "*m*," you say "*mmmmmm*" and keep saying it until I remove my finger'.

Use of gestural or verbal signals which prompt student responses facilitates choral responding. Teachers may say a word such as '*class*' or use a physical sign such as dropping their hand or pointing to a stimulus to elicit responses. Students learn that the selected cue means they are to respond immediately. If the question requires a brief period of thinking, the teacher holds up her hand during the 'think time', then drops it when a response is desired.

The teacher provides a brief period of time between asking a question and signaling for a response; she varies the length of time depending upon the complexity of the question. As the purpose of a session shifts from acquisition to fluency, the time between a question and the signal for a response is decreased. Questions which require more 'thinking' time than 10 seconds probably should not be used in a choral responding format (Heward et al., 1989).

As students respond, the teacher listens attentively and scans the students' mouths to determine if they appear to be responding correctly. When correct responses have been given, the teacher provides immediate feedback by saying something such as, 'Good, the sound of *m* is *mmmmm*'. The feedback should be brief so as to not interrupt the pace and flow of instruction; the teacher goes immediately to the next trial (i.e., question and response sequence). When one or more students make an error during CR, the teacher corrects their response by providing a model. If the correct response is sequential in nature, the teacher models the entire sequence of responses so that students are not inadvertently confused. For example, if the students are signaled to rote count from 1 to 5, and one student says, '1, 2, 3, 5, 4', the teacher does not correct by simply saying, '5'. If she did so, the student might conclude that the correct response is, '1, 2, 3, 5, 4, 5'. Rather, the teacher repeats the entire sequence of numbers, '1, 2, 3, 4, 5', then has the group repeat the sequence. After a few intervening trials, the teacher repeats trials that contained incorrect responses earlier in the lesson.

As noted, once student responses are consistently correct during a session, the teacher begins calling on individual children to respond. The teacher asks the question, then selects a child to respond. Asking the question first is a strategy which serves to maintain the attention of the entire group longer than calling a child's name and then asking the question.

Group responding also can be used to turn some educational games into efficient instructional activities (Wesson, Wilson, & Mandlebaum, 1988). Games can be altered so that all students have the opportunity to respond to every question. For example, in a board game format where students must make a correct response in order to move their board marker, the teacher can give each player two cards on which are written 'Yes' and 'No'. After an individual player makes a response, the teacher asks all members of the group if the response was correct; members of the group respond by holding up their 'Yes' or 'No' card in unison. Teachers sustain the 'Yes' and 'No' responses with praise or other reinforcing consequences. In arithmetic games where students are required to compute a response, providing players with individual chalk boards or magic slates on which to record their answers (which are held up in unison after the teacher signals for a response) is another strategy for promoting unison responding.

Evaluating Student Progress

Formative evaluation employs frequent evaluation and modification of educational programs if the data indicate a lack of sufficient student progress. Research by Fuchs and Fuchs (1986) has demonstrated 'that the use of systematic formative evaluation procedures...increase academic achievement (p.206)'. A variety of methods exist for gathering formative evaluation data.

Levels-of-assistance charting may be used in the evaluation of student progress in learning skill chains (Wolery et al., 1988). These charts contain each step in the behavior chain and levels of assistance (indicated by letters adjacent to the step description) (see Figure 1) which are arranged in order from most to least supportive (i.e., from full manipulation to independent performance). For each training trial after completion of the 0 second time delay phase of instruction, the teacher circles the symbol which represents the least supportive prompt necessary to obtain a correct response. Connecting lines between training trials creates a graph which shows progress toward independent performance of each step in the task analysis over time. Charting also assists the teacher in determining what level of prompt is likely to be necessary during any given trial; however, it is recommended that the prompt selected first be somewhat less supportive than the one needed during the last trial. For example, if a correct response was obtained after a model during the previous trial, the teacher may want to provide a gesture in an attempt to obtain a response during the present trial since a gesture is one step closer to independence on the prompt hierarchy shown in Figure 1.

Figure 1: Levels-of-Assistance Chart for Evaluating Student Progress in Learning Skill Chains

Name	*Sheryl*
Task analysis chart for	*making popcorn*

Step Description	I=independent V=verbal G=gestural M=model P=partial physical F=full manipulation

1. Gets electric popper from cupboard	I I I I I I I I I I I I I
	V V V V V V V V V V V V V
	G G G G G G G G G G G G G
	M M M M M M M M M M M M M
	P P P P P P P P P P P P P
	F F F F F F F F F F F F F

2. Gets popcorn and oil from cupboard	I I I I I I I I I I I I I
	V V V V V V V V V V V V V
	G G G G G G G G G G G G G
	M M M M M M M M M M M M M
	P P P P P P P P P P P P P
	F F F F F F F F F F F F F

3. Measures popcorn and puts it into popper	I I I I I I I I I I I I I
	V V V V V V V V V V V V V
	G G G G G G G G G G G G G
	M M M M M M M M M M M M M
	P P P P P P P P P P P P P
	F F F F F F F F F F F F F

4. Measures oil and puts it into popper	I I I I I I I I I I I I I
	V V V V V V V V V V V V V
	G G G G G G G G G G G G G
	M M M M M M M M M M M M M
	P P P P P P P P P P P P P
	F F F F F F F F F F F F F

5. Puts lid on popper	I I I I I I I I I I I I I
	V V V V V V V V V V V V V
	G G G G G G G G G G G G G
	M M M M M M M M M M M M M
	P P P P P P P P P P P P P
	F F F F F F F F F F F F F

6. Plugs popper into wall outlet	I I I I I I I I I I I I I
	V V V V V V V V V V V V V
	G G G G G G G G G G G G G
	M M M M M M M M M M M M M
	P P P P P P P P P P P P P
	F F F F F F F F F F F F F

Date of Observation   9/1   9/5   9/9 9/17 9/21 9/26

Figure 1: Levels of Assistance Chart for Evaluating Student
Progress in Learning Skill Chains (continued)

7. When popping is	I	I	I	I	I	I	I	I	I	I	I	I	I
finished unplugs	V	V	V	V	V	V	V	V	V	V	V	V	V
popper	G	G	G	G	G	G	G	G	G	G	G	G	G
	M	M	M	M	M	M	M	M	M	M	M	M	M
	P	P	P	P	P	P	P	P	P	P	P	P	P
	F	F	F	F	F	F	F	F	F	F	F	F	FF
8.Pours popcorn into	I	I	I	I	I	I	I	I	I	I	I	I	I
a bowl	V	V	V	V	V	V	V	V	V	V	V	V	V
	G	G	G	G	G	G	G	G	G	G	G	G	G
	M	M	M	M	M	M	M	M	M	M	M	M	M
	P	P	P	P	P	P	P	P	P	P	P	P	P
	F	F	F	F	F	F	F	F	F	F	F	F	F

Date of Observation   9/1   9/5   9/9   9/17 9/21 9/26

SMALL GROUP AND INDEPENDENT WORK

Methods of promoting student achievement in the context of small group and individual learning activities are discussed in this section including tutoring, classwide peer tutoring, cooperative learning, modifying traditional lectures, learning centers, and controlling rates of errors. Formative evaluation procedures applicable to small group and individual learning activities are described.

Tutoring

The use of tutoring has been shown to be positively related to increased levels of achievement among high-risk children and students with disabilities (Slavin, Karweit, & Madden, 1989). Few instructional approaches have the historical and empirical validation of effectiveness as the use of tutors in the educational process. Tutoring – instruction involving a dyad (i.e., tutor and tutee) – is delivered on a one-to-one basis using specially designed and sequenced curricular materials or nonprogrammed materials. Traditionally, schools have utilized older students, adult volunteers, or paraprofessionals as tutors, although recent evidence suggests that same-age peer tutoring (Delquadri et al., 1986; Franca et al., 1990; Hendrickson, 1983) and peer-mediated strategies using same-age peers (Kohler et al., 1989; Sugai & Chanter, 1989) may be effective. To date, most tutoring programs have required the tutor to have a 4th–6th grade reading level.

In addition to academic and general cognitive gains, tutoring programs are credited with positively affecting student self-esteem and social skill development (Ehly & Larsen, 1980). One important and frequently overlooked outcome of peer tutoring programs is that the tutor also benefits from the process of tutoring (Hendrickson, 1983; Slavin et al., 1989). Slavin and his colleagues attribute the greater success of some tutoring programs to the training of the tutors and the intensity with which instruction was delivered. Successful tutoring programs reported by Slavin et al. implemented tutoring three to five times a week, with the majority using tutoring five times a week.

Delquadri and his colleagues (1986) reported that the success of peer tutoring may be attributed to several features of the procedure. First, peer tutoring increases student opportunity to respond. There is also a greater likelihood for increased achievement when teachers select the skills to be practiced during peer tutoring than when skills are dictated by some other source such as district curriculum guides. Third, the application of behavioral principles (e.g., positive reinforcement and feedback on performance) is related to improved student outcomes.

Teachers function more as instructional managers and facilitators in the delivery of instruction when tutoring is used. In addition to training the tutors, teachers generally are responsible for (a) identifying the objectives of the program; (b) selecting tutor-tutee pairs; (c) designing, administering, and/or overseeing a system for monitoring student progress; (d) selecting and organizing the tutoring material; (e) observing tutor performance; (f) providing support and feedback to student teams; and, (g) doing whatever is necessary to maintain a positive and enthusiastic learning environment (Hendrickson, 1983).

Classwide Peer Tutoring

Delquadri et al. (1986) have devised a procedure referred to as classwide peer tutoring that incorporates features described above. Prior to beginning peer tutoring, students are trained in the procedures to be used. During training, the teacher carefully describes and models the peer tutoring process for the students, then has them practice each step until the peer tutoring sessions are functioning smoothly. In classwide peer tutoring, a specific portion of the school day (for example, 30 minutes) may be devoted to practicing skills viewed as important by the teacher. Students are divided into two teams, with members of each team subdivided into pairs who alternate being tutor and tutee. For example, during the first 10 minutes of the tutoring period, one student serves as tutor, the other as tutee. Following the first segment of time, student pairs switch roles for 10 minutes. The final 10 minutes are spent adding individual and team points earned for academic engagement and appropriate behavior during tutoring. New teams are established each week so that students have the opportunity to work with a variety of peers.

During daily tutorial sessions, the tutor obtains responses from the tutee and provides corrective feedback or reinforcement for correct responses. Reinforcement involves both praise and the awarding of points in the following manner: after each response, circle two points on the point card (see Figure 2) for each initially correct response, one point for correct responses following a correction given by the tutor, or the 0 for an incorrect response that the tutee was unable to correct after feedback. The teacher or teacher associate moves among the pairs of students to award bonus points to students (either tutor or tutee) who are demonstrating a high level of engagement and to provide assistance where needed.

At the end of each tutoring session, students compute the number of points earned (i.e., the number of points circled) on their individual cards, then each team sums the points earned by team members to obtain a team total. Team point totals are posted on a bulletin board each day; on Friday of each week, the winning team for the week is announced. The steps in daily tutorial sessions are summarized in Table 6.

Figure 2: Point Card for Peer Tutoring

Name _____	Date _____
1. 0 1 1	16. 0 1 1
2. 0 1 1	17. 0 1 1
3. 0 1 1	18. 0 1 1
4. 0 1 1	19. 0 1 1
5. 0 1 1	20. 0 1 1
6. 0 1 1	21. 0 1 1
7. 0 1 1	22. 0 1 1
8. 0 1 1	23. 0 1 1
9. 0 1 1	24. 0 1 1
10. 0 1 1	25. 0 1 1
11. 0 1 1	26. 0 1 1
12. 0 1 1	27. 0 1 1
13. 0 1 1	28. 0 1 1
14. 0 1 1	29. 0 1 1
15. 0 1 1	30. 0 1 1
Bonus Points: 1 1 1 1 1	Total Points: _____

Cooperative Learning

Johnson, Johnson, Holubec, and Roy (1984) observed that classroom learning in most schools takes place in competitive or individualistic settings. In competitive settings, it is assumed that some students will succeed while others will fail. In individualistic settings, each person is 'on his or her own'; students

Table 6: Steps in Conducting a Tutorial Session

First 10 Minutes

Step 1	The tutor provides a stimulus for tutee (e.g., holds up a flash card).
Step 2	The tutee responds.
Step 3	The tutor determines the correctness of the tutee's response. If the response is correct, the tutor circles two points on the point card. If the response is incorrect (or no response is given), the tutor models the correct response, then asks for a second response from the tutee.
Step 4	The tutee responds.
Step 5	The tutor determines the correctness of the tutee's second response. If the response is correct, the tutor circles one point on the point card. If the response is incorrect (or no response is given), the tutor models the correct response, then proceeds to the next stimulus.
Step 6	During this part of the session, the teacher or associate circulates around the room, periodically awarding bonus points to tutors and tutees for acceptable work.

Second 10 Minutes

The students reverse tutor/tutee roles and proceed with the same steps as outlined for the first 10 minutes of the session.

Third 10 Minutes

Step 1	Students sum the points on their individual cards.
Step 2	Students on each team calculate the total number of points earned by their respective teams.
Step 3	After each tutoring session, the teacher posts the team points on a bulletin board. At the end of the week, daily points are totaled to determine the winning team for the week.

---

are primarily concerned about themselves. In cooperative learning settings, positive interdependence is encouraged. That is, goals are structured so that students learn to be concerned about how well all members of the group have learned skills or concepts. Each individual member of the cooperative learning group is accountable for learning, but it is the group's responsibility for each member to achieve the assigned goal. Johnson et al. (1984) have reported that levels of achievement among students working in cooperative learning groups is frequently higher than achievement among students working alone or in competition with each other.

In order for cooperative learning groups to be effective, the teacher must structure the environment so that:

1. Objectives for the group activity are clearly specified.

2. Decisions concerning the placement of students into groups have been made before beginning the activity.

3. Group tasks and learning activities are clearly explained.

4. Groups are monitored carefully to determine if students need task assistance (i.e., information or questions answered about the task) or process assistance (i.e., help with interpersonal and group interaction skills).

5. An evaluation of each group is conducted by the teacher to determine if the goal was achieved and if acceptable interpersonal skills were utilized in the process of achieving the goal.

Working in cooperative learning groups is an evolutionary process in which students gradually learn the skills necessary in order to work effectively together. In the initial stages of cooperative learning, groups should be given short tasks that can be completed during one session. During these initial sessions, the teacher needs to be available to model skills and provide guidance. During the beginning stages of learning how to learn cooperatively, students should have the opportunity to work in a variety of groups.

Cooperative learning groups might be used in the process of teaching students about using telephone directories. Prior to direct instruction concerning the use of directories, students must be skilled in alphabetization. During an initial direct instruction lesson, the teacher might present the purposes and organization of telephone books. In a subsequent lesson, the teacher could focus on using the index to entries in the yellow pages. In this lesson, the teacher would model how to generate possible key words that could be looked up in the index to find a desired listing or service (e.g., plumbers). Next, she would model using the yellow pages to find the actual listings associated with the key words. Following the direct instruction portion of the lesson, students are assigned to cooperative learning groups for practice in finding yellow page listings for a service named by the teacher. Students within each group are encouraged to summarize the problem-solving steps for members of their individual groups (e.g., 'What is the first thing we should do? What do we do next?'). They brainstorm to identify possible key words, and finally they list several entries from the yellow pages. The teacher monitors group work to answer questions, provide prompts, and facilitate positive group participation among *all* members of each group. After group work is completed, the teacher leads a discussion about what each group learned and the procedures they found to be most helpful in completing the task successfully.

Lecture-Pause Procedures

A frequent means of providing instruction to students in elementary, middle, and secondary school settings is verbal presentation of information by the classroom teacher. Unfortunately, many students experience frustration and failure trying to assimilate and retain information presented in the lecture mode. Students with attention, memory, information processing deficits, and/or insufficient background knowledge are likely to have difficulty learning from lecture formats. Although many factors may impinge upon a student's ability to learn from lectures, Rowe (1976) proposed that loss of information may be the result of memory lapses. To offset these memory lapses, she proposed a series of pauses during which times students discuss the lecture and share notes. In 1986, Hughes, Hendrickson, and Hudson modified the process described by Rowe for use with underachieving and high achieving middle school students. These investigators documented the potential power of the lecture-pause procedure in enhancing the recall of factual information for both groups of students. Subsequently the lecture-pause procedure was adapted further for use in teaching elementary and middle school students with behavioral and mild mental/learning disabilities (Hendrickson, 1987).

The lecture-pause procedure breaks lectures into smaller than usual time segments. Lecture segments of 6–8 minutes are followed by pauses of 2–4 minutes. During the lecture, students listen, ask questions, take notes, and engage in behavior typically associated with a traditional lecture mode. At the sound of a bell or timer, the teacher stops lecturing, and the students gather together in preassigned groups of three to discuss the lecture. During the pause, students interact according to guidelines established by the teacher (e.g., they ask questions of each other, discuss what they can remember of the lecture, and prompt and reinforce one another for contributing to the discussion).

The process of discussing the content of the lecture at short intervals provides students with an opportunity to review as well as gain clarification on any misunderstood points. The pause (a) provides the students with an opportunity to restate or paraphrase information presented by the teacher; (b) lessens the likelihood of the student becoming overwhelmed; (c) provides opportunity for verbal rehearsal of information; and, (d) enables students to interact in a legitimate, productive manner during 'work' time. The pause segment also enables the teacher to observe and interact with students in a supportive manner. Teachers move around the room prompting and reinforcing student teams and individuals for desired behavior, for example, 'Can you think of one thing I talked about during the lecture (prompt)?' 'Hilda, you thought of an excellent question to ask Lia (individual praise)', and 'This team is terrific at making every minute count (group praise)'. In all, the lecture-pause procedure appears to (a) facilitate student acquisition and recall of basic skill and content area information, (b) provide opportunity to practice memory building habits, (c) encourage cooperation, and (d) teach related academic (e.g., note-taking) and social (e.g., turn-taking) skills (Hendrickson, 1987).

Any subject may be taught using the lecture-pause procedure. Lecture-pause has shown to be effective for improving student recall of science, language arts, arithmetic, social studies, and grammar lessons (Hendrickson & Bedinger, 1987). Teachers have employed the lecture-pause procedure when using instructional films. The lecture-pause procedure can be used as a primary instructional format, a preview process, a review process, or a means of providing occasional variety in the instructional format once the students have learned the procedure.

Creating teams

Student teams for the pause segment are identified before the lecture begins. Each team is comprised of three students. Each triad consists of a student who, relatively speaking, is a high performer, an average student, and a student who is high risk or low performing. Teams can be assigned and maintained across time or changed on a daily basis. During training of the students, the teacher emphasizes the equal responsibility of each member of the team.

Employing a team facilitator

When teaching students with special needs, several modifications have been found to be helpful for increasing the success of the lecture-pause technique. One of the most helpful adaptations has been to assign one member of each team to be the team 'facilitator' (Hendrickson & Bedinger, 1987). Team facilitators are given special recognition by the teacher and the responsibility of asking questions or stimulating discussion in other ways. Facilitators may be rotated weekly or daily. Each member of the team has the potential to serve successfully as the team facilitator.

In addition to creating the team facilitator role, teachers have found it helpful to link on-going behavior management systems and/or systems for promoting academic growth to the lecture-pause process. For example, positive feedback for appropriate behavior during all phases of the lecture-pause process always is warranted. In addition, the teacher may decide to award points for individual or group participation during the pause. Points, tokens, and teacher praise might follow attentive listening, active participation, and even note taking. To directly promote academic growth, students might earn special privileges based on their free recall test scores (see free recall test, p.34).

Table 7 contains suggestions for planning and training students and implementing the lecture-pause procedure. In addition to these suggestions, the teacher may wish to use the pause to teach students how to take notes.

To do this, the teacher creates a form which has two distinct spaces for taking notes. All students get a form with identical front and back copy. During the pause, each student is asked to write three to five words, phrases, or key concepts discussed by the teacher. Students assist each other in remembering the lecture through their discussion. They encourage each other to finish the note-taking assignment because teams in which all members have completed three notes, for example, are rewarded with points, teacher recognition, or some other consequence of worth to the students. Teams with members who have not completed the note-taking assignment do not receive the special reward.

Table 7: Suggestions for Using the Lecture-Pause Procedure

Planning

1. Initially choose one class period for training students in the lecture-pause procedure. Consider this an experimental phase and identify strategies that seem to work best for training your students. Work in a content area and with the group of students with whom you feel most comfortable and effective.
2. Plan to use the lecture-pause procedure two to three times each week in the same subject area.
3. Prepare the lesson to fit the lecture-pause process by dividing your lecture into two segments of relatively equal content.
4. Prepare overhead transparencies for teaching students about the lecture-pause procedure.
5. Make a short list of rules the students will need to follow during the lecture and during the pause. Include any information on points or rewards that may be tied to following the rules. Keep the rules positively stated. Hand out the list of rules to your students while discussing them.
6. Prepare any student-use material that will be employed during a typical lesson and introduce the students to this material during the initial training sessions (e.g., note-taking forms).
7. Decide in advance which students will be grouped together for the pause segments.
8. Plan to use a direct instruction approach when training the students and when lecturing. Remember to include an advance organizer, a rationale, a demonstration/model, guided practice, independent practice, corrective and positive feedback during the lesson, and a post organizer or brief review at the end of the lesson.

Table 7: Suggestions for Using the Lecture-Pause Procedure (continued)

Training Students and Implementing the Lecture-Pause Procedure

1. Introduce the basic features of the lecture-pause procedure to your students using a direct instruction approach. Introduce and clarify any rules. Watch for and praise students following the rules!
2. Take care in describing the pause procedure. Discuss the role of the facilitator – they are students who have the ability to be good leaders, can listen well, show respect for others, and know how to ask for assistance. Stress that everyone has equal responsibility in keeping the discussion going, however, it is the facilitator's job to ask questions and keep the others involved when the discussion wanes.
3. Rotate the team facilitator so that all members have an opportunity to be facilitators. During the initial training phase, select students who are likely to be cooperative and serve as good role models.
4. Practice the lecture-pause procedure using real content (e.g., a social studies lesson) and provide students with feedback on their performance. Use each segment of the practice session to provide prompts and feedback on behavior expected of the class as a whole, the pause teams, and individual students. Be sure to use student names when praising. Be sure to move into close proximity and to establish eye contact with any student who may need to be reprimanded for breaking a behavioral rule.
5. Establish and maintain enthusiasm by being enthusiastic. Contingency contracts may be useful for motivating some learners.
6. Give a free-recall test after each lesson. Score the tests as soon as possible so that you remember the content of the lesson for the day. Challenge students and/or teams to increase the amount of information they recalled once you have established a baseline on their performance.

The free recall test

At the end of the second lecture, the teacher summarizes the information presented for the day. Next, the students work independently for 2 to 3 minutes (this should be consistent across days) and write down everything they can remember without looking at their notes or talking to other students. The free recall tests are scored by the teacher. Usually, one point is awarded for each appropriate content word (e.g., nouns, adjectives, action verbs, and adverbs). An additional point is awarded for each phrase, complete sentence, or diagram. These points are tallied and can be charted by the student. The points should be used in arriving at the student's grade for the class. Speaking into an audio-tape recorder may be used as an alternative response to writing the free recall test. Oral responses, tape-recorded or given on a one-to-one basis to the teacher, require more teacher involvement than written responses. However, oral responding is a good alternative for poor or non-writers. Oral responding also may be used as a supplemental assessment strategy.

In sum, the lecture-pause procedure is a modified form of the traditional lecture and may have special promise for teaching students with learning difficulties.

Learning Centers

Children labelled mildly retarded exhibit a wide range of educational needs. Their diverse needs often require that the special education teacher group students for instructional purposes, which in turn creates a challenge concerning how to engage students who are not in the direct instruction group during some portions of lessons. Although it may be a relatively simple task to keep students busy, the responsible teacher recognizes that all students should be *successfully engaged* in activities which enhance their learning of functional skills and concepts. This section contains a description of how class periods (e.g., reading) can be divided into three segments, each of which engage children in activities related to the subject but do not require direct teacher instruction.

One method of engaging students in meaningful instructional activities is through the use of learning centers to reinforce and extend skills and concepts taught in small group teacher-directed instruction (Evans, Evans, Gable, & Schmid, 1991; Frank, 1974). When creating such a learning center, the teacher begins by identifying an area of the curriculum in which a group of students receive direct instruction. Next, the teacher lists the skills/concepts which already have been taught during direct instruction and identifies activities which can be utilized to provide students with drill and practice or applications of these skills. The teacher should consider the following factors when establishing learning center activities.

1. Determine each student's stage of learning: acquisition, fluency, or generalization. Avoid including skills in a classroom learning center which children are still acquiring. Instead, provide students with activities designed to increase fluency or promote generalization.

2. Select activities in which it is possible to provide students with performance feedback on a frequent basis. Possible feedback mechanisms include answer sheets, taped messages on an audiocassette, language master cards, and use of peer tutors.

3. Avoid typical paper-and-pencil worksheet and workbook activities.

4. Establish and practice rules for student behavior at learning centers. What responsibilities do students have? How can they get assistance if they need it? Do they have any choices in the selection of learning center activities? What is the sequence of activities they are to complete?

5. Take advantage of the motivational aspects of instructional games. Most students enjoy learning through games and are motivated to attend to and complete/win games. Game formats such as trail games, bingo, concentration, and dominoes can be used by small groups and individually to practice many different skills and concepts (Frank, 1974). Examples of various game formats are provided in Table 8.

Table 8: Game Formats for Learning Centers

Trail Format

Skill	Game
Fraction recognition	Any trail game board may be used. Students take turns picking cards which have drawings of fractional parts of various whole objects (e.g., $2\frac{1}{2}$). The student whose turn it is calls the answer, and all students count the fractional parts together. The correct answer is shown on the back of the fractional card. The teacher intermittently reinforces the group (or individuals) for participating in the group feedback procedure. If the player's peers judge the response to be correct, the player may move one space on the board.

Bingo Format

Skill	Game
Naming capitals of states	Students have different bingo cards with the name of a state in each square. After individual cards containing state capitals are drawn in turn, the player reads the card and tells the state for which it is the capital. Other players hold up a 'Yes' or 'No' card to indicate their judgment concerning the correctness of the player's response. After the group determines what the correct state is, they all cover that state if it appears on their individual bingo card. If they cannot agree, no space is covered on anyone's bingo card and play continues.

Table 8: Game Formats for Learning Centers (continued)

Concentration Format

Skill	*Game*
Basic arithmetic facts	A group of cards (e.g., 10–20, depending upon the students' ability to remember) are prepared, half with individual problems and half with the corresponding answers. Problems are placed in one array, answers in another. Students take turns exposing cards, one from each array, and indicating whether the answer 'matches' the problem. The other players then write on individual chalk boards what they each think is the correct answer to the problem and show their answer to the player. After the group determines the correct answer (by calculator, if necessary), the player keeps the pair of cards if correct or returns them to the arrays if incorrect.

Domino Format

Skill	*Game*
Identifying the value of various coins	A group of cardboard dominoes which have a mixture of coin pictures (e.g., 1, 5, 10 and 25) in various locations on the domino pieces are needed. Five dominoes are distributed to each player, and one domino is placed in the middle of the table. Each player takes a turn matching a domino (either picture to picture or picture to value) to those already played. Other players turn over a 'Yes' or 'No' chip to indicate their judgment concerning the correctness of the player's response. If the group determines that the response is correct, the domino stays; if the response is incorrect, it must be returned to the player's pile. Play continues until one person has played all dominoes.

After materials have been prepared, integrate the learning center activities into the daily classroom schedule of the group of students for whom the materials have been designed. Students should be informed about and practice using all learning center materials/equipment to ensure that they can proceed without close teacher supervision.

If students are grouped for direct instruction and will be attending the learning centers with the same students, consider using a rotation schedule where students remain together during an entire instructional period (e.g., mathematics). Each instructional group (with different instructional objectives) moves through the learning centers, independent seatwork, and teacher-led direct instruction activities in a pre-specified sequence. The instructional period may be divided into three segments: (a) direct instruction, (b) individual work at each student's desk, and (c) learning center work (i.e., a center is specially prepared for students in each group). A modified form of peer tutoring that is supervised by a teacher associate may be substituted for individual work as one of the three segments of the instructional period. When a teacher associate is not available, alternative means of giving feedback may be designed. For example, if students are practicing sight words for reading, the stimuli (i.e., sight words) may be written on language master cards with the correct response recorded on the magnetic strip. When the student is not sure of the correct response, the card can be run through the language master to obtain the answer. Another alternative is to create a correction center in which there are answer keys or activities designed to lead students to the correct answers. Usually a different student is taught to manage this center during each of the three segments of the class period.

To begin any class period, the teacher works with the least able group. The most able group receives an assignment (e.g., an activity related to the previous day's work) to be completed at their desks/tables (or the students are divided into pairs for peer tutoring), and the remaining group begins the period at a learning center. At the end of the first time segment (e.g., 20 minutes), the three groups rotate. Students in the direct instruction group go back to their desks to complete the assignment given by the teacher, the group who completed the follow-up assignment goes to a learning center, and the students who have been at a learning center come to the teacher for direct instruction. At the end of the second time segment, students rotate once again; thus, each group participates in three diverse, yet meaningful activities each period. Regularly, new activities are introduced into the learning centers to reflect new instructional objectives and to keep interest levels high.

Controlling Rate of Errors

How can teachers approximate errorless learning when students are working independently? One method for reducing errors is to use a stimulus-modification procedure in which stimulus characteristics of the instructional task are systematically altered to initially make the task easy and then progressively more difficult (Wolery et al., 1988). The procedure illustrated in Figure 3 concerns the alteration of arithmetic worksheets. Initially, the sheets are constructed to prompt the student to correctly solve problems (Brown & Frank 1990). Preparation of each worksheet first requires careful analysis of the steps needed to successfully solve the problems. These steps, organized sequentially, are written at the top of the worksheet. Next, an abbreviated checklist of the steps is placed adjacent to each problem on the page. A mnemonic device is taught to correspond with the abbreviated checklist to assist children in remembering how to complete the task (Mastropieri, Scruggs, & Levin, 1985). One such mnemonic strategy for facilitating memory of a series of instructions is to select a word whose letters correspond, in order, to the first letter in each of the sentences containing instructions (e.g., STAR might correspond to Stop, Think about what you are going to do, Assess your choices, Respond with your best choice.) Another mnemonic strategy is to teach children a list of steps in completing a task, all of which begin with the same letter. An example of this type of mnemonic device is illustrated in the term, 'The 3 Rs'. Most people, when asked the meaning of 'The 3 Rs', would respond with 'reading, writing, and arithmetic'.

Figure 3: Sample Worksheet for Prompting Correct Student Responses

---

Name _____   Date _____

Remember: S – Start in the ones column.

A – Add the numerals together.

S – Should I carry a numeral?

H – Have I carried the correct numeral?

__ S	__ S	__ S	__ S
__ __ __ A	__ __ __ A	__ __ __ A	__ __ __ A
__ __ __ S	__ __ __ S	__ __ __ S	__ __ __ S
__ __ __ H	__ __ __ H	__ __ __ H	__ __ __ H

2 3 3	1 6 5	4 1 9	5 5 3
+ 3 4 9	+ 2 8 7	+ 1 4 4	+ 2 2 2

Students begin a worksheet by looking at the first step in the list of directions at the top of the page. Once the correct column has been identified, the student places a check mark on the line next to the S (i.e., corresponding to S in the one's column) above the first problem. The student then reads the second step in the checklist at the top of the page, which prompts the student to add the two numerals in the one's column. A check mark is placed on the line above the one's column and next to the A after completion of this step. After all steps have been completed and checked off, the student moves to the next problem.

Students may be taught to use the specially designed worksheets by teacher modeling. The checklist and mnemonic devices are discussed briefly and then problems worked at the chalk board by the teacher who verbally mediates each step in the procedure. Once students become proficient in solving the problems with guidance, the checklist at the top of the page is removed and students are encouraged to rely on the mnemonic strategy (SASH) for remembering how to solve the problems. Finally, the abbreviated checklists which prompt students to use the mnemonic device are removed.

Another method for increasing student accuracy in responding during independent work involves the use of positive practice overcorrection in combination with positive reinforcement (e.g., Frank et al., 1987; Matson et al., 1982; Ollendick et al., 1980; Stewart & Singh, 1986). This procedure can be illustrated in the context of spelling practice. Students are given spelling words on individual cards (each student may have a unique set of word cards); words are traced carefully with a pencil, a task which requires that students focus their attention on the letters of each word in sequence. After students feel they can remember to spell a traced word from memory, they cover the word card and write the word once on a practice sheet (see Figure 4). Next, they compare their written response on the practice sheet with the word card, letter for letter in sequence. If the word has been correctly spelled, the student acknowledges the correct response by drawing a star or happy face in the circle provided, then moves on to the next spelling word. When the response is incorrect, the student draws a horizontal line through the circle to indicate an incorrect response. Next, the student *erases* the word from the practice sheet, copies it directly from the word card into the space, and recopies the word four more times on the practice sheet.

A third method for reducing errors during independent work is to intersperse known and unknown items (within a skill area) on practice materials (Neef, Iwata, & Page, 1980). For example, when practicing math facts, known and unknown combinations are alternated on a worksheet. This arrangement of known and unknown facts should result in a situation where the student seldom makes more than one consecutive incorrect response.

Evaluating Student Progress

One opportunity for gathering formative evaluation data is to directly observe student application of skills/concepts during games. Obtaining performance data in this context has two important features. First, students enjoy playing games as a part of learning new skills (McFarland, 1979); thus, behavior management problems may be minimized, and the need for teacher intervention reduced. Second, during game play, students are applying skills learned through direct instruction; thus correct use of these skills suggests that some generalization has taken place.

Figure 4: Sample Spelling Practice Sheet
(Positive Practice Overcorrection and Positive Reinforcement)

Name _____ Date _____

Figure 5 presents a data collection form which can be used to record the responses of one or more students simultaneously. Recording may be done by the teacher or a peer tutor. Tallies of correct and incorrect responses are made on the data sheet. This particular sheet can be used to record simultaneously the responses of three different students who are playing a game, or the responses over three sessions of one child who is playing the game with a peer.

The procedure for evaluating student progress in the context of playing a game is illustrated below with an example. Assume a student is working toward the short-term objective:

Figure 5: Sample Data Collection Form

	Form 1	Form 2	Form 3
Name	Steven	Steven	Steven
Date	9/1	9/4	9/6
Objective:	Telling time to the hour.	Telling time to the hour.	Telling time to the hour.

+ = correct - = incorrect

Trials / Responses

Trial	9/1	9/4	9/6
1.	+	+	+
2.	+	+	+
3.	+	+	+
4.	−	−	+
5.	+	+	+
6.	−	+	+
7.	+	+	+
8.	+	+	+
9.	−	−	−
10.	−	+	+
11.	+	+	+
12.	−	+	+
13.	+	−	−
14.	+	+	+
15.	+	+	+
16.	−	+	−
17.	+	−	+
18.		+	+
19.		+	+
20.			+
21.			+
22.			
23.			
24.			
25.			
26.			
27.			
28.			
29.			
30.			

	9/1	9/4	9/6
No. correct / No. responses	= 11/17 x 100 = 65 %	= 15/19 x 100 = 79 %	= 18/21 x 100 = 86 %
Comments:	Confused 6/9 and 4/5	Confused 6/9 and 4/5 again but improved!	Reached criterion level for one session.
Recorder:	Jamison	Jamison	Jamison

Given 20 clock flashcards, each with the time set to the hour, the student will be able to tell which numeral the hour hand is pointing to with 85 per cent accuracy on three consecutive sessions.

Further assume that a group of students (or one student and a peer tutor) plays a game designed to provide practice in identifying the numeral to which the hour hand on a clock is pointing for the purpose of achieving the short-term objective. In this game, the players take turns drawing flashcards containing a clock face. In order to advance along a game board, each player must identify the numeral to which the hour hand is pointing. As individual students take turns, the correctness of each response is recorded on the data sheet.

At the conclusion of the game in which formative evaluation data are gathered, the teacher computes the percentage of correct responses made by a student by counting the number of +'s in the circles, dividing by the numeral next to the last circle checked (i.e., the total number of responses during the game by the player), and multiplying by 100. In order to obtain maximum use from data sheets, the teacher records observations of errors at the bottom of the sheet. Observations recorded in the Comment section are used in planning instruction to correct any detected error patterns. Figure 5 illustrates three data sheets completed for one student across three game sessions. Note that the student had some difficulties during the first session in responding correctly as demonstrated by the performance level of 65 per cent correct. The teacher commented that the student was confusing numerals 6 and 9, and numerals 4 and 5. Following some additional instruction with special emphasis on discriminating between 6s and 9s and between 4s and 5s, a peer tutor and the student once again played the game. As illustrated in Figure 5, the student's performance level increased to 79 per cent correct, just below the criterion level of acceptability stated in the short-term objective. After further instruction on discriminating between 6s and 9s and between 4s and 5s, the game activity was repeated, with the student surpassing the criterion level. Since the short-term objective states that a performance level of at least 85 per cent must be demonstrated *on three consecutive sessions* (indicating a level of maintenance of the skill over time) the game should be played at least two more times in the next few days.

SUMMARY

The literature on effective teaching and direct instruction provides guidelines and specific strategies for improving the quality of education for students with mild mental disabilities. Research on best practices indicates that instruction directed by teachers, targeting specific skills, and delivered to small groups is particularly efficacious (Slavin et al., 1990). In providing teacher-directed instruction an instructional paradigm which includes (a) orienting the student to the content of the lesson, the objectives and procedures to be followed; (b) careful demonstration of the new skill or concept combined with visual representations of the task and checks for understanding; (c) structured practice in which students respond to questions and receive feedback and praise; (d) guided practice in which students work semi-independently under close teacher supervision; and (e) independent practice during which the student works without direct supervision and receives delayed feedback constitutes the major elements of a direct instruction approach (Joyce & Weil, 1986). Two aspects of direct instruction that appear to account for much of the growth experienced by students include the immediate provision of performance feedback and the increased amount of successfully engaged time. Teachers are strongly encouraged to modify their teaching and structure classroom learning activities to enhance both the quality and timing of performance feedback their students receive and the amount of time students are engaged successfully in practicing appropriate academic skills.

Numerous recommendations for improving student feedback and increasing academically engaged time were discussed in this chapter including the importance of planning lessons to follow the direct instruction paradigm, maintaining a brisk teaching pace, using questions effectively, minimizing student errors, maximizing choral responding (particularly during the acquisition stage of learning), and monitoring student progress on a continuous basis. To promote learning of students not involved in teacher-directed instruction, several suggestions were made including (a) employing tutoring or classwide tutoring systems, (b) designing cooperative learning activities, (c) using the lecture-pause procedure, (d) organizing learning centers, (d) minimizing student errors through material design, and (e) maintaining an objective system of monitoring student performance.

REFERENCES

Anderson, L., Evertson, C., & Emmer, E. (1980). Dimensions in classroom management derived from recent research. *Journal of Curriculum Studies, 12,* 343–346.

Berliner, D., & Rosenshine, B. (1976, February). *The acquisition of knowledge in the classroom: Beginning teacher evaluation study.* (Tech. Rep. IV-1). San Francisco, CA: Far West Laboratory for Educational Research and Development.

Brophy, J. (1979). Teacher behavior and its effects. *Journal of Educational Psychology, 71,* 733–750.

Brophy, J. (1983). Classroom organization and management. *Elementary School Journal, 83,* 254–285.

Brophy, J., & Evertson, C. (1977). Teacher behavior and student learning in second and third grades. In G. Borich (Ed.), *The appraisal of teaching: Concepts and process* (pp.79–95). Reading, MA: Addison-Wesley.

Brown, D., & Frank, A. (1990). Let me do it! – Self-monitoring in solving arithmetic problems. *Education and Treatment of Children*, 13, 239–248.

Carnine, D. (1981). High and low implementation of direct instruction teaching techniques. *Education and Treatment of Children*, 4, 43–51.

Carnine, D., & Silbert, J. (1979). *Direct instruction reading*. Columbus, OH: Charles E. Merrill.

Carnine, D., Silbert, J., & Kameenui, E. (1990). *Direct instruction reading* (2nd ed.). Columbus, OH: Merrill Publishing Company.

Darch, C., & Gersten, R. (1986). Direction setting in reading comprehension: A comparison of two approaches. *Learning Disability Quarterly*, 9, 235–243.

Delquadri, J., Greenwood, C., Whorton, D., Carta, J., & Hall, R. (1986). Classwide peer tutoring. *Exceptional Children*, 52, 535–542.

Duffy, G. (1983). From turn taking to sense making: Broadening the concept of reading teacher effectiveness. *Journal of Educational Research*, 76, 134–139.

Ehly, S., & Larsen, S. (1980). *Peer tutoring for individualized instruction.* Boston, MA: Allyn and Bacon.

Englert, C. (1983). Measuring special education teacher effectiveness. *Exceptional Children*, 50, 247–254.

Englert, C. (1984). Effective direct instruction practices in special education settings. *Remedial and special education*, 5 (2), 38–47.

Evans, W., Evans, S., Gable, R., & Schmid, R. (1991). *Instructional management for detecting and correcting special problems*. Boston, MA: Allyn and Bacon.

Fisher, C., Berliner, D., Filby, N., Marliave, R., Cahen, L., Dishaw, M., & Moore, J. (1978). *Teaching and learning in elementary schools: A summary of the beginning teacher evaluation.* San Francisco, CA: Far West Regional Laboratory for Educational Research and Development.

Franca, V., Kerr, M.M., Reitz, A.L., & Lambert, D. (1990). Peer tutoring among behaviourally disorderd students: Academic and social benefits to tutor and tutee. *Education and Treatment of Children*, 13 (2), 109–128.

Frank, A. (1974). Centering interest on student interest centers. *Teaching Exceptional Children*, 7 (1), 4–8.

Frank, A. (1989). Counting skills – a foundation for early mathematics. *Arithmetic Teacher*, 37 (1), 14–17.

Frank, A., Wacker, D., Keith, T., & Sagen, T. (1987). Effectiveness of a spelling study package for learning disabled students. *Learning Disabilities Research*, 2, 110–118.

Fuchs, L., & Fuchs, D. (1986). Effects of systematic formative evaluation: A meta-analysis. *Exceptional Children*, 53, 199–208.

Gall, M. (1970). The use of questions in teaching. *Review of Educational Research*, 40, 707–721.

Hall, R., Delquadri, J., Greenwood, C., & Thurston, L. (1982). The importance of opportunity to respond in children's academic success. In E. Edgar, N. Haring, J. Jenkins, & C. Pious (Eds.), *Mentally handicapped children: Education and training* (pp.107–140). Baltimore, MD: University Park Press.

Hendrickson, J., & Stowitschek, C. (1980). Teacher use of diagnostic questioning and modeling in language development. *Journal of Special Education Technology*, 4, 17–27.

Hendrickson, J. (1983). Low achievers teach low achievers: A peer-mediated approach for teaching basic skills. *International Journal of Instructional Media*, 10 (3), 189–200.

Hendrickson, J. (1987, January). *Rising to the challenge: Florida's model prevention programs.* Florida Public Schools Conference, Daytona, FL.

Hendrickson, J., & Bedinger, S. (1987). Teacher training module: The lecture-pause procedure. *Model Adjustment Program (MAP) Monograph* (Serial No. 10). School Board of Alachua County, Gainesville, FL.

Heward, W., Courson, F., & Narayan, J. (1989). Using choral responding to increase active student response. *Teaching Exceptional Children, 21* (3), 72–75.

Hughes, C., Hendrickson, J., & Hudson, P. (1986). The pause procedure: Improving factual recall from lectures by low and high achieving middle school students. *International Journal of Instructional Media, 13* (3), 217–226.

Joyce, B., & Weil, M. (1986). *Models of teaching* (3rd ed.). Englewood Cliffs, NJ. Prentice-Hall.

Kohler, F.W., Schwartz, I.S., Cross, J.A., and Fowler, S.A. (1989). The effects of two alternating peer intervention roles on independent work skills. *Education and Treatment of Children, 12* (3), 205–218.

Lee, J., O'Shea, L., & Dykes, M. (1987). Teacher wait-time: Performance of developmentally delayed and non-delayed young children. *Education and Training in Mental Retardation, 22,* 176–184.

Mastropieri, M., Scruggs, T., & Levin, J. (1985). Maximizing what exceptional children can learn: A review of keyword and other mnemonic strategy research. *Remedial and Special Education, 6* (2), 39–45.

Matson, J., Esveldt-Dawson, K., & Kazdin, A. (1982). Treatment of spelling deficits in mentally retarded children. *Mental Retardation, 20,* 76–81.

McFarland, T. (1979). *Development of a coin skills curriculum for educable mentally retarded children.* Unpublished doctoral dissertation, The University of Iowa.

Neef, N., Iwata, B., & Page, T. (1980). The effects of interspersal training versus high-density reinforcement on spelling acquisition and retention. *Journal of Applied Behavior Analysis, 13,* 153–158.

Ollendick, T., Matson, J., Esveldt-Dawson, K., & Shapiro, E. (1980). Increasing spelling achievement: An analysis of treatment procedures utilizing an alternating treatments design. *Journal of Applied Behavior Analysis, 13,* 645–654.

Rosenshine, B. (1980). How time is spent in elementary classrooms. In C. Denham & A. Lieberman (Eds.), *Time to learn* (pp.107–126). Washington, DC: National Institute of Education.

Rosenshine, B. (1983). Teaching functions in instructional programs. *Elementary School Journal, 83,* 335–352.

Rowe, M. B. (1976). The pausing principle – two invitations to inquiry. *Research on College Science Teaching, 5,* (4), 258–259.

Schuster, J., & Gritten, A. (1990). Using time delay with task analyses. *Teaching Exceptional Children, 22* (4), 49–53.

Silbert, J., Carnine, D., & Stein, M. (1990). *Direct instruction mathematics* (2nd ed.). Columbus, OH: Merrill Publishing Company.

Sindelar, P., Bursuck, W., & Halle, J. (1986). The effects of two variations of teacher questioning on student performance. *Education and Treatment of Children, 9* (10, 56–66.

Sindelar, Q., Espin, C., Smith, M., & Harriman, N. (1990). A comparison of more and less effective special education teachers in elementary-level programs. *Teacher Education and Special Education, 13,* 9–16.

Slavin, R., Karweit, N., & Madden, N. (1989). *Effective programs for students at risk.* Boston, MA: Allyn and Bacon.

Smith, D. D. (1989). *Teaching students with learning and behavior problems.* (2nd ed.). Englewood Cliffs, NJ: Prentice Hall.

Stallings, J., & Kaskowitz, D. (1974). *Follow through classroom observation evaluation, 1972–73.* Menlo Park, CA: Stanford Research Institute.

Stevens, R., & Rosenshine, B. (1981). Advances in research on teaching. *Exceptional Education Quarterly, 2,* 1–9.

Stewart, C., & Singh, N. (1986). Overcorrection of spelling deficits in moderately mentally retarded children. *Behavior Modification, 10,* 355–365.

Stowitschek, J., Stowitschek, C., Hendrickson, J., & Day, R. (1984). *Handbook of direct teaching tactics for exceptional children.* Gaithersburg, MD: Aspen Systems Corportation.

Sugai, J., & Chanter, C. (1989). The effects of training students with learning and behavior disorders to modify the behavior of their peers. *Education and Treatment of Children, 12* (2), 134–151.

Wesson, C., Wilson, R., & Mandlebaum, L. (1988). Learning games for active student responding. *Teaching Exceptional Children, 20* (2), 12–14.

Wolery, M., Bailey, D., & Sugai, G. (1988). *Effective teaching: Principles and procedures of applied behavior analysis with exceptional students.* Boston, MA: Allyn and Bacon.

COMPUTER APPLICATIONS IN THE SCHOOLS FOR STUDENTS WITH MILD DISABILITIES: COMPUTER-ASSISTED INSTRUCTION AND COMPUTER-MANAGED INSTRUCTION

Lynn S. Fuchs and Rose M. Allinder

In the 1970s, the introduction of computers to school environments to support educational goals represented a major innovation (Rieth, 1979), and the use of computers to facilitate student achievement appeared to hold great promise. Computers have been heralded for their capacity to effect individualization of instruction (Hannaford & Taber, 1982), present small increments of information systematically (Chiang, 1978), provide immediate feedback (Bennett, 1982), increase pupil motivation (Budoff & Hutten, 1982) and attention to task (Rieth, 1986), permit repetition and overlearning (Chiang, 1978), and store and manage large amounts of information that might be used in the instructional planning process (Baker, 1978).

The purpose of this chapter is to review research on computer applications in the schools, involving pupils with mild disabilities within two major categories: computer-assisted instruction and computer-managed instruction.

With computer-assisted instruction, the computer is employed as an indirect learning tool. Students interact with computers while the computer provides instruction. With computer-managed instruction, the computer is employed as an indirect learning tool. As students interact with the computer, it stores information about pupil performance; the computer organizes the stored data to provide assessment profiles and instructional recommendations to the teacher.

COMPUTER-ASSISTED INSTRUCTION

The promise for the computer as a direct learning tool may explain current focus within special education development and practice on computer-assisted instruction (CAI) – or the use of computers to provide instruction directly (Finch, 1972). There are several types of CAI, including tutorial, drill-and-practice, and simulation. Tutorial CAI is designed to aid acquisition of new skills and knowledge. Through the use of tutorial software, the student (a) is introduced to a concept and given opportunity to recall and apply the concept, (b) practices, recognizing the concept, and (c) produces the knowledge or skill without prompts (Behrmann, 1984). Drill-and-practice, the most frequently used type of CAI (Gerber, 1986), provides the student opportunities to master and become proficient at skills. Drill-and-practice software provides intensive practice, immediate feedback, and correction on specific skills in which a student needs drill (Bardenstein, 1982). The third type of CAI, simulation, provides opportunities to study characteristics of real phenomena by modeling the properties of these phenomena (Budoff & Hutten, 1982).

The use of computers with students with disabilities has become almost commonplace. Surveys of the availability of computers indicate that over 85 per cent of classrooms for students with disabilities use computers as part of their education program (Cosden, 1988). CAI has been championed as a way to help students by increasing (a) attention to task (Carman & Kosberg, 1982), (b) motivation (e.g., Ellis & Sabornie, 1986), (c) academic responding time (Perkins,1988), and (d) self-concept (Furst, 1983).

Given the growth of and the interest in using computers with children with disabilities, it is not unexpected to find this topic frequently addressed in the literature. Despite the large number of articles regarding the 'hows' and 'whys' of CAI, surprisingly few published studies exist that document the effectiveness of CAI to supplement or supply instruction to students with disabilities.

In this section, we review recent empirical investigations regarding the effectiveness of CAI on the acquisition and maintenance of math skills of students with learning problems. In order to evaluate the effectiveness of CAI with special populations in a thorough and judicious manner, we have restricted our review to studies judged to be both relevant and of high methodological standards (see Slavin, 1986). The studies we selected met the following criteria:

(a) students with disabilities were the primary subjects; (b) academic performance was the major dependent variable of interest; and (c) the CAI treatment lasted at least four weeks. For studies that utilized a group design, three additional criteria were stipulated. First, a control group consisting of students approximately the same age as students receiving CAI were included (Campbell & Stanley, 1963). Second, both the control and treatment groups consisted of more than one teacher (Cook & Campbell, 1979). Third, descriptive and/or inferential statistics were reported. Studies that utilized a single subject design also were judged according to an additional criterion: Multiple baseline designs were required to introduce the intervention to new baseline series only when the criterion-level had been reached in the already exposed series (Tawney & Gast, 1984).

These criteria were used in an attempt to select well-designed and well-implemented studies with minimal threats to either internal or external validity. The use of these criteria resulted in the exclusion of studies that used response time as the dependent variable (Goldman & Pellegrino, 1987; Schnorr, 1989); that had only one teacher per condition (Trifiletti, Firth, & Armstrong, 1984); that did not report inferential or descriptive statistics (Vitello & Bruce, 1977); that did not include a control group (Messerly, 1986); and that did not introduce the treatment in a sequential manner in a multiple baseline design (Chiang, 1986).

The resulting sample of four published studies was judged to meet the criteria specified and thus represent studies designed and implemented with minimal threats to validity. The use of only published studies may present a publication bias (Light & Pillemer, 1984); however, we chose to use only published studies so readers would have access to the studies reviewed and be able to evaluate the results presented and possibly implement recommendations and strategies investigated. Nevertheless, readers should be aware that only published studies are included here. The review of the individual studies is followed by a critique of this body of literature.

Review of CAI Math Studies

The first study involved 40 students classified as having emotional disabilities (Carman & Kosberg, 1982). These students were between the ages of 7 and 14, attended a residential school, and were judged of normal intelligence but at least two years behind in math. Students were randomly assigned to two groups: one received CAI and the other did not. The instructional year was divided into three equal 8-week parts. The CAI group received CAI during the first and third 8-week periods; during the second 8-week period, they received teacher-directed math instruction. The non-CAI group received teacher-directed math instruction during the first and last 8-week periods of the school year; they received CAI during the second 8-week period of the year.

CAI in this study consisted of two elements: drill-and-practice software and computer-managed-instruction (CMI) software. Drill-and-practice was a supplement to classroom instruction and was supplied through software programs. The CMI program provided for pretesting and posttesting capabilities, diagnostic-prescriptive capabilities, student-tracking capabilities, report-generating capabilities. Students' math performance was measured at the end of each of the three 8-week periods of the school year with the Stanford Achievement Test (SAT; Gardner, Rudman, Karlsen, & Merwin, 1982). Data were compared using the Wilcoxen matched pairs test (see Hayes, 1973).

Results indicated that following the first and second 8-week periods of the year, the group that had received CAI displayed significantly higher math gains on the SAT. However, following the third 8-week period of the school year, neither the CAI nor the non-CAI group had significant differences in math gain scores. The authors suggested that during the first two 8-week periods students were motivated by the newness and excitement associated with computers and, thus, learned more. By the third 8-week period, this newness and excitement had lessened and learning suffered. The authors also suggested that the lack of difference following the third 8-week period might be due to the fact that this time period was for April to June, a time when learning is lessened for all students. The authors concluded that the rate of math learning can be accelerated by the combination of CAI and CMI, but not maintained (Carman & Kosberg, 1982).

A second study of the effects of CAI was conducted with 250 elementary students with learning disabilities in grades 1 through 6 (McDermott & Watkins, 1983). This sample included all students in classes for students with learning disabilities within one school district. Of these students, 126 served as a control group and received conventional instruction from their special education teachers; 41 students served as a CAI control and received spelling CAI and conventional math instruction; and the remaining 38 students received math CAI. All CAI students, including CAI control students, were distributed among eight special education teachers in two schools.

Math CAI consisted of instruction provided individually to students through 'multilevel-multifunctional microcomputer programs covering the range from fundamental to advanced elementary mathematics' (McDermott & Watkins, 1983, p.83). The intervention lasted an entire school year, from September to May. Math performance was measured individually using the math portion of the Wide Range Achievement Test (WRAT; Jastak & Jastak, 1978) and in groups with the California Achievement Test (CAT; 1977). Data were analyzed through repeated-measures analyses of covariance using standard-score achievement indices and through 1 pretest-posttest achievement gains. Results did not indicate an interaction effect for method of instruction (CAI vs. non-CAI) and student achievement. The authors concluded that CAI was not more effective for elementary and junior high level students who have learning disabilities than traditional remedial instruction was.

A third investigation of the effects of CAI on the math skills of students with disabilities involved a 16 year-old male high school student (Howell, Sidorendko, & Jurica, 1987). This student had been judged to be significantly behind his peers in math and to be highly motivated to learn multiplication facts. The investigation consisted of two single subject studies. The first study lasted only 13 days and will not be reviewed here since it did not last a sufficient length of time.

In the second part of this study, a reversal design (ABAC) was used to compare the effects of (a) traditional math instruction and a tutorial software program and (b) traditional math instruction and a combination of teacher instruction and drill-and-practice software. Student responses were measured in both a timed and untimed condition. The tutorial software program incorporated the use of 'gradual recall' techniques in which the student was presented with multiplication problems, asked to say the problem either aloud or to himself, and then directed to remove a part of the problem from the screen and rework the problem. The combination of teacher instruction and drill-and-practice software consisted of (a) teacher directions for a specific strategy for working multiplication problems with 9 as a factor and (b) the application of drill-and-practice software in which the student answered 20 randomly generated problems containing the factors he did not know.

Results indicated that the tutorial software decreased the number of errors the student made; however, several sessions were needed before positive changes were noted. The combination of teacher instruction and drill-and-practice software resulted in a more immediate decrease in the number of errors made. Follow-up probes given after the combination intervention ended revealed that the student continued to answer the problems without errors. Comparable results were seen in both the timed and untimed condition. The authors concluded that the student's performance had been influenced positively but that software alone was not sufficient in eliciting durable results: A combination of teacher-directed intervention and CAI software proved to be most effective.

The final study reviewed for this chapter examined the effects of CAI on 160 mildly disabled and regular education students between the ages of 7 and 14 (Hasselbring, Goin, & Bransford, 1988). In this study, nondisabled students served as a control group and did not receive CAI; students with disabilities served in either a CAI or non-CAI group. Students in the CAI group practiced daily at computers; students in the non-CAI group received teacher-directed math instruction.

CAI consisted of software that was designed to improve students' automaticity of math facts by (a) tailoring instruction for each student based on their performance initially, (b) controlling the amount of time students had to respond, and (c) moving students from an instructional level to drill-and-practice in small, sequential steps. This CAI treatment differed from those in previous studies in that the software was designed specifically to provide drill-and-practice on known facts only and to incorporate principles of effective instruction during the acquisition phase of instruction (Hasselbring & Goin, 1989).

Results indicated that students in the CAI group displayed a 73 per cent increase in the number of facts recalled from memory; little or no change was seen in either of the two non-CAI groups in the number of facts recalled for this same time period. The authors concluded that the combination of drill-and-practice and recall training provided by the software was effective in developing automaticity in recalling math facts.

Commentary

Similarities and differences abound in these studies of the effectiveness of CAI with students with learning problems in math. Similarities center on design features and reported outcomes. Differences center on the CAI interventions and outcome measures.

Similarities

Because all studies relied on volunteers as participants, the problem of generalizability is common to all. Further threats may be evident in studies in which teachers participated in both CAI and non-CAI groups (Carman & Kosberg, 1982) or were in close proximity to teachers in the nonCAI group (McDermott & Watkins, 1983). In the McDermott and Watkins (1983) study, students received either spelling or math CAI as determined by random assignment. Since the eight teachers who administered the treatment were located in two schools, the threat of diffusion of treatment or compensatory treatment of non-CAI groups could have affected results. Similarly, in the Carman and Kosberg (1982) study, teachers alternated on an 8-week basis between CAI and nonCAI conditions. The possibility of diffusion of treatment is very possible in this study since a combination of CAI and CMI was used; teachers could continue to use the diagnostic-prescriptive information provided by CMI during the non-CAI period. Future research in this area should use a sufficiently large number of participants in separate facilities and thus attempt to reduce these threats.

The second similarity in these studies is the tendency to combine different types of CAI. Only one study (McDermott & Watkins, 1983) investigated the effects of a single type of CAI. This study indicated that tutorial CAI alone was no more or less effective than was traditional math instruction. A second study (Howell et al., 1987) also investigated the effects of tutorial CAI, as well as a combination of teacher-directed instruction and drill-and-practice CAI. These authors concluded that tutorial CAI alone was not as effective as was a combination of teacher-directed instruction and drill-and-practice CAI. The remaining studies either combined types of CAI (tutorial and drill-and-practice; Hasselbring et al., 1988) or combined CAI and CMI (Carman & Kosberg, 1982). Results from these studies' indicated that treatments that combined types of CAI, and thus placed an emphasis on effective instructional practices, were more effective.

Several authors have stressed the importance of these results by emphasizing the need to combine teacher-directed instruction and CAI (e,g., Carlson & Silverman, 1986; Carman & Kosberg, 1982; Gourgey, 1987; Howell et al., 1987; McDermott & Watkins, 1983). Unfortunately, surveys of actual practice in schools indicate that special education students are most likely to use drill-and-practice CAI (Cosden, 1988; Cosden, Gerber, Semmel, Goldman, & Semmel, 1987). Future research should continue investigating how to increase the effectiveness and feasibility of CAI in the classroom.

Differences

A major difference among these four studies is the type of design used. Three studies (Carman & Kosberg, 1982; Hasselbring et al., 1988; McDermott & Watkins, 1983) used a group design; the remaining study (Howell et al., 1987) used a reversal design. The appropriateness of this type of design should be examined carefully since the dependent variable in this study was of an academic nature, and thus not likely to reverse when the treatment was withdrawn. Future research that utilizes single subject designs to investigate the effectiveness of CAI with disabled students in academic areas should use a multiple baseline design with successive introduction of the treatment.

A second major difference among these studies is the type of outcome measures used. Two studies (Carman & Kosberg, 1982; McDermott & Watkins, 1983) compared student performance on standardized assessments; the remaining studies (Hasselbring et al., 1988; Howell et al., 1987) compared number of math facts students answered correctly while working on the computer. This difference is interesting to note given that the former set of studies reported mixed results regarding the effectiveness of CAI while the latter set of studies reported that CAI was effective. It is possible that the difference in outcomes between these two sets of studies is an artifact of the way in which the skills were assessed. Given the problems students with disabilities exhibit regarding generalization (e.g., Kazdin, 1975), it is not possible to assume that math skills demonstrated at the computer will automatically generalize to other classroom media (Carlson & Silverman, 1986). Additional research may be warranted which applies generalization strategies to the transferring of math facts learned at the computer to other classroom media.

Related to the type of outcome measure used is the timing of the measurements. Carman and Kosberg (1982) reported math gains for students receiving CAI for the first and second 8-week periods of the school year; no gains were noted for students for the third 8-week period of the year. Gains were reported also for students receiving CAI for 21 sessions (Howell, 1987) or for 49 days (Hasselbring et al., 1988). In contrast, no differences were reported between CAI and traditional math instruction when outcome measures were taken after 7 months (McDermott & Watkins, 1983). These differences after varying amounts of time using CAI may be due, in part, to the novelty effect associated with computers (Bardenstein, 1982). As the novelty and newness of computer-use erodes, students may not be as motivated and, thus, learning may suffer (e.g., Carman & Kosberg, 1982; Cosden et al., 1987; Messerly, 1986). While research on the relationship between motivation and computer-use over along period of time indicates that this may be a highly complex interaction (Malouf, 1987), results from these studies suggest that as CAI was used in these studies, it lacked the ability to sustain motivation over a long period of time.

Results from one of these studies (Carman & Kosberg, 1982) indicate that teachers, as well as students, may be affected by this phenomenon. This study reported declining effects in math after several weeks' exposure to computers in a treatment that combined CAI and CMI. Just as it is not possible to conclude that CAI alone was responsible for the gains during the first two 8-week periods, it is not possible to assume that the waning of the attraction of the computer alone was responsible for the lack of difference in the third 8-week period. Teachers' use of CMI diagnostic information may have contributed to increased student growth in math during the first two 8-week periods. Even as the motivating effect of the computer for students may have faded by the last 8-week period, it is possible that teachers' use of CMI during the third 8-week period may have declined, for similar or dissimilar reasons, and thus resulted in lack of growth during this time.

A third difference among these studies concerns the scope of instruction. In the Howell et al. (1987) and Hasselbring et al. (1988) studies, students were taught relatively well-restricted sets of skills, i.e., math facts. Both of these studies reported that CAI was effective in helping students master facts. In the Carman and Kosberg (1982) and McDermott and Watkins (1983) studies, students were presumably taught a wider array of skills; since the studies lasted an entire year, students would be expected to have been exposed to more than just math facts. Carman and Kosberg (1982) reported that the effectiveness of CAI seemed to diminish after a long period of time to the point that no difference between CAI and non-CAI was reported at the end of the year. McDermott and Watkins (1983) also reported no difference between CAI and conventional math instruction after a year's application. These results suggest that CAI may not be effective for any and all types of math skills but may be most effective when used judicially and sparingly in the acquisition of certain math skills.

Conclusion

The current state of research yields both guidelines and unanswered questions for practitioners and researchers interested in maximizing education of students with disabilities. First among these is the finding that CAI drill-and-practice alone is not effective in helping students with learning disabilities in the area of math. Only when combined with either teacher-directed instruction or with a tutorial aspect were positive results found (Carman & Kosberg, 1982; Hasselbring et al., 1988; Howell et al., 1987). This is a very important consideration given the body of research that indicates that CAI drill-and-practice comprises the majority of computer experiences for students with disabilities (e.g., Christensen & Cosden, 1986; Cosden, 1988; Cosden et al., 1987; Gerber, 1986; Mokros & Russell, 1986). Practitioners should be made aware of the need to meld the two approaches in order to facilitate math gains. Further research is needed that continues to investigate the design and implementation of software that incorporates effective teaching strategies.

A second guideline for planning effective instruction for students with disabilities stems from the indications in these studies that while CAI is motivating for students, this motivation factor may not be durable. Practitioners should consider using CAI only when it meets specific objectives for an individual student, instead of on a nondiscriminating basis; CAI may be least effective when used solely as a motivation tool. Additional research regarding under which circumstances CAI is most effective and efficient is needed.

A final area of investigation of the effective use of CAI for facilitating acquisition of math skills by students with disabilities concerns the need for further research that, when comparing CAI and traditional teacher-directed math instruction, details exactly what 'traditional teacher-directed math instruction' is. None of the studies we reviewed in this section gave information regarding what CAI was compared to. Such information is needed in order to determine if CAI is more or less effective than good, bad, or indifferent math instruction. That may be the most important question of all: Is CAI as good as, or better than, how special education teachers normally teach math? Results of the current research suggest that CAI may beat least as effective as traditional math instruction and may be more effective with certain math subskills (i.e., math facts). However, without more specific information regarding to what CAI is compared, it is difficult to give a definitive answer to this most basic question.

COMPUTER-MANAGED INSTRUCTION

Available research questions the effectiveness of CAI as a substitute for teacher-directed instruction. Additionally, current financial exigencies in many school systems, along with the high costs associated with each student utilizing a terminal for relatively long periods of time during every instructional lesson, may preclude wide implementation of CAI. These considerations suggest the potential value of an alternative major computer use to improve the effectiveness of educational environments – computer-managed instruction.

The finding that CAI may improve achievement of school-age pupils primarily as a supplement to, rather than a substitute for, teacher-delivered instruction supports more recent paradigms for studying computers. These paradigms stress the teacher as manager of the instructional environment, who integrates a host of effective teaching variables, including CAI, to produce student achievement (see Lieber & Semmel, 1985; Rieth, 1986). These alternative conceptualizations, stressing the importance of the teacher as the manager of available instructional resources, suggest the potential importance of an alternative major use of computers, which not only holds great promise as a tool for facilitating teachers' management of the complex instructional environment, but also requires fewer computers and lower associated costs: computer-managed instruction (CMI).

CMI encompasses the educational goals, the curriculum, the instructional model, the teacher, and a management information system to assist teachers in tracking pupil progress and scheduling student learning activities for individualized instruction (Baker, 1978). With sophisticated CMI programs, (a) the teacher enters into the computer initial information about the pupil and the instructional program as well as an educational goal, which is rooted in the curriculum and within an instructional model, (b) the computer then automatically generates and administers tests, which demonstrate strong psychometric properties, to track pupil progress toward goal accomplishment, and (c) the computer periodically provides feedback to the teacher concerning progress toward the goal, adequacy of the current instructional program, and possible strategies for improving the instructional program, so that the teacher can manage the instructional environment, including CAI applications, more effectively.

CMI, therefore, potentially supports teachers' management of the instructional process and improves the feasibility of data-based instructional management and curriculum-based progress monitoring programs, which have been shown to be effective in designing useful individualized educational programs (Fuchs & Fuchs, 1986). Below, we review literature on CMI within two subcategories. First, we provide a brief overview of early research on CMI. Second, we review more recent research on CMI applications to Curriculum-Based Measurement.

Early Research on CMI

Considerable resources have been allocated (a) to developing early CMI systems for regular education (see, for example, Chapin et al., 1975; Flanagan et al., 1975; Kelly, 1968; Westinghouse Learning Corporation, 1975) and for special education math (Hofmeister, 1986) and behavior management programs (Hofmeister, 1986) and (b) to discussing potential benefits of CMI (see, for example, Baker, 1978; Broderick, 1976; Daykin, Gilfillan, & Hicks, 1975; Finch, 1972; Hasselbring & Hamlett, 1985). Nevertheless, adequate resources have not been allocated toward developing of an effective reading or spelling CMI program that uses current computer capabilities. Additionally, research fails to address the effectiveness of CMI compared with traditional management approaches or to focus on the effects of alternative CMI structures.

A thorough search of the literature, involving a computer search of three on-line data bases (*ERIC, Comprehensive Dissertation Abstracts,* and *Psychological Abstracts*) and a manual search of six technology journals (*Association of Educational Data Systems Journal, Computers in Education, The Computing Teacher, Educational Technology, Electronic Learning,* and *School Microcomputing Bulletin*) and six special education journals (*Exceptional Children, Journal of Learning Disabilities, Journal of Special Education, Journal of Special Education Technology, Learning Disability Quarterly,* and *Remedial and Special Education*) for the years 1976 through summer 1986 revealed only two relevant published studies.

O'Neil, Hedl, Richardson, and Judd (1976) conducted an uncontrolled evaluation of one CMI approach, conducted with undergraduate students enrolled in an educational psychology course. Findings indicated that 78–96 per cent of students achieved at least 75 per cent or better on certain portions of the program. Dick and Gallagher (1972) explored two elements of CMI with college-age nondisabled pupils: fixed versus self-determined order of progression through 20 course-related tasks, and instructor versus computer administered and scored tests. Results indicated no significant differences between the groups on exams or on time taken to complete the course. However, cost analyses revealed that computer testing was less expensive than instructor testing.

Recent Research on CMI Applications to Curriculum-Based Measurement

Although Dick and Gallagher (1972) provide tentative evidence for potential cost benefits of CMI, neither study contributes important information to our understanding of the effectiveness of CMI or of which CMI elements contribute differentially to student achievement or to teacher behavior and decision making. A more recent line of research has focused on CMI within the context of Curriculum-Based Measurement (CBM). CBM is a measurement methodology where in teachers routinely measure student progress toward IEP goals on curriculum-related tasks; and, when measurement data indicate student progress toward those goals is inadequate, practitioners modify instructional programs in an attempt to improve academic gains (Deno, 1985).

There is strong and broad consensus as well as a diverse research base demonstrating that curriculum-based progress monitoring enhances the effectiveness of special education. The literatures on Direct Instruction (e.g., Gersten, Carnine, & White, 1984), applied behavior analysis (e.g., Lovitt, 1981; Rieth, Polsgrove, & Semmel, 1981), precision teaching (White & Haring, 1980), general special education (e.g., Fuchs et al., 1984), effective schools (Eubanks & Levine, 1983; Hoffman & Rutherford, 1984), and special education effective teaching (e.g., Goodman, 1985; Peters & Lloyd, 1986; Peterson et al., 1985) all identify curriculum-based progress monitoring as an essential component of effective special education.

Despite the US legal mandate (P.L. 94–142) as well as the importance of CBM for effective special education, surveys as well as observations of special education practitioners indicate they fail to use systematic monitoring procedures: Rather, they prefer unsystematic impressions (Fuchs & Fuchs, 1984; Wesson et al., 1984). Moreover, although teachers express confidence in the accuracy of those impressions, research indicates their informal evaluations about student progress tend to be inaccurate and to overrate student performance (Fuchs & Fuchs, 1984). This frequently results in maintenance of ineffective instructional programs for pupils with disabilities.

In summarizing research on teacher decision making, Shavelson and Stern (1981) attempt to explain teachers' tendency for unrealistic optimism concerning their pupils' achievement and the success of their instructional programs. Shavelson and Stern suggest that classroom environments are extremely complex settings where, without the benefit of an objective database, teachers tend to apply heuristics that simplify, albeit often incorrectly, the decision making process. As Shavelson and Stern indicate and as others concur (e.g., Einhorn & Hogarth, 1978), such heuristics readily incorporate positive, confirming input, but fail to integrate sources of negative, disconfirming feedback. Such heuristics frequently result in the decision that student progress is adequate and programmatic development unnecessary. Such a decision making process mitigates against effective special education practice, because teachers fail to revise inadequate programs.

Given a methodology with which teachers can accumulate an objective database to enhance the effectiveness of the programs they provide to pupils with disabilities, one must question why practitioners fail to implement CBM. Research suggests that, although teachers acknowledge such monitoring would enhance their effectiveness, they believe the time-consuming nature of the process is prohibitive and the technical rigor is problematic (Wesson et al., 1984). Observations of teachers implementing curriculum-based progress monitoring corroborate practitioners' perceptions (Fuchs et al., 1987).

The application of CMI to CBM represents a promising strategy for facilitating the feasibility of implementing this monitoring methodology. Computers, which can process large amounts of information, have the capacity to collect, store, graph, analyze, and provide feedback statements and recommendations to teachers concerning pupil progress toward goals and instructional modifications.

Over the past 7 years, we have conducted a research program investigating CMI applications to CBM. Below, we provide an overview of CMI applications we have developed during this time to support CBM implementation. Then, we summarize our research findings within four categories: (a) effects of automatic analysis of graphed data on teacher efficiency and satisfaction and on teachers' use of CBM information, (b) effects of automatic data collection programs on CBM efficiency and satisfaction, (c) effects of supplementary skills analysis on teacher efficiency and satisfaction, on teacher planning, and on student achievement, and (d) effects of automatic instructional recommendations, via expert systems, on teacher efficiency and satisfaction, on teacher planning, and on student achievement.

Description of CMI applications to CBM

CMI applications to CBM comprise four components:

- data-management software that automatically stores, graphs, and analyzes CBM scores;
- data-collection programs that (a) generate CBM tests, (b) administer and score tests and then provide test feedback as students work at the computer, without teacher assistance, and (c) automatically save the scores and student responses for teacher use within the data-management program;
- skills analysis software that systematically analyzes the student response database and provides information about the types of skills students have and have not mastered; and
- expert systems that use information from the student performance database and from other sources in order to recommend specific instructional strategies for enhancing student progress.

Programs incorporating the first three components are available to readers in spelling (Fuchs, Hamlett, & Fuchs, 1990c) and math (Fuchs, Hamlett, & Fuchs, 1990a). A program incorporating the first two components is available to readers in the area of reading (Fuchs, Hamlett, & Fuchs, 1990b).

Effects of automatic analysis of student graphs

Research has addressed effects of automatic analysis of student graphs with respect to efficiency of the CBM process, teacher satisfaction, and teachers' implementation of the CBM system. During 1985–1986, the efficiency of data-management software was assessed (Fuchs, Fuchs, Hasselbring, & Hamlett, 1987). Twenty special educators were assigned randomly to a CBM condition in which they used computerized data-management or to one in which they managed their student performance data by hand. Observations of teachers implementing CBM in reading, spelling, and math indicated that these CMI applications reduced teacher efficiency due to the extra steps required by the teachers with data-management software. After they measured and scored student tests, teachers had to go to a computer, load the software, enter identifying information to the computer, enter test dates and scores, save data, and view or print graphs. By contrast, the noncomputer teachers only had to place symbols at appropriate places on the graph. Although the software required additional time, teachers were more satisfied with CBM in the computerized data-management condition.

Regardless of the extent to which computers may affect the amount of time required for CBM or the extent to which teachers are satisfied with the process, our research indicates that computers may remove practitioners from the assessment information. Consequently, CMI may reduce teachers' meaningful implementation of CBM. During 1985–1986, Fuchs (1988) investigated this possibility, comparing CBM with and without computerized data-management, within the context of two data-analysis strategies. One approach, goal-based evaluation, was relatively simple, requiring teachers to modify instruction when a student's progress was lower than the goal. The second, more difficult strategy required teachers to introduce an instructional adjustment every month, compare the effectiveness of different phases, build effective strategies, and eliminate less effective methods. Teachers who implemented CBM without data-management CMI applications implemented CBM equally well with both data-analysis strategies. Teachers with computerized data-management, however, implemented the more difficult data-analysis method less well than the easier method. Findings indicated that teachers' involvement with data (ie., graphing, drawing trend lines, and applying the logic of data analysis) may be important to accurate CBM implementation.

So, computer applications may distance practitioners from the assessment database and there by limit effective interpretation of the information. Consequently, in 1986–1987, Fuchs, Fuchs, and Hamlett (1989a) investigated strategies for enhancing practitioner involvement within CMI. Two forms of teacher feedback were employed. With 'standard feedback', the computer simply showed the analysis to the teacher and provided recommendations concerning the need to change the goal or the instructional program. In the second, 'enhanced' feedback condition, practitioners inspected computer graphs independently, formulated their own decisions, and entered decisions into the computer. The software then provided corrective feedback and explained the correct decision. Teachers in this enhanced feedback group implemented data analysis significantly more accurately.

Consequently, as CMI programs free practitioners from test generation, measurement, scoring, graphing, and data analysis, it may be important to identify methods for maintaining teachers' meaningful involvement with student assessment information. Structuring software so that teachers are required to inspect their students' graphs carefully on their own and review the logic of data analysis may represent one method of facilitating this involvement.

Effects of automatic data collection

In 1988, Fuchs, Hamlett, Fuchs, Stecker, and Ferguson (1988) investigated the efficiency of the second CMI application, automatic data collection programs. Twenty special educators used CBM in reading, spelling, and math for 15 weeks. Half the teachers collected data by hand and entered student scores in a data-management program; in the other condition, students worked directly on computers for automatic data collection, and scores were saved on the data-management program. Observations of students during automatic data collection and of teacher during data-management activities indicated that teachers spent dramatically and significantly less time in measurement and evaluation when data were collected by computers. Given a caseload of 20 pupils, with each pupil measured twice weekly in three academic areas, teachers would save 5 hours per week in measurement activities if they use computers to collect data. Additionally, with automatic data collection, teachers were more satisfied with CBM.

Effects of skills analysis

Effects of the third CMI application, skills analysis, were assessed in 1987–1988 (Fuchs, Fuchs, & Hamlett, 1989b; Fuchs, Fuchs, Hamlett, & Allinder, 1991b; Fuchs, Fuchs, Hamlett, & Stecker, 1990). Twenty special educators used computers for automatic data collection and for data management. In each academic area, half of the teachers received graphed and skills analyses of student performance, and the other half received only graphed analysis. With respect to efficiency, findings indicated that teachers who received graphed and skills analysis spent more time reviewing student assessment information – largely because there was more information to view. They were, however, more satisfied with the procedures with both types of computerized analyses.

Additionally, our research indicates that, across reading, spelling, and math, student achievement differences accrue due to the skills analysis programs. During 1987–1988, teachers used CBM with computerized data management with enhanced feedback and automatic data collection. Half of the teachers received the graphed analysis only, and the other half received the graphed analysis along with skills analyses. In each area, students whose teachers received the supplementary skills analysis achieved better, with statistically and practically important differences (Fuchs, Fuchs, & Hamlett, 1989b; Fuchs, Fuchs, Hamlett, & Allinder, 1991b; Fuchs, Fuchs, Hamlett, & Stecker, 1990). Although these supplementary skills analyses are performed efficiently and accurately by computers, the process is time consuming and unreliable when performed by humans. So, it appears that computers can be used to provide supplementary skills analysis that is unavailable and that enhances the extent to which teachers can make sound instructional decisions to boost student achievement.

Effects of expert systems

Effects of the fourth CMI application expert systems, were evaluated during 1988–1989. For each academic area, half of the participating teachers used expert systems to help determine how to revise student programs when CBM data indicated inadequate student progress. The other half formulated instructional adjustments using their own judgment. In math, for example, the expert systems entered into dialogue with the teacher, requesting information about the student's graphed performance, skills analysis, work habits, and previous instructional program, and the teacher's curriculum priorities. Based on the teacher's responses, the program identified skills for instruction, instructional strategies, skills for mixed probe drill, and motivational strategies.

With respect to the efficiency of and teacher satisfaction with CBM, we found that teachers spent more time with CBM activities when teachers used the expert system to help determine the nature of their instructional changes. Interestingly, however, despite this additional time, teacher satisfaction with the CBM process increased with use of the expert systems.

Achievement effects associated with the expert systems varied as a function of content area. In math (Fuchs, Fuchs, Hamlett, & Stecker, 1991), effects supporting the expert system were more impressive. Teachers who used the expert system designed better instructional programs, which incorporated attention to a more diverse set of skills, which relied on a more varied set of instructional design features. Additionally, students in the expert system experimental groups achieved significantly and dramatically better than students in the nonexpert system, CBM group and better than the control (i.e., non-CBM) group.

In reading (Fuchs, Fuchs, Hamlett, & Ferguson, 1992), effects differed for instructional planning and for achievement. Teachers in the expert system CBM group planned instructional programs that incorporated more reading skills and that utilized more instructional methods. With respect to achievement, students in the expert system group achieved reliably better than nonexpert system CBM pupils and than control students on outcome measures involving written retells, an outcome measure that mirrored expert system teachers' greater use of written story grammar and retell instructional activities. On other reading outcome measures (i.e., oral reading fluency and maze), however, both CBM groups achieved comparably well and better than the control group.

Results in the area of spelling (Fuchs, Fuchs, Hamlett, & Allinder, 1991a) were least supportive of the expert system. Nonexpert and expert system teachers both effected reliably better achievement outcomes than both the control teachers; however, the two CBM groups' achievement was not reliably different. Our analysis of teachers' instructional plans indicated that teachers in the expert system relied on practice routines recommended by the expert system to a great extent, and utilized teacher-directed instruction recommendations less frequently. The expert system, in the absence of instructional recommendations, ended up providing more teacher-directed instruction in spelling. Consequently, the expert system advice did not substantially add to or improve decisions formulated by the teachers.

SUMMARY

Several patterns in our CMI research program warrant summary. With respect to the effects of CMI on the efficiency of ongoing systematic monitoring programs, data-management systems *alone* do not appear to improve the efficiency of the monitoring process. When computers are used to prepare, administer, and score the measurements, however, teacher time devoted to CBM is substantially reduced. Additionally, supplementary analysis, such as skills analysis and use of expert systems, necessitates additional time. Interestingly, regardless of actual effects of computer applications on the efficiency of the CBM process, teachers uniformly support CMI applications, as indicated by their satisfaction as expressed in questionnaires.

With respect to teacher involvement in the process, our research indicates use of CMI programs may, in fact, reduce teachers' meaningful use of assessment information, and strategies for maintaining teacher involvement in CBM may be necessary, as software frees teachers from collecting, scoring, and analyzing their students' assessments. In terms of achievement, when CMI programs supplement quantitative graphed summaries of student performance with more qualitative descriptions of student performance, such as skills analyses (which are difficult if not impossible for practitioners to conduct by hand), teacher planning and student achievement improves. Finally, use of expert systems may enhance teacher planning and student achievement. However, the efficacy of each specific expert system must be evaluated; our pattern of results does uniformly support the effectiveness of expert systems.

Consequently, it appears that computers can be used to improve CBM efficiency, implementation, and student achievement outcomes. However, it is not always possible to anticipate how specific CMI applications will affect the assessment process. Systematic research exploring effects of specific applications appears necessary, and software developed in line with empirical findings may continue to be helpful in enhancing teachers' systematic use of assessment information.

Research reported in this paper was supported, in part, by Grants #G008530198, #G008730087, and #H023E900020 from the US Department of Education, Office of Special Education Programs, to Vanderbilt University.

REFERENCES

Bardenstein, L. (1982). MELBORP (Math drill and practice). *American Annuals of the Deaf, 127,* 659–664.

Baker, F. B. (1978). *Computer managed instruction: Theory and practice,* Englewood, Cliffs, NJ: Educational Technology Publications.

Baldwin, V. (1976). Curriculum concerns. In M. A. Thomas (Ed.). *Hey, don't forget about me.* Reston, VA: Council for Exceptional Children.

Behrmann, M. (1984). Types of computer applications. In M. Behrmann (Ed.), *Handbook of microcomputers in special education,* (pp.47–64). San Diego, CA: College-Hill Press.

Bennet, R. E. (1982). Applications of microcomputer technology to special education. *Exceptional Children, 49,* 106–114.

Budoff, M., & Hutten, L. R. (1982). Microcomputers in special education: Promises and pitfalls. *Exceptional Children, 48,* 123–128.

California Achievement Test (1977). Monterey, CA: CTB/McGraw-Hill.

Campbell, D. T., & Stanley, J. C. (1963). *Experimental and quasi-experimental designs for research.* Boston, MA: Houghton Mifflin.

Carlson, S. A., & Silverman, R. (1986). Microcomputers and computer-assisted instruction in special education classrooms: Do we need the teacher? *Learning Disabilities Quarterly, 9,* 105–110.

Carman, G. 0., & Kosberg, B. (1982). Educational technology research: Computer technology and the education of emotionally handicapped children. *Educational Technology, 22,* 26–30.

Chapin, J. D., Lorenz, T., Anglin, J. A., & Grass, B. (1975). An interactive management information system for support of individualized instruction. Paper presented at the annual meeting of the American Educational Research Association.

Chiang, A. (1978). *Demonstration of the use of computer assisted instruction with handicapped children* (Report No. 446-AM-66076A). Arlington, VA: RMC Research Corp. (ERIC Document Reproduction Service No. ED 166 913)

Chiang, B. (1986). Initial learning and transfer effects of microcomputer drills on LD students' multiplication skills. *Learning Disability Quarterly, 9*

Christensen, C. A., & Cosden, M. A. (1986). The relationship between special education placement and instruction in computer literacy skills. *Journal of Educational Computing Research, 2,* 299–306.

Cook, T. D., & Campbell, D. T. (1979). *Quasi-experimentation: Design and analysis issues for field settings.* Boston, MA: Houghton Mifflin.

Cosden, M. A. (1988). Microcomputer instruction and perceptions of effectiveness by special and regular education elementary school teachers. *Journal of Special Education, 22* 242–253.

Cosden, M. A., Gerber, M. M., Semmel, D. S., Goldman, S. R., & Semmel, M. I. (1987). Microcomputer use within microeducational environments. *Exceptional Children, 53,* 399–409.

Deno, S. L. (1985). Curriculum-based measurement: The emerging alternative. *Exceptional Children, 52, 219–232.*

Dick, W., & Gallagher, P. (1972). System concepts and computer-managed instruction: An implementation and validation study. *Educational Technology, 12,* 33–38.

Einhorn, H. J., & Hogarth, R. M. (1978). Confidence in judgment: Persistence of the illusion of validity. *Psychological Review, 85,* 395–416.

Ellis, E. S., & Sabornie, E. J. (1986). Effective instruction with microcomputers: Promises, practices, and preliminary findings. *Focus on Exceptional Children, 19,* 1–16.

Eubanks, E. E., & Levine, D. U. (1983). A first look at effective schools projects in New York City and Milwaukee. *Phi Delta Kappa, 64,* 697–702.

Finch, J. M. (1972). An overview of computer-managed instruction. *Educational Technology, 12,* 38–46.

Flanagan, J. C., Shanner, W. M., Brudner, H. G., & Marker, R. W. (1975). An individualized instructional system: PLAN. In H. Talmadge (Ed.), *Systems of individualized instruction.* Berkeley: McCutchan.

Fuchs, L. S., Deno, S. L., & Mirkin, P. K. (1984). The effects of frequent curriculum-based learning. *American Educational Research Journal, 21,* 449–460.

Fuchs, L. S. (1988). Effects of computer-managed instruction on teachers' implementation of systematic monitoring programs and student achievement. *Journal of Educational Research, 81, 294–304.*

Fuchs, L. S., Fuchs, D. (1984). Criterion-referenced assessment without measurement: How accurate for special education? *Remedial and Special Education, 5* (4), 29–32.

Fuchs, L. S., Fuchs, D., & Hamlett, C. L. (1989a). Computers and curriculum-based measurement: Effects of teacher feedback systems. *School Psychology Review, 18,* 112–125.

Fuchs, L. S., Fuchs, D., & Hamlett, C. L. (1989b). Monitoring reading growth using student recalls: Effects of two teacher feedback systems. *Journal of Educational Research, 83,* 103–111.

Fuchs, L. S., Fuchs, D., Hamlett, C. L., & Allinder, R. M. (1991a). Effects of expert system advice within curriculum-based measurement on teacher planning and student achievement in spelling. *School Psychology Review, 20,* 49–66.

Fuchs, L. S., Fuchs, D., Hamlett, C. L., & Allinder, R. M. (1991b). The contribution of skills analysis to curriculum-based measurement in spelling. *Exceptional Children, 57,* 443–452.

Fuchs, L. S., Fuchs, D., Hamlett, C. L., & Ferguson, C. (1992). Effects of expert system consultation within curriculum-based measurement using a reading maze task. *Exceptional Children, 58,* 436–450.

Fuchs, L. S., Fuchs, D., Hamlett, C. L., & Stecker, P. M. (1991). Effects of curriculum-based measurement and consultation on teacher planning and student achievement in mathematics operations. *American Educational Research Journal, 28,* 617–641.

Fuchs, L. S., Hamlett, C. L., & Fuchs, D. (1990a). *Monitoring Basic Skills Growth: Basic Math.* Austin, TX: PRO-ED.

Fuchs, L. S., Hamlett, C. L., & Fuchs, D. (1990b). *Monitoring Basic Skills Growth: Basic Reading.* Austin, TX: PRO-ED.

Fuchs, L. S., Hamlett, C. L., & Fuchs, D. (1990c). *Monitoring Basic Skills Growth: Basic Spelling*. Austin, TX: PRO-ED.

Fuchs, L. S., Hamlett, C. L., Fuchs, D., Stecker, P. M., & Ferguson, C.(1988). Conducting curriculum-based measurement with computerized data collection: Effects on efficiency and teacher satisfaction. *Journal of Special Education Technology, 9* (2), 73–86.

Fuchs, L. S., Fuchs, D., Hasselbring, T. S., & Hamlett, C. (1987). Effects of computerization of data-based instruction on teacher efficiency. *Journal of Special Education Technology 8* (4), 14–27.

Furst, M. (1983). Building self-esteem. *Academic Therapy, 19,* 11–16.

Gardner, E. F., Rudman, H. C., Karlsen, B., & Merwin, J.C. (1982). *Stanford Achievement Test.* Cleveland, OH: Psychological Corporation.

Gerber, M. M. (1986). Teaching with microcomputers. *Academic Therapy, 22,* 117–124.

Gersten, R., Carnine, D., & White, W. A. T. (1984). The pursuit of clarity: Direct instruction and applied behavior analysis. In W. L. Heward, T. E.Heron, D. S. Hill, & J. Trap-Porter (Eds.), *Focus on behavior analysis in education* (pp.38–57). Columbus, OH: Merrill.

Goldman, S. R., & Pellegrino, J. W. (1987). Information processing and educational microcomputer technology: Where do we go from here? *Journal of Learning Disabilities, 20,* 144–154.

Goodman, L. (1985). The effective schools movement and special education. *Teaching Exceptional Children, 17,* 102–105.

Gourgey, A. F. (1987). Coordination of instruction and reinforcement as enhancers of the effectiveness of computer-assisted instruction. *Journal of Educational Computing Research, 3,* 219–230.

Hannaford, A. E., & Taber, F. M. (1982). Microcomputer software for the disabled: Development and evaluation. *Exceptional Children, 49,* 137–144.

Hasselbring, T. S., & Hamlett, C. (1985). Planning and managing instructional: Computer-based decision making. *Teaching Exceptional Children, 16,* 248–252.

Hasselbring, T. S., & Goin, L. T. (1989). Use of computers. In G. A. Robinson,J. R. Patton, E. A. Polloway, & L. R. Sargent (Eds.), *Best Practices in Mild Mental Retardation* (pp.395–412). Reston, VA: Division on Mental Retardation-Council for Exceptional Children.

Hasselbring, T. S., Goin, L. I., & Bransford, J. D. (1988). Developing math automaticity in learning handicapped children: The role of computerized drill and practice. *Focus on Exceptional Children, 20,* 1–7.

Hayes, W. L. (1973). *Statistics for the social sciences* (2nd ed.). New York: Holt Rinehart.

Hoffman, J. V., & Rutherford, W. L. (1984). Effective reading programs: Acritical review of outlier studies. *Reading Research Quarterly, 20,* 79–92.

Hofmeister, A. M. (1984a). *Development of a microcomputer/videodisc aided math instructional management system for mildly handicapped children.* Final report to the U. S. Department of Education, Office of Special Education, Project #G008101536. Logan: Utah State University.

Hofmeister, A. M. (1984b). *Classroom behavior consultant.* Logan: Utah State University.

Hofmeister, A. M., & Lubke, M. M. (1986). Expert systems: Implications for the diagnosis and treatment of learning disabilities. *Learning Disability Quarterly, 9,* 133–137.

Howell, R., Sidorendko, E., & Jurica, J. (1987). The effects of computer use on the acquisition of multiplication facts by a student with learning disabilities. *Journal of Learning Disabilities, 20,* 336–341.

Jastak, F., & Jastak, S. (1978). *Wide Range Achievement Test.* Wilmington, DE: Jastak Associates.

Kazdin, A. E. (1975). Response maintenance and transfer of training. In A. E. Kazdin (Ed.), *Behavior modification in applied settings* (pp.212–228). Homewood, IL: Dorsey Press.

Kelly, A. C. (1968). An experiment with TIPS: A computer-aided instructional system for undergraduate education. *The American Economic Review, 58,* 446–457.

Lieber, J., & Semmel, M. I. (1985). Effectiveness of computer application to instruction with mildly disabled learners: A review. *Remedial and Special Education, 6,* 5–12.

Light, R. J., & Pillemer, D. B. (1984). *Summing up: The science of reviewing research.* Cambridge: Harvard University Press.

Lovitt, T. C. (1981). Notes on behavior modification. *Journal of Special Education, 15,* 395–400.

Malouf, D. B. (1987). The effect of instructional computer games on continuing student motivation. *Journal of Special Education, 21,* 27–38.

McDermott, P. A., & Watkins, M. W. (1983). Computerized vs. conventional remedial instruction for learning-disabled pupils. *Journal of Special Education, 17,* 81–88.

Messerly, C. (1986). The use of computer-assisted instruction in facilitating the acquisition of math skills with hearing-impaired high school students. *Volta Review, 88,* 67–77.

O'Neil, H. R., Heldl, J. J., Richardson, F. C., & Judd, W. A. (1976). An affective and cognitive evaluation of computer managed instruction. *Educational Technology, 16,* 29–34.

Perkins, V. L. (1988). Effective instruction using microcomputers. *Academic Therapy, 24,* 129–136.

Peters, E., & Lloyd, J. (1986). Effective instruction: Critical components of teaching. *Teaching Exceptional Children, 19,* 46.

Peterson, D. L., Albert, S. C., Foxworth, A. M., Cox, L. S., & Tilley, B. K. (1985). Effective schools for all students: Current efforts and directions. *Teaching Exceptional Children, 17,* 106–111.

Rieth, H. (1979). *An analysis of the instructional and contextual variables that influence the efficacy of computer-based instruction for mildly handicapped secondary students.* (Available from H. Rieth, Box 328, Peabody College, Nashville, TN 37203.)

Rieth, H. (1986). Computers in special education survey. (Available from H. Rieth, Box 328, Peabody College, Nashville, TN 37203.)

Rieth, H. J., Polsgrove, L., & Semmel, M. I. (1981). Instructional variables that make a difference: Attention to task and beyond. *Exceptional Education Quarterly, 2* (3), 61–72.

Schnorr, J. M. (1989). Practicing math facts on the computer. *Teacher Education and Special Education, 12,* 65–69.

Shavelson, R., & Stern, P. (1981). Research on teachers' pedagogical thoughts, judgments, decisions, and behavior. *Review of Educational Research, 51,* 441–454.

Slavin, R. E. (1986). Best evidence synthesis: An alternative to meta-analytic and traditional reviews. *Educational Researcher, 15,* 5–11.

Stowitschek, J. J., & Stowitschek, C. E. (1984). Once more with feeling: The absence of research on teacher use of microcomputers. *Exceptional Education Quarterly, 4,* 23–29.

Tawney, J. W., & Gast, D. L. (1984). *Single subject research in special education.* Columbus, OH: Merrill.

Taylor, R. P. (Ed.). (1980). *The computer in the school: Tutor, tool, tutee.* New York: Teachers College Press.

Tindal, G., Fuchs, L. S., Christenson, S., Mirkin, P. K., & Deno, S. L. (1981). *The relationship between student achievement and teacher assessment of short- or long-term goals* (Research Report No. 61). Minneapolis: Institute for Research on Learning Disabilities. (ERIC Document Reproduction Service No. ED 218 246)

Trifiletti, J. J., Firth, G. H., & Armstrong, S. (1984). Microcomputers versus resource rooms for LD students: A preliminary investigation of the effects on math skills. *Learning Disabilities Quarterly, 7, 69–76.*

Trow, W. C. (1977). Educational technology and the computer. *Educational Technology, 17, 18–21.*

Vitello, S. J., & Bruce, P. (1977). Computer-assisted instructional programs to facilitate mathematical learning among the handicapped. *Journal of Computer-Based Instruction, 4,* 26–29.

Wesson, C., King, R. P., & Deno, S. L. (1984). Direct and frequent measurement of student performance: If it's good for, why don't we do it? *Learning Disability Quarterly, 7, 45–48.*

Westinghouse Learning Corporation (1975). *The PLAN Curriculum – Overview Language Arts.* New York: Author.

White, 0. R. (1974). *Evaluating the educational process.* Seattle: University of Washington, Child Development and Mental Retardation Center, Experimental Education Unit.

White 0. R., & Haring, N. G. (1980). *Exceptional teaching* (2nd ed.). Columbus, OH: Merrill.

SOCIAL SKILLS:
REVIEW AND IMPLICATIONS FOR INSTRUCTION FOR STUDENTS WITH MILD MENTAL RETARDATION

Lori Korinek and Edward A. Polloway

Social competence has frequently been cited as a critical component of life adjustment (e.g., Epstein & Cullinan, 1987; Neel, 1988). In particular, the importance of social competence and related personality features has been stressed for individuals who have mental retardation or other developmental disabilities (e.g., Balla & Zigler, 1979). As a consequence, social skills instruction has increasingly been recognized as a key component to be included in intervention programs for students who are mildly mentally retarded.

In this chapter, we seek to address a series of three aspects of this topic. First, attention is given to a review of recent research which illustrates the nature of social and behavioral problems experienced by individuals with retardation. Second, we discuss considerations for selection of curricular programs available to facilitate the training of social skills. Third, attention is given to specific instructional approaches in the social domain. Finally, the concluding section focuses on the general implications of this discussion.

It is important to initially acknowledge current realities concerning the population that is the focus of our discussion. School programs for students with mild mental retardation have experienced substantial changes since the mid-1970s in terms of the nature of the students that they identify and serve. These changes have altered significantly traditional presumptions about the characteristics of this group (Polloway & Smith, 1988). Reasons for population change include various factors such as definitional changes and sociopolitical factors which have brought about an overall decrease in prevalence in programs for student with mild mental retardation (Polloway & Smith, 1983).

Federal data provide a general indication of the magnitude of the numerical decreases that have occurred in the prevalence of students served as mentally retarded. For example, between the school years 1976–77 and 1986–87, for the ten years immediately following the passage of PL 94–142, virtually all states and territories showed a decline in the number of children served in such school programs with the overall national decrease eventually being well over 30 per cent (Algozzine & Korinek, 1985; MacMillan, 1989; U. S. Department of Education, 1989).

Specifically, the numerical 'cure' (Reschly, 1988) that this decrease in prevalence reflects has been effected by the declassification of many students previously served as mildly mentally retarded and described as the highest functioning or most 'adaptive' in what used to be called *educable* mentally retarded (EMR) programs and by the restrictiveness in eligibility procedures for other subsequently referred children who were considered borderline cases (Mascari & Forgnone, 1982; Polloway, 1984). As a consequence, programs in those states where significant reductions in prevalence estimates have been noted are now likely to be serving a population that MacMillan and Borthwick (1980) have described as 'a more patently disabled group' (p.155) and include individuals who are more likely to exhibit multiple disabilities (Forness & Polloway, 1987).

Given the limited research attention focused on students identified as having mild mental retardation in the 1970s and 1980s (Haywood, 1979; Prehm, 1985), relatively limited data are available on the current population in terms of social functioning levels as well as related concerns for appropriate school placements, various demographic variables, and curricular needs (Epstein, Polloway, Patton, & Foley, 1989). This concern is particularly important since the significant population shift described above calls into question the validity of the rich experimental foundation developed in past decades, thus leaving it of questionable value for evaluating current issues (Gottlieb, 1982; MacMillan, 1989; MacMillan, Meyers, & Morrison, 1980).

SOCIOBEHAVIORAL DEFICITS
IN MILD MENTAL RETARDATION

There has traditionally been a high degree of professional agreement that persons with mild mental retardation exhibit social, behavioral, and emotional difficulties to a greater extent than would be reported within the general population (Beier, 1964; Heber, 1964; Patton & Polloway, 1990; Reese-Dukes & Stokes, 1978; Szymanski, 1980). In their classic volume on this topic, Balthazar and Stevens (1975) indicated that the prevalence of emotional and behavioral disorders in persons with mental retardation was likely to range between 10–30 per cent. The problem of differential diagnosis (Benton, 1964; Schloss, 1984) has been seen as but one result of the occurrence of such adjustment problems. Regardless of the relationship between the two disabling conditions, it is clear that adjustment problems have often historically been a significant contributing factor in decisions to refer students for mental retardation programs (Polloway & Patton, 1990).

Because of the importance of social concerns in persons who are mentally retarded, several notable attempts have been made to conceptualize the construct of social competence (e.g., Greenspan, 1979; Sargent, 1989) as well as to define its role in relation to the general concept of mental retardation (e.g., St. Claire, 1989). Greenspan (1990) recently proposed a revised model of social competence that is divided into two sub-constructs. The first, entitled *intellectual aspects*, includes practical and social intelligence. Practical intelligence refers to 'the ability to maintain and sustain oneself as an independent person in managing the routine activities of daily living' (Coulter & Polloway, 1989, p.1), whereas social intelligence focuses on the 'ability to understand social expectations and the evaluation of other persons, and to judge appropriately how to conduct oneself in social situations' (Coulter & Polloway, 1989, p.2). Greenspan's (1979) original model included social comprehension, social insight, judgment, and communication, whereas the revised model deals with the general areas of awareness and skill. The second sub-construct of the revised model, *personality aspects*, focuses on style aspects of competence. These include temperament and character, which together focus on attention, calmness, niceness, and responsibility (Greenspan, 1990).

Sargent (1989) developed another important model of social competence derived in part from Greenspan's work. The three components of Sargent's model include: *social affect* (appearance of an individual to others), *social skills* (specific behaviors that are central to interpersonal interactions), and *social cognition* (intelligence inclusive of the individual's understanding and being able to respond appropriately to various social situations). Social skills curricula must attend to these varied dimensions of social competence to meet the needs of students with mental retardation.

These attempts at model-building represent positive developments for understanding social competence and, to some degree, mental retardation in general. However, despite these models and the common presumptions about the existence of social competence problems in individuals with mild mental retardation, there have been relatively few recent studies of such problems (Polloway, Epstein, & Cullinan, 1985). The primary educational research base in this area was developed in the 1960s and 1970s and derived from comparisons between students placed in special vs. regular class based programs (e.g., Kehle & Guidubaldi, 1978; Luftig, 1980; for reviews, see Cegelka & Tyler, 1970; Corman & Gottlieb, 1978; Polloway, 1984). The data reported in such efficacy studies do not provide a substantive base for forming generalizations about the nature of specific sociobehavioral problems, since they are characterized by wide variance both in methodology and findings. Additionally, their focus was mainly on the effects of specific service delivery models rather than an analysis of specific behaviors. As a consequence, limited confirmation exists on the prevalence and nature of specific problems in children and adolescents with mild mental retardation (e.g., MacMillan, 1982; Matson & Breuning, 1983).

RESEARCH ON PROBLEM AREAS

In seeking to elucidate the nature of social deficits, we have chosen to review more current research according to a broad definition of such deficits. Therefore, cited in the review below are studies which attend to the social arena inclusive of research on related concerns such as behavioral disturbances and specific personality traits which hold relevance for social competence.

Since the 1970s, one approach that has been used to study the sociobehavioral area is the Behavior Problem Checklist (BPC) (Quay, 1977; Quay & Peterson, 1975, 1983), a rating scale of 55 specific problem areas. The instrument has been widely used with a variety of populations (see Quay & Peterson, 1983) including a series of studies examining behavior problems of students with mental retardation (e.g., Cullinan, Epstein, & Dembinski, 1979; Cullinan, Epstein, Matson, & Rosemier, in press; Matson, Epstein, & Cullinan, 1984). For example, Cullinan et al. (in press), factor analyzed data from adolescent students and reported that those identified as retarded exhibited significantly more problems within the domains of conduct disorder and personality problem. Matson et al. (1984) reported that the behavior problems obtained from factor analysis data from adolescents with mental retardation included the dimensions of conduct problems, attention-deficit disorder, socialized delinquency, personality problems and depression.

Based on another study using the BPC, Polloway and colleagues (1985) reported that students with mental retardation were more likely to exhibit behavioral and emotional problems than were their non-disabled peers. A total of 330 such comparisons were analyzed with 40.6 per cent indicative of significantly more problems in the students with mental retardation. Overall, elementary school pupils with mild retardation differed from their same sex peers on the most items, with a significant difference found for this group on 30 of 55 items for males and 36 of 55 items for females. As age increased, the number of differences in the prevalence of behavior problems between the two groups lessened.

Comparative findings were particularly instructive in the area of self-concept. The relevant literature in this area has generally indicated that students with mild retardation report lower levels of self-efficacy than do their peers (see Simeonsen, 1978). To the extent that any self-report instruments reflect items dealing with competence in specific skills (e.g., academic), it could be concluded that such self-appraisals would be accurate at least in that limited context. Findings from Polloway et al. (1985) provide support for the existence of low self-concept as evaluated by teachers on items which encourage a focus on specific skill deficiencies (e.g., lacks self-confidence, feels inferior). All age and sex comparisons between students identified as mentally retarded v. non-retarded were significant.

Another factor analytic study utilizing the BPC was reported by Epstein, Cullinan, and Polloway (1986). They found that students who were identified as mildly mentally retarded were likely to display the following patterns of adjustment problems, ordered by significance: aggression, attention disorder, anxiety-inferiority, and social incompetence, with the aggression factor clearly being the most pronounced. Students identified as mildly mentally retarded could be differentiated from their non disabled peers at each age and sex level for the first three factors. The social incompetence factor had not been identified in previous research. The items comprising this factor (e.g., social withdrawal, sluggishness, fixed expression) are rarely evaluated on adaptive behavior scales.

Research conducted on using other methodologies such as teacher reports has also confirmed the presence of social and behavioral problems in students with mild mental retardation. In their study investigating sociobehavioral characteristics of elementary and secondary students with mild mental retardation, Polloway, Epstein, Patton, Cullinan, and Luebke (1986) reported mixed findings relative to social status. Whereas over half of the students were rated by their teachers as either popular or at least accepted, between 21 and 29 per cent of each of the four age X sex samples were seen as either neglected or rejected. These findings complement studies reported by Gottlieb and his colleagues. Gottlieb and Budoff (1973) reported that the more inappropriate that the behavior was, the more likely that the individual demonstrating the behavior would be rejected. Gottlieb, Semmel, and Veldman (1978) indicated that rejection results from the non-disabled students' perception of the inappropriate nature of overt behavior rather than academic incompetence, thus emphasizing a key social consideration in integration efforts and underscoring the need for instruction in social skills and social competence for students who are mentally retarded.

More recently, Epstein, Polloway, Patton, and Foley (1989) provided descriptive data on the characteristics of elementary students with mild mental retardation. The data were derived from individualized education programs (IEPs) on a variety of traits and services provided to a population of 107 students. They reported that distractibility and other attention-related items were the most often listed behavioral characteristics. Further, over 80 per cent of the students had identified social and/or behavioral problems while 7 per cent had been identified as also being eligible for services in the area of behavior disorders. Epstein et al. (1989), indicated that the latter figure may have been a conservative estimate based on the prevailing tendency to identify an individual student within only one of the traditional categories of mild disabilities. Nevertheless, the figure is consistent with Balthazar and Stevens' (1975) estimate noted earlier that 10–30 per cent of persons with mental retardation have emotional or behavioral disorders as a secondary disability.

The issue of dual diagnosis and significant sociobehavioral and psychological disorders in individuals with mild mental retardation was further investigated by Forness and Polloway (1987). Their study focused on the presence of psychiatric and physical diagnoses in such students. Analyzing a group of students referred to a tertiary care program, they reported that over 75 per cent of the students qualified for a psychiatric diagnosis. Included in this population were students identified as: within the autistic spectrum (i.e., autism or pervasive developmental disorders); with primary diagnoses of conduct disorders and attention deficits; with initial referrals for attentional or conduct disturbance but subsequent diagnosis revealing affective or schizophrenic disorders; and, with identification as having been sexually or physically abused. These data are reinforced by the reality of psychosocial stressors within the students' homes. Forness and Polloway (1987) indicated at least a moderate-to-severe level of environmental stress overall with subsequent fair-to-poor levels of psychosocial adaptation.

While the sample in the above study is not representative of the total population of students with mild retardation (i.e., since clients were referred through three agencies for specialized services), it did represent about one in every 8 or 9 such students served within the center's catchment area. Given an average class size of 8–15 students in mild mental retardation programs, these findings suggest the possibility that one or several such students might be enrolled in each classroom.

The possible linkages between mental retardation and behavior disorders including social deficits continues to be an area warranting further consideration. Reiss, Levitan, and McNally (1982) theorized that increased risk of emotional/behavioral problems should be expected because these individuals must face social adjustment problems equipped with limited problem-solving skills. The general findings across studies in the sociobehavioral domain reinforce the importance of curricular attention to social competence. It is apparent that students with mental retardation and related disabilities have unique educational needs that place them at risk for poor adult outcomes if appropriate interventions are not employed (Linden & Forness, 1986).

RESEARCH ON CURRICULAR ASPECTS

What are the implications for curriculum design of the findings of sociobehavioral difficulties experienced by students with mild mental retardation? It is illustrative to initially consider the findings of Epstein et al. (1989) on individualized education program (IEP) goals. Clear emphasis on academic goals was found in students' IEPs as consistent with prior analyses (e.g., McBride & Forgnone, 1985). Although in elementary programs this may not be surprising, the limited emphasis on social-emotional skills are of concern, especially when considered in conjunction with their finding of the absence of transition and career development goals. Elementary programs should provide preparation for subsequent environments by focusing on horizontal transitions (i.e., to mainstream classes) and vertical transitions (to later grades), thus laying a foundation for future programming in life skills (Jaquish & Stella, 1986; Polloway, 1987; Silverman, Zigmond, & Sansone, 1981). The virtually exclusive emphasis on academic skills is consistent with data reported by McBride and Forgnone (1985) who found that only 1–4 per cent of the IEP objectives written for middle school students with mild mental retardation reflected either career-vocational or socio-behavioral domains. Given the fact that Edgar (1987, 1988) has reported that a minority of the graduates of programs for students with mild mental retardation surveyed were employed, engaged in training, or living independently, the need for a shift in curricular orientation seems evident.

Polloway and Smith (1988) argued for the critical importance of social skills training both for the facilitation of school integration efforts and for the potential benefits for adult outcomes. Social skills have been defined as 'responses which, within a given situation, prove effective, or in other words, maximize the probability of producing, maintaining, or enhancing positive effects for the interactor' (Foster & Ritchey, 1979, p.626). Thus, training efforts focused on social skills acquisition are concerned with the development of skills necessary to overcome situations in classrooms, on the job, and in other areas that prevent assimilation (Masters & Mori, 1986). Several studies further provide an educational context for this concern.

MacMillan and Borthwick (1980) indicated that mainstreaming did not appear feasible when applied to students identified under the increasingly common restrictive definitions of mild mental retardation; integration efforts were generally limited to nonacademic periods during the instructional day.

Although more recent work raises some questions about this assertion their findings can be interpreted as support for the importance of social skills training as a complement to academic instruction as the key factor in the establishment of successful integrated programs.

In a widely cited early study, Reese-Dukes and Stokes (1978) reported on a program in which 33 students with mild mental retardation were completely mainstreamed into regular classes. Degree of social acceptance was determined through a sociometric scale. In all areas evaluated, the children with mild mental retardation received significantly lower social acceptance scores than did their peers. Two implicit conclusions can be identified: regular class placement should be reconsidered or training must be provided to assist in the adjustment and acceptance of students when mainstreamed. As Polloway and Patton (1986) stated, 'we can either sell out the concept or preferably strive toward a way to make it work' (p.1).

Luftig's (1980) review of the effects of placement on the self-concept of students with retardation concluded that students with higher IQ scores (i.e., 71–85) were more successful in regular classes whereas those with lower scores (i.e., 49–70) with poor reading skills maintained higher levels of self-concept in special classes. Given that students representing the former group would now rarely be placed in mild mental retardation programs, the key finding for our discussion concerns the latter students. Luftig (1980) concluded '...to place a child in an educational environment in which he cannot maintain feelings of self-worth may actually increase rather than decrease the restrictiveness in the school environment' (p.14).

In general, it seems increasingly clear that the success or failure of students with mild disabilities in regular classes is related to social competence. Gresham's (1982, 1983, 1984) reviews of over 40 studies on integration led to his conclusion that children with disabilities interact infrequently and often negatively with their nondisabled peers. Essentially, many pupils have been placed in mainstream settings without the necessary social skills to succeed and gain acceptance from their peers. Again, this can either be seen as an indictment of integration or, more appropriately, as a call for curricular attention (Polloway & Patton, 1986). As Sargent (1989) indicated, such research does not 'urge abandonment of mainstreaming' but rather creates the 'case for teaching social skills to pupils with disabilities for the purpose of enhancing their ability to benefit from integration' (p.272).

In the discussion that follows, attention is given to programs designed to teach social skills. Although limited data on the effectiveness of social skills programs are generally available (Epstein & Cullinan, 1987), the approaches highlighted have been identified as having the potential for greatest success.

CONSIDERATIONS FOR SELECTING SOCIAL SKILLS AND CURRICULA

The presence of social skill deficits and the need for instruction in this area for students with mental retardation are clear. Precisely how to assess individual needs and plan instruction for particular students may be less obvious. The practitioner is often left to determine the specific skills to teach, materials to use, and sequences of instruction to ensure mastery and generalization. This dilemma is especially true in school systems that have not designed or adopted a comprehensive social skills curriculum or that place the responsibility for program content with the classroom teacher. Particularly for such situations, the following considerations are suggested as important in the design or selection of social skills curricula.

Targeting Specific Needs

Although lack of social competence among individuals with mental retardation has been well documented, it cannot be assumed that all students are in need of training in all skills (Polloway et al., 1986). Social skills instruction should target the specific interactional skills most needed by the particular students for whom training is intended. Various measures can be used to assess social functioning, including adaptive behavior scales, rating scales, checklists, and interviews completed by teachers, parents or, in some cases, peers, as well as student self-reports, inventories, or simulations in which students are asked to respond to specific social situations. Observation of students' social competence in natural settings and environmental assessment of expectations/skills needed in more integrated settings are essential to validate the results of more formal assessments and to pinpoint the most beneficial targets for training. When data on individual students are aggregated and compared, those skills needed by the greatest number of students may be likely targets for group instruction.

Priority for initial instruction should be given to skills most needed by students in their immediate interactions and that will enhance the likelihood of successful integration with nondisabled peers (Morgan & Jensen, 1988; Polloway & Patton, 1986; Polloway & Smith, 1988; Sargent, 1989). Nelson (1988) suggested that educators begin by teaching students behaviors that will 'naturally elicit desired responses from peers and adults' (p.21). At the elementary and middle school level, these behaviors may include sharing, smiling, asking for help (McConnell, 1987), attending, turn-taking, following directions, and problem-solving (Cartledge & Milburn, 1980; Gottlieb, 1982; Odom & McEvoy, 1988) – skills which are important to gaining social acceptance and which apply across multiple settings (see review by McEvoy, Shores, Wehlby, Johnson, & Fox, 1990). At the secondary level, based upon extensive research documenting critical social demands on adolescents, Hazel, Schumaker, Sherman, and Sheldon-Wildgen (1981) identified critical skills as those of giving positive and negative feedback, accepting negative feedback, resisting peer pressure, problem-solving, negotiation, following instructions, and conversation. Community-related and work-related social skills may also assume priority at the upper high school level (Jaquish & Stella, 1986; Polloway, 1987). The social skills programs mentioned throughout this chapter to illustrate various concepts typically include a variety of peer-related, adult-related, and self-related skills to assist in decision-making and instruction. If such commercially produced programs are used, care must be taken to select those programs that address skills most needed by the students under consideration. Supplemental programs/skills may be needed to effect a match between student needs and instruction.

Selection of target skills should also correspond closely to local school, cultural, and community norms/expectations as determined by school personnel, parents, and other community members. Involving these stakeholder groups in determination of essential social competencies helps to ensure the social appropriateness/validity of instructional targets (Gresham, 1986; Morgan & Jensen, 1988) and elicits support for program efforts. Behaviors identified by these constituent groups are also more likely to be reinforced in the students' natural environments, both in and out of school.

Promotion of Social Competence as Well as Social Skills

Another consideration in designing or selecting a social skills curriculum for students with mild mental retardation is the degree to which it promotes social competence as well as social skills (Sargent, 1989; Schumaker, Pedersen, Hazel, & Meyen, 1983). As explained earlier in this chapter, social skills are specific behaviors that facilitate interpersonal interactions and maintain a degree of independence in daily functioning. Social competence involves the use of those skills at the right times and places, showing social perception, cognition, and judgment of how to act in a particular situation and how to adjust one's behavior to meet different situations (Greenspan, 1979, 1990; Kerr & Nelson, 1989; Sargent, 1989). A limited focus on skill training without addressing competence issues decreases the likelihood that the student will maintain the skills or generalize them to settings and interactions beyond the classroom. Instruction must make obvious to the student the salient characteristics of situations in which the skills are useful and appropriate, as well as afford the student ample opportunities to practice making social judgments and demonstrating skills across different situations (Haring, 1988; Sargent, 1988).

Accommodation of Learning Characteristics

While a curriculum or program may be well-suited to students with mild mental retardation in terms of the skills addressed, its utility also depends upon the degree to which the program accommodates the learning characteristics of this population such as low achievement and self-concept, limited self-management ability, a history of failure, and difficulties with cue discrimination, attention, memory, abstract thinking, problem solving, and generalization (Baroff, 1986; Epstein et al., 1989; Langone, 1986; Patton & Polloway, 1990; Polloway et al., 1985; Schumaker et al., 1983). Design features or adaptations of programs/materials that help to compensate for these difficulties include program structure, low readability and writing requirements, motivation and reinforcement aspects, direct instruction of skills, practice opportunities, and maintenance/ generalization activities.

Structure

Headings and advance organizers to orient students' attention to key content topics and upcoming material, careful task analysis of skills, sequencing from easy to more difficult material, clear presentation of sub-skills, explanations, and examples, and cues to guide responding (e.g., pictures, page numbers, examples, study guides) help to facilitate successful student use of the materials and skill acquisition. Small steps, simple directions, lack of excess detail, and frequent review further enhance the usability of curricula and minimize negative effects of mental retardation in relation to social skills acquisition (Gast, 1987; Schumaker et al., 1983; Sargent, 1988).

Manageable reading and writing requirements

The readability and language level of the material will, in part, determine the degree to which students can derive meaning from social skills curricula. Ease of reading, simple language, glossaries of key terms, video- or audiotapes of printed materials, pictorial cues, and minimal required writing are features that minimize the students' limitations in relation to the materials, yet convey the information in an understandable manner. Materials that employ a variety of learning modalities also enhance interest for students in a class where learning styles are likely to vary (Sargent, 1988; Schumaker et al., 1983).

Motivation and reinforcement

Students with mild mental retardation, like their counterparts in general education, tend to perform better when motivated to do so or when they can clearly see the purpose for learning and demonstrating the skills being taught (Baumeister & Brooks, 1981). Instructional materials, therefore, should also include suggestions for motivating students, rationales that can be adapted to particular populations, and a variety of chronologically age-appropriate activities that invite and maintain student attention through novelty and active participation in learning. Reinforcement of social skills enhances the likelihood that they will be used again. Social skills programs should address skills that, when performed by students, elicit positive responses (natural reinforcement) from others in their environment. Additional reinforcement may also be needed during initial phases of instruction.

Various commercial programs incorporate motivation and reinforcement in different ways. The *ASSET Social Skills Program for Adolescents* (Hazel et al., 1981), for example, emphasizes teacher- and student-identified rationales and incorporates goal-setting for learning the social skills included in the curriculum. Similarly, *The Prepare Curriculum* (Goldstein, 1988) includes the provision of a rationale for learning as the first step in each session on problem solving. Considerable guidance is also provided for the teacher on management and reinforcement of student behavior. The *ACCEPTS* program (Walker et al. 1983), and the *RECESS* program (Walker et al., 1978) include a management system wherein points earned during training can be redeemed for minutes of free time. Additional suggestions are made for informal contracts and alternative reinforcers. Certificates are awarded in the *Skillstreaming* program (Goldstein, Sprafkin, Gershaw, & Klein, 1980). Peer instruction, cognitive behavior modification, group contingencies for individual performance, and home contingencies are techniques for motivating and reinforcing students employed in *Project SISS: Systematic Instruction of Social Skills* (Sargent, 1988). These programs provide models for designing or adapting social skills materials to address motivation and reinforcement requirements of effective instruction.

Specific training of skills and discriminations

Evidence of limited social competence among populations of students with mental retardation makes direct instruction of social discriminations and skills a critical feature of curricula in this area (Castles & Glass, 1986; Colvin & Sugai, 1988; Cullinan & Epstein, 1985; Hollinger, 1987; McGinnis & Goldstein, 1984; Stephens, 1978). This emphasis represents a shift from the focus of many of the earlier affective education and values clarification programs which emphasised feelings, attitudes, self-esteem, and appreciation of others. Activities (e.g., stories, discussion) were often awareness-oriented with little direct demonstration, practice, and monitoring of actual skill acquisition or application of skills in natural environments. While awareness activities are important in the context of social interactions, they are insufficient for achieving lasting behavioral change (Castles & Glass, 1986; Sargent, 1988; Schumaker et al., 1983; Stowitschek & Powell, 1980). Care must be exercised to select programs that will meet the skill acquisition and social competence objectives required for successful interaction.

Sufficient examples and opportunities for practice

Typically, students with mild mental retardation require more repetitions, demonstrations, and examples than their nondisabled peers in order to understand and master a concept or skill. Many of the available social skills curricula suggest use of relevant examples, modeling, and practice activities, but the degree to which the program activities are provided and appropriate for particular groups of students varies considerably from program to program. In many cases, it is left to the trainer to devise relevant demonstration and practice activities for the skills under study. The challenge is to provide sufficient repetition and practice to master skills, yet keep students motivated and interested in the training. Some programs have attempted to do this by structuring practice sessions in game-type formats, including videotaped examples/nonexamples of specific behaviors and demonstrations of skills (e.g., *ASSET*, Hazel et al., 1981; *ACCEPTS*, Walker et al., 1983), offering scripted or semi-scripted role plays (e.g., *Getting Along With Others*, Jackson, Jackson, & Monroe, 1983; *ACCESS*, Walker, Todis, Holmes, & Horton, 1988), or role-play suggestions (e.g., *Social Skills for Daily Living*, Schumaker, Hazel, & Pederson, 1988; *Getting Along With Others*, Jackson et al., 1983), and using comic books illustrating the skills under study (*Social Skills for Daily Living*, Schumaker et al., 1988).

Maintenance and generalization procedures

Possibly the greatest challenge in teaching social skills is ensuring maintenance and generalization of those skills to situations outside the classroom. Unless specific plans for generalization across persons, materials, and settings are instituted, the chances of achieving skill generalization are minimal (Haring, 1988; Rutherford & Nelson, 1988; Schloss, Schloss, Wood, & Kiehl, 1986; Stokes, & Baer, 1977). Available social skills programs incorporate a variety of generalization techniques including varying training cues and reinforcement, training in alternate settings, teaching self-monitoring strategies, and programming common stimuli in generalization settings. For example, in the *ACCEPTS* (Walker et al., 1983) and *PEERS* (Hops et al., 1978) programs, peers are enlisted to provide opportunities to students to demonstrate newly acquired skills during recess. *Social Skills for Daily Living* (Schumaker et al., 1988) uses surprise assignments wherein peers or others engage trainees in naturalistic interactions that provide practice for skills outside the classroom. Homework assignments to practice generalization are part of the *ASSET* curriculum (Hazel et al., 1981), *ACCESS* (Walker et al., 1988), *Skillstreaming* (Goldstein et al.,

1980), *Getting Along With Others* (Jackson et al., 1983) and several other programs.

Provision of Direction and Support for the Teacher

Social skills programs and materials vary greatly in the degree of detail and amount of field test information provided to educators to help them select and implement social skills instruction. Often a program will provide a general overview of skills covered, teaching methods, and progress monitoring, with few specific explanations or supplemental materials to support instruction. Effective implementation may rely heavily on teacher background, training, instructional expertise, and time available to develop the needed lessons, evaluation forms, and support materials. While the skills addressed may be highly relevant and the general suggestions helpful, the teacher may find lesson planning time-consuming. Lack of detailed information or need for additional training may also limit the use of the program by instructional assistants, volunteers, peer tutors, and others. This may, in turn, hamper generalization by limiting the number of trainers and settings for instruction (Carter & Sugai, 1989).

Another consideration under teacher support is the 'adaptability factor' or ease with which the material can be adapted to meet unique needs of individual students or groups. For example, how easily can questions be added, example situations modified, or instruction be geared toward either individuals or groups? Are instructional objectives, review lessons, enrichment activities, study guides, answer keys, and/or vocabulary development exercises included (Gast, 1987)? Most programs serving students with mild disabilities include a wide range of student abilities and needs. The more suggestions and alternatives provided the teacher to assist him/her in tailoring the program to specific needs and individualizing within a group context, the more efficient the preparation to implement social skills instruction.

Unfortunately, programs with detailed lessons, student support materials, audiovisual components, and ready-to-use assessment and evaluation systems tend to cost more, both initially and to maintain. Teachers must decide whether the cost can be justified in terms of student benefit, teacher time, and available resources. In the final analysis, the program or curriculum that offers the best match between student needs, environmental demands, teacher support, and budgetary constraints will be the program of choice. Realistically, a program that ranks high on some variables may not meet other requirements, and no single program is likely to be completely satisfactory. The teacher is left to compare and contrast available curricula and make a decision as to the *most* appropriate curriculum for the given situation or to combine and adapt aspects of different curricula. To assist in program selection, Carter and Sugai (1989) suggest using a checklist of important components/features (e.g., skills addressed, nature and level of materials, cost, ease of use, assessment and generalization procedures, field test data, etc.) to analyze and compare the different social skills programs on the dimensions identified as critical for a particular training situation. The program that incorporates the most desirable features or that seems to be the most adaptable for the resources available would be the logical choice for selection. Actually trying a curriculum or program prior to adoption, if possible, is a final step toward determination of its suitability.

INSTRUCTIONAL METHODOLOGY FOR SOCIAL SKILLS DEVELOPMENT

Current approaches to instruction that hold promise for effectively developing social skills involve direct instruction of skills, metacognitive problem-solving, or optimally, a combination of the two. Direct instruction of social skills focuses more narrowly on specific skills and discriminations and resembles effective academic instruction. This approach seems necessary for specific behavioral change among most students with mild disabilities (Cartledge & Milburn, 1980; Colvin & Sugai, 1988; Cullinan & Epstein, 1985; McGinnis & Goldstein, 1984; Morgan & Jensen, 1988; Rathjen, 1984; Stephens, 1978). Programs emphasizing interpersonal social-cognitive processes/problem-solving concentrate on applications to a wider range of conditions and situations. Training attempts to improve students' abilities to identify problems, and to generate, weigh and select alternative solutions that best fit the presenting conditions. Such decision-making is essential to help students meet the variety of situations they will likely encounter and to apply successfully specific social skills which they have acquired (Elias & Maher, 1983; Michelson & Mannarino, 1986; Vaughn, Ridley, & Cox, 1983).

Since the mid-1970s, many social skills programs published (see reference list) have included both specific skill development as well as problem-solving elements. Sargent (1988) cautions, however, that no single program or approach is sufficient to guarantee social competence. Educators must continually address and reinforce social competence in all aspects of education afforded students with mild/moderate mental retardation.

With this caution clearly in mind, the following section represents a composite social skills instructional sequence based on techniques used in programs proven successful with various groups of students who are mentally retarded. Most of these programs employ a combination of methods including demonstration, guided practice, and application activities. Such multifaceted approaches tend to enhance instructional effectiveness and durability, and appeal to a wider range of students and situations (Carter & Sugai, 1989; Schumaker, et al., 1983). The sequence could be used to teach skills that meet assessed student needs and that improve social functioning in present and future environments. The instructional steps include: (a) introduction of skill and rationale, (b) discussion of situations and examples, (c) identification of skill steps, (d) modeling, (e) rehearsal, and (f) generalization.

Introduce Skill and Rationale

In introducing a new skill, students should be told what the skill entails, how it relates to previously learned skills, and why they should learn it. This provides an advance organizer for instruction (Lenz, Alley, & Schumaker, 1987) and helps invest students in the training. Once students have a clear definition of the skill under discussion, attention should be focused on the rationale for learning the skill. Students should be guided in seeing the importance and benefits of using the skill in their daily routines, as well as the negative consequences of not using the skill or continuing to use less effective means for dealing with social interactions.

Rationales can be worded as causal statements to show students the connection between their behavior and consequences (e.g., 'If [positive behavior], then [positive consequence].' 'If [negative behavior], then [negative consequence].' (Schumaker, Hazel, & Deshler, 1988)). Rationales should also be concrete, short term, personally relevant, believable, and directly related to present demands made of the student in school or non-school environments. Too often educators use rationales that are abstract, long-term, and reflective of their values rather than the students'. Clarifying the immediate benefits of the skills in terms directly related to daily interactions (e.g., 'If you make a friend, you're more likely to have someone with whom to eat lunch.') is likely to be more meaningful and persuasive. Having students provide their own rationales following teacher modeling further enhances involvement and commitment to learning and using the skill.

Discuss Situations and Examples

Students with mild mental retardation tend to be less attuned to subtle cues that guide social behavior in interpersonal interactions (Epstein, Cullinan, & Polloway, 1986). Specific attention must be focused upon developing these discriminations. Discussing the general characteristics and presenting cues of situations in which the skill would be useful, as well as specific examples of situations from the students' current experiences where the skill is needed or would make them more successful in meeting their goals, helps students to see the immediate benefits of the training. With teacher prompting, students should be guided in formulating their own examples of situations in which skill performance is beneficial. This also promotes commitment to and responsibility for their own learning.

Use of specific examples contrasted with nonexamples of the target skill can also be effective for highlighting alternative ways of behaving in a social situation and the advantages of employing the more effective skill (e.g., *ACCESS*, Walker et al., 1988 *ACCEPTS*, Walker et al., 1983; *Getting Along With Others*, Jackson et al., 1983). This procedure also helps students to discriminate the critical attributes of a skill and likely reactions to its performance.

Identify Skills Steps

After the skill, rationale, and possible applications have been discussed, a more in-depth analysis of each skill step, including related verbal and nonverbal behaviors, takes place. Skill steps can be listed on the board, an overhead transparency, or skill cards for student reference. These same steps can be used as a checklist to give feedback, self-evaluate, and monitor progress throughout training. The number of steps should be limited for ease of remembering, but be sufficiently detailed to prompt performance of all necessary subcomponents of the skill. Some educators (e.g., Hazel et al., 1981; Schumaker et al., 1988) recommend that students verbally rehearse the skill steps until they can recite them rapidly and accurately from memory before moving to behavioral rehearsal of the skill. In other programs, students write skill steps, rehearse them via unison reading, or are allowed to refer to skill steps or cue cards until these prompts are no longer needed to perform the skill (e.g., *SISS*, Sargent, 1988). In any case, students must reach a level of automaticity with skill steps to successfully employ the skill in actual situations (Alley & Deshler, 1979; Schumaker et al., 1983).

Model the Skill

In combination with other techniques, modeling or demonstrating the appropriate behavior has repeatedly been found to enhance skill acquisition and increase instructional effectiveness (Bandura, 1977; Carter & Sugai, 1988; Morgan & Jensen, 1988; Kerr & Nelson, 1989; Schumaker et al., 1983), and to be more successful than coaching alone for teaching social skills (LaGreca, Stone, & Bell, 1983). Live models (adults or peers), videotapes, movies, puppets, and books have been used to model social behaviors. The model should be clear, unambiguous, accurate, reproducible, and adaptable (Eisler & Frederiksen, 1980). When peer models are used, they are more effective when perceived by trainees as being helpful, friendly, high status, but similar to trainees in characteristics such as race, gender, and age (Carter & Sugai, 1988; Michelson & Mannarino, 1986).

Rehearse with Feedback and Reinforcement

When students have demonstrated their understanding of skill steps by identifying or labeling each step of the target skill performed by the model, students must practice the skill to mastery. Active student involvement through role plays, with teacher reinforcement for correct performance and corrective feedback for aspects of performance that are omitted or in need of improvement, builds fluency with the skill. Initially, commercially available or teacher-written scripts of the role play situations may facilitate student performance (Gaylord-Ross & Haring, 1987). Training may then move to less structured, nonscripted practice of student-generated situations and examples with teacher coaching. As previously mentioned, checklists of skill steps may be used to monitor performance, guide feedback, and promote self-evaluation.

Extra practice may be needed on particular steps of the skill. Sargent (1988) recommends use of feedback cards during role-plays to focus attention on one subskill at a time. Having students give each other feedback or videotaping role plays for student use in self-evaluation are additional techniques to provide feedback and reinforce correct performance. Practice to criterion in role-play situations is essential. If mastery is not attained in the controlled training situation, the likelihood that the skill will be used effectively in non-training situations is minimal.

Generalize to Other Settings and Situations

Generalization activities that promote transfer of skills from training conditions to new settings and interactions are a critical part of training. Application of skills learned to non-training situations is the ultimate goal and measure of successful social skills instruction.

A variety of generalization techniques have been suggested including: (a) training in the natural setting where skills will be used or training in sequential settings until generalization to all desired settings is observed; (b) programming common stimuli and feedback used in the situations where generalization is desired; (c) sequentially varying the stimuli used in training until generalization to all related stimuli occurs; (d) using a variety of cues, prompts, materials, trainers, and settings for training; (e) introducing the student to natural maintaining contingencies, or teaching functional skills that are likely to be reinforced outside instruction and ensuring that the learner experiences this reinforcement; (f) fading artificial reinforcers used during training so the student is responding to the level and type of reinforcement likely to be present in natural situations; (g) reinforcing generalization of target skills when it is observed in other settings; (h) training students to solicit reinforcement; and (i) teaching mediational strategies such as self-instruction and self-monitoring to assist generalization (Carter & Sugai, 1989; Haring, 1988; Nelson, 1988; McConnell, 1987; Sargent, 1988; Shores, 1987; Stokes & Baer, 1977). Research has shown that all of these techniques are effective with at least some students with mild to moderate mental retardation (Haring, 1988; Liberty & Billingsley, 1988). However, which generalization techniques are *most* efficient and effective with particular individuals and social behaviors has yet to be established. In light of this situation, incorporation into training of some of the generalization strategies judged by the teacher to be most likely to succeed with his/her pupils, along with careful monitoring of generalization to measure effectiveness and need for program adjustment is warranted.

White (1988) has suggested several ways to monitor generalization. These include providing opportunities for students to demonstrate the skill in environments where the skill is desired during and after training, asking others in the environment whether the skill is being used, and direct observation by the teacher or others in the settings of importance. Nelson (1988) and Morgan and Jensen (1988) further underscore the need for collaboration between general and special education teachers to ensure monitoring, generalization, and maintenance of social skills in mainstream environments.

Peers may also be trained to facilitate generalization by initiating positive social interactions and prompting, cuing, and reinforcing their less skilled classmates in a variety of settings (McConnell, 1987; Kerr & Nelson, 1989; Hollinger, 1987). *ACCEPTS* (Walker et al., 1983), *PEERS*, (Hops et al., 1978), and *Social Skills for Daily Living* (Schumaker et al., 1988) are examples of programs that employ peers to promote generalization. Group-oriented contingencies in which the student's peer group shares in reinforcers earned by the student for demonstrating the desired behavior is another frequently used strategy to elicit peer support (e.g., *ACCEPTS*, Walker et al., 1983; *PEERS*, Hops et al., 1978; *RECESS*, Walker et al., 1978). Care must be taken, however, to ensure that the target student is capable of performing the behavior before group contingencies are employed.

Several programs include homework assignments where students apply skills practiced in class at home (e.g., *ASSET*, Hazel et al., 1981; *Getting Along With Others*, Jackson et al., 1983; *ACCESS*, Walker et al., 1988; *Skillstreaming*, Goldstein et al., 1980). Instructions for homework assignments should be clear and sufficiently detailed to allow the student to demonstrate the behavior successfully and allow others in the out-of-class setting to monitor performance. The student should also have demonstrated mastery of the social skill sequence in more controlled training situations before expecting his or her successful performance in other settings.

Self-recording, follow-up discussion of attempts to apply the skill to new situations, and teacher feedback generally accompany homework assignments. Parents or other adults in the generalization settings can report on students' performance of skills at home, in other classes, vocational settings, or the community using checklists, homenotes, or periodic reliability checks on student self-recording through observation. Positive consequences can be provided for accuracy and effective performance of target skills. Problem-solving and extra practice of skills is recommended when difficulties are encountered in the generalization setting (Cartledge & Kleefeld, 1989). Periodic review and positive practice of behaviors are also needed if students' social skills deteriorate after formal training is completed.

Collaboration between general and special educators to teach social skills in the context of the general education classroom (Bauwens, Hourcade, & Friend, 1989) is another strategy to help ensure maintenance and generalization of students' social skills. That is, rather than training students in the special education setting and hoping that skills will transfer to more integrated settings, both teachers can cooperatively teach students social skills as part of the general class curriculum. One instructor might teach certain components of the instructional sequence and the other teacher cover the remaining steps. Or one teacher might serve as the primary instructor, while the other teacher follows up with small group activities to learn the skill steps, rehearse the skill, or plan applications. The enhanced possibilities for modeling, generalization, service to students at-risk for social failure but not identified as handicapped, and a more accurate match between setting demands and actual training are strong arguments for collaborative teaching of social skills.

SUMMARY

There is little question that teachers must complement their focus on academic, linguistic, and vocational training with a like commitment to social skills training. As Balla and Zigler (1979) stated: 'if it were possible to change the personality structures of many retarded persons, they might become self-sustaining members of society rather than consigned to a life of dependency and neglect' (p.163). Clearly, findings of social deficits and related behavioral concerns should have important implications for curriculum design.

There is a significant likelihood that a large number of students in mental retardation programs experience varied problems in addition to mental retardation that collectively require a comprehensive curriculum designed to respond to their needs. The curriculum cannot solely be academic-remedial in orientation, but rather must also focus on concerns for social and daily living skills. More specifically, the curriculum should focus on the development of necessary vertical and horizontal transition skills to respectively facilitate the students' entrance into regular programs and subsequent school and community settings. The development of adequate social skills must be a key part of such a comprehensive curriculum for students with mild mental retardation (Polloway, Patton, Epstein, & Smith, 1989). This is not a new message for persons in special education; rather it evokes memory of the statement made two decades ago by Harvey Dingman (1973):

The really important question, then, is what is to be taught as 'social competence'. The skills crucial for independence living – getting along with people and utilizing social abilities – are not attained in programs for the retarded designed solely to provide an academic education. (p.90)

REFERENCES

Algozzine, B., & Korinek, L. (1985). Where is special education for students with high prevalence handicaps going? *Exceptional Children, 51,* 388–394.

Alley, G., & Deshler, D. D. (1979). *Teaching the learning disabled adolescent: Strategies and methods.* Denver: Love Publishing.

Balla, D., & Zigler, E. (1979). Personality development in retarded persons. In N. R. Ellis (Ed.), *Handbook of mental deficiency: Psychological theory and research* (2nd ed.) (pp.143–168). Hillsdale, NJ: Lawrence Erlbaum Associates.

Balthazar, E. E., & Stevens, H. A. (1975). *The emotionally disturbed, mentally retarded: A historical and contemporary perspective.* Englewood Cliffs, NJ: Prentice Hall.

Bandura, A. (1977). *Social learning theory.* Englewood Cliffs, NJ: Prentice-Hall.

Baroff, G. S. (1986). *Mental retardation: Nature, cause and management* (2nd ed.). Washington: Hemisphere Publishing Corporation.

Baumeister, A. A., & Brooks, P. H. (1981). Cognitive deficits in mental retardation. In J. M. Kauffman & D. H. Hallahan (Eds.), *Handbook of special education* (pp.87–107). Englewood Cliffs, NJ: Prentice-Hall.

Bauwens, J., Hourcade, J. J., & Friend, M. (1989). Cooperative teaching: A model for general and special education integration. *Remedial and Special Education, 10*(2), 17–22.

Beier, D. C. (1964). Behavioral disturbances in the mentally retarded. In H. Stevens & R. Heber (Eds.), *Mental retardation: A review of research* (pp.453–487). Chicago, IL: University of Chicago Press.

Benton, A. L. (1964). Psychological evaluation and differential diagnosis. In H. A. Stevens & R. Heber (Eds.), *Mental retardation: A review of research* (pp.16–56). Chicago, IL: University of Chicago Press.

Carter, J., & Sugai, G. (1989). Social skills curriculum analysis. *Teaching Exceptional Children, 22*(1), 36–39.

Carter, J., & Sugai, G. (1988). Teaching social skills. *Teaching Exceptional Children, 20*(3), 68–71.

Cartledge, G., & Kleefeld, J. (1989). Teaching social communication skills to elementary school students with handicaps. *Teaching Exceptional Children, 22*(1), 14–17.

Cartledge, G. & Milburn, J. F. (1980). *Teaching social skills to children.* New York: Pergamon.

Castles, E., & Glass, C. (1986). Training in social and interpersonal problem-solving skills for mildly and moderately mentally retarded adults. *American Journal of Mental Deficiency, 19,* 35–42.

Cegelka, W. J., & Tyler, J. L. (1970). The efficacy of special class placement for the mentally retarded in proper perspective. *Training School Bulletin, 67*(1), 33–67.

Colvin, G., & Sugai, G. (1988). *Proactive strategies for managing social behavior problems: An instructional approach.* Eugene, OR: University of Oregon.

Corman, L., & Gottlieb, J. (1978). Mainstreaming mentally retarded children: A review of research. In N. R. Ellis (Ed.), *International review of research in mental retardation* (Vol. 9) (pp.251–275). New York: Academic Press.

Coulter, D. L., & Polloway, E. A. (1989). Definition and diagnosis in mental retardation. Unpublished manuscript.

Cullinan, D., & Epstein, M. H. (1985). Behavioral interventions for educating adolescents with behavior disorders. *The Pointer, 30*(1), 4–7.

Cullinan, D., Epstein, M. H., & Dembinski, R. J. (1979). Behavior problems of educationally handicapped and normal pupils. *Journal of Abnormal Child Psychology, 7*, 495–502.

Cullinan, D., Epstein, M. H., Matson, J. L., & Rosemier, R. A. (in press). Behavior problems of mentally retarded and non-retarded adolescent pupils. *School Psychology Review.*

Dingman, H. F. (1973). Preface: Social performance of the mentally retarded. In R. K. Fyman, C. E. Meyers, & G. Tarjan (Eds.), *Sociobehavioral studies in mental retardation.* (pp.iii–ix). Monograph of the American Association on Mental Deficiency.

Edgar, E. (1988). Employment as an outcome for mildly handicapped students: Current status and future directions. *Focus on Exceptional Children, 21*(1), 1–8.

Edgar, E. (1987). Secondary programs in special education: Are many of them justifiable? *Exceptional Children, 53*, 555–561.

Eisler, R. M., & Frederiksen, L. W. (1980). *Perfecting social skills: A guide to interpersonal behavior development.* New York: Plenum Press.

Elias, M., & Maher, C. (1983). Social and affective development of children: A programmatic perspective. *Exceptional Children, 49*, 339–346.

Epstein, M. H., & Cullinan, D. (1987). Effective social skills curricula for behaviorally disordered students. *Pointer, 31*(2), 21–24.

Epstein, M. H., Cullinan, D., & Polloway, E. A. (1986). Patterns of maladjustment among mentally retarded children and youth. *American Journal of Mental Deficiency, 91*, 127–134.

Epstein, M. H., Polloway, E. A., Patton, J. R., & Foley, R. (1989). Mild retardation: Student characteristics and services. *Education and Training in Mental Retardation, 24*, 7–16.

Forness, S. R., & Polloway, E. A. (1987). Physical and psychiatric diagnoses of pupils with mild mental retardation currently being referred for related services. *Education and Training in Mental Retardation, 22*, 221–228.

Foster, S. L., & Ritchey, W. L. (1979). Issues in the assessment of social competence. *Journal of Applied Behavior Analysis, 12*, 625–638.

Gast, K. B. (1987). Commercial curricula for the mildly handicapped: Considerations and review. *Teaching: Behaviorally Disordered Youth, 3*, 36–41.

Gaylord-Ross, R., & Haring, T. (1987). Social interaction research for adolescents with severe handicaps. *Behavioral Disorders, 12*, 264–275.

Goldstein, A. P. (1988). *The prepare curriculum: Teaching pro-social competencies.* Champaign, IL: Research Press.

Goldstein, A. P., Sprafkin, R. P., Gershaw, N. J., & Klein, P. (1980). *Skillstreaming the adolescent.* Champaign, IL: Research Press.

Gottlieb, J., (1982). Mainstreaming. *Education and Training of the Mentally Retarded, 17*, 79–82.

Gottlieb, J., & Budoff, M. (1973). Social acceptability of retarded children in non-graded schools differing in architecture *American Journal of Mental Deficiency, 78*, 15–19.

Gottlieb, J., Semmel, M. I., & Veldman, D. J. (1978). Correlates of social status among mainstreamed mentally retarded children. *Journal of Educational Psychology, 70*, 396–405.

Greenspan, S. (1990, May). A redefinition of mental retardation based on a revised model of social competence. Paper presented at the annual meeting of the Academy on Mental Retardation.

Greenspan, S. (1979). Social intelligence in the retarded. In N. R. Ellis (Ed.), *Handbook of mental deficiency: Psychological theory and research* (2nd ed.) (pp.483–531). Hillsdale, NJ: Lawrence Erlbaum.

Gresham, F. M. (1986). Conceptual issues in the assessment of social competence in children. In P. S. Strain, M. J. Guralnick, & H. M. Walker (Eds.), *Children's social behavior: Development, assessment, and modification*. New York: Academic Press.

Gresham, F. M. (1984). Social skills and self-efficacy for exceptional children. *Exceptional Children, 51*, 253–261.

Gresham, F. M. (1983). Social skills assessment as a component of mainstreaming placement decisions. *Exceptional Children, 49*, 331–336.

Gresham, F. M. (1982). Misguided mainstreaming: The case for social skills training with handicapped children. *Exceptional Children, 48*, 420–433.

Haring, N. (Ed.). (1988). *Generalization for students with severe handicaps: Strategies and solutions*. Seattle, WA: University of Washington Press.

Haywood, H. C. (1979). Editorial. What happened to mild and moderate mental retardation? American Journal on Mental Deficiency, 83, 429–431.

Hazel, J. S., Schumaker, J. B., Sherman, J. A., & Sheldon-Wildgen, J. (1981). *ASSET: A social skills program for adolescents*. Champaign, IL: Research Press.

Heber, R. (1964). Personality. In H. A. Stevens & R. Heber (Eds.), *Mental retardation: A review of research* (pp.143–174). Chicago: University of Chicago Press.

Hollinger, J. D. (1987). Social skills for behaviorally disordered children as preparation for mainstreaming: Theory, practice, and new directions. *Remedial and Special Education, 8*(4), 17–27.

Hops, H., Guild J. J., Fleischman, D. H., Paine, S. C., Street, A., Walker, H. W., & Greenwood, C. R. (1978). *PEERS: Procedures for establishing effective relationship skills*. Eugene, OR: Center for Behavioral Education of the Handicapped, University of Oregon.

Jackson, N. F., Jackson, D. A., & Monroe, C. (1983). *Getting along with others: Teaching social effectiveness to children*. Champaign, IL: Research Press.

Jaquish, C., & Stella, M. A. (1986). Helping special students move from elementary to secondary school. *Counterpoint, 7*(1), 1.

Kehle, T. J., & Guidubaldi, J. (1978). Effect of EMR placement models on affective and social development. *Psychology in the Schools, 15*, 275–282.

Kerr, M. M. & Nelson, C. M. (1989). *Strategies for managing behavior problems in the classroom* (2nd ed.). Columbus, OH: Merrill.

LaGreca, A., Stone, W., & Bell, C. (1983). Facilitating the vocational-interpersonal skills of mentally retarded individuals. *American Journal of Mental Deficiency, 88*, 270–278.

Langone, J. (1986). *Teaching retarded learners*. Boston: Allyn and Bacon.

Lenz, B. K., Alley, G. R., & Schumaker, J. B. (1987). Activating the inactive learner: Advance organizers in the secondary content classroom. *Learning Disability Quarterly, 10*, 53–67.

Liberty, K., & Billingsley, F. (1988). Strategies to improve generalization. In N. G. Haring (Ed.), *Generalization for students with severe handicaps: Strategies and solutions* (pp.143–176). Seattle: University of Washington Press.

Linden, B. E., & Forness, S. R. (1986). Post-school adjustment of mentally retarded persons with psychiatric disorders: A ten-year follow-up. *Education and Training of the Mentally Retarded, 21,* 157–164.

Luftig, R. L. (1980). The effect of differential education placements on the self-concept of retarded pupils. Paper presented at the annual meeting of the American Educational Research Association. (ERIC Document Reproduction Service No. ED 196 198).

MacMillan, D. L. (1989). Mild mental retardation: Emerging issues. In G. Robinson, J. R., Patton, E. Polloway, & L. Sargent, (Eds.), *Best practices in mild mental retardation* (pp.1–20). Reston: CEC-MR.

MacMillan, D. L. (1982). *Mental retardation in school and society* (2nd ed.). Boston: Little, Brown.

MacMillan, D. L., & Borthwick, S. (1980). The new educable mentally retarded children: Can they be mainstreamed? *Mental Retardation, 18,* 155–158.

MacMillan, D. L., Meyers, C. E., & Morrison, G. M. (1980). System-identification of mildly mentally retarded children: Implications for interpreting and conducting research. *American Journal of Mental Deficiency, 85,* 108–115.

Mascari, B. G., & Forgnone, C. (1982). A follow-up study of EMR students four years after dismissal from the program. *Education and Training of the Mentally Retarded. 17,* 288–292.

Masters, L. F., & Mori, A. A. (1986). *Teaching secondary students with mild learning and behavior problems.* Rockville, MD: Aspen.

Matson, J. L., & Breuning, S. E. (Eds.) (1983). *Assessing the mentally retarded.* New York: Grune & Stratton.

Matson, J. L., Epstein, M. H., & Cullinan, D. (1984). A factor analytic study of the Quay-Peterson scale with mentally retarded adolescents. *Education and Training of the Mentally Retarded, 19,* 150–154.

McBride, J. W., & Forgnone, C. (1985). Emphasis of instruction provided LD, EH, and EMR students in categorical and cross-categorical programming. *Journal of Research and Development in Education, 18*(4), 50–54.

McConnell, S. R. (1987). Entrapment effects and the generalization and maintenance of social skills training for elementary school students with behavioral disorders. *Behavioral Disorders, 12,* 252–263.

McEvoy, M. A., Shores, R. E., Wehlby, J. H., Johnson, S. M., & Fox, J. J. (1990). Special education teachers' implementation of procedures to promote social interaction among children in integrated settings. *Education and Training in Mental Retardation, 25,* 267–276.

McGinnis, E., & Goldstein, A. (1984). *Skillstreaming the elementary child.* Champaign, IL: Research Press.

Michelson, L., & Mannarino, A. (1986). Social skills training with children: Research and clinic application. In P. S. Strain, M. J. Guralnich, & H. M. Walker (Eds.), *Children's social behavior: Development, assessment, and modification* (pp.373–406). Orlando, FL: Academic Press.

Morgan, D. P., & Jensen, W. R. (1988). *Teaching behaviorally disordered students: Preferred practices.* Columbus, OH: Merrill.

Neel, R. S. (1988). Implementing social skills instruction. *Behavior Disorders in Our Schools, 3*(1), 13–18.

Nelson, C. M. (1988). Social skills training for handicapped students. *Teaching Exceptional Children, 20*(4), 19–23.

Odom, S., & McEvoy, M. A. (1988). Integration of young children with handicaps and normally developing children. In S. Odom & M. Karnes (Eds.) *Early intervention for infants and children with Handicaps: An Empirical Base.* Baltimore, MD: Paul H. Brookes.

Patton, J. R., & Polloway, E. A. (1990). Mild mental retardation. In N. G. Haring & L. McCormick (Eds.), *Exceptional children and youth* (5th ed.) (pp.195–237). Columbus, OH: Merrill.

Polloway, E. A. (1987). Early age transition services for mildly mentally retarded individuals. In R. Ianacone & R. Stodden (Eds.), *Transitional issues and directions for individuals who are mentally retarded* (pp.11–24). Reston, VA: Division of Mental Retardation, Council for Exceptional Children.

Polloway, E. A. (1984). The integration of mildly retarded students in the schools: An historical review. *Remedial and Special Education, 5*(4), 18–28.

Polloway, E. A., Epstein, M. H., & Cullinan, D. (1985). Prevalence of behavior problems among educable mentally retarded students. *Education and Training of the Mentally Retarded, 20*, 3–13.

Polloway, E. A., Epstein, M. H., Patton, J. R., Cullinan, D., and Luebke, J. (1986). Demographic, social, and behavioral characteristics of students with educable mental retardation. *Education and Training of the Mentally Retarded, 21*, 27–34.

Polloway, E. A., & Patton, J. R. (1990). Biological causes. In J. R. Patton, M. Berne-Smith, & J. S. Payne (Eds.), *Mental retardation* (3rd ed.) (pp.117–159). Columbus, OH: Merrill.

Polloway, E. A., & Patton, J. R. (1986). Social integration: The goal and the process. *AAMD Education Division Newsletter, 2*(1), 1–2.

Polloway, E. A., Patton, J. R., Epstein, M. H., & Smith, T. E. C. (1989). Comprehensive curriculum: Program design for students with mild handicaps. *Focus on Exceptional Children, 21*(8), 1–12.

Polloway, E. A., & Smith, J. D. (1988). Current status of the mild mental retardation construct: Identification, placement, and programs. In M. C. Wang, M. C. Reynolds, & H. J. Walberg (Eds.). *The handbook of special education: Research and practice* (Vol. II, pp.1–22). Oxford, Eng: Pergamon Press.

Polloway, E. A., & Smith, J. D. (1983). Changes in mild mental retardation: Population, programs, and perspectives. *Exceptional Children, 50*, 149–159.

Prehm, H. H. (1985, January). *Education and training of the mentally retarded*: Mid-year report to the board of directors of CEC-MR. Unpublished manuscript.

Quay, H. C. (1977). Measuring dimensions of deviant behavior: The behavior problem checklist. *Journal of Abnormal Child Psychology, 5*, 277–287.

Quay, H. C., & Peterson, D. R. (1983). *The interim manual for the revised behavior problem checklist.* Coral Gables, FL: University of Miami.

Quay, H. C., & Peterson, D. R. (1975). *Manual for the behavior problem checklist.* Unpublished manuscript.

Rathjen, D. P. (1984). Social skills training for children: Innovations and consumer guidelines. *School Psychology Review, 13*, 302–310.

Reese-Dukes, J. L., & Stokes, E. H. (1978). Social acceptance of elementary educable mentally retarded pupils in the regular classroom. *Education and Training of the Mentally Retarded, 13*, 356–361.

Reiss, S., Levitan, G. W., & McNally, R. J. (1982). Emotionally disturbed, mentally retarded people: An underserved population. *American Psychologist, 37*, 361–367.

Reschly, D. (1988). Assessment issues, placement litigation and the future of mild mental retardation classification and programming. *Education and Training in Mental Retardation, 23*, 285–301.

Rutherford, R. B. J., Jr., & Nelson, C. M. (1988). Applied behavior analysis in education: Generalization and maintenance. In J. C. Witt, S. N. Elliott, & F. M Gresham (Eds.), *Handbook of behavior therapy in education* (pp.227–324). New York: Plenum.

Sargent, L. (1989). Instructional interventions to improve social competence. In G. Robinson, J. R. Patton, E. A. Polloway, & L. Sargent (Eds.), *Best practices in mild mental retardation* (pp.265–287). Reston, VA: CEC-MR.

Sargent, L. (1988). *Project SISS* (systematic instruction of social skills) (2nd ed.). Des Moines: Iowa Department of Public Instruction.

Schloss, P. J. (1984). *Social development of handicapped children and adolescents*. Rockville, MD: Aspen Publishing.

Schloss, P. J., Schloss, C. N., Wood, C. E., & Kiehl, W. S. (1986). A critical review of social skills research with behaviorally disordered students. *Behavioral Disorders, 12*, 1–14.

Schumaker, J. B., Hazel, J. S., & Deshler, D. D. (1988). *Keys to success in social skills instruction*. Lawrence, KS: Excel Enterprises.

Schumaker, J. B., Hazel, J. S., & Pederson, C. S. (1988). *Social skills for daily living: A curriculum*. Circle Pines, MN: American Guidance Service.

Schumaker, J. B., Pederson, C. S., Hazel, J. S., & Meyen, E. L. (1983). Social skills curricula for mildly handicapped adolescents: A review. *Focus on Exceptional Children, 16*(4), 1–16.

Shores, R. E. (1987). Overview of research on social interaction: A historical and personal perspective. *Behavioral Disorders, 12*, 233–241.

Silverman, R., Zigmond, N., & Sansone, J. (1981). Teaching coping skills to adolescents with learning problems. *Focus on Exceptional Children, 13*(6), 1–20.

Simeonsen, R. J. (1978). Social competence. In J. Wortis (Ed.), *Mental retardation and developmental disabilities: An annual review* (Vol. X) (pp.130–171). New York: Brunner-Mazel.

St. Claire, L. (1989). A multidimensional model of mental retardation: Impairment, subnormal behavior, role failures, and socially constructed retardation. *American Journal of Mental Retardation, 94*, 88–96.

Stephens, T. M. (1978). Social skills in the classroom. Columbus, OH: Cedars Press.

Stokes, T. F., & Baer, D. B. (1977). An implicit technology of generalization. *Journal of Applied Behavior Analysis, 10*, 349–367.

Stowitschek, J. J., & Powell, T. H. (1980). *Materials for teaching social skills to handicapped children: An analytic review*. Technical Report No. 50. Logan, UT: Developmental Center for Handicapped Persons, Utah State University.

Szymanski, L. S. (1980). Psychiatric diagnosis of retarded persons. In L. S. Szymanski & P. E. Tanquay (Eds.), *Emotional disorders of mentally retarded persons: Assessment, treatment, and consultation* (pp.61–81). Baltimore: University Park Press.

U. S. Department of Education. (1989). *Eleventh annual report to Congress on the implementation of the Education of All Handicapped Children Act*. Washington, DC: U. S. Government Printing Office.

Vaughan, S., Ridley, C., & Cox, J. (1983). Evaluating the efficacy of an interpersonal skills training program with children who are mentally retarded. *Education and Training of the Mentally Retarded, 18*, 191–196.

Walker, H. M., McConnell, S. R., Walker, J., Holmes, D., Todis, B., & Golden, N. (1983). *ACCEPTS: A curriculum for effective peer and teacher skills*. Austin, TX: Pro-Ed.

Walker, H. M., Street, A., Garrett, B., Crossen, J., Hops, H., & Greenwood, C. R. (1978). *RECESS (Reprogramming environmental contingencies for effective social skills): Manual for consultants*. Unpublished manuscript. Eugene, OR: Center for Behavioral Education of the Handicapped, University of Oregon.

Walker, H. M., Todis, B., Holmes, D., & Horton, G. (1988). *ACCESS: Social skills curriculum*. Austin, TX: Pro-Ed.

White, O. (1988). Probing skill use. In N. G. Haring (Ed.), *Generalization for students with severe handicaps* (pp.129–141). Seattle WA: University of Washington Press.

COGNITIVE-BEHAVIORAL INTERVENTIONS

In this section we present an overview of self-regulatory techniques that have been used with students who have mild mental retardation. We have identified cognitive-behavioral techniques that are commonly tested in the literature: self-instruction, self-recording, and combinations of these. Each of these is described in subsequent sections.

 Self-Instruction

Self-instruction is a procedure which consists of teaching a student to verbalize a sequence of questions and answers as she completes a task. The process of teaching students to instruct themselves typically follows the course described by Meichenbaum (1977):

- An adult performs a task while describing aloud the various steps he is taking;
- The child performs the same task under the direction of the adult;
- The child performs the task alone while describing aloud the steps she is taking;
- The child performs the task while whispering the steps to herself;
- The child performs the task without verbalizing the steps aloud, though she is encouraged to think through the steps involved in the task.

Using the Meichenbaum (1977) course of self-instruction, Graham and Harris (1989) taught students with learning disabilities to guide themselves through the steps of a strategy for composing an argumentative essay. As they approached the essay, students used self-instruction to help them remember these steps in writing: (a) define the problem, (b) plan the essay, (c) evaluate the essay, (d) praise yourself when you finish. This technique not only helped students to write a better essay, it also served as a prompt to help them remember the steps in writing future essays. For example, students spontaneously applied the procedure in a subsequent creative writing assignment.

Self-Recording

Self-recording procedures, like those of self-instruction, require a teacher to model the technique. However, in self-recording, students and their teachers address a particular behavior such as answering problems correctly. The student decides whether that behavior has occurred or is occurring at a given time, and then records the results of that assessment.

Many studies have demonstrated that the behavior of students who use this procedure changes; it may either increase desirable behaviors or decrease undesirable ones. For example, Lloyd, Bateman, Landrum, and Hallahan (1989) studied two different self-recording procedures. Each time a tape-recorded tone sounded during independent work sessions, students either recorded whether they were attending to task or the number of problems completed. In the attention condition, when the students heard the tones, they asked themselves whether they had been paying attention to their assigned work and recorded their answers. In the work productivity condition, the pupils also heard tones but asked themselves how many problems they had completed and recorded their answer to that question. Although these students preferred to record their attentive behavior, self-recording of both behaviors resulted in clear and salutary changes in academic productivity and attention to task as assessed independently by the teacher and observers.

Combined Procedures

In many studies, investigators have combined diverse procedures. They may use traditional behavioral interventions (e.g., a token economy) as well as cognitive-behavioral techniques in an intervention package. Or, they may introduce combinations of self-instruction, self-recording, and other techniques (self-reinforcement) in order to change behavior.*

For example, Cameron and Robinson (1980) combined self-instruction and self-reinforcement in their efforts to improve the math performance of students with behavioral disorders. The students learned how to use self-instruction techniques during independent work time; as they completed their math assignments, they checked their work and gave themselves one point for each correct answer. They exchanged the points for special activities immediately after the session. Not only did students' on-task behavior during math time increase as a result of this combination of techniques, but also their accuracy in math performance improved dramatically.

One salient strength of cognitive-behavioral techniques lies in their applicability to different areas of classroom performance. Indeed, researchers and practitioners have successfully applied these techniques to academic areas such as reading, mathematics, and writing, as well as in areas related to academics such as attending to task and out-of-seat behavior.

CLASSROOM APPLICATIONS

The intervention procedures described in the previous section have been applied to the instruction of children and youth with mild mental disabilities in class-

---

*   Likewise, researchers have introduced cognitive-behavioral procedures to modify social and vocational behaviors. However, in this chapter, we shall address the use of these techniques solely in academic arenas and in areas closely related to academics for students with mild mental abilities.

Table 1: Studies of Classroom Applications of Cognitive-Behavioral Interventions

		Area of Application		
Technique	*Related Behaviors*	*Reading*	*Writing*	*Math*
Self-instruction	Burgio, Whitman, & Johnson (1980)	Borkowski & Varnhagan (1984)		Albion & Salzberg (1982)
				Johnston, Whitman, & Johnson (1980)
				Keogh, Whitman, & Maxwell (1988)
				Leon & Pepe (1983)
				Vanluit (1987)
				Whitman & Johnston (1983)
Self-recording	Blick & Test (1987)	Chiron & Gerken (1983)	Anderson-Inman, Paine, & Deutchman (1984)	
	Howell, Rueda, & Rutherford (1983)			
	Nelson, Lipinski, & Boykin (1978)			
	Sugai & Rowe (1984)			
Combination	Horner & Brigham (1979)	Knapczyk & Livingston (1973)		
	Shapiro, McGongile, & Ollendick (1980)			
	Robertson, Simon, Pachman, & Drabman (1979)			
	Shapiro & Klein (1980)			

room situations. In this section, we describe those applications in the areas of (a) academic-related behavior, (b) reading, (c) writing, and (d) arithmetic.

Table 1 shows studies we found that applied cognitive-behavioral interventions to the classroom learning problems of children and youth with mild mental disabilities. In this table, we classified individual studies according to the intervention used and the area to which it was applied.

We selected only studies that took place in a classroom and that targeted an academic or academic-related behavior, excluding those studies which addressed vocational behaviors. We organized the following sections according to areas of application.

In Table 1, we identified studies according to the target behavior addressed in each. All of the target behaviors are academic (reading, writing, mathematics) or related to academic proficiency (e.g., attending) and, thus, influence the success of a student in classroom situations.

Academic-Related Behaviors

We defined academic-related behaviors as those which are correlated with successful performance in school. Behaviors such as attending to task, volunteering answers, and following teacher directions are examples of behaviors we considered related with students' academic success (e.g., Cobb, 1972; Cobb & Hops, 1973). Because teachers judge behaviors such as these to be important for classroom success (e.g., Kauffman, Lloyd, & McGee, 1989), we regarded them as appropriate targets for instruction. The academic-related behavior most frequently chosen as a focus for cognitive-behavioral procedures is attention to task.

In the following sections, we review studies that have addressed academic-related behaviors for change using cognitive-behavioral techniques. In our search of the literature, we did not locate studies that employed self-instruction to modify academic-related behaviors of students with mild mental retardation. Therefore, we will only discuss studies that used self-recording and combinations of intervention techniques in these sections.

Self-recording

Several studies that have addressed academic-related behaviors have used self-recording techniques. For example, Blick and Test (1987) used self-recording with high school students, two of whom were identified as having mild mental retardation. Blick and Test taught the students to record four on-task behaviors: looking at the teacher or at a movie, talking with the teacher, reading assigned material, and writing for an assignment. The students recorded whether

---

We searched the PYSCLit data base from January 1980 to March 1992 as well as examining other reviews and discussions (e.g., Harris, 1982; Lloyd, 1988; Taylor, 1988).

Combined interventions

Knapcyzk and Livingston (1973) used combinations of behavioral and cognitive-behavioral techniques, assessing the effects of both self-recording and a token economy on the accuracy with which students with mild mental retardation completed reading assignments. Generally, the students read one story and answered comprehension questions pertaining to it each day. The students recorded their percentages of accuracy and earned tokens commensurate with their accuracy in answering the questions. When this procedure was introduced, the percentage of correct responses on comprehension questions increased dramatically.

Writing

In addition to reading, we also found studies addressing the language arts area of writing. Writing has many component areas, including handwriting, spelling, and composition. Although there are many applications of cognitive-behavioral techniques to these areas (e.g., Harris, Graham, & Pressley, 1992), few of these studies have been conducted with students who have mild mental retardation. In the following paragraph we describe one study that used these techniques with students with mental retardation.

Anderson-Inman, Paine, and Deutchman (1984) introduced a self-recording procedure to 9- and 10-year-old students with mild mental retardation to increase the transfer of skills necessary to produce a neat paper. Anderson-Inman et al. identified specific features that made written work visually attractive, taught the students to use these features, and then taught the students to record whether they used these features in their own work. The students recorded the occurrence of nine features by checking from a list those that they had incorporated in their paper. Results of this study demonstrated that the introduction of the self-recording procedure improved performance on all of the nine features.

Mathematics

Although many cognitive-behavioral techniques have been used in the area of mathematics with populations of pupils with other disabilities (e.g., learning disabilities; see Lloyd & Keller, 1989), the only cognitive-behavioral technique that we found used with children with mild mental retardation in mathematics was self-instruction. We review several studies that used this technique with mathematic skills.

Following the procedure for self-instruction that Meichenbaum (1977) described, Leon and Pepe (1983) introduced self-instruction techniques to elementary school students, 42 of whom were identified as having mild mental retardation, to teach them mathematical computation skills. Leon and Pepe found that self-instruction was an effective way of teaching students to solve arithmetic problems; it was, in fact even more effective than traditional, teacher-directed instruction. They found that students who learned to employ the procedure demonstrated generalization of arithmetic skills to a new setting.

Although, the students in their study employed self-instruction techniques with varying degrees of success, Leon and Pepe (1983) found that they prompted one another to use the procedure. These peer-generated prompts contributed to the transfer across settings. This result illustrates a distinct advantage of teaching pupils skills in a group setting. Not only was teaching self-instruction in a group situation an effective use of the teacher's time, but also it provided discriminative stimuli (in the form of peers) for using the procedure under other circumstances.

Similarly, Whitman and Johnston (1983) successfully taught students with mild mental retardation to use self-instruction to complete arithmetic tasks in a group setting. As Leon and Pepe (1983) did, they adapted Meichenbaum and Goodman's (1971) techniques by teaching students to ask themselves questions as they completed arithmetic tasks. These questions ranged from general to specific as the students worked the problem; as they first approached the problem, for instance, they asked themselves, 'What kind of problem is this?' Then, as they moved through the problem, they both answered their initial question ('It's an add problem; I can tell by the sign') and prompted themselves further ('Now what do I do?'). Whitman and Johnson found that students' math skills improved as a result of using this procedure.

Albion and Salzberg (1982) also studied the effects of self-instruction on students' correct completion of math tasks. In this study, they taught students both general and specific strategies. The general strategies consisted of prompts to help the students get started (e.g., 'Remember to work slowly and carefully'; 'Keep my eyes on my paper'), but specific self-instructions were directly related to the math assignment (e.g., 'First I look at the two numbers in the right column. Let's see, 8 + 6.')

DISCUSSION

The research we have reviewed provides a basis for recommendations about future research and for conclusions about the usefulness of cognitive-behavioral intervention procedures. In the subsequent parts of this section, we address each of these matters.

Research

Although we find the results of the studies we have reviewed encouraging, our enthusiasm for the application of cognitive-behavioral techniques must be tempered by at least four factors:

- There are few studies
- There is little systematic research
- There has been little study of generalization
- There have been few studies of individualization.

We address each of these in the following subsections.

Limited database

Only three cells in our Table 1 have more than one study in them. Most cells include only one study or no studies. With all of the promise of cognitive-behavioral interventions for pupils with mild mental retardation, we find it discouraging that we could find so few studies.

One reason for this, of course, is that we limited our review to those studies in which pupils with mild mental retardation served as subjects. Studies with children and youth identified as having learning disabilities, attention deficits, behavior disorders, or other disabilities can fruitfully be combined with this literature. When this is done, there is a more substantial data base upon which to build the case for the effectiveness of cognitive-behavioral techniques. To the extent that these other literatures apply to children and youth with mild mental retardation, we feel safe in saying that there is ample reason for optimism about the usefulness of these techniques.

Nevertheless, it would be beneficial to have a more comprehensive database from which to work in developing recommendations for practice. We clearly need studies, for example, of combinations of cognitive-behavioral techniques in the areas of writing and mathematics. Such techniques almost surely would produce benefits, but what combinations of techniques would produce the greatest benefits? What are the unique features of (a) pupils with mild mental retardation, (b) reading, writing and mathematics, and (c) instructional formats that must be addressed when designing self-regulation interventions?

Furthermore, there is at least one technique – self-reinforcement – that has not been studied at all with pupils with mild mental retardation. self-reinforcement, which has been used with other special education populations (e.g., Lovitt & Curtiss, 1969), actually incorporates two distinct procedures: self-determination of reinforcers and self-delivery of reinforcers.[*] As with other cognitive-behavioral techniques, self-reinforcement shifts the responsibility from the teacher to the pupil. Pupils may arrange the contingency requirements, deliver the

---

[*] Theoretically, self-consequation also includes self-determination and self-delivery of punishment, but these aspects of punishment, rightfully, have not been studied in classrooms.

reinforcers, or do both. This is in contrast, of course, to typical school situations, where teachers alone determine the contingencies of the consequation and the reinforcement or punishment.

Chiron and Gerken (1983) taught mildly mentally retarded students to color a rung on a ladder, which they kept on their desks, as they completed a reading assignment. When students completed all of their assignments (and thus all of the rungs on the ladder), they gave themselves a star at the top of the ladder, praised themselves, and displayed the ladder in the classroom. This procedure allowed students to view the results of their work and to praise themselves, saying: 'I've done a good job; I'm doing well'. The Chiron and Gerken study illustrates why we think that self-reinforcement is a technique worthy of study with pupils who have mild mental retardation.

Absence of systematic study

Systematic study of variables associated with the success of cognitive-behavioral techniques with pupils with mild mental retardation is absent for the most part. Only the work of Whitman and his colleagues using self-instruction with mathematics represents an organized approach to the problem. We need fewer one-shot studies and more studies that analyze phenomena in an orderly fashion.

Given the nature of their learning deficits, combinations of techniques are likely to emerge as particularly beneficial for these pupils. But, it is still important to conduct components analysis (Jones, Nelson, & Kazdin, 1977). When an intervention package consists of multiple components, which one or combination of components causes the effects? For example, suppose that we study a procedure that is a combination of (a) goal setting, (b) self-recording, (c) self-instruction, and (d) self-reinforcement. From our study, we learn that this package causes substantial improvements in the written expression of pupils, both in the pupils' special education classroom and in a mainstream setting. We might reasonably wonder whether it would be possible to obtain similar benefits by only using one or two of these components (e.g., self-recording and self-reinforcement), or we might wonder whether the benefits of the combination of procedures do not transfer to the mainstream classroom unless all of the components are included. Such analyses would be beneficial.

Inadequate generalization

Not only do we need more analyses of the contributions of various components to generalization, but also we simply need more study of generalization. We found too few studies that addressed this putative benefit of cognitive-behavioral interventions. As Whitman argued (1990), generalization of skills from one (training) environment to another is difficult for these pupils, and self-regulation provides a potential way to foster it.

Many studies have incorporated generalization features (for example, teaching pupils self-instruction on a limited set of arithmetic problems and measuring their performance on other un-trained problems), but, we found few studies directly examining generalization in a broader sense (e.g., transfer across settings). The Leon and Pepe (1983) study is an exception in this regard. The techniques in this study clearly merit further examination. Other studies have addressed the matter of generalization with other populations and types of tasks (e.g., Gow, Ward, & Balla, 1986; Gow & Ward, 1985). Future studies in this area should routinely incorporate measures of transfer.

Few studies of individualization

Despite the need to make interventions fit the characteristics of students with mild mental retardation, we also found little evidence that researchers were specifically tailoring cognitive-behavioral treatments to this population. For example, the memory deficits of pupils with mild mental retardation have been well documented (Borkowski, Peck, & Damberg, 1983), leading to the conclusion that interventions should accommodate this learner characteristic.

We need research about the contributions of these variables to the effects of cognitive-behavioral treatments. Perhaps the results will be similar to those reported with other populations (e.g., Borkowski, Weyhing, & Carr, 1988), in which case we would recommend their inclusion in treatment packages; or perhaps the results will be different. But, we can not know without the evidence that studies of such questions will provide.

Practice

The deficits in the literature to which we have alluded in the foregoing section also temper the strength of our recommendations for practice. Therefore, the suggestions we offer should be considered tentative by those who wish to apply them.

For that reason, our first recommendation is that teachers closely monitor the effects of these interventions. The best way to do this is to use curriculum-based assessment procedures to document and monitor the appropriateness and effectiveness of an intervention (Howell & Morehead, 1987; Truesdell, 1987). Monitoring of performance in this manner will also alert teachers that an intervention may need to be modified: If it is working, keep using it. If it is not working, try something else. In the absence of compelling research, using such an assessment system will permit teachers to make informed decisions about the usefulness of particular interventions for particular students.

Best practice, if not detailed research, also dictates that we structure teaching to meet the needs of individual learners. This is no less true when using cognitive-behavioral techniques. Students with mild mental retardation come to the learning situation with varying degrees of competence. Hence, it is necessary to assess beginning skill levels and develop interventions based on such assessment. For instance, when using a self-recording strategy to decrease errors in written work, teachers should determine the severity of the mistakes for each student. Informal observation will help identify specific aspects of the behavior that require attention and set priorities for intervention. One student may only make such mistakes on arithmetic assignments but another may make such mistakes on both arithmetic and composition assignments. Some students may need more practice trial than other students. Systematic observation should allow teachers to establish frequencies of the inappropriate behavior or number of practice trials needed and to measure the effectiveness of the treatment.

Cognitive-behavioral strategies have not yet and probably will not supplant the need for highly effective instruction in basic skills. We think that the procedures and programs of Direct Instruction (DI; see Engelmann, Becker, Carnine, & Gersten, 1988) should be used at least to teach skills such as basic decoding, computation, spelling, capitalization, punctuation, and so forth. Tarver (1986) argued that teachers should use cognitive behavioral strategies to teach more integrative, higher-order skills after using DI for teaching arbitrary, fundamental skills. We suspect that students will benefit from a sequence of instruction in which concepts and operations are introduced using more teacher-directed instruction (e.g., DI) and then responsibility for practice and application is systematically made more student directed (e.g., self-instruction).

In general, in fact, we think that many of the principles of effective instruction are important to the successful use of cognitive-behavioral interventions. Some students will need frequent cues and prompts before they learn to perform self-instructional skills independently. To accommodate these special needs, teachers must (a) model the self-instructional behaviors during the initial phases of implementation, (b) provide many additional opportunities for guided practice, and (c) give corrective feedback throughout the implementation period (Deshler & Schumaker, 1986). They must ensure that the pupils can perform the self-regulatory strategies on their own; this means teachers must require the students to demonstrate correct performance, not that they simply say 'Yes' when asked if they know what to do.

SUMMARY

Cognitive-behavioral techniques such as those discussed in this chapter hold considerable promise for improving the academic and task-related behavior of pupils with mild mental retardation. Our examination of the literature leads us to conclude that these techniques warrant more extensive study, particularly study of whether they actually foster generalization of skills or how they can be modified so that they do so. Also, we found a need for further study of the adaptation of these techniques to fit the characteristics and needs of pupils with mild mental retardation.

Despite the need for additional research, we think that cognitive-behavioral techniques have sufficient empirical support to merit use with students. Applications of these techniques should be constrained by the need to teach pupils pre-requisite skills using other techniques, plan instruction according to individuals' needs, and incorporate the procedures of effective instruction. In addition, teachers should monitor the effects of cognitive-behavioral techniques just as they should with any other intervention they use.

REFERENCES

Albion, F. M., & Salzberg, C. L. (1982). The effect of self-instructions on the rate of correct addition problems with mentally retarded children. *Education and Treatment of Children, 5*, 121–131.

Anderson-Inman, L., Paine, S. C., & Deutchman, L. (1984). Neatness counts: Effects of direct instruction and self-monitoring on the transfer of neat-paper skills to nontraining settings. *Analysis and Intervention in Developmental Disabilities, 4*, 137–155.

Bijou, S. W. (1963). Theory and research in mental (developmental) retardation. *Psychological Record, 13*, 95–110.

Blick, D. W., & Test (1987). Effects of self-recording on high-school students' on-task behavior. *Learning Disability Quarterly, 10*, 203–213.

Borkowski, J. G., & Cavanaugh, J. C. (1979). Maintenance and generalization of skills and strategies by the retarded. In N. R. Ellis (Ed.), *Handbook of mental deficiency: Psychological theory and research* (2nd ed., pp.569–617). Hillsdale, NJ: Erlbaum.

Borkowski, J. G., Peck, V. A., & Damberg, P. R. (1983). Attention, memory, and cognition. In J. L. Matson & J. A. Julich (Eds.), *Handbook of mental retardation* (pp.479–497). New York: Pergamon.

Borkowski, J. G., & Varnhagan, C. K. (1984) Transfer of learning strategies: Contrast of self-instructional and traditional training formats with EMR children. *American Journal of Mental Deficiency, 38*, 369–379.

Borkowski, J. G., Weyhing, R. S., & Carr, M. (1988). Effects of attributional retraining on strategy-based reading comprehension in learning-disabled students. *Journal of Educational Psychology, 80*, 46–53.

Burgio, L. D., Whitman, T. L., & Johnson, M. R. (1980). A self-instructional package for increasing attending behavior in educable mentally retarded children. *Journal of Applied Behavior Analysis, 13*, 443–459.

Cameron, M. I., & Robinson, V. M. J. (1980). Effects of cognitive training on academic and on-task behavior of hyperactive children. *Journal of Abnormal Child Psychology, 8*, 405–419.

Campione, J. C. (1989). Assisted assessment: A taxonomy of approaches and an outline of strengths and weaknesses. *Journal of Learning Disabilities, 22*, 151–165.

Campione, J. C., & Brown, A. L. (1978). Toward a theory of intelligence: Contributions from research with retarded children. *Intelligence 2,* 279–304.

Chiron, R., & Gerken, K. (1983). The effects of a self-monitoring technique on the locus of control orientation of educable mentally retarded children. *School Psychology Review, 12,* 87–92.

Cobb, J. A. (1972). Relationship of discrete classroom behaviors to fourth-grade academic achievement. *Journal of Education Psychology, 63,* 74–80.

Cobb, J. A., & Hops, H. (1973). Effects of academic survival skill training on low achievement first graders. *Journal of Educational Research, 63,* 108–113.

Deshler, D. D. & Schumaker, J. B. (1986). Learning strategies: An instructional alternative for low-achieving adolescents. *Exceptional Children, 52,* 583–590.

Engelmann, S., Becker, W. C., Carnine, D. W., & Gersten, R. (1988). The Direct Instruction Follow Through Model: Design and outcomes. *Education and Treatment of Children, 11,* 303–317.

Garber, H. L., & Heber, R. (1982). Prevention of cultural-familial mental retardation. In A. M. Jeger & R.S. Slotnick (Eds.), *Community mental health and behavioral ecology: A handbook of theory, research, and practice* (pp.217–230). New York: Plenum.

Gow, L., Ward, J., & Balla, J. R. (1986). The use of verbal self-instruction training to promote indirect generalization. *Australia and New Zealand Journal of Developmental Disabilities, 12,* 123–132.

Gow, L., & Ward, J. (1985). The use of verbal self-instruction training for enhancing generalization outcomes with persons with an intellectual disability. *Australia and New Zealand Journal of Developmental Disabilities, 11,* 157–168.

Graham, S., & Harris, K. R. (1989). Improving learning disabled students' skills at composing essays: self-instructional strategy training. *Exceptional Children, 56,* 201–214.

Hallahan, D. P. (Ed.). (1980). Using cognitive strategies with exceptional children [Entire issue]. *Exceptional Education Quarterly, 1,*(1).

Hallahan, D. P., & Reeve, R. E. (1980). Selective attention and distractibility. In B. K. Keogh (Ed)., *Advances in special education* (Vol. 1, 141–181). Greenwich, CT: JAI Press.

Harris, K. R. (1982). Cognitive-behavior modification: Application with exceptional students. *Focus on Exceptional Children, 15*(2), 1–16.

Harris, K. R., Graham, S., & Pressley, M. (1992). Cognitive-behavioral approaches in reading and written language: Developing self-regulated learners. In N. N. Singh & I. L. Beale (Eds.), *Current perspectives in learning disabilities: Nature, theory, and treatment* (pp.415–451). New York: Springer-Verlag.

Horner, R. H., & Brigham, T. A. (1979). The effects of self-management procedures on the study behavior of two retarded children. *Education and Training of the Mentally Retarded, 41,* 18–24.

Howell, K. W., & Morehead, M. K. (1987). *Curriculum-based evaluation for special and remedial education: A handbook for deciding what to teach.* Columbus, OH: Merrill.

Hughes, J. N., & Hall, R. J. (Eds.). (1989). *Cognitive behavioral psychology in the schools.* New York: Guilford.

Jason, L. A., Thompson, D., & Rose, T. (1986). Methodological issues in prevention. In B. A. Edelstein & L. Michelson (Eds)., *Handbook of prevention* (pp.1–19). New York: Plenum.

Johnston, M. B., & Whitman, T. (1987) Enhancing math computation through variations in training format and instructional content. *Cognitive Therapy and Research, 11,* 381–397.

Johnston, M. B., Whitman, T. L., & Johnson, M. (1980). Teaching addition and subtraction to mentally retarded children: A self-instruction program. *Applied Research in Mental Retardation, 1*, 141–160.

Jones, R. T., Nelson, E. R., & Kazdin, A. E. (1977). The role of external variable in self-reinforcement. *Behavior Modification, 1*, 147–178.

Kauffman, J. M. (1991). Restructuring in sociopolitical context: Reservations about the effects of current reform proposals on student with disabilities. In J. W. Lloyd, N. N. Singh, & A. C. Repp (Eds.), *The regular education initiative: Alternative perspectives on concepts, issues, and methods* (pp.57–66). Sycamore, IL: Sycamore.

Kauffman, J. M., Lloyd, J. W., & McGee, K. A. (1989). Adaptive and maladaptive behavior: Teachers' attitudes and their technical assistance needs. *Journal of Special Education, 23*, 185–200.

Keogh, D. A., Whitman, T. L., & Maxwell, S. E. (1988). Self-instruction versus external instruction: Individual differences and training effectiveness. *Cognitive Therapy and Research, 12*, 591–610.

Knapcyzk, D. R., & Livingston, G. (1973). Self-recording and student teacher supervision: Variables within a token economy. *Journal of Applied Behavior Analysis, 6*, 481–486.

Ledwidge, B. (1978). Cognitive behavior modification: A step in the wrong direction? *Psychological Bulletin, 85*, 353–375.

Leon, J. A., & Pepe, H. J. (1983). Self-instructional training: Cognitive behavior modification for remediating arithmetic deficits. *Exceptional Children, 50*, 54–60.

Lindsley, O. R. (1964). Direct measurement and prosthesis of retarded behavior. *Journal of Education, 147*, 62–81.

Lloyd, J. W. (1988). Direct academic interventions in learning disabilities. In M. C. Wang, M. C. Reynolds, & H. J. Walberg (Eds.), *Handbook of special education: Vol. 2. Research and practice: Mildly handicapped condititions* (pp.345–366). London: Pergamon.

Lloyd, J. W., Bateman, D., Landrum, T. J., & Hallahan, D.P. (1989). Self-recording of attention versus productivity. *Journal of Applied Behavior Analysis, 22*, 315–323.

Lloyd, J. W., & Keller, C. E. (1989). Effective mathematics instruction. *Focus on Exceptional Children, 21*(7), 1–10.

Lovitt, T. C., & Curtiss, K. A. (1969). Academic response rate as a function of teacher- and self-imposed contingencies. *Journal of Applied Behavior Analysis, 2*, 49–53.

Meichenbaum, D., & Goodman, J. (1971). Training impulsive children to talk to themselves: A means of developing self-control. *Journal of Abnormal Psychology, 77*, 115–126.

Meichenbaum, D. (1977). *Cognitive-behavior modification.* New York: Plenum.

Nelson, R. O., Lipinski, D. P., & Boykin, R. A. (1978). The effects of self-recorders' training and the obtrusiveness of the self-recording device on the accuracy and reactivity self-monitoring. *Behavior Therapy, 9*, 200–208.

Osborne, S. S., Kosiewicz, M. M., Crumley, E. B., & Lee, C. (1987). Distractible students use self-monitoring. *Teaching Exceptional Children, 19*, 66–69.

Ramey, C. T., MacPhee, D., & Yates, K. O. (1982). Preventing developmental retardation: A general systems model. In D. K. Detterman & R. J. Sternberg (Eds.), *How and how much can intelligence be increased?* (pp.67–119). Norwood, NJ: Ablex.

Ramey, C. T., Bryant, D. M., Campbell, F. A., & Sparling, J. J. (1989). Early intervention for high-risk children: The Carolina Early Intervention Program. *Prevention in Human Services, 7*(1) 33–57.

Repp, A. C. (1983). *Teaching the mentally retarded.* Englewood Cliffs, NJ: Prentice-Hall.

Robertson, S. J., Simon, S. J., Pachman, J. S., & Drabman, R. S. (1979). Self-control and generalization procedures in a classroom of disruptive retarded children. *Child Behavior Therapy, 1,* 347–362.

Shapiro E. S., & Klein, R. D. (1980). Self-management of classroom behavior with retarded/disturbed children. *Behavior Modification, 4,* 83–97.

Shapiro, E. S., McGonigle, J. J., & Ollendick, T. H. (1980). An analysis of self-assessment and self-reinforcement in a self-managed token economy with mentally retarded children. *Applied Research in Mental Retardation, 1,* 227–240.

Sugai, G., & Rowe, P. (1984). The effect of self-recording on out-of-seat behavior of an EMR student. *Education and Training of the Mentally Retarded, 19,* 23–28.

Tarver, S. G. (1986). Cognitive behavior modification, direct instruction and holistic approaches to the education of students with learning disabilities. *Journal of Learning Disabilities, 19,* 369–375.

Taylor, R. L. (1988). Psychological intervention with mildly retarded children: Prevention and remediation of cognitive deficits. In M. C. Wang, M. C. Reynolds, & H.J. Walberg (Eds.), *Handbook of special education: Vol. 2. Research and practice: Mildly handicapped conditions* (pp.59–75). London: Pergamon.

Truesdell, L. A. (1987). Curriculum-based assessment: Process and application. *Reading, Writing, and Learning Disabilities, 3,* 281–289.

VanLuit, J. E. H. (1987). Teaching impulsive children with arithmetic deficits in special education: A self-instructional training program. *European Journal of Special Needs Education, 2,* 237–246.

Whitman, T. L. (1987). Self-instruction, individual differences, and mental retardation. *American Journal of Mental Deficiency, 92,* 213–223.

Whitman, T. L. (1990). Self-regulation and mental retardation. *American Journal of Mental Retardation, 94,* 347–362.

Whitman, T., & Johnston, M. B. (1983). Teaching addition and subtraction with regrouping to educable mentally retarded children: A group self-instructional training program. *Behavior Therapy, 14,* 127–143.

TEACHING STUDENTS WITH MILD MENTAL RETARDATION

Thomas E. Scruggs and Margo A. Mastropieri

The four chapters in this section – on effective teaching, social skills, cognitive-behavioral techniques, and computer-managed instruction – provide important and detailed information on the best current practices for students with mild mental retardation. Each chapter describes an important aspect of special education for this population, well-supported by recent research evidence. Taken together, they should be of valuable service to those who seek to become special education teachers, as well as those currently teaching who seek to become better special education teachers.

Each of these chapters shares a common theme with the others: the view that students with mild mental retardation *can* learn efficiently, given that instruction is systematic, goal-oriented, directly provided, and carefully monitored. Nevertheless, the chapters are sufficiently different in their immediate content that we discuss them separately, noting commonalities when possible.

EFFECTIVE INSTRUCTION

Hendrickson and Frank provide a general framework on the instruction of students with mild disabilities, often referred to as *effective instruction*. Initially established with learners of more average abilities learning basic skills (see Brophy & Good, 1986; and Rosenshine & Stephens, 1986, for reviews), these teaching practices have also been shown to be strongly related to achievement of students with mild mental retardation. Important components of effective instruction, as described by Hendrickson and Frank, include teacher-directed, group formats; high levels of student engagement and student-teacher interaction; appropriate pace, questioning and feedback; and the structured use of peers and learning centers to enhance learning. A substantial amount of research evidence now supports the effectiveness of this approach for special education (Mastropieri & Scruggs, 1987). Overall, the most positive findings have been that teachers can and do make a difference in the level of achievement attained by their students, and that systematic attention to these effective teaching variables, by any teacher, can raise student achievement.

One concern which has been raised about this instructional model, at least in its applications to nonhandicapped learners, is its 'unabashedly empirical and nontheoretical tenor' (Shulman, 1986, p.13). Although 'process-product' researchers themselves have not offered a 'theory' of effective teaching, there do exist some empirical generalizations about learning and intelligence which shed some light on the reasons why many of these 'effective teaching' variables have been so successful with students with mild mental retardation. These generalizations are based in large part upon new interpretations of the work of Woodrow in the 1930s and 1940s (Jensen, 1989). Jensen (1989, p.52) re-evaluated this literature and concluded that learning is more highly related to general intelligence (that is, lower-IQ students will be least successful) when: (a) the *amount of time* for learning is fixed for all students; (b) learning trails are *paced slowly*; (c) the content requires *mastery of earlier learning* and *simultaneous integration* of a number of different elements; (d) achievement is measured at an *early stage of learning*; (e) learning is *insightful*, involving 'catching on', or 'getting the idea'; (e) the content is positively *age-related*, in that it is more easily learned by older, rather than younger children; (f) the learning task permits *transfer* from previous learning; and (g) the content is *meaningful* in that it is related to other knowledge or experience already possessed by the learner.

It can be readily seen that the conditions described above are, unfortunately, highly descriptive of typical classroom environments, and this may explain why teachers commonly equate intelligence with competence in school learning. Special education teachers can increase the achievement of students with mild mental retardation by manipulating these variables, primarily in the way described by Hendrickson and Frank, as well as other 'effective instruction' advocates. A most important variable, and one mentioned prominently by Hendrickson and Frank, is *successfully engaged time*. Maximizing learning time directly addresses the first point above, and suggests that, with higher time allocations, students with mild disabilities can achieve more like their nondisabled peers. Cooperative learning and peer tutoring programs as described by

Hendrickson and Frank can also provide additional learning time; indeed, a meta-analysis conducted by Cook, Scruggs, Mastropieri, and Casto (1985–1986) lends support to the positive facilitative effects of students with mild disabilities as either tutors or tutees.

Appropriate pace, as described by Hendrickson and Frank, is also a critical variable in teaching students with mild disabilities. Although rapid pace may be of great importance in the early stages of fact or skill acquisition, modifications in pacing may be more appropriate at later stages, or for different learning objectives.

Careful task structuring and analysis can effectively address the points dealing with hierarchical learning tasks and those requiring simultaneous integration of information. With appropriate modifications in the sequence in which tasks are presented and mastered, academic underachievement due to intellectual limitations can be minimized. Teaching that assures automaticity, or fluency of responding (see Mastropieri & Scruggs, 1987), before introducing new tasks, can also minimize problems. The performance of students with mild mental retardation also will be less pronounced if achievement is assessed at this later stage, rather than an early stage of learning. Curriculum-based, formative evaluation, as described in the chapter by Fuchs and Allinder (Chapter 3), is also beneficial in that performance can be measured at *all* stages of learning.

In developmental, constructivist, or discovery-oriented classroom approaches (Julyan, 1989), learning frequently may require intentional, conscious mental effort; may require insight, 'catching on', or 'getting the idea'; and may utilize tasks that are age-related or developmentally sensitive. Under such circumstances, learning is likely to be correlated with general intelligence, in that students with intellectual impairments probably will be less successful. The 'effective teaching' model described by Hendrickson and Frank provides a sharp contrast with constructivist models, and as such, is more likely to be successful with students with mild mental retardation in promoting basic skills acquisition.

The effective instruction model was validated on basic skills areas, in which there is little room for discovery. One does not easily 'discover' new vocabulary words, irregular word spellings, sound-symbol correspondence, or coin values. In order for these facts and skills to be acquired by students with mild mental retardation, structured, direct teacher presentations are necessary. Not only does this presentation style lower the intellectual requirement for assimilating the information, it is a more efficient way for students to learn information that is not easily revealed through logical deduction.

Nevertheless, students with mild mental retardation also need to learn to think and discover things for themselves. To this extent, promoting both inductive and deductive reasoning, by modeling, prompting and testing these skills, is important for students with intellectual impairments. However, such 'less-directive' teaching has thinking processes and not content acquisition as its final aim. Special education teachers should be careful not to confuse the two purposes, and corresponding teaching procedures.

Hendrickson and Frank acknowledge the problem of transfer, or generalization, in special education. Students with mild mental retardation are commonly observed to exhibit difficulties transferring previously-acquired skills to new tasks (Scruggs & Mastropieri, 1984), and, according to Jensen's generalizations, students with lower IQ will be less likely to succeed in environments that assume transfer will spontaneously occur. Programming for generalization has been an important component of special education for years, and for which a variety of techniques are available (Rutherford & Nelson, 1988; Mastropieri & Scruggs, 1984; 1987; 1990).

Finally, content that is presumed to be meaningful is more easily learned by higher-IQ than lower-IQ students. The probable reason for this is that students with higher intellectual ability are able to establish connections between new content and their existing knowledge systems. Students with mild disabilities are less able to form such connections.

One particularly successful technique for enhancing the integration of new content, which has recently received much research attention, is mnemonic instruction (Scruggs & Mastropieri, 1990). Mnemonic instruction serves to establish firmer ties between known and to-be-learned information by reconstructing unfamiliar stimulus components to more concrete and meaningful forms and integrating these with the learner's prior knowledge base. Although mnemonic techniques may seem very complex, they have been used to greatly increase the learning and memory of students with mild mental retardation in areas such as vocabulary, science, and social studies (see Scruggs & Mastropieri, 1990; and Mastropieri & Scruggs, in press, for reviews).

COGNITIVE-BEHAVIORAL TECHNIQUES

Lloyd, Talbott, Tankersley, and Trent describe the use of cognitive-behavioral techniques to improve the classroom performance of students with mild retardation. This approach is in no way incompatible with the overall instructional model described by Hendrickson and Frank. In fact, the model is extended in that Lloyd et al. recommend that students be trained to transfer effective instructional techniques to their own learning. Important components of cognitive-behavioral techniques include: effective use of time, pace, self-questioning, feedback, as well as task-analysis. Since students with mental retardation have been shown to have particular difficulty with transfer, systematic training in this area is especially important.

One specific problem with research in cognitive-behavioral techniques, mentioned by Lloyd et al., is that there has been so little of it. Lloyd and Landrum (1990) recently conducted a thorough review of the self-recording research literature. Of 37 studies identified, only five included students with mental retardation as subjects, either exclusively or in conjunction with students with other disabling conditions. The remainder utilized primarily students with learning, behavior, or attentional deficits, with students with learning disabilities (LD) being represented most frequently. Lloyd et al. argue that research with other students with mild disabilities can be used to support the general use of cognitive-behavioral techniques with students with mental retardation. This is undoubtedly true; however, issues involving the *specific* use of cognitive-behavioral techniques are less well developed. While students with learning disabilities are similar to students with mild mental retardation to the extent that their academic achievement is typically well below grade level, they may be, on average, two standard deviations ahead of students with mild mental retardation in the area of psychometric intelligence. Such a large difference may have strong implications for cognitive-behavioral tasks, in light of their emphasis on independent execution of cognitive skills. Elsewhere (Mastropieri & Scruggs, 1987), we have written of three major components of cognitive-behavioral techniques: the student must (a) *realize* when the specific strategy is called for, (b) correctly *recall* the steps involved in the strategy, and (c) effectively *execute* these steps to accomplish the task. In some of our cognitive-generalization training (e.g., Scruggs & Mastropieri, in press), we have seen that students with mild mental retardation may have difficulty with all three of these components, and particularly the first: identifying the correct time and place for specific strategy execution. While there is no reason to believe that students with mild mental retardation cannot ultimately learn to execute cognitive-behavioral techniques, future research can provide important information regarding specific details of training these students to use cognitive-behavioral techniques.

The effective instruction model has been criticized for being too 'teacher-directed', in that the teacher controls the format, pace, and content of instruction. With the use of cognitive-behavioral techniques, responsibility for learning shifts, when appropriate, to students, who can also learn to master the steps to independent thinking, feedback, and monitoring. When these techniques are successful, and they frequently are, they can help provide the skills necessary for independent functioning, a primary goal of special education.

SOCIAL SKILLS

Korinek and Polloway describe procedures very similar to those described by Hendrickson and Frank, and Lloyd et al., for teaching social skills. They make a compelling case for the need for such training, and argue that learners with mild mental retardation, like other learners, perform better when they are motivated to do so and see the purpose of exhibiting the behaviors being trained. This is also true, of course, with academic-vocational learning and cognitive-behavioral training. The more individual students understand and share the purpose of education, the more positive effort they are likely to make.

Korinek and Polloway discuss curricular aspects of social skills training. It may also be important to consider the interaction between the interpersonal characteristics of students with mild retardation and other school curriculum, particularly with respect to mainstreaming considerations. We (Mastropieri & Scruggs, 1990) are presently undertaking a project which considers the characteristics of students with disabilities with respect to curricular demands of mainstream science education. Unfortunately, the vast majority of science education classes employ teacher lecture and independent textbook reading and study as the dominant instructional activities, an approach which is unlikely to produce mainstreaming success. Not only is this approach sharply criticized by major scientific organizations (Rutherford & Ahlgren, 1990), it is substantially less effective than those approaches which de-emphasize textbook learning in favor of hands-on activities (Shymansky, Kyle, & Alport, 1983). Hands-on science approaches are likely to be much more accommodating to individual differences because (a) they base much of their learning on concrete experience, rather than abstract reasoning from texts, and (b) they typically employ cooperative learning groups (see the Hendrickson and Frank chapter) who work collaboratively on science activities. Students with mild retardation have the opportunity to succeed in such settings if (a) the task is not so open-ended and unstructured that they can not understand it, and (b) they have sufficiently well-developed social competence to enable them to work effectively with other, non-handicapped students. This level of social competence is unlikely to be exhibited without training, and involves understanding where and when to make a contribution to the group activity, asking for assistance when necessary, taking turns, and sharing laboratory apparatus. Students with mild disabilities who have had cooperative learning experiences in special education settings will have had more opportunity to practice these skills than those who have not. While it is difficult to imagine many students with mild mental retardation succeeding in classrooms where independent study of textbooks is required, socially competent students with disabilities may have a much greater chance of succeeding in hands-on, group learning situations.

COMPUTER-MANAGED INSTRUCTION

Fuchs and Allinder discuss a critically important topic in the effective instruction of students with mild mental retardation: systematic, formative evaluation, and computer technology recently developed to improve the efficiency of these practices. In a meta-analysis, Fuchs and Fuchs (1986) demonstrated the positive effect of formative evaluation on student learning. The reason for this may well have to do with the increased attention provided to the learning patterns of individual students. Although the 'effective instruction' model has provided special education teachers with a wealth of information for improving student learning in general, relatively little information regarding the specific learner is provided. Addressing individual differences on a truly individual level requires performance monitoring of each student. Curriculum-based, formative evaluation procedures (e.g., Fuchs, 1986; Fuchs & Fuchs, 1986) provide an effective way of doing this. No matter how well validated a treatment is in the research literature, it is of little utility unless it can be demonstrated to be effective with the individual learner in the classroom, through formative evaluation procedures.

In spite of the successes of formative evaluation, one complaint has been that the procedures are very time-consuming, particularly when dealing with large numbers of students. Computer-managed instruction (CMI), is offered as a positive alternative to collecting, recording, and evaluating data by hand. With CMI technology, student data can be stored, graphed, and analyzed; tests can be generated, administered, scored, and feedback provided; and student performance analyzed for skills which have been and have not been mastered to date. Such technology has the promise of revolutionizing the process of individual data collection, and initial research has shown the effectiveness of this technology. If there is any drawback, it seems to have been that it has sometimes worked *too* well – that some direct teacher involvement with data may be important for improving teacher decision-making.

The relative lack of research involving students with mild mental retardation may be less of a problem than the lack of such research in other areas previously discussed. The specific interventions, after all, are on teachers of students with mild disabilities, and as such may contain more direct implications for teachers of students with mild mental retardation. Although some of the tasks, and perhaps graphed lines of progress may differ, the positive outcomes of such techniques are likely to be similar.

Most of the research on curriculum-based, formative evaluation, and computer-managed instruction has focused on students' acquisition of basic skills, such as reading, spelling, and math. The use of such measurement techniques in content instruction, such as social skills, science and social studies, would seem to be a particularly interesting avenue for future research. Such inquiry offers special challenges, because of the different demands of such content. In science, for example, students are expected to learn relevant facts and concepts, apply process skills to scientific experiments, and develop products based on their own projects. Such behaviors may not lend themselves as easily to formative evaluation techniques of the sort used on basic skills assessment, and may be even more difficult to manage with computer assistance.

Additionally, science educators have called for different types of evaluation which do not seem easily compatible with formative evaluation techniques. These techniques include open-ended and embedded questions (Harmon, 1990), group assessment (Johnson & Johnson, 1990), and portfolio assessment (Collins, 1990). Although all these techniques have the purpose of gathering information thought to be unattainable on traditional 'objective' tests, they should somehow allow for reliability and validity in assessment, and the monitoring of progress toward broadly stated goals and objectives. The extent to which these approaches can be combined with direct and continuous measurement techniques could provide profitable future research questions.

SUMMARY

The four chapters in this section provide a wealth of important information on best current practices in special education with students with mild mental retardation. Taken together, they provide an overall view of instruction with is comprehensive, systematic, and effective. Although further research is needed in all the areas described above, at this point it can be stated that teaching of the type described in this section – including effective modeling, prompting, and feedback; social skills training; cognitive-behavioral techniques; and curriculum-based, formative evaluation with computer assistance – is very likely to result in academic and social success for students with mild mental retardation. The degree of future implementation of these variables in special settings across the country will in large part define the future effectiveness of special education.

REFERENCES

Brophy, J., & Good, T. (1986). Teacher behavior and student achievement. In M.C. Wittrock (Ed.), *Handbook of research on teaching* (3rd ed., pp.328–375). New York: Macmillan.

Collins, A. (1990). Portfolios for assessing student learning in science: A new name for a familiar idea? In A. B. Champagne, B. E. Lovitts, & B. J. Calinger (Eds.), *Assessment in the service of instruction* (pp.157–166). Washington, DC: American Association for the Advancement of Science.

Cook, S. B., Scruggs, T. E., Mastropieri, M. A., & Casto, G. (1985–1986). Handicapped students as tutors. *Journal of Special Education, 19,* 483–492.

Fuchs, L. S. (1986). Monitoring progress of mildly handicapped pupils: Review of current practice and research. *Remedial and Special Education, 7*(5), 5–12.

Fuchs, L. S., & Fuchs, D. (1986). Effects of systematic formative evaluation: A meta-analysis. *Exceptional Children, 53,* 199–208.

Harmon, M. (1990). Fair testing issues: Are science education assessments biased? In A. B. Champagne, B. E. Lovitts, & B. J. Calinger (Eds.), *Assessment in the service of instruction* (pp.29–60). Washington, DC: American Association for the Advancement of Science.

Jensen, A. (1989). The relationship between learning and intelligence. *Learning and Individual Differences, 1,* 37–62.

Johnson, D. W., & Johnson, R. T. (1990). Group assessment as an aid to science instruction. In A. B. Champagne, B. E. Lovitts, & B. J. Calinger (Eds.), *Assessment in the service of instruction* (pp.149–156). Washington, DC: American Association for the Advancement of Science.

Julyan, C. L. (1989). Messing about in science: Participation, not memorization. In W. G. Rosen (Ed.), *High-school biology today and tomorrow* (pp.184–193). Washington, DC, National Academy of Science Press.

Lloyd, J. W., & Landrum, T. J. (1990). Self-recording and attending to task: Treatment components and generalization effects. In T. E. Scruggs, & B. Y. L. Wong (Eds.), *Intervention research in learning disabilities* (pp.235–262). New York: Springer-Verlag.

Mastropieri, M. A., & Scruggs, T. E. (1984). Generalization: Five effective strategies. *Academic Therapy, 19*, 427–432.

Mastropieri, M. A., & Scruggs, T. E. (1987). *Effective instruction for special education*. Austin, TX: Pro-Ed.

Mastropieri, M. A., & Scruggs, T. E. (1990). *Decision-making guidelines for facilitating mainstreaming success in science*. Proposal funded by the U.S. Department of Education, West Lafayette, IN: Purdue University, Department of Educational Studies.

Mastropieri, M. A., & Scruggs, T. E. (in press). *Teaching students ways to remember: Strategies for learning mnemonically*. Cambridge, MA: Brookline Books.

Rosenshine, B., & Stephens, R. (1986). Teaching functions. In M. C. Wittrock (Ed.), *Handbook of research on teaching* (3rd ed., pp.376–391). New York: Macmillan.

Rutherford, F. J., & Ahlgren, A. (1990). *Science for all Americans*. New York: Oxford University Press.

Rutherford, R. B., & Nelson, C. M. (1988). Generalization and maintenance of treatment effects. In J. C. Witt, S. N. Elliott, & F. M. Gresham (Eds.), *Handbook of behavior therapy in education* (pp.277–324). New York: Plenum.

Scruggs, T. E., & Mastropieri, M. A. (1984). Issues in generalization: Implications for special education. *Psychology in the Schools, 21*, 397–403.

Scruggs, T. E., & Mastropieri, M. A. (1990). The case for mnemonic instruction: From laboratory investigations to classroom applications. *Journal of Special Education, 24*, 7–29.

Scruggs, T. E., & Mastropieri, M. A. (in press). Classroom applications of mnemonic instruction: Acquisition, maintenance, and generalization. *Exceptional Children*.

Shulman, L. S. (1986). Paradigms and research programs in the study of teaching. In M. C. Wittrock (Ed.), *Handbook of research on teaching* (3rd ed., pp.3–36). New York: Macmillan.

Shymansky, J. A., Kyle, W. C. Jr., & Alport, J. M. (1983). The effects of new science curricula on student performance. *Journal of Research in Science Teaching, 20*, 387–404.

PART II

STRATEGIES FOR TEACHING STUDENTS WITH MORE SEVERE LEVELS OF MENTAL RETARDATION

RESEARCH BASIS OF INSTRUCTIONAL PROCEDURES TO PROMOTE SOCIAL INTERACTION AND INTEGRATION

Thomas G. Haring

Social interaction is fundamental to effective living. Generalized communication and social interaction skills are necessary for independently engaging in many critical events such as asking directions or ordering food. Moreover, one of the major reasons for the loss of employment by persons with disabilities is due to inappropriate social behavior (Chadsey-Rusch, 1990). Most fundamentally social behavior such as communication, play, or giving and receiving social reinforcement, is the basis of our construction of reality. Social interaction, being the major means of receiving reinforcement and feedback about behavior, shapes our conceptions of what is true or not true; good or not good; and safe or unsafe. Skinner (1957) observed that, 'It is because our behavior is important to others that it eventually becomes important to us' (p.314).

Understanding and shaping social interaction ought to be fundamental to education – unfortunately, it is not. Many intervention models are based on a simple operational principle: If its broken, fix it. This pragmatic logic underlies most efforts in special education and behavior analysis. A student who has trouble learning to read lacks critical discriminations, cognitive strategies and perceptual skills and so is given a special program. A child with extreme oppositional behavior and who is disruptive to the class is viewed as unable to control his own behavior and is referred to a behavior specialist of some type. Teachers expect students to learn and behave in situationally appropriate ways. Those who do not, are defined as having a problem. In essence, special services are given when problems exist and 'when someone complains effectively enough to provoke a behavior change program' (Baer, 1986, p.121). Special services are created to directly reduce complaints. This is most easily accomplished by removing the child with special needs from the classroom of the complainer. Unfortunately, although complaints are effectively reduced, it is not clear that the child benefits in any substantial way from this arrangement.

Special education and other specialized services have evolved to fix problems that challenge the coping skills of teachers. Arranging a child's experiences to build a complex repertoire of social interaction skills does not fit easily into this logic. Will an increased social repertoire work immediately and effectively to solve a pressing problem in behavior? Are students who are socially withdrawn and noncommunicative disturbing to teachers? Probably not. To most adults in a school, social interaction is rarely defined as a primary goal of education. A child who lacks social abilities, but who creates few learning or behavioral challenges for the teacher is unlikely to ever receive referrals for special services. If our model of services continues to be based on remediation of problems that are viewed as within the child (not within the child's interaction with the environment) and if the school systems' response to problems (i.e., teacher complaints) continues to be removal of the child from regular classes, a serious commitment to understanding and intervening upon social interaction behavior is not likely to occur.

Fortunately, there is an increasing appreciation of the limitations that remedial models of intervention and the logic of segregation place on promoting development. Social integration is increasingly being defined as a primary outcome for children with disabilities (cf, Meyer, Peck, & Brown, 1991; Peck, Odom & Bricher, 1992). The solving of problems through removal and segregation of children with challenging learning and developmental differences is no longer being viewed as a legally acceptable solution. Increasingly, the focus of systems' change efforts is to maintain all students with disabilities within regular settings, and provide the needed support services directly in the mainstream. A major reason for this policy change is to bring students with disabilities into contact with the normal forces of socialization, and provide normal patterns of social contacts to facilitate the formation of friendships and other social relationships. As the purposes and goals of special education change, new intervention strategies are needed to achieve these goals.

The purpose of this chapter is to review recent developments in the systematic instruction of social skills that facilitate these desired outcomes. This review will cover current issues and research in the areas of assessing social interaction skills, development of targets for intervention, and evaluation of programs that seek to influence social interactions and relationships. This review is guided by a specific model of social interchanges that acknowledges the need to analyze contextual characteristics of settings in which interactions occur, the competence and effectiveness of the social interchange behaviors of participants, and the relationship between social exchanges and peer relationships.

OVERVIEW OF SOCIAL SKILLS TRAINING

Historical Perspective

Few would argue that social development isn't fundamental, or that social development isn't learned through interactions within the environment as well as by direct instruction and guidance. Yet, in planning instruction for students with disabilities, the systematic instruction and measurement of social behavior is a phenomena of relatively recent history. Although earlier researchers and curriculum developers recognized problems in socialization, the functioning of the child was analyzed in terms of internal psychological constructs rather than in terms of interaction with others. Subsequently, instructional events were organized around these underlying psychological processes. For example, in an early methods text on learning disabilities, Myers and Hammill (1969), discuss instructional methods within chapters that are organized by the leading psychological theories of that time concerning the causation of learning disabilities. Thus, the chapters discuss methods of evaluation and instruction of skills relevant to perceptual motor systems, phonics, language development, and evaluation of speech, language, academic skills, and cognitive development. Although difficulties and immaturity in development of social relationships are frequently described as characteristics of students with learning disabilities, these problems were generally considered to be 'side-effects' of deeper disorders underlying the developmental processes.

Bender (1949) attributed the social adjustment problems of children with learning disabilities to two primary underlying causes. Under one hypothesis, motor disorders in a child, which are present because of minimal brain dysfunction, create prolonged dependency on the mother which inhibits more normal peer relationships and emotional stability. Under the second hypothesis, perceptual or intellectual problems in cognitive processing impede the child's efforts to accurately perceive the social world leading to frustration, misinterpretations of reality, and ultimately, maladaptive behavior. The focus of instruction is directed at repairing or retraining the underlying psychological or academic difficulties, with little systematic analysis or instruction of social interchanges.

This earlier viewpoint concerning the need for social skills training for students with mild disabilities has changed considerably over the past two decades (e.g., MacMillan & Morrison, 1984).

The field of evaluation and instruction for persons with mental retardation and other more severe disabilities has traditionally placed a higher premium on socialization (e.g., Cruikshank & Johnson, 1967). However, efforts to systematically teach social interaction behavior were not documented or widely promoted until the mid 1970s (e.g., Strain, Cooke, & Appolloni, 1976). Although the need for, and importance of, social skill training for students with severe disabilities has been acknowledged for a decade, the curriculum model most widely used for learners with severe disabilities does not reflect a process that is particularly mindful of, or sensitive to, the need for instruction in this area.

Current Approach to Curriculum Development

Within current instructional approaches for students with moderate, severe, and profound disabilities, the most prevalent model for selecting instructional objectives is based on ecological inventories. For example, Falvey et al. (1979) introduced an ecological model for generating curriculum with the following steps:

1. List current and potential environments that a student is likely to encounter.

2. List specific sub-environments within each environment.

3. List activities that occur in each sub-environment that a student may need to learn to increase independence.

4. List specific skills required to participate in the activities.

5. Conduct a discrepancy analysis between the skills needed to participate in activities and the student's current skills to identify instructional objectives.

While the focus of the ecological model does not preclude social skill learning, this model has been applied most frequently in the area of instruction of response chains needed for specific job requirements, or specific living skills within domestic and community settings. Although the instruction of social interchange skills is not inconsistent with this model, this model does not directly promote the instruction of social interchanges because:

1. The model directs us to analyze the physical parameters of the environment and the tasks to be accomplished rather than the social parameters of the environment. For example, the model does not direct the interventionist to analyze who is typically in that environment, what expectations they might have for social interactions, or in what ways a person with

disabilities can fit socially into this setting, perhaps in non-normative yet acceptable ways.

2. Skills are assumed to be specific to smaller micro-environments and sub-environments rather than generic across environments. While this is true of many production-type responses, social skills such as greetings, initiating interactions, sharing materials, commenting on events occurring in the environment, or maintaining conversation are more frequently generic across social environments rather than specific to environments. The instruction of skills such as these requires a consistent program of intervention across settings and across years of effort. In addition, students with severe disabilities often require more comprehensive techniques to build the motivation to respond socially (e.g., Koegel & Koegel, 1988). Making social responding important to children, as with the skills listed above, must be viewed as a shaping process across environments rather than as an isolated skill that can be taught in one specific setting.

3. Skills that increase independence are implicitly and explicitly the focus of instruction, not social interchange skills. The skills needed to participate in an activity are generally motoric responses that are task analyzed rather than social/communicative responses. Social responses are rarely considered to be critical for participation within an environment.

The last five to ten years have witnessed a substantial re-appraisal of traditional curriculum models that stress remediation of skill deficiencies, repair of cognitive deficits, and instruction of independent living skills as the sole educational outcome of concern for learners with severe disabilities. Instead, nearly all curriculum models now include the targeting of peer interactions as fundamental curriculum components (e.g., Gaylord-Ross & Holvoet, 1985; Sailor & Guess, 1983). A major reason that social skills are emerging as an important emphasis is that social skills are seen as facilitating integration.

Focus on Social Integration

Social development and school and community integration form an interactive process of habilitation for students with disabilities. School and community integration facilitates social skill development by providing peers as models for appropriate behavior (e.g., Egel, Richmand, & Koegel, 1981), by providing increased opportunities to practice social skills across multiple settings, and by offering social interaction contexts that are more interesting and more responsive than contexts provided in segregated environments (cf. Calkins, Dunn, & Kulgen, 1986; Snell & Eichner, 1989). Conversely, increased social interaction skills, frequently acquired through systematic instruction, allow for more meaningful (and more dignified) interaction with nondisabled people within integrated settings. Thus, increased social development facilitates integration and, in turn, increased integration provides for greater opportunities for social development.

There are some other important reasons to view social interaction interventions as primary features of instructional programs for persons with disabilities.

1. Parents identify social relationships and the development of friendships as primary concerns (e.g., Strully & Strully, 1986). The development of social interchanges and increases in social competence facilitate friendships and relationships with peers.

2. Current models of service delivery reject earlier models of a continuum of services that lead from more segregated environments to more integrated environments. Instead, current models call for the integration of all people with disabilities directly into typical environments with the support that is needed to learn and participate. Thus, rather than changing environments along a continuum of restrictiveness as students learn and develop, students are placed directly in less restrictive environments and the degree of support in the environment is changed as students learn and develop. As the model of service delivery is progressively changed from a model focused on specialized services and preparing for integration, to a model that stresses the delivery of services within the context of typical settings, the need for social skills increases. The failure to engage in reciprocal social responding in normalized settings can be stigmatizing and can lead to social isolation and *defacto* segregation of students with disabilities.

3. Social interactions enhance participation in many activities of daily life. For example, it is desirable to engage in simple social exchange behaviors when making purchases. For many students with severe disabilities, the social responses that are needed in integrated settings lag far behind the task analyzed skills needed for functional activities in those environments (e.g., Haring, Kennedy, Adams, & Pitts-Conway, 1987). Indeed, the nonverbal exchange behaviors that are characteristic of completing a purchase are identical in function to exchange behaviors and turn taking in playing a game, or holding a conversation and are equally social in that they involve a reciprocal exchange of responses between two people.

4. The instruction of social interchange skills may lessen the need for programming based on behavioral control of aberrant responses. There is evidence that the maladaptive behaviors of many people with disabilities may in fact serve communicative functions. Maladaptive behavior can be replaced by functionally equivalent social/communicative behavior to reduce the level of problem behavior rather than specific programs designed to reduce the behavior directly (Carr & Durand, 1985) .

As integration becomes viewed as a primary educational outcome that requires active efforts to promote, the need to develop our existing technologies of behavior change to assist individuals with severe disabilities in achieving a socially integrated lifestyle becomes apparent. Social skill training can be a significant means of promoting integration (Brady & McEvoy, 1989), as well as social relationships (Haring, 1991). Within the next section, the research supporting intervention to promote social interaction between students with disabilities and their nondisabled peers is reviewed.

PROMOTING INTEGRATION THROUGH SOCIAL INTERACTION INTERVENTION

In an important early study, Guralnick (1980) examined the patterns of social interactions between children with severe disabilities and peers. This study indicated that nondisabled peers prefer to interact with other nondisabled peers, and that active integration efforts are needed to promote interactions (cf. Stainback & Stainback, 1981). Similarly, Haring and Lovinger (1989) more recently found that preschool-aged students are frequently unresponsive to the typical (i.e., baseline) social initiations of children with severe disabilities. However, once more competent social initiations had been taught within the context of appropriate toy play, the responsiveness of the peers rose to a level that was positive and supportive. Not only are many nondisabled children unresponsive to students with severe disabilities in the absence of intervention, in many intervention studies published over the last several years, the initial level of social behavior assessed during baseline phases prior to intervention has tended to be low.

The tendency for initial levels of interaction to be low is indicated in Figure 1. This figure shows the mean levels of social interaction during baseline and treatment conditions for ten published research studies conducted between 1982 and 1989. To construct this figure, a literature search was conducted to identify ten research studies that fulfilled the following criteria:

1. A time-based measurement system was employed for at least part of the data analysis. The use of a common measure for the dependent variable allowed an analysis of the overall amount of time that students with developmental disabilities spent in focused social interaction with non-handicapped peers. Because these studies used time-based measures (i.e., either percent intervals based on time sampling, or duration of interaction) as a dependent measure, direct comparisons across studies are possible without using transformational techniques such as Meta-Analysis to calculate effect sizes (e.g., White, Rusch, Kazden, & Hartman, 1989). It should be noted however, that although time-based measures were employed across the studies, the definitions of social engagement, though highly similar across studies, were not identical.

2. All studies included students with severe disabilities and measured interactions with nondisabled peers (or in one case, siblings).

3. All studies included a baseline and at least one intervention phase that involved some form of social-behavioral intervention directed either toward social skill instruction of the student with disabilities, or teaching peers to initiate and maintain interactions.

4. All studies had interpretable experimental designs that reflected current editorial standards for design, measurement, and reliability.

Initially, studies were selected based on a review of all social interaction research published in the *Journal of Applied Behavior Analysis* and the *Journal of The Association for Persons with Severe Handicaps* from 1980 to 1989. This search yielded a total of six research studies that met the above criteria. An additional four studies were found through searches of other journals to bring the total to ten. Citations and characteristics of the studies selected for this analysis are given in Table 1.

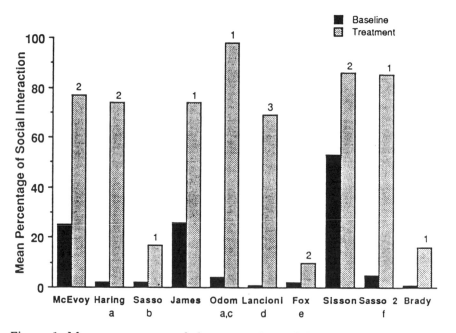

Figure 1. Mean percentages of time spent in social interaction and social engagement across ten published studies conducted between 1982 and 1989.

(a) Duration data were converted to percentage data, (b) Includes means for both low status students and high status students, (c) Includes sum of teacher antecedent and peer initiation data, (d) Represents the sum of all data points (both tutors and probers), (e) Represents the percent intervals with extended interactions, (f) Represents mean percent across all three interventions.

Figure 1 shows that the initial baseline levels of social interaction across these ten studies ranged from 1 per cent of the recording intervals to 52 per cent with a mean of 12.1 per cent. For example, in the study by McEvoy et al. (1988) in which three children with autism were integrated into early childhood settings, two of the children in the study never initiated an interaction during baseline. During intervention phases across the ten studies, the range in mean percentages of intervals with interactions was from 10 per cent to 98 per cent with a mean = 61.7 per cent. To place this number in a perspective, Greenwood, Walker, Todd, and Hops (1981) found that the natural rate norms for social interaction for nonhandicapped preschoolers ranged between 53 per cent and

Table 1: Citations and Characteristics of Studies Reviewed In Figure 1

Author(s)	Year	Sample Size	Population
1. McEvoy, Nordquist, Vey, Twardosz, Heckamen, Wehby & Denny	1988	3	Kindergarten Autism
2. Haring & Lovinger	1989	2	Kindergarten Autism
3. Sasso & Rude	1987	8	Elementary-age Severe Retardation and Autism
4. James & Egel	1986	3	Preschool Mental Retardation and Cerebral Palsy
5. Odom & Strain	1986	3	Preschool Autism
6. Lancioni	1982	3	Elementary-age Mental Retardation
7. Fox, Shores, Lindeman, & Strain	1986	3	Preschool Down Syndrome and Social Isolates
8. Sisson, Babeo, & Van Hasselt	1988	5	Elementary-age Blind & Multiple Handicaps
9. Sasso, Hughes, Swanson & Novak	1987	1	Elementary-age Multiple Handicaps
10. Brady, Shores, McEvoy, Ellis, & Fox	1987	2	Elementary-age autistic

69 per cent. The mean rate across these ten studies during intervention phases represents a normalized rate of interacting.

Figure 1 shows that five studies employed interventions based on peer initiation strategies, where the primary focus of the intervention was to increase the social initiation of nondisabled peers. Four of the studies employed a social skill training strategy directed at the child with disabilities and one study used a combined strategy. Interestingly, the mean for studies that employed a peer initiation strategy (58%) did not differ significantly from the mean for studies that employed a social skills training strategy or combined approach (62%). Thus, training that is focused either on peers or on students with disabilities seems equally effective in increasing the rates of interaction to normalized levels (a t-test of the difference between means yielded a p .05).

Initiation training and peer initiation training interventions have been employed over a wide range of participants with moderate and severe disabilities including: Children with autism, severe mental retardation, moderate mental retardation, physical disabilities, and sensory impairments with mental retardation. Although this range is impressive, these results should not be viewed as conclusive evidence regarding the external generality of intervention across populations because the diagnostic category of autism is over-represented in this research (five out of ten studies included students with autism). In addition, all studies that were reviewed were conducted with preschool or elementary-age students. The research base in the social interaction intervention literature continues to be built with populations of students who are younger. As has been pointed out, procedures used for younger children may not be appropriate or effective with older students (e.g., Gaylord-Ross, Haring, Breen, & Pitts-Conway, 1984). Finally, it should also be noted that it was not possible to analyze these data for the degree of disability of participants. It is currently unknown how effect may differ for students who are more severely disabled.

In summary, these data indicate that in the absence of social interventions, the rate of social engagement within integrated settings is relatively low. In half of the studies, the initial baseline level of interaction was near zero. When social interventions were begun (regardless of the target being the peers or the students with disabilities), rates of social engagement generally approached normalized rates of interaction. Based on these and related findings that have employed frequency-based measures (e.g., Breen, Haring, Pitts-Conway, & Gaylord-Ross, 1985; Gaylord-Ross, et al., 1984; Odom, Hoyson, Jamieson, & Strain, 1985) it can be concluded that one obstacle to social integration is the initial low competence level of students with severe disabilities and the comparatively low rate of social initiation that these students receive from nondisabled students. It has been consistently demonstrated that, in the absence of structured integration activities and social skill training programs, meaningful levels of social interaction may not occur. In the next sections of this chapter, procedures that have been experimentally shown to increase social interactions and social skills are reviewed.

INTERVENTION PROCEDURES

Contextual Variation

An important factor in conducting social interaction training and in promoting social interaction is the context for interaction (Haring, 1991). Contexts can be analyzed as to both physical parameters and social parameters. Physical parameters vary as to the richness in opportunities for interaction and in the degree of support for interaction provided by the setting or materials. Some toys or activities are designed to directly promote social interchanges. For example, in playing on a see-saw, two children must coordinate their behavior in a socially reciprocal fashion, otherwise the activity can not proceed. Activities that require joint interaction such as playing Frisbee, handball, or interactive games, are referred to as cooperative activities. Other toys or more passive activities, such as watching TV, do not occasion high levels of social interchange or may encourage more isolated play.

In addition to physical parameters such as types of activity or toys that influence the degree of interactions, aspects of *social* context also affect the amount of interaction. Peck (1989) has provided an analysis of the importance of social contextual variables. In his review, Peck stresses the importance of the *transactional* nature of interaction. That is, a defining feature of social interaction is the interplay between interactants such that there is a continual adjustment and adaptation of responding between both members of a dyad. One consequence of this viewpoint is that the focus of the social interaction problem changes from an emphasis on skill deficits of the child with disabilities, to an emphasis on characteristics of the social interaction patterns shared across interactants that may be leading to less functional or mature interactions. That is, the social responses produced by a person with disabilities are not viewed as indicative of skills deficits that are inherent to the individual, but instead, are a result of adaptations made between the child and others in the environment. Thus, one focus of intervention is to change the social contextual characteristics of the environment to occasion different behavior. In Peck's analysis, social contextual characteristics such as child directedness and responsiveness to child-initiated interactions (Koegel, Dyer, & Bell, 1987), peer characteristics (Bednersh & Peck, 1986), task variation (Dunlap, 1984), interaction style (Mirenda & Donnellan, 1986), and compliance with child preferences and choice-making (Peck, 1985) are variables for analysis and change.

Haring, Breen, and Weiner (in preparation) assessed aspects of the social and physical environment to determine the degree of support for social interactions across classroom, school, and community contexts. Within this analysis, the major contextual variables assessed were teacher directedness and structure for interactions and focus of the activity. Teacher directedness was categorized in one of three ways: a) teacher-directed activities, b) episodes that were organized with an activity, but not teacher directed; and c) nondirected free-time interactions), and focus of the activity (instruction, or recreation leisure). The focus of the intervention was categorized as either task – related or recreational in nature. Social behavior such as frequency of social initiation, and number of interaction turns (either verbal conversational turns, or nonverbal object exchange turns) were recorded. In addition, the natural richness of each context was assessed by judging the number of opportunities for interaction and whether or not they were actually utilized in an interaction.

An example of the data analysis from this study is presented in Figure 2. The upper panel of this figure shows the mean opportunities for interaction (for 41 participants) across the three setting variables investigated in the study: Community, school, or classroom settings. Within this analysis, classroom contexts were analyzed separately from school contexts. Classrooms contexts included both special education classrooms and mainstreamed classrooms. School contexts included, breaks between classes in the hallways, eating lunch, and times spent in nonclassroom settings before and after school.

An opportunity for an interaction was defined as any conventionally appropriate event in which an interaction could occur. For example, a verbal or nonverbal initiation from a peer is an opportunity to interact. These data show that community and school settings offer substantially greater opportunities for social interaction than do classroom settings. The lower panel in Figure 2 represents the differences in opportunities for interaction across two conditions of activity focus (Recreation vs. Task) and three conditions of structure (*Non* indicates nonstructured, *CO* indicates that context was organized but interactions were not directly prompted, and *TD* indicates that the teachers directed or prompted interaction between the students). Thirty minutes of data were selected for each student across five different contextual conditions. A repeated measures ANOVA was performed with the five context variables as repeated measures, and the group variable as an independent variable. The data analysis showed a significant difference between setting variables: Community, school, and classroom $F(2, 38) = 7.82$, p $.001$. There was not a significant difference between activity and structure variables (Recreation-Nonstructured activities, Recreation-context organized, Recreation-teacher directed, Task-context organized, and Task/Teacher directed) $F(2, 8) = 1.06$, p $.37$. Visual inspection of the means across the activities indicates that the least effective contextual conditions were recreation contexts with the context organized by the teacher, but no teacher direction of social interaction. The most effective contextual conditions were

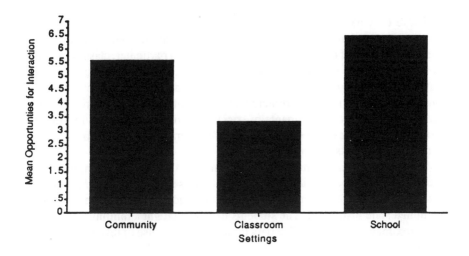

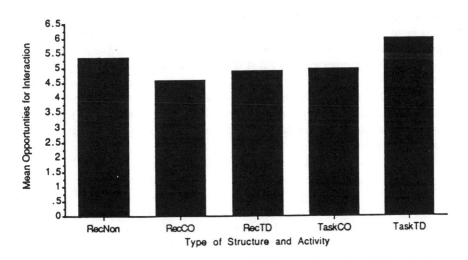

Figure 2. Upper panel: Mean number of opportunities for social interaction across three types of settings: Community, classroom and school. *Lower panel:* Mean number of opportunities for social interaction across five contextual variables.

RecNon means recreational contexts that are nonstructured, RecCO means recreational contexts where the context is organized by the teacher (but behavior is not prompted), RecTD means recreational contexts that are teacher directed, TaskCO means task contexts that are organized by the teacher (but behavior is not prompted), and TaskTD means task contexts that are teacher directed.

recreational contexts when there was no teacher structure and in task contexts that were teacher directed.

These data have implications for the design of social skill programs and planning integration activities. The settings for social interactions significantly affect the number of opportunities for interaction. In particular, classrooms have substantially fewer opportunities for interactions, while school contexts have nearly double the opportunities for interaction. Teacher support (nonstructured, context organized, or teacher directed) and focus of activity (recreation vs. task) were less important determinants of social behavior than was the location for the interactions. The greatest opportunities for interaction occur in nonstructured recreational contexts within the school.

Research by Warren and Rogers-Warren (1983) supports the importance of setting events on communicative behavior. In this study, wireless microphones were used to record the use of noun labels by students with severe retardation living in a state institution. The students had been taught a minimum repertoire of approximately 15 words. The data indicated that the use of this repertoire was highly associated with specific settings. In particular, the resident's classroom had the highest percentage of labels used under natural conditions (a mean of 78 per cent of the labels taught were observed within the classroom on at least one occasion) while the living unit and dining hall settings of the institution were associated with fewer labels used (mean = 44 per cent). The authors examined the relationship of the antecedent adult behavior to this language use of the residents. The number of times that the students were asked to respond was approximately 10 times greater in the classroom setting than in the other settings combined. The rate of adult verbalizations was also substantially greater in the classrooms. This study supports the contention that opportunities to respond is an important variable that might be functionally related to communicative and social responding.

Summary

There have been some recent efforts to specify and investigate the effects of variation in physical and social contexts on interaction. As specific activities, contexts, and peers are identified for individual students with disabilities, a next step in designing social interaction programs is to plan instruction to support and teach skills needed by the student to participate in activities. The ability of a student with disabilities to more independently participate in activities is important because it allows peers to focus their time during the interaction on more purely social commenting, rather than instruction. Fortunately, there is a research literature on conducting instruction to teach basic play and leisure skills that can serve as a context for interaction.

Teaching Play Repertoires

The most natural context for social interaction among younger children is play time. Whitman, Mercurio, and Caponigri (1970) conducted one of the first studies concerning teaching social responses to persons with severe mental retardation within a play context. Within this study, students were taught to roll balls and pass blocks to each other with prompts and reinforcement. The instruction of social skills within play contexts is dependent on several factors. First, activities and settings for instruction need to be found through environmental inventories and interviews that identify opportunities for play with persons who are not disabled. For younger children, this is a comparatively easy task as most play occurs within predictable and supervised places. Second, once settings and activities have been identified, students need to be taught to engage in the response sequences necessary to participate in this play or activity. Under current best practices models (e.g., Meyer, Eichinger, & Park-Lee, 1987), this instruction needs to occur directly within the criterion settings, not as a prerequisite for entering that setting. Third, the need for the students with disabilities to receive social skill instruction, particularly in the area of initiating and maintaining play responses should be analyzed. Finally, the need to develop peer mediated interventions to increase rates of social engagement needs to be analyzed. The area of social interaction during freetime or structured play time is probably the most thoroughly researched area in the literature.

Recreational and leisure programming

For older students, recreational and leisure activities provide a natural context for engaging in social leisure interactions. Nietupski, Hamre-Nietupski, and Ayres (1984) provide a review of the research that has been conducted concerning the instruction of leisure and play skills to persons with severe and profound disabilities. Among the conclusions drawn by Nietupski et al. are that: (a) nonschool, integrated sites should be surveyed for leisure skills as well as school sites; (b) task analysis is a proven technology that provides persons with severe and moderate handicaps the ability to engage in a wide variety of games and activities; and (c) skills should be selected for instruction based on a criteria of normalcy for engagement in these skills by nondisabled peers, and with regard to skills that can be used across settings.

A variety of skills have been taught using task-analytic methods including table games (Marchant and Wehman, 1979); toy play (Favell, 1973; Haring, 1985); pinball machine use (Hill, Wehman, & Horst, 1982); videogames (Sedlak, Doyle, & Schloss, 1982); physical fitness skills (Stainback, Stainback, Wehman, & Spangiers, 1983); and recess skills (Hiroshige, 1989). It is apparent that, at least for students who are moderately to severely mentally retarded and who have relatively normal motor development, that a sufficiently wide array of skills can be taught. In conducting training in basic play skills or social leisure skills, the major goal is to give students a familiar context within which to interact. While training organized around the skills needed to perform a game or activity are important, many students with severe disabilities require interventions that teach social interaction skills directly, in addition to skills needed for participation.

As greater focus is placed on the importance of training social skills within natural interaction contexts, it will become increasingly important to look at natural leisure contexts in a much finer-grained manner. For example, Hughes (1989) recently conducted a study describing the rules that a specific group of children at one elementary school follow in playing what would seem to be a simple game – foursquare. It turns out that foursquare is not a simple game. The glossary for this study lists 100 rules that comprise this game as it is played in one school. In addition, players frequently change, adapt, and elaborate different aspects of the game on an ongoing basis. The rules can change as specific children who are friends, or not friends, enter the game (a major purpose of *ad hoc* rule changes is to keep your friends in the game, or get nonfriends out rapidly, so that one peer group can dominate the play). Players of foursquare are not randomly selected clusters of children. They comprise several interrelated social networks who engage in foursquare regularly. Thus, in conducting intervention research, it is important to recognize the finer-grained rules (including the social rituals) and social interrelationships that control the game. For example, players who are standing in line have a role to play during games such as participating in disputes, voting on whether a player is out, calling for changes in the rules, and counting for players when 'second saves' are allowed. Intervention needs to include learning the formal rules of the game (which are actually quite simple), learning the highly specific and changeable rules and rituals as practiced on a specific school site, and gaining access to a social network (i.e., being a friend with members of a sub-group who regularly play).

Initiation Training

One of the most common strategies to increase social interaction is teaching students with disabilities to initiate interactions. As reviewed in Figure 1, this strategy has a history of effectiveness across investigations that is comparable to the effectiveness of peer initiation training. Gaylord-Ross and Haring (1987) discuss the advantages of teaching initiations:

1. *Increased Probability of Successful Interactions*. The student with severe disabilities has more control over interactions. This is important because the student can initiate interactions around activities within which they are competent rather than passively waiting for peer initiations which may or may not match their current interests and level of competence.

2. *Increased Independence*. The student is less dependent on nondisabled peers to engage in interactions. The social image of the disabled person may be enhanced because of greater control over interactions.

3. *Increased Frequency of Interaction*. Teaching social initiation skills to students with severe handicaps results in increased levels of social behavior compared to baseline levels within natural contexts (e.g., Haring & Lovinger, 1989).

There is a strong correlation between rate of talking and rate of language acquisition in normally developing young children (Nelson, 1973) and children with disabilities (Hart & Risley, 1980). It is therefore tempting to believe that teaching students to initiate verbal interactions would not only increase the rate of social exchanges, but might also facilitate more basic semantic, syntactic, or pragmatic language development. The critical issue here is to determine if increasing the number of social and communicative events that a student participates in across the day also has more general effects on language development. Warren and Kaiser (1988) propose three criteria for evaluating such general effects of intervention: (a) Does the intervention result in increases in the formal measures of language (e.g., syntax, or vocabulary size)? (b) Does the intervention result in increased use of social language such as increases in the number of types of requests demonstrated? and (c) Is there evidence that the intervention results not only in the acquisition of the targeted responses, but increases in the learning rates of other communicative functions or forms? Relatedly, does the intervention result in increased generalization of these and related nontargeted communicative forms or functions across persons or settings? To date, the major focus of the research literature in both the social interaction intervention and communication areas has primarily documented the acquisition and generalization of specific targeted functions, rather than the more general effects that are possible. Clearly, more longitudinal research in this area is highly warranted.

In one of the first investigations on teaching initiations, Stokes, Baer, and Jackson (1974) used a multiple exemplar training format with institutionalized adults to teach generative greeting responses. Within this study, participants were prompted to initiate interactions to one staff member and, after the training criterion was met, probes were conducted with people who had not participated in instruction. If generalization did not occur to all staff members targeted, instruction was begun with another staff member. Teaching with additional staff members continued until generalization to all staff was observed.

While training an initial greeting response is an important first step in teaching social interaction skills, initiation responses such as saying 'Hi' and gestural waves result in interactions that last only a few seconds. Additional training procedures are needed to teach more elaborate interactions of extended durations. An initial study that taught initiation skills that resulted in more extended interactions and that was not dependent on conversational skills was conducted by Gaylord-Ross et al. (1984). Within this study, three nonverbal activities were selected around which students with autism could initiate interactions within a high school setting. The three activities, playing a hand held videogame, listening to a Sony Walkman, and sharing gum, were age-appropriate activities that nondisabled students as well as the students with autism enjoyed. The students with autism were trained to approach nondisabled students and offer to share the objects as a means to initiate interactions. Training was conducted with peer 'confederates' while the data reported was with untrained nondisabled peers naturally encountered within a courtyard setting as part of the normally scheduled midmorning break. The results indicated that, prior to training, the students with autism never initiated interactions. During the initiation training phase, two of the students initiated interactions at least once during each break, while the third student initiated an average of two interactions per break. Importantly, the mean duration of interactions indicated that the students and the peers interacted for extended periods of time. Breen et al. (1985) extended the findings of the earlier study by applying the same model of teaching object-centered initiations within breaktime settings in community job sites. In this research, students with autism were taught to make coffee and offer it to co-workers.

Initiation training strategies are fundamental to social interaction training approaches. As these procedures have been developed and extended, it is clear that some initiations, for example offering a toy as a bid to start playing, can result in interactions of extended durations, while other initiations result in briefer interactions. An important current trend in social skills research is to teach responses to students with severe disabilities that can be used to extend and elaborate interactions. For an example of this approach, Haring, Roger, Lee, Breen, and Gaylord-Ross (1986) trained students to initiate verbal interactions within a cafeteria setting in an elementary school. Wildman, Wildman, and Kelly (1986) report a similar study that targeted several classes of conversation extension responses such as asking questions of one's partner and giving information about oneself. The training was shown to be effective in increasing conversational competence which was independently confirmed with social validity ratings. Downing (1987) was also successful in teaching a generic ability to extend conversational interactions by modeling and reinforcing responses from conversational partners that were relevant and meaningful to the topic under discussion.

Hunt, Alwell, and Goetz (1988) demonstrated that not only could elaboration responses be taught (in this case defined as conversational 'turns'), but that the teaching of such responses resulted in decreases in socially inappropriate behaviors. In the approach used by Hunt et al., students with severe disabilities were given personalized picture books containing photographs of favorite activities, family members and pets at home, and other highly salient pictures to the student. The student was then taught to initiate interactions by showing the book to peers. Because the pictures are highly meaningful to the individual students, it is more likely that extended duration interactions will occur and that the students with disabilities will be more highly motivated to communicate about the topics in the pictures.

In summary, social initiation and interaction extension and elaboration skills are an important means to increase levels of social interactions within natural settings. Within these interventions it is critical to assess not only the increases in frequencies of social behaviors, but also increases in the normalized quality of social interactions that result from training. Without ongoing monitoring of effectiveness, direct social skill training (such as initiation training) might produce limited generalization, and initiation skills that have non-normalized or ineffective characteristics (e.g., Berler, Gross, & Drabman, 1982).

A major weakness of this literature is the lack of demonstrated relationships between the acquisition of specific skills and the attainment of the larger objectives for the training of these skills; that is, increased social acceptance. One important way to assess the effects of initiation training interventions is to assess the immediate effects of the initiation of the response on the peer (e.g., Fox, Shores, Lindeman, & Strain, 1986). Initiation strategies that result in more generally positive responses from peers can then be identified. In addition, it is critical to assess the duration as well as frequencies of interaction to identify social contexts and initiation strategies.

Simply increasing raw initiation rates, though relatively easy to accomplish in applied settings, needs to be carefully evaluated for each individual. In some cases, simply increasing initiation rates without a focus of the quality and meaningfulness of the initiation may not achieve the effect that is desired. For example, if the initiation rate is increased for a student, but the initiations are stigmatizing or directed inappropriately at strangers, it is possible that the intervention would do more harm than good. Clearly, measures of contextual appropriateness, and the reactions of others in the students social milieu are important to monitor (e.g., Warren, Rogers-Warren, & Baer, 1976). In addition, intervention to increase social and communicative initiations should be coupled with other interventions designed to increase the quality of interactions.

Teaching initiation skills is one of the most basic approaches to social intervention. A closely related approach is to increase the frequency of interaction through teaching others in the school or classroom to increase their initiations toward students with disabilities. This strategy is referred to as Peer Initiation Intervention.

Peer Initiation Intervention

As shown in Figure 1, peer initiation interventions also have an extensive history of effectiveness in promoting increased social interaction of children with disabilities (e.g., Hendrickson, Strain, Trembly, & Shores, 1982). Within these strategies nondisabled peers are trained to initiate interactions with students with disabilities. Research has documented that these strategies result in increases in the social interactions between students with disabilities and their peers. These effects have shown to be robust across students with autism (Strain, Kerr, & Ragland, 1979; Odom & Strain, 1986), children with behavior disorders (Strain & Fox, 1981), children with mental retardation (Lancioni, 1982), and students with severe disabilities (Young & Kerr, 1979). Peer initiation procedures can be applied within school settings or within home settings by siblings (James & Egel, 1986).

The major focus of peer initiation strategies is to teach peers to organize play episodes, share toys, respond positively to social responses, and engage in play. The peer serves as a social facilitator for the student with disabilities to enter and participate in play or social interactions. In some cases, peer initiation interventions have resulted not only in increases for targeted students, but also produced 'spillover' effects to nontargeted students (Strain, Shores, & Kerr, 1976). Sasso and Rude (1987) showed that the status of the peers used within the intervention influenced other peers to interact with the disabled student. Sasso, Hughes, Swanson, and Novak (1987) investigated a technique in which nondisabled peers were trained to reinforce untrained nondisabled peers for initiating interactions with students who are disabled. The results indicated that the procedure was effective in increasing the level of interaction and that teacher prompting of interaction was largely unnecessary.

Research by Odom, Hoyson, Jamieson, and Strain (1985) illustrates some potential problems with the application of peer initiation interventions. In this research, peers were trained to initiate social interactions by organizing play situations, sharing toys, requesting toys, assisting in activities, and complimenting the social behavior of the students with disabilities. Following training, the students' social initiations and interactions with disabled peers were observed and the results indicated that the peer intervention package produced rapid increases in the frequency of positive initiations. Generalization probes were then conducted within other contexts, and prompts and reinforcers were not given within the probes. Under unprompted conditions, the nondisabled peers did not interact appreciably with the disabled peers. In addition, a component analysis was conducted by systematically adding and withdrawing the prompting and the reinforcement procedures within the three criterion contexts. Results indicated that the positive interactions were dependent on the use of prompts and rewards by the teacher within those settings.

It appears from these data that the nondisabled peers who participate may not develop an increased 'intrinsic motivation' to interact with disabled peers. Studies have not yet been conducted to demonstrate that the peers value the interactions with the disabled students, view them as more normalized, or have increased their likelihood of interacting with them in the absence of being directed to do so by the teacher. Unfortunately, few studies investigating any social interaction training strategies of any type have been attempted to document the impact of intervention of relationships, sociometric status, or social perceptions. A major role for future investigation into peer initiation strategies will be to better assess peer perceptions of interventions on an ongoing basis to build stronger peer commitment to the interventions. In addition, it is clear that these interventions should include components that affect attitude change and promote discussions of the importance of friendship as an ongoing component of interventions.

It may also be important to begin to examine what motivates peers without disabilities to interact with and become friends with peers with disabilities. The study by Odom et al. (1985) suggests that teacher direction and rewards may play a large role. Research should begin to target other factors that might also play a role. For example, increasing peer support among other nondisabled friends may be an important component. It would be fruitful to employ more qualitative interview techniques to study the self-stated motivational perceptions of students who have engaged in longer-term friendship interactions with disabled students to better understand how and why these relationships are maintained.

Instruction of Pivotal Social Skills

Pivotal skills are responses that set the occasion for the emergence of, or changes in, other response classes that would not have occurred had the pivotal response not been learned. The concept of pivotal responses includes the idea that some responses are so fundamental that the instruction of one response class directly promotes a more wide-spread developmental improvement far beyond the response class trained (e.g., Koegel & Koegel, 1988). Intervention in social responding can entail the teaching of such pivotal responses. For example, for a student who is socially isolated and anxious within social contexts, behaviors (such as stereotypic responding) that reduce social contact by increasing a child's ability to ignore the social world (e.g., attending solely to an idiosyncratic body movement, posture, or object manipulations) are highly reinforced because they cause a reduction in contact with the aversive aspects of the social world. If, as a result of a social skills training or a peer initiation program, a student is directly prompted to participate in the social world and the student finds that this participation is rewarding, a fundamentally different set of response classes (e.g., playing and initiating social interactions) might result. Many social interaction responses are potentially pivotal to more dramatic changes in the course of a student's development. Clearly, responses that can be most pivotal to creating widespread changes in development should be targeted. In addition to initiation training and peer initiation programs, there are other intervention strategies that show the potential for creating pivotal changes in many interrelated response classes.

Self-monitoring responses

Self-monitoring is a process that includes: (a) Discriminating correct from incorrect examples of a target behavior (i.e., establishing a performance standard); (b) observing your own behavior or the results of a performance; (c) evaluating your behavior against the standard; (d) self-recording the performance; and (e) self-reinforcement (Koegel & Koegel, 1988). Thus, self-monitoring itself consists of a series of responses. Once these responses are taught, they mediate the performance of other responses. For example, students can be taught to self-monitor their own initiation of social responses. A standard of performance can be created such as a goal to initiate five conversations per school day. Students can subsequently record each instance of social initiation and receive feedback and reinforcement from others when the successful attainment of this performance standard is reported. Self-monitoring has been widely shown to be teachable to students with moderate and mild disabilities. One area where it has been widely applied is in increasing work productivity (e.g., Ackerman & Shapiro, 1984).

There are several examples of the use of self-monitoring in the area of social and communicative skills. Gajar, Schloss, Schloss, and Thompson (1984) used a self-monitoring procedure to increase the conversational appropriateness of youths who suffered head injuries. Assessment of conversational behavior prior to intervention indicated that these students engaged in confabulatory and preservative responding, excessive self-disclosures, interruptions, and inappropriate laughter. During a training phase, the students were given feedback through a visual stimulus whenever their conversation was appropriate or inappropriate. During the self-monitoring phase, students used a toggle switch to self-monitor their own perception of appropriate conversational behaviors. The self-monitoring increased the levels of appropriate conversational responding to levels comparable to same-age nondisabled students in the same context. Although there may be some difficulties in applying this technology under more natural conditions, the study shows that even quite complex behaviors and very subtle social discriminations can be self-monitored by persons with disabilities.

Liberty (1985) investigated the use of a self-monitoring procedure to increase question answering in students with severe disabilities. In this study, students with severe disabilities used hand counters and wrist counters to self-record two word answers to questions. The results indicated that wearing the self-monitoring devices controlled responsiveness. Case studies of the application of self-monitoring to increase responsiveness to questions from others have also been reported by Koegel and Koegel (1988).

A major issue in self-monitoring for students with severe disabilities is that it is probably possible to self-monitor only one response class at a time rather than multiple response classes. Therefore, it is important that the response selected for self-monitoring be as pivotal as possible so that broader changes in socialization can be promoted. In addition, another issue with self-monitoring systems is whether or not they can be faded while the level of social responding remains reasonably high. There are relatively few examples of studies in which self-monitoring procedures are systematically faded. Indeed, most demonstrations of self-monitoring show that the self-monitoring system controls responding. This means that when the systems are withdrawn, the behavior typically returns to baseline levels. Finally, the overall success of self-monitoring is dependent on the reinforcement that the students receive for engaging in the self-monitored behaviors. This can occur in two ways. First, behaviors should be selected that others in the student's environment would naturally reinforce, or would reinforce more strongly if prompted to do so. A second (not mutually exclusive) approach is to reward the students for reporting the self-monitored responses at periodic intervals, however, if students are dependent on this type of reinforcement rather than the former, the probability of successfully fading the self-monitoring program will be quite low.

In summary, intervention approaches that combine the logic of teaching pivotal skills with the use of self-monitoring as a system to promote generalization and use of the skills under natural conditions is a potentially powerful technology. Although considerably more experimental work is needed in this area, a promising foundation for future practice has been laid.

Teaching generative scripts

Another pivotal response is to teach students to follow scripted interaction patterns that can be applied across multiple settings. For example, a simple interaction script such as approach, greet, offer interactive object, and terminate interaction can be taught and used across a variety of settings and materials. The script is generative because an almost infinite number of objects (e.g., hand held videogames, picture communication books, or cups of coffee) can be inserted within the chain across various contexts. Once the students have learned this sequence of behaviors across multiple examples and across multiple settings, new objects that can structure interactions will frequently be spontaneously introduced by students. This type of social initiation strategy was employed within the study by Gaylord-Ross et al. (1984) and Breen et al. (1985).

Goldstein, Wickstrom, Hoyson, Jamieson, and Odom (1988) investigated the instruction of sociodramatic script training to promote interaction. Examples of scripted sociodramatic activities that these authors have investigated include a shoe store activity, and a magic show. Within these interventions, scripts are produced that include roles for three students. For example, within the magic show script, there are the roles of magician, magician's assistant, and volunteer from the audience. The teacher supplies all the needed props for carrying out the play, and teaches the participants to recite lines that correspond to each role. In addition, the teacher encourages elaboration of scripted lines and spontaneous changes in the play. The data indicate that the level of social interaction and language use increases dramatically under these conditions. This intervention may be effective, not only because of the facilitative effects of teacher direction and structure, but because of the familiarity of the scripted context over time, reinforcement for elaboration, and the overall enjoyment and reinforcing quality of putting on a play.

Age-appropriate 'hanging out'

'Hanging out' is a pivotal skill for adolescents. The adolescent credo is that good things happen to those that hang out...nothing ever happens to those who do not. Fortunately, hanging out is dependent on few responses, and these responses are relatively easy to teach. Critical responses for students at this age level are: (a) identifying the members of your clique, (b) identifying where your clique hangs out, (c) hanging out and looking cool, and (d) following your group as it moves. All of these responses are readily teachable to students with severe disabilities. For example, Haring, Breen, and Laitinen (1989) taught adolescent girls to identify age-appropriate teenage fashions and choose those items when on shopping trips to the mall.

The most critical component of hanging out is to identify and support the entry of students with severe disabilities into extant cliques of nonhandicapped students. Fortunately, there are starting to be some excellent models to follow in setting up peer support networks.

An innovative friendship program was developed by Breen, Lovinger, and Haring (1989). At La Colina Jr. High School in Santa Barbara, students with severe handicaps are assigned to a special education classroom, but attend regular education classes such as art and physical education, and all noncurricular activities (e.g., lunch and breaks between classes). In addition to these efforts to include the students with severe disabilities in the mainstream of the school, there is also a program designed to create supported friendships. Within this program, nondisabled students are recruited every school year to participate in a supported friendship program. The program is called the Partners At Lunch (PAL) Club. The program is structured with several unique characteristics. First, the nondisabled students are asked to make a minimum commitment of time that is purposely kept low. For example, a student may commit to a minimum of one, two, or three lunch periods per week. Students may exceed the minimum commitment at any time; however a procedure to limit time commitment at first was instituted because many students initially over-committed to the program and became dissatisfied after a month or so of participation. By keeping the initial commitment lower, the majority of the students have successfully maintained a friendship for at least a year.

A second unique aspect of the program is that entire peer groups are recruited for participation, not just individuals. As the program typically functions, the student with severe disabilities spends the lunch period with a peer group, and follows that peer group throughout its normal social interaction patterns. A third unique feature is that peer groups meet with the students and the teacher during one afternoon each week after school for social/leisure interactions. The PAL Club is a recognized afterschool club that is formally sanctioned by the student council, as are other school clubs such as the Chess Club or French Club. The teacher typically brings in an age-appropriate feature length film or taped segments of music videos and provides refreshments. During this time, the teacher informally interviews the peer groups to determine how the non-monitored lunchtime interactions are proceeding. This provides the teacher with the opportunity to identify potential problems and provide specific suggestions for how to handle the problems in the future. In addition it provides the opportunity to identify training objectives for social skills or critical skills that are perceived by the peers as requiring intervention.

Hanging out is a pivotal response class for adolescents with severe disabilities. While the responses needed to appropriately hang out are minimal, an active effort is needed to integrate students with disabilities into intact peer groups. Simply sending students into a typical school lunchroom or courtyard and expecting integration and inclusion to occur is unlikely to result in successful interactions. A major reasons for social behavior intervention is to not only teach a social interaction skill, but to set the occasion for ongoing social interactions. Ultimately, it is hoped that teaching pivotal skills, increasing the frequency and quality of interactions, and increasing the rate of social contacts will result in attainment of friendships. The relationship between social intervention and formation of relationships is therefore critical to evaluate.

RELATIONSHIP BETWEEN SOCIAL INTERVENTION AND RELATIONSHIPS

As discussed in the beginning of this chapter, there are a number of interrelated reasons for the systematic instruction of social interaction skills. These reasons include the need to promote social development and the fact that social interaction forms the basis for social integration. Although social interaction is an important goal in and of itself, for most people social interaction, as it relates to quality of life, is defined as interacting with friends and acquaintances. Unfortunately, the ability to engage in social interaction does not, in and of itself, mean that social relationships will follow. The review of recent experimental efforts to promote interaction and teach social skills has shown that these skills can be taught. Unfortunately, most research conducted to date has been concerned with demonstrating the possibility of teaching these skills, not the use of these skills, once taught, within stable social networks.

The use of social skills within stable social networks is the ultimate end product of intervention. As such, it is important that techniques to promote social skill development as well as measure and support social networks be developed. Currently, there are four major ways to assess the strength of a person's participation in social networks: (a) assessment of acceptance, (b) assessment of friendship patterns, (c) assessment of social participation, and (d) qualitative interview methods.

Assessment of Acceptance

The major approach to assessing peer acceptance is through questionnaires. The construct referred to as Social Willingness for Interaction (Voeltz, 1980, 1982) has been well replicated. Within social willingness questionnaires, students are asked to rate how likely or willing they would be to engage in specific activities with a person with disabilities. The items are ranked on a scale that ranges from most casual to progressively more involved or intimate interactions. For example, a lower intensity item might be the willingness to sit next to a person with disabilities in a mainstreamed class, while a more intimate item would assess the willingness to attend a school dance accompanied by a person with disabilities.

From Voeltz's research, it is clear that in schools where contact with persons with disabilities is promoted, the overall levels of willingness for interaction among the entire student body increases. However, the degree of social willingness shown by students may not be dependent on the type of contact that students experience. Haring, Breen, Pitts-Conway, Lee, and Gaylord-Ross (1987) investigated the effects of participating as a peer tutor to participating in friendship-based program. Within this research, students who participated as peer tutors were taught to implement task analytic instruction with students with disabilities within a community-based, integrated school program. Students in the friendship-based program (who attended the same school as the peer tutors) interacted daily with the students with disabilities within recreational leisure games and activities. Both experimental groups showed substantially greater social willingness than a low contact control group. However, there was not a significant difference in willingness between the two experimental groups. A difference between the groups was not detectable because both groups showed extremely high willingness for interaction that was near the ceiling of the scale.

Assessment of Friendship

Most attempts to assess friendships have involved the use of peer nomination measures. To conduct these assessments, students are asked to nominate who is, or is not a friend among the people they know. For example, Hiroshige (1989) asked elementary-aged children the following questions in order to assess the friendship networks of students with severe physical disabilities who were mainstreamed:

1. Who would you like to play with?

2. Who would you not like to play with?

3. Who are your friends?

4. Who are not your friends?

5. Who would you invite to your birthday party?

6. Who would you not invite to your birthday party?

In conducting this survey, students are asked to list at least three children for each question.

Positive nominations are requested (e.g., Who would you play with?) as well as negative nominations (e.g., Who would you not like to play with?). Positive nominations allow an analysis of the friendship patterns and the identification of peer groups in which a student participates. Peer groups can be defined on the basis of a high rate of mutual nominations of members of the group. The level of popularity of individual members of a group can also be assessed by the level or number of nominations by other members of the group. Students who are *rejected* by peers are those that receive higher rates of negative nominations, while students who are *neglected* are those that are not nominated either positively or negatively. Frequently, students with disabilities fall into the neglected category (MacMillan & Morrison, 1984).

Social Participation

The purpose of assessing social participation is to assess the degree to which a student actually attends and participates in activities with nondisabled peers in school and community settings. Assessing social participation is essentially a process of documenting the types of interactions a person is experiencing and with whom they are interacting. The purpose of assessing social participation is to ensure that students are given sufficient opportunities to practice skills and develop relationships.

Kennedy, Horner, and Newton (1990) tested a system that documented the social contacts of persons with disabilities living in group homes with nondisabled members of the community. The system was used as an ongoing evaluation tool to encourage staff members to initiate more social activities with nondisabled peers. Frequently, social interactions initiated by staff members were with their own friends. Within school settings, simple frequency counts of the number of activities per week with peers would be a good measure of social participation.

Qualitative Research Methods

Qualitative research methods are also well suited to assess the degree of social participation and strength of relationships with nondisabled peers. Qualitative assessment methods can include observations of interactions as well as interviews with nondisabled participants who interact with students with disabilities. Qualitative methods are most useful for understanding the impact of interventions or interactions on the participants. Through the interview process, students explain the meaning of interaction from their own perspective and values. These methods are particularly well suited to better understand the nature of friendships that result from integration efforts and how the participants view and value the input from teachers in supporting interactions.

Qualitative methods can be used in at least two ways. One important use of interview methods is to assess the perceptions of peers prior to the design of intervention. Peers frequently have unique ideas as to targets for intervention and contexts for interactions that would be overlooked by adults in the school setting. Second, interview methods can be used after interventions to collect more impressionistic data as to the value of the intervention. For example, students can be asked if they noticed that an intervention on social skills had taken place and if this intervention made interacting with another student more or less pleasant. Students can also give valuable feedback to assess whether or not skills are actually being used under unsupervised conditions and whether of not the student's current social behavior matches the environment well or is stigmatizing.

Chadsey-Rusch and Rusch (1987) have done extensive work in the area of social behavior in vocational settings using qualitative research methods. They have studied variables such as the characteristics of the physical environment, the organizational climate, and the effects of intervention on social skill use. The impact of using observational, interview, and other qualitative methods to guide theory development and practice is also occurring within the design of residential programs (e.g., Zetlin, & Turner, 1985) as well as in planning and assessing the efforts of school systems to become more integrated (Murray-Seegert, 1989). Given the interactional nature of social development, it is critical to assess the impact and meaning of the interactions from the perspective of the peers.

SUMMARY AND CONCLUSIONS

The history of research in social skills acquisition has demonstrated that social skills can be taught and generalized in school and community settings. In fact, several methods, such as teaching initiations and peer initiation training, have long histories of effectiveness in creating levels of behavior that are normative. In addition, there is an emerging technology that can be used to assess the degree of social integration that is occurring for individual students as well as the strength of friendships and networks that a person experiences. The greatest weakness in the literature is that efforts to teach social and communicative responding have not been well linked with efforts to assess the impact of these interventions on others in the student's environment.

A primary conclusion of this review is that efforts to promote social development and social interactions need to be more concerned with investigating the impact of these interventions on peers in terms of increased willingness for interaction, increased social participation, and changes in their perceptions of their relationships to persons with disabilities. It should be noted that these questions are different than those traditionally asked through social validation research (e.g., Van Houton, 1979). Social validation research has typically provided data concerning whether or not a behavior is occurring at a normative rate (e.g., Greenwood et al., 1981), and whether or not people (frequently expert judges, teachers, or university students) can discriminate improvements in a behavior after intervention (e.g., Haring et al., 1986). Generally, social validity measures assess the frequency and effectiveness of the social behavior; they do not assess whether or not the persons in the students' immediate social ecology value the changes. Because one important outcome of social training efforts is to support friendships and integration into existing social networks, it is imperative that these effects be measured in ways beyond more traditional assessments of social validity. Once these effects are measured, it will then become incumbent on school systems to develop interventions that increase these variables (the social perception variables and valuation of the student), and discontinue program practices that do not contribute in some way to these outcomes.

Of the areas reviewed, the following practices, procedures and methods warrant increased focus in the experimental literature.

Social interventions for students with the most severe disabilities

Conspicuously absent in the review of instructional research are interventions that have included or are relevant to persons with profound disabilities. In particular, increased research in areas such as augmentative communication systems with peers as interactants is particularly needed (e.g., Wacker, Wiggins, Fowler, & Berg, 1988).

Stronger documentation of the effects of intervention on relationships

As reviewed above, a sufficient assessment methodology exists to assess social networks, acceptance, and relationships. These methods should be employed after intervention to assess the impact of intervention on peers. In addition, once data collection systems are more fully developed, experimental research can focus on the effectiveness of collecting, sharing, and analyzing these data on teachers' efforts to create opportunities for interactions. Teacher and administrative evaluations should consider these data as important aspects of performance evaluation.

Increased participation by peers in intervention design

Reports of peers participating in design of intervention, targeting of responses for instruction, or helping to assist in conducting interventions are rare. In addition, this can be conceived of as an independent variable and questions can be asked such as, 'does peer participation in the design of intervention increase intervention effectiveness and commitment of peers to interacting with persons with disabilities?' If students can participate socially in integrated settings, and are accepted in a peer network (with or without support from teachers) there is less need to focus on smaller social responses. In fact, as relationships develop, peers are frequently willing to overlook many behaviors that adults would assume to be stigmatizing or unusual.

Focus on pivotal behaviors

Although there are effective intervention strategies to increase highly specific social responses such as eye contact, and answering common questions such as 'how are you?' (e.g., Tara, Matson, & Leary, 1988), there needs to be an increased focus on teaching social skills that increase social participation and that are more pivotal to social development. Responses such as self-monitoring, hanging out, initiating interactions and generative scripts are examples of more pivotal response interventions.

Identification of richer contexts for interaction

Contextual variation is an important variable in promoting social development. Both physical and social parameters affect social interchanges. Peers are the primary determiners of the social contexts within natural settings. Thus, interventions focused on changing peer responsiveness, peer initiation, and peer participation within natural school contexts are an important focus of intervention. As contexts are identified for interaction, teachers should analyze the activities taking place in those contexts to teach skills needed for participation.

Instruction of social behavior is a potentially important means to support integration as well as providing a basis for development of communicative and conversational skills. However, the conceptualization and implementation of social skills instruction, as well as the focus of research, needs to shift to a greater concern with behavior under natural contexts and greater concern with the use of skills in social relationships in order to be more relevant to social integration as a primary instructional outcome. By assessing more global outcome variables such as peer perceptions, participation in social networks, and peer acceptance, of skills in social relationships in order to be more relevant to social integration as a primary instructional outcome. By assessing more global outcome variables such as peer perceptions, participation in social networks, and peer acceptance, we will do a better job of identifying those instructional processes that effect positive outcomes. Because the perceptions and behavior of peers and the fine-grained characteristics of natural contexts are the keys to this process, ultimately this means that researchers in the area of social integration need to become better integrated themselves into the social fabric of the schools, more careful observers of contexts, and more attentive to nondisabled peers including their needs and their perceptions of our efforts.

In developing a scientific data-based approach to creating social integration, the first step is to carefully articulate the outcomes that are most desired. Once agreement as to the validity of goals is reached, the effects of interventions in achieving theses goals needs to be assessed on an ongoing basis. As the goals of intervention become clearer, the development of approaches that act most directly in achieving those goals also becomes increasingly clear. In the area of social interaction research interventions that act directly to increase participation in cohesive social networks are the most critical and the most lacking. Building effective practices to directly support relationships is the major challenge for future research.

REFERENCES

Ackerman, A. M., & Shapiro, E. S. (1984). Self-monitoring and work productivity with mentally retarded adults. *Journal of Applied Behavior Analysis, 17*, 403–407.

Baer, D. M. (1986). In application, frequency is not the only estimate of the probability of behavior units. In T. Thompson & M. D. Zeiler (Eds.), *Analysis and integration of behavioral units* (pp.117–136). Hillsdale, NJ: Lawrence Erlbaum Associates.

Bednersh, F., & Peck, C. A. (1986). Assessing social environments: The effects of peer characteristics on the behavior of students with severe handicaps. *Child Study Journal, 16*, 315–329.

Bender, L. (1949). Psychological problems of children with organic brain disease. *American Journal of Orthopsychiatry, 25*, 2024–2025.

Berler, E. S., Gross, A. M., & Drabman, R. S. (1982). Social skills training with children: Proceed with caution. *Journal of Applied Behavior Analysis, 15*, 41–54.

Brady, M. P. & McEvoy, M. A. (1989). Social skills training as an integration strategy. In R. Gaylord-Ross (ed.), *Integration strategies for students with handicaps* (pp.213–232). Baltimore MD: Paul H. Brookes.

Brady, M. P., Shores, R. E., McEvoy, M. A., Ellis, D., & Fox, J. J. (1987). Increasing social interactions of severely handicapped autistic children. *Journal of Autism and Developmental Disabilities, 17*, 375–391.

Breen, C., Lovinger, L., & Haring T. G. (1989, Dec). PAL (Partners At Lunch) club: Evaluation of a program to support social relationships in a junior high school. Paper presented at the 16th Annual TASH Conference, San Francisco, CA.

Calkins, C. F., Dunn, W., & Kultgen, (1986). A comparison of preschool and elderly community integration/demonstration projects at the University of Missouri Institute for Human Development. *Journal of The Association for Persons with Severe Handicaps, 11*, 276–285.

Carr, E. G., & Durand, V. M. (1985). Reducing behavior problems through functional communication training. *Journal of Applied Behavior Analysis, 18*, 111–126.

Chadsey-Rusch, J. (1990). Teaching social skills on the job. In F. R. Rusch (Ed.), *Supported employment: Models, methods, and issues* (pp.161–180). Sycamore, IL: Sycamore Publishing Co.

Chadsey-Rusch, J., & Rusch, F. R. (1987). Social ecology of the work place. In R. Gaylord-Ross (Ed.), *Vocational education for persons with handicaps* (pp.234–256). Palo Alto, CA: Mayfield.

Cruickshank, W. M. & Johnson, G. O. (1968). *Education of exceptional children and youth.* Englewood Cliffs, NJ: Prentice Hall.

Downing, J., (1987). Conversation skills training: Teaching adolescents with mental retardation to be verbally assertive. *Mental Retardation, 25*, 147–155.

Dunlap, G. (1984). The influence of task variation and maintenance tasks on the learning and affect of autistic children. *Journal of Experimental Child Psychology, 37*, 41–64.

Egel, A. L. Richmand, G., & Koegel, R. L. (1981). Normal peer models and autistic children's learning. *Journal of Applied Behavior Analysis, 14*, 4–12.

Falvey, M., Ferrara-Parrish, P., Johnson, F., Pumpian, I., Schroeder, J., & Brown, L. (1979). Curricular strategies for generating comprehensive longitudinal and chronological age-appropriate functional vocational plans for severely handicapped adolescents and young adults. In L. Brown, M. Falvey, D. Baumgart, I. Pumpian, J. Schroeder, and L. Gruenewald (eds.), *Strategies for teaching chronological age-appropriate functional skills to adolescents and young adult severely handicapped students*, (Vol. 9, Part 1). Madison, WI: Madison Metropolitan School District, 102–161.

Favell, J. (1973). Reduction of stereotypes by reinforcement of toy play. *Mental Retardation, 11*, 21–23.

Fox, J., Shores, R., Lindeman, D., & Strain, P. (1986). Maintaining social initiation of withdrawn handicapped and nonhandicapped preschoolers through a response-dependent fading tactic. *Journal of Abnormal Child Psychology, 14*, 387–396.

Gajar, A., Schloss, P. J., Schloss, C. N., & Thompson, C. K. (1984). Effects of feedback and self-monitoring on head trauma youth's conversational skills. *Journal of Applied Behavior Analysis, 17*, 343–352.

Gaylord-Ross, R., & Haring, T. G. (1987). Social interaction research for adolescents with severe handicaps. *Behavior Disorders, 12*, 264–275.

Gaylord-Ross, R. J., Haring, T. G., Breen, C., & Pitts-Conway, V. (1984). The training and generalization of social interaction skills with autistic youth. *Journal of Applied Behavior Analysis, 17*, 229–247.

Gaylord-Ross, R., & Holvoet, J. F., (1985). *Strategies for educating students with severe handicaps.* Boston: Little, Brown, and Company.

Goldstein, H., Wickstrom, S., Hoyson, M., Jamieson, B., & Odom, S. (1988). Effects of sociodramatic play training on social and communicative interaction. *Education and Treatment of Children, 11*, 97–117.

Greenwood, C. R., Walker, H. M., Todd, N. M., & Hops, H. (1981). Normative and descriptive analysis of preschool freeplay social interaction rates. *Journal of Pediatric Psychology, 4,* 343–367.

Guralnick, M. J. (1980). Social interactions among preschool children. *Exceptional Children, 40,* 248–253.

Haring, T. G. (1991). Social relationships. In Meyer, L., Peck, C. A., & Brown, L. (Eds.) *Critical issues in the lives of people with severe disabilities.* (pp. 195–218). Baltimore, MD: Paul H. Brookes.

Haring, T. G. (1985). Teaching between-class generalization of toy play behavior to handicapped children. *Journal of Applied Behavior Analysis, 18,* 127–139.

Haring, T. G., & Breen, C. (1991). Units of analysis of social interaction outcomes in supported education. *Journal of The Association for Persons with Severe Handicaps., 14,* 255–262.

Haring, T. G., Breen, C., & Laitinen, R. E. (1989). Stimulus class Formation and concept learning: Establishment of within- and between-set generalization and transitive relationships via conditional discrimination procedures. *Journal of The Experimental Analysis of Behavior, 52,* 13–25.

Haring, T. G., Breen, C., Pitts-Conway, V., Lee, M., & Gaylord-Ross, R. J. (1987). Adolescent peer tutoring and special friend experiences. *Journal of The Association for Persons with Severe Handicaps, 12,* 280–286.

Haring, T. G., Breen, C., & Weiner, J. (manuscript in preparation). Effects of context on opportunities for interaction, social initiation, and duration of interaction in integrated settings.

Haring, T. G., Kennedy, C. H., Adams, M., & Pitts-Conway (1987). Teaching generalization of purchasing skills across community settings to autistic youth using videotape modeling. *Journal of Applied Behavior Analysis, 20,* 89–96.

Haring, T. G., & Lovinger, L. (1989). Promoting social interaction through teaching generalized play initiation responses to preschool children with autism. *Journal of The Association for Persons with Severe Handicaps, 14,* 58–67.

Haring, T. G., Roger, B., Lee, M., Breen, C., & Gaylord-Ross, R., (1986). Teaching social language to moderately handicapped students. *Journal of Applied Behavior Analysis, 19,* 159–171.

Hart, B., & Risley, T. R. (1980). In vivo language training: Unanticipated and general effects. *Journal of Applied Behavior Analysis, 12,* 407–432.

Hendrickson, J. M., Strain, P. S., Trembly, A., & Shores, R. E. (1982). Interactions of behaviorally handicapped children: Functional effects of peer social initiations. *Behavior Modification, 6,* 323–353.

Hill, J., Wehman, P., & Horst, G. (1982). Toward generalization of appropriate leisure and social behavior in severely handicapped youth: Pinball machine use. *Journal of The Association for Persons with Severe Handicaps, 6,* 34–44.

Hiroshige, J. A. (1989). Effects of direct instruction of social skills and peer facilitation on free play at recess of students with physical disabilities. Unpublished doctoral dissertation, University of California, Santa Barbara.

Hughes, L. A. (1989). Foursquare: A glossary and 'native' taxonomy of game rules. *Play & Culture, 2,* 103–136.

Hunt, P., Alwell, M., & Goetz, L. (1988). Acquisition of conversation skills and the reduction of inappropriate social interaction behaviors. *Journal of The Association for Persons with Severe Handicaps, 13,* 20–27.

James, S. D., & Egel, A. L., (1986). A direct prompting strategy for increasing reciprocal interactions between handicapped and nonhandicapped siblings. *Journal of Applied Behavior Analysis, 19,* 173–186.

Kennedy, C. H., Horner, R. H., & Newton, J. S. (1990). The social networks and activity patterns of adults with severe disabilities. *Journal of The Association for Persons with Severe Handicaps 15,* 86–90.

Koegel, R. L., Dyer, K., & Bell, C. K. (1987). The influence of child-preferred activities on autistic children's social behavior. *Journal of Applied Behavior Analysis, 20,* 243–252.

Koegel, R. L., & Koegel, L. K. (1988). Generalized responsivity and pivotal behaviors. In R. H. Horner, G. Dunlap, & R. L. Koegel (Eds.) *Generalization and maintenance: Life-style changes in applied settings* (pp.41–66). Baltimore MD: Paul H. Brookes.

Lancioni, G. E. (1982). Normal children as tutors to teach social responses to withdrawn mentally retarded schoolmates: Training, maintenance, and generalization. *Journal of Applied Behavior Analysis, 15,* 17–40.

Liberty, K. (1985). Teaching retarded students to reinforce their own behavior: A review of process and operation in the current literature. In N. G. Haring (Ed.) *Investigating the Problem of Skill Generalization* (pp.88–106). Seattle, WA: Washington Research Organization.

MacMillan, D. L., & Morrison, G. M. (1984). Sociometric research in special education. In R.L. Jones (Ed.), *Attitude and attitude change in special education: Research and practice.* Reston VA: Council for Exceptional Children.

Marchant, J., & Wehman, P. (1979). Teaching table games to severely retarded children. *Mental Retardation, 17,* 150–151.

McEvoy, M. A., Nordquist, V. M., Vey, M., Twardosz, S., Heckaman, K., Wehby, J., & Denny, K. R. (1988). Promoting autistic children's peer interaction in an integrated early childhood setting using affection activities. *Journal of Applied Behavior Analysis, 21,* 193–200.

Meyer, L. H., Eichinger, J., & Park-Lee, S. (1987). A validation of program quality indicators in educational services for students with severe disabilities. *The Journal of The Association for Persons with Severe Handicaps, 12,* 251–263.

Meyer, L. H., Peck, C. A., & Brown, L. (1991). *Critical issues in the lives of people with severe disabilities.* Baltimore, MD: Paul H. Brookes.

Mirenda, P., & Donnellan, A. (1986). Effects of adult interaction style on conversational behavior in students with severe communicative problems. *Language, Speech, and Hearing Services in Schools, 17,* 126–141.

Murray-Seegert, C. (1989). *Nasty girls, thugs, and human beings like us: Social relations between severely disabled and nondisabled students in high school.* Baltimore, MD: Paul H. Brookes.

Myers, P. I., & Hammill. D. D. (1969). *Methods for learning disorders.* New York: John Wiley & Sons.

Nelson, K. (1973). Structure and strategy in learning to talk. *Monographs of the Society for Research in Child Development, 38* (#1–2, Serial No. 149).

Nietupski, J. A., Hamre-Nietupski, S., & Ayres, B. (1984). Review of task analytic leisure skills training efforts: Practitioner implications and future research needs. *Journal of The Association for Persons with Severe Handicaps, 9,* 88–97.

Odom, S. C., Hoyson, M., Jamieson, B., & Strain, P.S. (1985). Increasing handicapped preschooler's peer social interactions: Cross setting and component analysis. *Journal of Applied Behavior Analysis, 18,* 3–17.

Odom, S. L., & Strain, P. S. (1986). A comparison of peer-initiation and teacher antecedent interventions for promoting reciprocal interactions of autistic preschoolers. *Journal of Applied Behavior Analysis, 19*, 59–72.

Peck, C. A. (1985). Increasing opportunities for social control by children with autism and severe handicaps: Effects on student behavior and perceived classroom climate. *Journal of The Association for Persons with Severe Handicaps, 10*, 183–193.

Peck, C. A. (1989). Assessment of social communicative competence: Evaluating environments. *Seminars in Speech and Language., 10*, 1–15.

Peck, C. A., Odom, S. M., & Bricker, D. D. (1992). *Integrating Young Children with Disabilities into Community Programs: Ecological Perspectives on Research and Implementation.* Baltimore: Paul H. Brookes Publishing Co.

Sailor, W., & Guess, D. (1983). *Severely handicapped students: An instructional design.* Boston: Houghton Mifflin Company.

Sasso, G. M., Hughes, C. G., Swanson, H. L. & Novak, C. G., (1987). A comparison of peer initiation interactions in promoting multiple peer initiators. *Education and Training in Mental Retardation, 22*, 150–155.

Sasso, G. M., & Rude, H. A. (1987). Unprogrammed effects of training high-status peers to interact with severely handicapped children. *Journal of Applied Behavior Analysis, 20*, 35–44.

Sedlak, R., Doyle, M., & Schloss, P. (1982). Video games: A training and generalization demonstration with severely retarded adolescents. *Education and Training of the Mentally Retarded, 17*, 332–336.

Sisson, L. A., Babeo, T. J., & Van Hasselt, V. B. (1988). Group training to increase social behaviors in young multihandicapped children. *Behavior Modification, 12*, 497–524.

Skinner, B. F. (1957). *Verbal Behavior.* New York: Appleton-Century-Crofts Inc.

Snell, M. E., & Eichner, S. J. (1989). Integration for students with profound disabilities. In F. Brown & D. H. Lehr (eds.), *Persons with profound disabilities: Issues and practices* (pp.109–138). Baltimore, MD: Paul H. Brookes.

Stainback, W., & Stainback, S. (1981). A review of research on interaction between severely handicapped and nonhandicapped students. *Journal of The Association for Persons with Severe Handicaps, 6*, 23–29.

Stainback, S., & Stainback, W., Wehman, P., & Spangiers, L. (1983). Acquisition and generalization of physical fitness exercises in three profoundly retarded adults. *Journal of The Association for Persons with Severe Handicaps, 8*, 47–55.

Stokes, T. F., Baer, D. M., & Jackson, R. L. (1974). Programing the generalization of a greeting response in four retarded children. *Journal of Applied Behavior Analysis, 7*, 599–610.

Strain, P. S., Cooke, T. P., & Apollini, T. (1976). *Teaching exceptional children: Assessing and modifying social behavior.* New York: Academic Press.

Strain, P. S., Kerr, M. M., & Ragland, E. V. (1979). Effects of peer-mediated social initiations and prompting/ reinforcement procedures on the social behavior of autistic children. *Journal of Autism and Developmental Disorders, 9*, 41–54.

Strain, P. S., & Fox, J. J. (1981). Peer social interactions and the modification of social withdrawal: A review and future perspective. *Journal of Pediatric Psychology, 6*, 417–433.

Strain, P. S., Shores, R. E., & Kerr, M. M. (1976). An experimental analysis of 'spillover' effects on the social interaction of behaviorally handicapped preschool children. *Journal of Applied Behavior Analysis, 9*, 31–40.

Strully, J. & Strully, C. (1986). Friendship and our children. *Journal of The Association for Persons with Severe Handicaps, 10*, 224–227.

Tara, M. E., Matson, J. L., & Leary, C. (1988). Training social interpersonal skills in two autistic children. *Journal of Behavior therapy and Experimental Psychiatry, 19*, 275–280.

Wacker, D. P., Wiggins, B., Fowler, M., & Berg, W. K. (1988). Training students with profound or multiple handicaps tp make requests via microswitches. *Journal of Applied Behavior Analysis, 21*, 331–344.

Warren, S. F., Rogers-Warren, & Baer, D. M. (1976). The role of offer rates in controlling sharing by young children. *Journal of Applied Behavior Analysis, 9*, 491–497.

Warren, S. F., & Kaiser, A. P. (1988). Research in early language intervention. In S. L. Odom & M. B. Karnes (Eds.), *Early intervention for infants and children with handicaps: An empirical base* (pp.89–108). Baltimore: Paul H. Brookes.

Warren, S. F., & Rogers-Warren, A. K. (1983). Setting variables effecting the generalization of trained vocabulary within a residential institution. In K. T. Kernan & R. B. Edgerton (Eds.). *Environments and behavior: The adaptation of mentally retarded persons* (pp. 257–282). Baltimore MD: University Park Press.

White, D. M., Rusch, F. R., Kazdin, A. E., & Hartmann, D. P. (1989). Applications of meta analysis in individual-subject research. *Behavioral Assessment, 11*, 281–296.

Whitman, T. L., Mercurio, J. R., & Caponigri, V. (1970). Development of social responses in two severely retarded children. *Journal of Applied Behavior Analysis, 3*, 133–138.

Wildman, B. G., Wildman, H. E., & Kelly, W. J. (1986). Group conversational skills training and social validation with mentally retarded adults. *Applied Research in Mental Retardation, 7*, 443–458.

Young, C. C., Kerr, M. (1979). the effect of a retarded child's initiations on the behavior of severely retarded school-aged peers. *Education and Treatment of the Mentally Retarded, 14*, 185–190.

Van Houton, R. (1979). Social validation: The evolution of standards of competency for target behaviors. *Journal of Applied Behavior Analysis, 12*, 581–593.

Voeltz, L. M. (1980). Children's attitudes toward handicapped peers. *American Journal of Mental Deficiency, 9*, 41–55.

Voeltz, L. M. (1982). Effects of structured interactions with severely handicapped peers on children's attitudes. *American Journal of Mental Deficiency, 86*, 380–390.

Zetlin, A. G., & Turner, J. L. (1985). Transition from adolescence to adulthood: Perspectives of mentally retarded individuals and their families. *American Journal of Mental Deficiency, 89*, 570–576.

MASSED TRIALS REVISITED: APPROPRIATE APPLICATIONS IN FUNCTIONAL SKILL TRAINING

Linda M. Bambara and Steven F. Warren

Within the past decade, instructional methods for individuals with moderate to severe developmental disabilities have evolved rapidly. Current 'best practices' in instructional methodology rest on several pedagogical assumptions. First, goals for instruction should be derived through ecological assessments of the individual's current and future life demands (Brown, Branston-McClean, Baumgart, Vincent, Falvey, & Schroeder, 1979). Second, entire tasks, activities, or routines should be targeted for instruction rather than isolated skills (Neel & Billingsley, 1989). However, if it is essential to focus on a single skill, then that skill should be integrated with and taught in the context of other related behaviors (Guess & Helmstetter, 1986). Third, targeted activities or skills should be chronologically age-appropriate (Brown, Branston, Hamre-Nietupski, Pumpian, Certo, & Gruenewald, 1979). Fourth, instruction should take place in-vivo, directly in the settings and activities that require the use of targeted tasks or skills (Falvey, 1989; Sailor, Goetz, Anderson, Hunt, & Gee, 1988). Fifth, and perhaps most importantly, instruction should result in functional outcomes (Horner, McDonnell, & Bellamy, 1986). That is, instruction should result in behaviors that are immediately useful and generalizable across a variety of real life tasks and activities.

Along with the acceptance of these assumptions about how and where instruction should take place, has come the development of 'new' instructional practices that best matched the pedagogy. In the area of trial sequencing, stress has been placed on the appropriateness of trial distribution, while the traditional massed trial training approach, as the principle method of instruction, has been largely rejected (Brown, Nietupski, & Hamre-Nietupski, 1976; Caro & Snell, 1989; Donnellan & Neel, 1986; Guess & Helmstetter, 1986; Mulligan, Guess, Holvoet, & Brown, 1980; Sailor, et al., 1988) In fact, the issue of distributed versus massed trial training has been presented as part of the dichotomy between functional and nonfunctional training (Guess & Noonan, 1982; Neel & Billingsley, 1989; Reichle & Keogh, 1986).

The emphasis on the use of distributed trial training and the move away from massed trial training came about for two interdependent reasons. First, the current instructional paradigm essentially dictates a distributed approach (see definitions and applications of distributed trial training later in this chapter). Training skills in-vivo, in the context of other behaviors (e.g., activity chains, skill clusters) and across settings and activities whenever functional opportunities arise, require that trial presentations for a single response be distributed across time and among other behaviors (Guess & Helmstetter, 1986). Massed trial training, with its emphasis on immediate trial repetitions of a single skill is not applicable.

Second, immersed in the tradition of early operant instructional technology, massed trials have been associated with rigid, artificial training conditions that are now known to mitigate against stimulus generalization (Koegel & Rincover, 1977; Rincover & & Koegel, 1975; Wahler, 1969). Procedures such as fixed trial formats, use of artificial cues and consequences, and presentation of the same stimulus event within 'distraction-free' settings have traditionally gone hand-in-hand with massed trial formats. Used predominantly in classrooms for students with severe disabilities, these procedures came about through the direct translation of laboratory research, where, during the 1960s and early 1970s, the focus was on demonstrating that persons with severe disabilities could learn through operant instructional techniques (Guess & Helmstetter, 1986). Further, acquisition and generalization were viewed as separate, distinct training issues, i.e., active programming for generalization typically occurred only after initial acquisition was achieved (Haring & Bricker, 1976; Sailor & Haring, 1977). As this laboratory based model to instruction was criticized and rejected for not resulting in functional skills and generalized outcomes, so was massed trial training.

Given the current emphasis on in-vivo, community-based and activity-based instruction, the authors are in full agreement with the tenet that massed trials should not be used as the primary method of instruction for individuals with severe disabilities. As previously indicated, the repetitious format is simply too discrepant from the way many skills and tasks are used in natural contexts to result in immediately functional and generalizable behaviors. However, this should not be interpreted to mean that massed trial training is an outdated, inappropriate technology that has no place in functional skill training. Rather than viewing distributed and massed trial training as dichotomous formats, choosing functional over non-functional interventions, the issue should be *how* and *when* the formats can be used in complimentary ways to train adaptive, functional behaviors in the most effective and efficient manner. Used in conjunction with distributed trial training in natural contexts, massed trials may offer a number of powerful benefits when appropriately matched to instructional purpose, the nature of target skill or task, and individual learner characteristics.

The purpose of this chapter is to explore functional uses of massed trial training for learners with severe disabilities. The chapter begins with a review of the definitions of massed and distributed trial training and a discussion of recent studies that compare the effectiveness of the two trial sequencing strategies. Next, providing illustrations from the training literature, specific suggestions for the appropriate uses of massed trial training and its potential benefits are discussed. Recommendations for avoiding certain troublesome caveats associated with massed trial instruction are also provided. The chapter ends with a discussion of future directions for research.

DIFFERENCES BETWEEN MASSED AND DISTRIBUTED TRIAL SEQUENCING

Precise, operationalized definitions of massed and distributed practice are difficult to present for two reasons. First, the terms are somewhat relational. That is, the identification of one is partially dependent on the other. Second, the terms are not static. Influenced by developments in curriculum and instruction, their definitions have evolved through the years.

The distinction between massed and distributed practice as presented in the early experimental psychology literature (circa 1900 to 1960), centered on the amount of time occurring between trial presentations or practice periods of a single task (Deese & Hulse, 1967). If little (a few seconds) or no time occurred between task trials, then practice was defined as massed. If periods of practice were broken up by periods of rest or periods of engagement in other tasks, it was defined as a distributed format. The length of time occurring between distributed practice on tasks (i.e., the intertrial interval) ranged anywhere from several minutes to several days, whereas the time occurring between massed trials typically ranged from 0 to 8 seconds (Bambara & Warren, 1984).

Contemporary definitions of massed and distributed trial sequencing have been strongly influenced by the relatively recent emphasis on activity and skill cluster instruction for individuals with severe disabilities. The definitions focus on the arrangement of discrete training trials, as opposed to periods of active practice; hence the terms distributed and massed *trial* training as opposed to massed and distributed *practice*. Training trials are defined as *distributed* when they are interspersed among other responses or training trials from other instructional programs such that trials from the same instruction program, task, or skill are not repeated in immediate succession (Guess & Helmstetter, 1986; Mulligan, et al., 1980; Snell & Browder, 1986). On the other hand, *massed trials* involves the immediate repetition of two or more trials for the same skill or task within a relatively short period of time (Bellamy, Horner, & Inman, 1979; Cuvo & Davis, 1983; Mulligan et al., 1980).

Applications of Distributed Trial Sequencing

The simplest illustration of distributed trial sequence, as presented by Mulligan et al. (1980), is to take one trial or skill from program 'X' and alternate it with another trial or skill from program 'Y' to achieve a distributed sequence: 'XYXYXYXYXYXY'. Presented out of context, distributed trials need not be related. However, when training occurs in-vivo, trial distribution takes on other relevant characteristics. Training trials are not just dispersed, but are also integrated with other task or activity related responses and are typically sequenced with these responses in a functional manner (Guess & Helmstetter, 1986; Snell & Browder, 1986).

There are several approaches to trial distribution in in-vivo training. In one approach, distributed trials are derived through a task analysis of functional routines and activities. Each subcomponent or substep in an activity chain can be viewed as a trial for one response (Cuvo & Davis, 1983; Snell & Browder, 1986). In a second approach, an isolated, yet frequently occurring skill is targeted for instruction and then integrated and sequenced with other responses across a range of relevant, functional activities. This approach to skill sequencing, which is reflected in the Individualized Curriculum Sequencing model (Guess & Helmstetter, 1986; Holvoet, Guess, Mulligan, & Brown, 1980) often results in trials for a single skill that are distributed within as well as across activities.

Common to both the first and second approach is the idea of 'clustering' discrete responses into natural chains of behavior where the completion of one response sets the occasion for the initiation of another. In a third approach, training trials are not sequenced, but are loosely dispersed among other activity related behaviors. Trial presentations arise 'incidentally' based on naturally occurring opportunities, rather than occurring in a fixed or predictable order with other skills. This strategy is exemplified in 'activity based programming' (Bricker & Cripe, 1989) and in 'milieu' language intervention (Warren & Bambara, 1989).

Applications of Massed Trial Training

When massed trials of an isolated skill or task are presented, training typically takes place out-of-context in simulated or classroom settings, usually as a separate or noncontingent component of an instructional program (Cuvo & Davis, 1983; Browder & Snell, 1987). However, with increased emphasis on in-vivo instruction, massed trial training has also been applied in natural settings when the target skill itself occurs in natural repetitions (e.g., use of pictures to select items from a grocery shelf in Horner, Albin, & Ralph, 1986), or when massed trials are used contingently to temporarily branch out of a distributed chain and remediate errors (see the section on 'difficult steps in a response chain' for a discussion). A more recent application of massed practice in in-vivo settings involves the repeated practice of entire task chains, such as operating a pinball machine several times in one training session (Hill, Wehman, & Horst, 1982). In this case completion of an entire task is viewed as one trial, even though training may occur on each subskill (Cuvo & Davis, 1983; Snell & Browder, 1986).

Whether presented out-of-context during isolated training sessions or in-vivo, massed trial training involves the repeated presentation of a single skill or task. The extent of stimulus and response variation that occurs across repeated trial presentations is influenced by serial and concurrent task sequencing (Cuvo, et al., 1980; Waldo, Guess, & Flanagan, 1982). If a within-task serial training approach is applied to massed trials, then the same stimulus event/response would be repeated trial after trial until criterion is achieved on that item (e.g., in a coin identification task, nickel would be trained to criterion first, before another coin is trained to criterion). If within-task response items are trained concurrently (e.g., presentation of nickel, dime, quarter, and penny would be rotated across trials within a training session), then more stimulus and response variation would be reflected across session trials.

COMPARATIVE EFFECTIVENESS OF MASSED AND DISTRIBUTED TRIAL TRAINING

Before summarizing the research that compares the effectiveness of massed and distributed practice on the learning of persons with severe disabilities, it is important to point out some critical limitations and gaps in the literature. First, no research is available on *how, when,* or *for whom* massed or distributed trial training should be used. Research has focused almost exclusively on determining which of the two trial sequencing formats is the better strategy per se, not how and under what conditions the two formats can be used to enhance instructional effectiveness and efficiency. Second, research that is directly applicable to the instruction of learners with severe disabilities is limited to a handful of studies. Although widely researched in the 1930s, 1940s, and 1950s, there is very little of the early experimental psychology literature on massed vs. distributed practice that is generalizable to the education of individuals with severe disabilities, due to vast discrepancies in the subject population (most studies used adults without disabilities), definitions of massed and distributed practice (as previously discussed), experimental tasks (most tasks were abstract such as 'pursuit rotor tracking' and 'paired associate' matching activities) and instructional purpose (most experiments were designed to explain theoretical phenomenon, e.g., response inhibition, rather than to address an applied problem) (Bambara & Warren, 1984).

Three contemporary studies that have evaluated the comparative effects of massed and distributed trial training on the learning of individuals with severe disabilities include a study conducted by Mulligan, Lacy, and Guess (1982) that involved 11 students with severe disabilities, and studies conducted by Dunlap and Koegel (1980) and Dunlap (1984) that involved two and five students with autism, respectively. Each of these studies included experimental tasks that are commonly employed in classrooms (e.g., holding a cup, sorting, sight word discrimination) and structured trial sequencing formats according to contemporary definitions. However, in all cases, both massed and distributed formats were taught in didactic training sessions. Distributed trials were not sequenced in any particular relationship as they would be if taught in natural settings. The primary findings of these studies are summarized below.

Acquisition

Two of the three studies measured rate of acquisition in terms of trials to criterion (Dunlap, 1984; Mulligan, et al., 1982). Neither study found differences between the two trial sequencing formats when all trials in the massed and distributed clusters contained unlearned or novel tasks. Apparently, either approach is effective in similar conditions.

Performance

While no differences were found in rates of acquisition, learner performance appeared to be differentially affected. Higher levels of correct responding and increased responsiveness to trial presentations were found with distributed trial training (Dunlap & Koegel, 1980; Mulligan et al., 1982). Further, Dunlap and Koegel (1980) and Dunlap (1984) found more positive displays of child affect (such as interest, happiness, and enthusiasm) under distributed trial training than massed trial training conditions, suggesting that poorer student performance under the massed trial approach is attributable to boredom. As will be discussed later, it is entirely possible that poorer performance under massed trial training may be caused by the inappropriate use of the technology (e.g., too many trials at one time). However, these outcomes suggest that the format should be applied with particular sensitivity to learner interest.

Composition Of Trial Sequences

Recent research also suggests that the *composition* of trials across distributed clusters and across trial repetitions of the same task is a potentially important variable that affects learning. Dunlap (1984) found quicker acquisition of target tasks when training trials were distributed among other tasks that were already learned (i.e., maintenance tasks) by the students than when distributed among other tasks that were also being trained for acquisition (there was no difference between the latter condition and massed trial training). In related research involving individuals with mild to moderate disabilities (Koegel & Koegel, 1986; Neef, Iwata, & Page, 1977; 1980) similar results were obtained for a variation of massed trial sequencing. That is, interspersing 'known' within-task items (such as spelling words) among similar 'unknown' within-task items was found to enhance acquisition when compared to repeated trial presentations of 'unknown' within-task items only.

One interpretation for this effect, whether it occurs in distributed or massed trial sequences, is that the interspersion of known tasks or within-task items allows the learner to experience frequent success and thus enhance the learner's motivation to learn new tasks (Dunlap, 1984; Dunlap & Dunlap, 1987). Applications to instruction will be discussed later.

In summary, the small data base directly comparing massed and distributed practice suggests that distributed practice may be more effective than massed trials even within traditional didactic training sessions. Furthermore, a larger data base (Horner, Meyer, & Fredericks, 1986) has identified a number of limitations with traditional didactic instruction in general. In addition to massed trial training, traditional didactic instruction is characterized by a high degree of teacher control and structure, emphasis on precision and specificity of training procedures, and incorporation of a high degree of differential reinforcement (Warren & Kaiser, 1988). There appear to be several inherent problems with didactic instruction that tend to make meaningful generalization difficult to achieve. These include: (a) an emphasis on structure and form of skills and a corresponding lack of emphasis on normal function and use (Spradlin & Siegel, 1982); (b) difficulty in ensuring a high degree of student attention and interest (Dunlap & Koegel, 1980); and (c) difficulty in teaching students to appropriately initiate newly learned skills (Halle, 1987). Most studies that have documented problems with didactic instruction have made no attempt to separate the effects of various components of this approach, such as massed practice. Nevertheless, this literature, combined with the studies reviewed above, raises the issue of whether massed practice is appropriate under any conditions.

Despite the problems identified above, we believe that massed trial training does have a number of useful applications as part of an overall instructional technology for learners with severe disabilities. In the following section we identify and discuss five appropriate applications of massed trial training. These applications are summarized in Table 1.

APPROPRIATE APPLICATIONS OF MASSED TRIAL TRAINING

'Natural' Massed Repetitions

One of the first considerations in determining the appropriateness of a massed trial format is how the target skill or response is used naturally across daily activities and routines. This may be best determined by answering two basic questions: First, how is the skill or response typically sequenced within age-appropriate activities? Is the skill typically integrated with other responses, and used across a variety of activities? Or, does the skill typically occur in repetitious clusters? Second, what is the critical effect (White, 1980) of the target behavior as an isolated, repeated response, or as a subskill in a functional activity? What purpose or function does the response or the entire activity chain serve *for the individual*

It is obvious that the majority of daily living activities require the coordination and integration of multiple' discrete responses, thus supporting the use of distributed trial sequencing formats. Indeed, as long as training under a distributed format is both effective and efficient there is probably no reason to consider an alternative sequencing format for most skills. However, there are numerous situations in which repetitions of an isolated skill does occur 'naturally' in everyday activities. Vocational skills, such as counting and sorting, motor skills such as stepping and pushing a wheelchair, domestic tasks such as buttoning clothing and sorting/folding laundry, and communication skills such as turntaking are a few examples of activities that require a learner to repeat the same response one after the other. Obviously, in-vivo massed trial training for skills such as these is the logical choice of training formats. Using a distributed sequence for teaching shirt buttoning, e.g., button one button, engage in another task, button another button, engage in another task, button a third button etc., simply does not make sense.

Consideration of 'critical effect' alone, in terms of facilitating meaningful outcomes for individuals (Evans & Scotti, 1989), may also indicate a massed trial training format. ' Stated another way, function should dictate the form and sequencing of a response. Functionality should be evaluated in terms of producing a reinforcing effect for the individual and should not be evaluated just on

Table 1: Appropriate Applications of Massed Trial Training

Application	Use	Primary Instructional Purpose
Natural Massed Repetitions	natural repetitious sequences (e.g., sorting, buttoning)	to match to natural sequences
	massing for critical effect (e.g., sustain rudimentary interactions rehearsal, enjoyment).	to facilitate desired learner outcomes
Difficult Steps in an Activity Chain	isolated warm-up of single steps	to enhance efficient learning of the entire chain
	contingent error correction	
Complex, Difficult Discriminations	remedially, to accentuate basic stimulus/response associations (e.g., rule-governed concepts).	to provide greater instructional control over antecedent and consequent stimuli
	warm-up sessions	to enhance effective and efficient learning of response *form* not function
		to avoid disrupting the flow of 'natural' interactions
Functional	teach generalized, as opposed to adaptive academic skills	same as complex discriminations (see above)
	warm-up sessions	to enhance fluency through drill and practice
Individual Characteristics	matched to individual needs	

Note: Massed trials may be used in-vivo or during isolated, didactic lessons. However, if used didactically, then in-vivo instruction should be programmed concurrently.

the basis of typical, age-appropriate routines (Evans & Scotti, 1989).Thus, if the repetition of a single response serves to bring about a desired effect for the individual, whether the effect be enjoyment, sustaining an interaction, or rehearsal, then massed trial training would be an appropriate selection. Teaching rudimentary interaction skills, such as turntaking in a social exchange (repeating an action to get 'more') or sustaining object engagement (e.g., tapping a toy to produce a reactive effect), are examples of goals that are seemingly dependent on the simplicity and redundancy of an activity to establish a critical effect of sustaining interactions (Reichle, York, & Eynon, 1989). Rehearsal, engaging in repetitions to perfect and refine, may enhance skill development, as well as bring about a sense of control and mastery for the learner. For example, although shoe-tying may be 'required' once a day, it is not uncommon to see young children repeatedly practice their emerging new skill until they get it just right. Rehearsal seems particularly well suited to the development of motor skills. In fact, there are numerous examples in sports training where individual skills (e.g., shooting baskets, pitching baseballs, serving tennis balls) are isolated and drilled to enhance mastery.

Difficult Steps in an Activity Chain

Not all responses in a task/activity analysis are equivalent in terms of the amount of training required for successful demonstration.Providing massed trials on a 'difficult' step in a response chain is one application of massed trials frequently discussed (Bellamy, et al., 1979; Browder, Hines, McCarthy, & Fees, 1984; Cuvo & Davis, 1983; Snell & Browder, 1986). A difficult step is simply defined as a response that requires substantially more training trials to criterion (Snell & Browder, 1986) or one that yields more errors during instruction (Browder, Snell, & Wildonger, 1988) than other responses in the activity chain.

The argument for the use of massed trials on difficult steps is one of efficiency. Although trial for trial comparisons between the two training formats revealed no differences in the rate of acquisition by learners with severe handicaps in the Mulligan et al. (1982) and Dunlap (1984) studies, massed trials on difficult steps may result in quicker acquisition of the entire response chain when considering the amount of instructional and learner time and effort required to repeat the chain until criterion is achieved on all subskills. For example, Browder et al. (1988) noted that the step of 'appropriate coin selection' yielded the most amount of errors out of a 10-step vending machine use task analysis for all the participants in their study. Although the researchers did not remove the difficult step from the chain, they did recognize 'post hoc' that isolated massed trials for the difficult step might have resulted in more efficient learning of the entire chain than training the difficult step within the chain only. The use of massed trials may be particularly advantageous when naturally occurring opportunities to train are limited to a few occasions per week.

Two general strategies for providing massed practice on difficult steps appear in the literature: 'warm-up' and error correction (Snell & Browder, 1986). Warm-up involves removing the difficult step from the chain, training the response didactically in a simulated or training setting (e.g., classroom), then reintegrating the response back into the activity chain. For example, Bowers, Rusch, and Hudson (1979) taught correct bus number identification in a partially simulated classroom activity before teaching an adult with severe disabilities independent bus riding in the community. In a similar approach, Browder, et al (1984) provided massed trials on functional sight-word reading in isolated lessons held before daily training on domestic skill sequences requiring sight-words.

Massed practice has also been used contingently as a consequence to incorrect responding for a number of community living skills (e.g., Cuvo, Veitch, Trace & Konke, 1978; Sprague & Horner, 1984; van den Pol, Iwata, Ivancic, Page, Neef & Whitley, 1981; Volgesburg & Rusch, 1979). For instance, during street crossing training, Volgesburg and Rusch (1979) implemented four trials of 'looking' whenever the trainee failed to look before crossing. In another example, van den Pol et al. (1981) used contingent massed trials, one repeated trial for each error made, while training restaurant ordering skills in the community.

There are no empirical guidelines suggesting which of the two strategies, error correction or warm-up, is the better practice. However, logically there are relative advantages and disadvantages to consider. With error correction, extra training occurs on the spot. The difficult response is never taken out of sequence, avoiding the additional step of reintroduction and the potential hazard of using massed trials as prerequisite for skill instruction in natural settings. On the other hand, in-vivo error correction may be impractical or impossible for some responses (e.g., it is not likely that a busy supermarket cashier would be willing to wait while the learner practices counting change) and potentially stigmatizing if correction cannot be done discreetly. Warm-up requires the scheduling of additional training sessions (in addition to in-vivo instruction), however, it affords the trainer increased instructional control compared to training under natural conditions. Moreover, because training on a difficult step occurs out of sequence, it allows training on the entire chain to flow efficiently from one response to another without significant interruption.

Complex, Difficult Discriminations

The ability to discriminate is at the heart of most learning tasks, including the development of concept formation (Keogh & Reichle, 1985). According to Zeaman and House (1963), discrimination is a two-step process requiring a learner to first differentially attend to a relevant stimulus(i), and second respond appropriately to that stimulus feature(s). Discrimination difficulties arise when a learner fails at either one or both steps of the discrimination process. Discrimination problems that arise during in-context, distributed trial sequenced instruction may be due to the inherent complexity of the discrimination task itself (see Bellamy et al., 1979) such as in 'minimal difference' (e.g., coin identification) and relational (e.g., 'big' vs. 'little') discriminations, as well as a number of other inhibiting factors associated with in-vivo instruction that may interfere with discrimination learning. These factors include: too few training trials occurring naturally to sufficiently facilitate acquisition, insufficient range of exemplars present in in-context training sites to teach appropriate responding across all relevant members of a stimulus class (Horner, et al., 1986), and the interference of powerful, competing environmental stimuli that may obscure the saliency of the discriminative stimulus (Bambara, Warren & Komisar, 1988; Horner & Billingsley, 1988).

When discrimination difficulty becomes evident during distributed trial, in-vivo instruction several alternatives may be appropriate. First, many of the traditionally recommended strategies for remediating discrimination problems (e.g. Bellamy, et al., 1979; Keogh & Reichle, 1985) can be applied directly to in-vivo settings with some creative environmental arrangement. This general approach to remediating discrimination difficulties would involve the explicit structuring of in-vivo antecedent events to increase the number of 'naturally' occurring opportunities, and improve the quality and saliency of stimulus exemplars (see Bricker & Cripe, 1989, for illustrations). The obvious advantage of this alternative would be to maintain the integrity between the targeted response and its function.

A second alternative would be to separate 'form' from 'function' and use massed trials remedially during isolated sessions to shape the topography of the target response. This alternative would be most appropriate when the primary instructional interest is in establishing a basic association between a discriminative stimulus and desired response, and not on teaching use. When used for this purpose, there may be several potential benefits of didactic massed trial training. First, the trainer is afforded increased options for selecting the most effective and efficient instructional procedure for the individual learner and skill. While feedback only procedures (such as the 'least to most' prompt hierarchy) can be easily integrated within the context of daily activities, many antecedent stimulus control procedures such as progressive time delay, stimulus shaping, and stimulus fading may be best presented in massed trial table-top activities because of the level of precision required in their implementation (Browder, Lalli, & Derr, 1989). Implementing these procedures in in-vivo, distributed formats may be quite difficult or impossible under some circumstances. It seems that the effectiveness of these procedures hinges on the close proximity of trials. Further, during massed trial didactic training an instructor may be better able to expose a learner to a full range of exemplars (Horner & McDonald, 1982), and be better able to present exemplars in a mix of easy-to-hard groupings and in juxtapositions with negative examples, as frequently suggested for remediating discrimination difficulties (Horner, et al., 1986; Keogh & Reichle, 1985).

A second potential benefit of didactic, massed trial training is that decontextualization of the skill alone may serve to enhance stimulus saliency and increase the learners attention to its critical dimensions. Although increasing stimulus saliency in-vivo is desirable, it is not always practical or possible, particularly when the surrounding environmental stimuli are competing with the learner's attention. Several 'in-vivo' studies (Bambara, et al., 1988; Billingsley & Neel, 1985; Horner & Budd, 1985) have reported difficulty overcoming powerful competing stimuli in the natural environment. Used remedially, didactic massed trial sessions may serve to strengthen the response enough to reduce the 'threat' of competing stimuli when the response is later trained in context.

An illustration of when massed trials would be appropriate for remediating difficult discriminations comes from our own experience with using 'milieu' or 'incidental' language training procedures for teaching young children with moderate levels of mental retardation to use prepositional phrases productively. In an unpublished pilot study, tthe authors trained prepositional phrases involving the concepts 'in', 'on', 'under', and 'beside' across two pragmatic functions, requesting and commenting. Training trials were dispersed throughout a structured play activity. While the authors were successful at increasing the spontaneous use of prepositional phrases involving concepts already in the children's receptive repertoire, they had limited success at teaching novel concepts 'besides' and 'under' incidentally. The number of training opportunities and the quality of exemplars arising naturally during the play activity were inadequate. Their attempt at 'enriching' the play activity by programming in a range of good exemplars, increasing the number of trial opportunities, and increasing stimulus saliency by pointing out relevant relational attributes, resulted in an undesirable stiltedness that significantly interrupted the flow of the activity despite their effort to maintain naturalness. Further, with increased interruption in the children's play, the children became less motivated to cooperate during teaching trials. It seemed that the children diverted their attention to surrounding play activities (which were more reinforcing) as prompting and error correction became more intrusive. Through continued persistence and creative programming, improved performance on a limited number of exemplars was eventually achieved. But at what expense? It might have been more efficient, less cumbersome, and more enjoyable to the children had the authors programmed several massed trial warm-up sessions to facilitate basic discriminative associations rather than 'beefing-up' the natural activity, and used the in-vivo incidental teaching paradigm to teach pragmatic applications in a more natural, uninterrupted format.

One approach to teaching some types of skills that are based on an underlying rule or structure is to conduct massed trial instruction using a matrix training format (Goldstein, 1985). Matrix training is a method of efficiently assuring that sufficient exemplars of a concept or rule are trained to the point at which generalization of the rule itself occurs. For example, to teach a child to combine color adjectives (e.g., red, green, yellow, blue) and objects (car, cup, ball, paper, etc.) combinations of adjectives and objects would be trained in a step-wise manner as shown in Figure 1. Generally, overlap among stimulus components is essential because it requires students to make the critical discriminations necessary for recombinative generalization to occur (Goldstein, 1985). This type of training format, when combined with massed practice, leads to the most efficient generalization (i.e., smallest number of training trials before generalization to untrained exemplars occurs). However, additional training using milieu or other approaches will probably be necessary to assure generalization to actual functional usage in natural environments. Nevertheless, when massed practice appears preferable, as in the example we provided above, then using a matrix approach with step-wise overlap training may minimize the amount of training necessary. Examples of this approach used with massed trial training can be found in studies by Goldstein (1983); Goldstein, Angelo, and Mousetis (1987); and Romski & Ruder (1984).

Objects

	Car	Cup	Ball	Paper	Hat	Truck
Red	X	X				
Green		X	X			
Yellow			X	X		
Blue				X	X	
Orange					X	X
Purple						X

(Color Adjectives)

Figure 1: A 6 x 6 color-adjective object matrix.

The X's in the cells denote training exemplars of color-object combinations. Note that the step-wise progression provides overlap of four color adjectives and four object stimuli (e.g., red car, red cup, green cup, green ball, yellow ball, etc.). The blank cells are untrained exemplars and may be used to assess recombinatory generalization.

Functional Academics

Providing repeated opportunities to develop and practice a specific response is particularly appropriate for functional academic training, especially when training *generalized* as opposed to *adaptive* academic skills (Browder & Snell, 1987). Generalized academic skills instruction follows a 'traditional' developmental skill sequence, similar to skill sequences used with students. For example, a skill sequence for telling time might include telling time to the hour, half-hour, at 15-minute intervals, 5-minute intervals, and 1-minute intervals. The goal of generalized academic training is to provide the learner with a sufficiently broad knowledge base that would be applicable across a range of situations. Adaptive academic training, on the other hand, restricts instruction to only those specific responses required by the student's daily living activities (e.g., reading sight-words on a washing machine and microwave) and frequently includes the use of academic prostheses (e.g., recognizing 'when it is time to do something' with the aid of environmental cues and pictorial time illustrations) bypassing the need for any academic knowledge.

With increased emphasis on in-vivo instruction and adapting performance objectives such that a response has immediate utility in natural settings (White, 1980, 1985), generalized academic instruction has been overlooked as an appropriate option for some learners with moderate and severe disabilities (Browder & Snell, 1987). Adaptive academic skills can be taught relatively easily within functional activities and natural sequences of behavior, because the target skill has been greatly simplified. However, training generalized academic skills demands a more concentrated, intensive training format because it involves lengthy skill building, complex discriminations, and considerably more conceptual development than adaptive skills.

Functional academic instruction is actually a subset of the complex discrimination category discussed above, thus the reasons for using massed trials for remediating discrimination difficulties apply here as well. In addition, massed trials for generalized academic instruction may be particularly useful for increasing fluency of responding through 'drill and practice' (Haring, Liberty, & White, 1980) and for training subskills that may not have immediate application, but serve as the foundation for other more functional responses (e.g., learning to count by 5s in order to tell time at 5-minute intervals). Further, academic training via a massed trial approach lends itself to the intermixing of review items with task items in acquisition training. As previously discussed, this intermixing of review items not only serves a maintenance and fluency building function for items already acquired by the learner, but may also have a facilitative effect on the acquisition of the 'new' untrained items of the same task (Koegel & Koegel, 1986; Neef et al., 1977; 1980).

To ensure that training for function is not overlooked and that the learner is provided with an immediately useful skill, it is best to schedule in-vivo training concurrently with didactic massed trial sessions (Browder & Snell, 1987). There are several different programming options. The first is to integrate the academic skill 'in training' with functionally appropriate opportunities occurring in context. Even though the skill in training may represent a subcomponent of a broader goal, with some environmental arrangement programming training for function can occur at most levels of an instructional skill sequence. For example, if an individual is learning to tell time to the hour, then the trainer can identify or arrange opportunities during the day when the learner would be 'required' to use this skill, perhaps to watch a favorite television show at 4 o'clock or set the table for dinner at 6 o'clock. If the individual is learning to sum nickels and dimes, then he/she may be required to use these coins while making small purchases at a store or vending machine. Modifications and expansions of in-context training opportunities would develop concurrently as the learner progresses up a skill sequence.

A second option is to teach an adaptive academic skill in-vivo (e.g., selecting the correct coins for vending machine use by matching coins to a sample glued on a cardboard prostheses), while the broader generalized skill (e.g., summing coins) is trained during isolated lessons. Form and function are developed simultaneously, but in a parallel rather than an integrated fashion. In the above example, the student learns the generalized concept that money is used to make purchases, and that coins are needed for vending machine use, while he/she is learning to count coins in a separate instructional activity. Additionally, simultaneous use of an adaptive skill allows immediate participation in in-vivo activities, and does not restrict access until the generalized skill is mastered. A third option is to use a combination of both the first and second options, integrating a subskill immediately in some situations, teaching the adaptive skill in other situations, while providing repeated practice opportunities to further develop skill form.

Learner Characteristics

Another consideration in the selection of trial sequencing approaches is the characteristics of the learner, specifically the level of mental retardation. That is, some children with severe levels of mental retardation may initially need massed trial instruction in order to establish the form of a given skill within their repertoire. However, any tendency to make guidelines about what particular instructional methodology should be applied given general characteristics such as level of mental retardation, should probably be avoided at present in view of the continuing lack of a reliable data base relevant to this issue. Instead, decisions should be based on the type of skill being targeted.

AVOIDING THE CAVEATS ASSOCIATED WITH MASSED TRIAL TRAINING

As previously discussed, massed trials may offer an appropriate training format across a range of situations. However, there are a number of 'pitfalls' commonly associated with their use that should be avoided if possible. These problems can be eliminated with appropriate, preventive programming.

Use Massed Trials Adjunctively

As emphasized throughout this chapter, massed trials, unless used to teach skills that occur in natural repetitions, should always be used as an *adjunct* to distributed trials in functional contexts. The inherent danger in using massed trials is that once taken out of context, the instructor may fail to integrate the skill with other responses, or use mastery under a massed trial approach as a prerequisite for skill training in natural settings, thereby restricting functional opportunities. The end result would be insufficient generalization. To avoid this problem, massed trial training should be programmed concurrently with natural sequenced instruction in functional contexts using one or more of the strategies previously discussed, e.g., warm-up sessions, error correction, adaptive skill training plus isolated massed trial sessions. The actual balance of the number of massed trial sessions to distributed trial sessions in-vivo is probably best determined on an individual basis with special consideration given to individual learning styles, instructional purpose and anticipated outcomes.

Be Sensitive to Learner Interest and Responsiveness

Massed trial instruction may potentially result in reduced learner motivation and boredom. As discussed, decreased responsiveness to trial presentations, greater error rates, and negative affect have been documented for learners with severe disabilities when compared to distributed trial sequences that were also presented didactically (Dunlap 1984; Dunlap & Koegel, 1980; Mulligan et al., 1982). However, these limitations may be attributed to extensive, over-presentation of trials, and rigid adherence to fixed reinforcement ratios, session length and presentation formats. For example, in their comparison of massed and distributed trials on the performance of two students with autism, Dunlap and Koegel (1980) presented detailed within session performance trends for one student. The data revealed some interesting patterns. At the beginning of each 30-minute training session and within the first 8 to 10 trial presentations, the student's correct responding under the massed trial condition was relatively high. But as the sessions progressed to include up to *64 massed trials,* performance proportionately decreased. This pattern of initial high rates of responding followed by a performance decline as the number of trials increased was replicated across skills and training sessions. The fact that higher levels of correct responding were regained at the beginning of a new training session, suggests that the attentional drop-off with massed trials was a function of the number of trial repetitions and was a temporary phenomenon, i.e., no carry over across sessions. Obviously the clinical validity of extending training sessions when learner interest and responsiveness declines is highly questionable. The extensive repetition of a single skill or behavior will eventually diminish the motivation and performance of even the most responsive individual.

The obvious implication is that when massed trials are used they should be presented in small doses within short periods of time. Determination of number of trial presentations should be guided by learner performance *during* the training session and not by a priori determinations. As long as the learner appears motivated and receptive to another trial, training can continue. Signs of resistance or performance decline should signal the immediate termination of a massed trial session. Depending on the nature of the skill, it is also possible to distribute small blocks of massed trials across the day. In any case, fixed notions about session length or the number of trial presentations should be avoided.

In addition to adjusting trial presentations to learner responsiveness, there are several other strategies that may enhance motivation. As previously discussed, intermixing known items with unknown acquisition items on academic tasks, may serve to lessen the demands of repeated trials and facilitate increased responding (Koegel & Koegel, 1986; Neef et al., 1977; 1980). Presenting trials in a game-like format is another strategy. There is no reason that didactic massed trial sessions should emulate the sterile, rigid formats of the laboratory experiments of yesteryear. Taking a skill out of its natural context provides instructors with unlimited options to creatively build new instructional contexts that are fun and enjoyable to students.

Another strategy, which is not a motivational technique in itself but would serve to reduce the total amount of time spent in massed trial training sessions, is to shape a response until it is brought under a desired level of instructional control that is conducive to in context training, rather than training for mastery under a massed trial format.For example, van den Pol et al. (1981) presented massed trials until the trainee demonstrated a response without the need for physical guidance. Once the response was brought under verbal instructional control, training for mastery (i.e., independent performance) continued within the activity chain format.

Program for Generalization Within Massed Trials

In the 1960s and 1970s, generalization strategies were typically not incorporated within massed trial training sessions (Stokes & Baer, 1977). However, programming for generalization can and should be incorporated in massed trial sessions and need not wait until a skill is trained in its natural distributed sequence. Although complete generalization from a massed trial format is not likely (i.e., the format is too dissimilar from the way distributed responses are typically used in natural environments), generalization is a multidimensional phenomenon and can be facilitated at some level (e.g., across relevant stimulus exemplars, across exemplars in a response class, across people) within a massed trial format.

Stokes and Baer (1977) and Stremel-Campbell and Campbell (1985) provide many empirically based guidelines on how to promote generalization from massed trial learning. Using real instead of simulated objects, presenting a range of relevant stimulus exemplars, varying antecedent cues, allowing variation in responses, and conducting massed trial training in-vivo (if feasible and non-stigmatizing for the learner) are a few examples.

At the onset of instruction, a generalization plan should be developed specifying the conditions under which the generalized response should occur and the specific techniques to be used to promote generalization (Stremel-Campbell & Campbell, 1985). When massed trials are selected as an adjunct to in-vivo instruction, the instructor should determine what generalization techniques to include in massed trial sessions from the overall plan. Depending on the specific purpose of using a massed trial format, it is conceivable to include all generalization strategies from the plan, making the training sessions very similar to the generalization conditions. For example, Horner and colleagues (1986) used massed trials to train one step of a generalized grocery item selection program by incorporating many of the conditions of the criterion activity into the massed trial training. That is, training was conducted in the grocery store, using a range of shopping list picture cues and actual grocery items. On the other hand, it may also make sense to limit the generalization programming techniques during mass trial sessions to focus on a particular generalization problem. For example, the instruction might opt to make massed trial training sessions very different from criterion settings to highlight appropriate responding to a specific stimulus cue. In this instance, irrelevant stimulus conditions might be held constant (e.g., setting, trainers), while the learner is exposed to multiple exemplars and nonexemplars of a particular object class. In either case, the point is that massed trial training and programming for generalization need not be considered mutually exclusive entities. Instructional purpose, not the selection of the training format, should determine how to program for generalization and how much stimulus variation to incorporate during massed trial training opportunities.

SUMMARY AND FUTURE DIRECTIONS
FOR RESEARCH

Historically, massed trials have been overused and misused, leading to the current emphasis on the appropriateness and desirability of trial distribution over massed trial instruction. However, it may be unwise to dismiss massed trial training as 'nonfunctional' without evaluating potentially appropriate applications within the contemporary framework of functional skill training. When used in conjunction with in-vivo distributed trial training and matched appropriately to instructional purpose, skill and learner characteristics, massed trials may serve to enhance instructional efficiency and effectiveness. Appropriate applications and the potential benefits of massed trials were illustrated with instructional examples taken from the training literature. However, research that addresses how, when, for whom, and for what skills massed trials can be used appropriately is virtually non-existent.

There are several critical areas in need of investigation. First, research is needed to evaluate the relative effectiveness and efficiency of massed trial training. Comparisons between in-vivo distributed instruction with an approach that combines massed trials and in-vivo distributed trials may yield information on whether massed trials indeed will enhance acquisition and facilitate more rapid learning of a specific response or an entire task chain. For example, preliminary data obtained on the productive language skills of 12 preschool children with moderate to severe cognitive disabilities suggest that a combined in-vivo plus one-to-one massed trial approach (approximately 30 minutes/day, 5 days/week) resulted in greater acquisition gains than in-vivo instruction alone (Fredericks, 1989). Comparative measures of language performance were taken in natural settings. Many more comparative investigations such as the one illustrated here are warranted. As suggested by Horner et al. (1986), effectiveness and efficiency should be measured in rigorous standards that are meaningful to instructors. Thus, an effectiveness measure might address how well a combined approach results in the demonstration of new behaviors in natural settings. Efficiency might be assessed by measuring trials to criterion, total instructional time, and cost effectiveness.

Second, research based guidelines are needed to assist in the appropriate selection and optimal implementation of massed trial approaches for specific learners, skills, and instructional purposes. Numerous questions exist including: Are certain skills more appropriate for a massed trial or a combined massed trial/distributed trial approach then others? What are the characteristics of these skills (e.g., complex discriminations, rule-governed concepts) and can they be identified Prior to instruction or must learning difficulties occur first in natural contexts? What are the advantages and disadvantages of using massed trials for error correction and warm-up? Are there specific learner characteristics for which massed trials are generally appropriate or inappropriate?

Third, particular attention should be paid to the composition and structure of massed trial sequences. Intermixing known with unknown within-task items was shown to have facilitative acquisition of academic tasks (e.g., Neef et al., 1977). On the other hand, extensive repetitions of the same response were found to have a deleterious effect on performance (Dunlap & Koegel, 1980). It appears that not all massed trial sequences are created equal. Continued research should identify other within format variables that may enhance or impede learning in order to optimize instruction and avoid common pitfalls.

Fourth, research is needed on how to optimize student attention in conjunction with massed practice. For example, what is the average number of trials that can be presented before student attention drops off? Does this average vary based on type of skill being trained, type of reinforcers used, cognitive level of the student, and so forth?

Fifth, and finally, given that massed practice may sometimes be the most appropriate method to use in instruction, how can it best be combined with in-vivo generalization techniques such as milieu instructional strategies, to promote efficient generalization to the student's actual skill repertoire in the natural environment? Massed practice might be used to establish quickly and efficiently an initial baseline of either general skills with students with severe disabilities or very specific skills with all types of students. Meanwhile, these students would receive milieu teaching (Warren & Kaiser, 1988) of the same skills to teach functional use and to ensure generalization and integration into the learner's natural usage repertoire. Hybrid approaches, perhaps developed within 'game like' formats, that retain many of the strengths of both massed and distributed (or didactic and milieu) teaching need to be extensively investigated.

CONCLUSION

Massed trial instruction is neither an inherently good or bad teaching approach. With many types of skills and in many situations it is clearly an inappropriate teaching strategy. However, in some situations massed trial training seems to have a number of advantages over distributed practice approaches. The real need is to further determine the strengths and limitations of this teaching approach through applied research.

REFERENCES

Bambara, L. M., Warren, S. F., & Komisar, S. (1988). The individualized curriculum sequencing model: Effects on skill acquisition and generalization. *Journal of the Association of Persons with Severe Handicaps, 13*, 8–19.

Bambara L. M., & Warren S. F. (1984). *A closer look at the individualized curriculum sequencing model.* Unpublished manuscript, Vanderbilt University, Nashville.

Bellamy, G. T., Horner, R. H., & Inman, D. P. (1979). *Vocational habilitation of severely retarded adults: A direct service technology.* Baltimore: University Park Press.

Billingsley, F. F., & Neel, R. S. (1985). Competing behaviors and their effects on skill generalization and maintenance. *Analysis and Intervention in Developmental Disabilities, 5,* 357–372.

Bowers, J., Rusch, F. R., & Hudson, C. (1979). Training a severely retarded young adult to ride the city bus to and from work. *AAESPH Review, 4* (l), 15–23.

Bricker, D., & Cripe, J. (1989). Activity-based intervention. In D. Bricker (Ed.), *Early intervention for at-risk and handicapped infants, toddlers, and preschool children* (2nd ed.) (pp.251–274). Palo Alto: Vort Corporation.

Browder, D., Hines, C., McCarthy, L. J., & Fees, J. (1984). A treatment package for increasing sight word recognition for use us daily living skills. *Education and Treatment of the Mentally Retarded, 19,* 191–200.

Browder, D. M., Lalli, J., & Derr T. (1989, May). *A comparison of stimulus control procedures for sight word acquisition.* Paper presented at the 113th Annual Meeting of the American Association on Mental Retardation.

Browder, D. M., & Snell, M. E. (1987). Functional academics. In M. E. Snell (Ed.), *Systematic instruction for persons with severe handicaps* (3rd ed.) (pp.436–468). Columbus, OH: Charles E. Merrill Publishing Co.

Browder, D. M., Snell, M. E., & Wildonger, B. A. (1988). Simulation and community-based instruction of vending machines with time delay. *Education and Training of the Mentally Retarded, 23,* 175–185.

Brown, L., Branston, M. B., Hamre-Nietupski, S., Pumpian, I., Certo, N., & Gruenewald, L. (1979). A strategy for developing chronological age-appropriate and functional curricular content for severely handicapped adolescents and young adults. *Journal of Social Education, 13,* 81–90.

Brown, L., Branston-McClean, M. B., Baumgart, D., Vincent, L., Falvey, M., & Schroeder, J. (1979). Using the characteristics of current and subsequent least restrictive environments in the development of curriculum content fur severely handicapped students. *AAESPH Review, 4,* 407–424.

Brown, L., Nietupski, J., & Hamre-Nietupski, S. L. (1976). The criterion of ultunate functioning. In M. A. Thomas (Ed.), *Hey, don't forget about me* (pp.2–15). Reston, VA: The Council for Exceptional Children.

Caro, P., & Snell, M. E. (1989). Characteristics of teaching communication to people with moderate and severe disabilities. *Education and Training of the Mentally Retarded, 24* (1), 63–77.

Cuvo, A. J., & Davis, P. (1983). Behavior therapy and community living skills. In R. Eisler & P. Miller (Eds.), *Progress in behavior modification* (Vol. 14) (pp.125–172). New York: Academic Press.

Cuvo, A. J., Klevans, L., Borakove, S., Borakove, L. S., VanLanduyt, J., & Lutzker, J. R. (1980). A comparison of three strategies for teaching object names. *Journal of Applied Behavior Analysis, 13,* 249–257.

Cuvo, A. J., Veitch, V. D., Trace, M. W., & Konke, J. L. (1978). Teaching change computation to the mentally retarded. *Behavior Modification, 2,* 531–548.

Deese, H., & Hulse, S. H. (1967). *Psychology of learning.* New York: McGraw-Hill.

Donnellan, A. M., & Neel, R. S. (1986). New directions in educating students with autism. In R. H. Horner, L. H. Meyer, & H. D. Bud Fredericks (Eds.), *Education of learners with severe handicaps* (pp.99–126). Baltimore: Paul H. Brookes.

Dunlap, G. (1984). The influence of task variation and maintenance tasks of the learning and affect of autistic children. *Journal of Experimental Child Psychology, 37,* 41–64.

Dunlap, L. K., & Dunlap, G. (1987). Using task variation to motivate handicapped students. *Teaching Exceptional Children, 19,* 16–19.

Dunlap, G., & Koegel, R. L. (1980). Motivating autistic children through stimulus variation. *Journal of Applied Behavior Analvsis, 13,* 619–627.

Evans, I. M., & Scotti, J. R. (1989). Defining meaningful outcomes for persons with profound disabilities. In F. Brown & D. H. Lehr (Eds.), *Persons with profound disabilities: Issues and practices* (pp.83–107). Baltimore: Paul H. Brookes.

Falvey, M. A. (1989). *Community-based curriculum : Instructional strategies for students with severe handicaps.* Baltimore: PAul H. Brookes.

Fredericks, H. D. (1989, October). *Integrated daycare?* Paper presented at the International Early Childhood Conference on Children with Special Needs, Minneapolis, MN.

Goldstein, H. (1983). Training generative repertoires within agent-action-object miniature linguistic systems with children. *Journal of Speech & Hearing Research, 26,* 76–89.

Goldstein, H. (1985). Enhancing language generalization using matrix and stimulus equivalence training. In S. F. Warren & A. K. Rogers-Warren (Eds.). *Teaching functional language* (pp.225–290). Baltimore: University Park Press.

Goldstein, H., Angelo, D. & Mousetis, L. (1987). Acquisition and extention of syntactic repertoires by severely mentally retarded youth. *Research in Developmental Disabilities, 8,* 549–574.

Guess, D., & Helmstetter, E. (1986). Skill cluster instruction and the individualized curriculum sequencing model. In R. H. Horner, L. H. Meyer, & H. D. Fredericks (Eds.), *Education of learners with severe handicaps* (pp.221–248). Baltimore: Paul H. Brookes.

Guess, D., & Noonan, M. J. (1982). Curricula and instructional procedures for severely handicapped students. *Focus on Exceptional Children, 14* (5), 1–12.

Halle, J. (1987). Teaching language in the natural environment to individuals with severe handicaps: An analysis of spontaneity. *Journal of the Association of Persons with Severe Handicaps, 12,* 28–37.

Haring, N. G., & Bricker, D. (1976). Overview of comprehensive services for the severely/profoundly handicapped. In N. G. Haring & L. Brown (Eds.), *Teaching the severely handicapped* (Vol. 1) (pp.17–32). New York: Gruen & Stratton.

Haring, N. G., Liberty, K. A., & White, W. R.(1980). Rules for data-based strategy decisions in instructional programs: Current research and instructional implications. In W. Sailor, B. Wilcox, & L. Brown (Eds.), *Methods of instruction for severely handicapped students* (pp.159–192). Baltimore: Paul H. Brookes.

Hill, J. W., Wehman, P., & Horst, G. (1982). Toward generalization of appropriate leisure and social behavior in severely handicapped youth: Pinballmachine use. *Journal of the Association for the Severely Handicapped, 6* (4), 38–44.

Holvoet, J., Guess, D., Mulligan, M., & Brown, F. (1980). The individualized curriculum sequencing model (II): A training strategy for severely handicapped students. *Journal of The Association for the Severely Handicapped, 5,* 337–351.

Horner, R. H., Albin, R. W., & Ralph, G. (1986). Generalization with precision: The role of negative teaching examples in instruction of generalized grocery item selection. *Journal of the Association for Persons with Severe Handicaps, 11* (4), 300–308.

Horner, R. H., & Billingsley, F. F. (1988). The effect of competing behavior on the generalization and maintenance of adaptive behavior in applied settings. In R. H. Horner, G. Dunlap, & R. L. Koegel (Eds.), *Generalization and maintenance* (pp.197–220). Baltimore: Brookes Publishing Co.

Horner, R. H., & Budd, C. M. (1985). Teaching manual sign language to a nonverbal student: Generalization of sign use and collateral reduction of maladaptive behavior. *Education and Training of the Mentally Retarded, 20,* 39–47.

Horner, R. H., & McDonald, R. S. (1982). Comparison of single instance and general case instruction in teaching a generalized vocational skill. *Journal of the Association for the Severely Handicapped, 7,* 7–19.

Horner, R. H., Meyer, L. H., & Fredericks, H. D. (Eds.), *Education of learners with severe handicaps.* Baltimore: Paul H. Brookes.

Horner, R. H., McDonnell, J. J., & Bellamy, G. T. (1986). Teaching generalized skills: General case instruction in simulation and community settings. In R. H. Horner, L. H. Meyer & H. D. Fredericks (Eds.), *Education of learners with severe handicaps* (pp.289–314). Baltimore: Paul H. Brookes.

Koegel, L. K., & Koegel, R. L. (1986). The effects of interspersed maintenance tasks on the academic performance in severe childhood stroke victim. *Journal of Applied Behavior Analysis, 19* (4), 425–430.

Koegel, R. L., & Rincover, A. (1977). Research on the difference between generalization and maintenance in extra-therapy responding. *Journal of Applied Behavior Analysis, 10,* 1–12.

Keogh, W. J., & Reichle, J. (1985). Communication intervention for the 'difficult-to-teach' severely handicapped. In S. F. Warren & A. K. Rogers-Warren (Eds.), *Teaching functional language* (pp.157–194). Baltimore: Paul H. Brookes.

Mulligan, M., Guess, D., Holvoet, J., & Brown, F. (1980). The individualized curriculum sequencing model (1): Implications from research on massed, distributed, or spaced trial training. *Journal of The Association for the Severely Handicapped, 5,* 299–323.

Mulligan, M., Lacy, L., & Guess, D. (1982). Effects of massed, distributed and spaced trial training on severely handicapped students' performance. *Journal of the Association for the Severely Handicapped, 7,* 48–61.

Neef, N. A., Iwata, B. A., & Page, T. J. (1977). The effects of known-item interspersal on acquisition and retention of spelling and sightreading words. *Journal Applied Behavior Analysis, 10,* 738.

Neef, N. A., Iwata, B. A., & Page, T. J. (1980). The effects of interspersal training versus high density reinforcement on spelling acquisition and retention. *Journal of Applied Behavior Analysis, 13,* 153–158.

Neel, R. S., & Billingsley, F. F. (1989). *Impact: A functional curriculum handbook for students with moderate to severe disabilities.* Baltimore: Paul H. Brookes.

Reichle, J., & Keogh, W. J. (1986). Communication instruction for learners with severe handicaps. In R. H. Horner, L. H. Meyer, & H. D. Bud Fredericks (Eds.), *Education of learners with severe handicaps* (pp.189–219). Baltimore: Paul H. Brookes.

Reichle, J., York, J., & Eynon, D. (1989). Influence of indicating preferences for initiating, maintaining, and terminating interactions. In F. Brown & D. H. Lehr (Eds.), *Persons with profound disabilities: Issues and practices* (pp.191–211). Baltimore: Paul H. Brookes.

Rincover, A. & Koegal, R. L. (1975) Setting generality and stimulus control in autistic children. *Journal of Applied Behavior Analysis, 8*, 235–246.

Romski, M. A., & Ruder, K. F. (1984). Effects of speech and sign instruction on oral language learning and generalization of action & object combinations by Downs's syndrome children. *Journal of Speech & Hearing Disorders, 49*, 292–702.

Sailor, W., Goetz, L., Anderson, J., Hunt, P., & Gee, K. (1988). Research on community intensive instruction as a model for building functional, generalized skills. In R. H. Horner, G. Dunlap, & R. L. Koegel (Eds.), *Generalization and maintenance* (pp.67–98). Baltimore: Brookes Publishing Co.

Sailor, W., & Haring, N. G. (1977). Some current directions in education of the severely/multiply handicapped. *AAESPH Review, 2*, 3–23.

Snell, M. E., & Browder, D. M. (1986). Community referenced instruction: Research and issues. *Journal of the Association for Persons with Severe Handicaps, 11* (1), 1–11.

Spradlin, J., & Siegel, G. (1982). Language training in natural and clinical enviroments. *Journal of Speech and Hearing Disorders, 47*, 2–6.

Sprague, J. R., & Horner, R. H. (1984). The effects of single instance, multiple instance, and general case training on generalized vending machine use by moderately and severely handicapped students. *Journal of Applied Behavior Analysis, 17*, 273–278.

Stokes, T. F., & Baer, D. M. (1977). An implicit technology of generalization. *Journal of Applied Behavior Analysis, 10*, 349–367.

Stremel-Campbell, K., & Campbell, C. R. (1985). Training techniques that may facilitate generalization. In S. F. Warren & A. K. Rogers-Warren (Eds.), *Teaching functional language* (pp.251–307). Baltimore: University Park Press.

van den Pol, R. A., Iwata, B. A., Ivancic, M. T., Page T. J., Neef, N. A., & Whitley, F. P. (1981). Teaching the handicapped to eat in public places: Acquisition, generalization, and maintenance of restaurant skills. *Journal of Applied Behavior Analysis, 14*, 61–69.

Volgesberg, R. T., & Rusch, F. R. (1979). Training severely handicapped students to cross partially controlled intersections. *AAESPH Review, 4*(3). 264–273.

Wahler, R. G. (1969). Setting generality: Some specific and general effects of child behavior therapy. *Journal of Applied Behavior Analysis, 2*, 239–246.

Waldo, L., Guess, D., & Flanagan, D. (1982). Effects of concurrent and serial training on receptive labeling by severely retarded individuals. *Journal of the Association for the Severely Handicapped, 1*, 33–39.

Warren S. F., & Bambara L. M. (1989). An experimental analysis of milieu language intervention: Teaching the action-object form. *Journal of Speech and Hearing Disorders, 54*, 448–461.

Warren, S. F. & Kaiser, A. P. (1988). Research in early language intervention. In S. M. Odom & M. B. Karnes (Eds.), *Early intervention for infants and young children with handicaps* (pp.89–108). Baltimore: Brookes Publishing Co.

White, O. R. (1980). Adaptive performance objectives: Form versus function. In W. Sailor, B. Wilcox, L. Brown (Eds.), *Methods of instruction for the severely handicapped* (pp.47–69). Baltimore: Brookes Publishing Co.

White, O. R. (1985). The evaluation of severely mentally retarded populations. In D. Bricker & J. Filler (Eds.), *Severe mental retardation: From theory to practice* (pp.161–184). Reston, VA; Council for Exceptional Children.

Zeaman, D., G House, B. J. (1963). The role of attention in retardate discrimination learning. In N. R. Ellis (Ed.), *Handbook of mental deficiency* (pp.159–223). New York: McGraw-Hill.

ESTABLISHING SPONTANEOUS VERBAL BEHAVIOR

Jeff Sigafoos and Joe Reichle

LANGUAGE INTERVENTION PROGRAMS

A number of comprehensive language intervention programs for persons with developmental disabilities were produced and became widely disseminated by the mid, 1970s. Several of these programs were designed primarily to teach speech to learners with autism or severe to profound mental retardation (e.g. Bricker & Bricker, 1970, 1974; Guess, Sailor, & Baer, 1974; Kent, 1974; Lovaas, 1977, MacDonald, 1976; MacDonald & Blott, 1974; Miller & Yoder, 1974; Stremel & Waryas, 1974). Either implicitly or explicitly all of these programs incorporated into their teaching methodology operant techniques, such as imitation, differential reinforcement, shaping and discrimination training. Differences among programs tended to occur in terms of orientation, content, and sequencing of training. Some programs were derived from cognitive-developmental and psycholinguistic theory (e.g. Bricker & Bricker, 1970, 1974; Miller & Yoder, 1974; Stremel & Waryas, 1974). Others were based largely on a functional- remedial logic (e.g. Guess, Sailor, & Baer, 1974; Kent, 1974; Lovaas, 1977). For more complete reviews of these programs see Guess (1980), Guess, Sailor, Keogh, and Baer (1976), and McCoy and Buckholt (1981).

Widespread implementation of these procedures brought to the forefront several new issues and problems. One problem was that some participants never spoke the targeted linguistic forms even after months of intensive intervention (Goetz, Schuler, & Sailor, 1979; Lovaas, Koegel, Simmons, & Long, 1973). The prognosis tended to be worse for learners who were not vocally imitative (Lovaas, 1977; Carr, 1982). In the absence of an imitative repertoire, attention shifted to teaching augmentative and alternative modes of communication which could be more readily prompted than could speech. For example, sign (Braam & Poling, 1983; Carr, 1982; Carr & Kologinsky, 1983; Reichle, Rogers, & Barrett, 1984) and graphic mode (Calculator & D'Altilio-Luchko, 1983; Reichle & Yoder, 1985; Romski, Sevcik, & Pate, 1988; Sigafoos, Doss, & Reichle, 1989) options are increasingly used with learners having developmental disabilities.

While augmentative modes solved the problem created by the absence of an echoic repertoire, the communicative repertoires taught to learners with severe disabilities, be they in vocal, gestural, or graphic modes, continued to be characterized as 'incomplete' (Sundberg, 1980, p.6), 'constrained' (Hubbell, 1977), and 'rote' (Schaeffer, 1978). Basically, the repertoires displayed by learners after systematic communication intervention did not correspond very well to the verbal behaviors characteristic of the linguistic community at large. There seemed to be something missing. One missing element was 'spontaneity'.

SPONTANEITY AND INDIRECT EFFECTS

Unlike actions which achieve their effects by direct contact with the physical world, verbal behaviors are effective only indirectly through the mediation of another (Skinner, 1957). Reaching for and grasping a cup of coffee is *directly* related to obtaining the cup. 'Asking' for a cup of coffee, however, is effective only *indirectly* through the mediation of a listener predisposed to deliver coffee upon request. One could 'ask' for coffee by producing speech, a manual sign, or by pointing to a line drawing of a cup of coffee, given, of course, that one is in the presence of an appropriately conditioned listener. Although topographically distinct (Michael, 1985), saying 'coffee', signing 'coffee', or pointing to a line drawing of a cup of coffee, may at times be functionally equivalent (Carr, 1988).

Because verbal behavior achieves its effects indirectly, it seems less tied to the immediate physical environment and hence more spontaneous. Hockett (1960) referred to the act of talking about things remote in space and time as displacement. Language was unique because of displacement. Whereas one could not obviously act directly upon things remote in space and time, displaced (indirect) acts are possible. Lennenberg (1967) referred to essentially the same indirectness as spontaneity, which he sees as characteristic of normal language development. Because verbal behaviors act indirectly upon the physical world and therefore do not *require* outward support, it is perhaps easy to see why such actions have often been attributed to internal 'linguistic' processes. Generally, these processes were considered to be biological in origin, and hence language is frequently said to emerge spontaneously as the speaker matures.

SPONTANEITY IN DEVELOPMENTAL DISABILITIES

Verbal repertoires taught to learners with developmental disabilities are frequently characterized by a lack of spontaneity (Carr, 1982; Carr & Kologinsky, 1983; Charlop, Schreibman, & Thibodeau, 1985; Gobbi, Cipani, Hudson, & Lapenta-Neudeck, 1986; Halle, 1987; Lovaas, Koegel, Simmons, & Long, 1973; Oliver & Halle, 1982; Schaeffer, 1978; Sosne, Handleman, & Harris, 1979). While it has been suggested that this lack of spontaneity reveals an inherent limitation of operant training procedures (Beisler & Tsai, 1983; Hubbell, 1977) and more generally the inherent limitations of contingency-oriented accounts of language (Lee, 1981b, 1988; Skinner, 1957), these same procedures are now being used to encourage the display of spontaneous verbal behavior in persons with developmental disabilities. The remainder of this chapter will review these efforts as well as the issues and problems involved in teaching spontaneous verbal behavior. The first problem aptly pointed out by Halle (1987) is to delineate the various ways the term 'spontaneous' has been applied.

DEFINITIONS OF SPONTANEITY

Various definitions have been offered for what constitutes 'spontaneous' communication. Most of these are definitions by default. One definition of spontaneous communicative acts is that they are those that occur in the absence of some cue, prompt, or imitative model. Speech in particular was often defined as spontaneous when it occurred in the absence of a model (Bricker & Bricker, 1974; Charlop, Schreibman, & Thibodeau, 1985; MacDonald, 1976; MacDonald, & Blott, 1974): for example, when the learner said 'apple' without being asked to 'Say apple'. Because programs designed to teach speech relied necessarily on vocal imitation training (Lovaas et al., 1966; Risley & Wolf, 1967), the intervention procedures brought the learner's speech repertoire under the control of models provided by the interventionist and often little else. Any speech produced without support of a prior cue to imitate was considered spontaneous (Koegel, O'Dell, & Koegel, 1987).

Communicative acts that occurred in the absence of explicit instructions (e.g. 'Tell me what you want'. 'What is this?') reflected another type of spontaneity (Beisler & Tsai, 1983; Gray & Ryan, 1973; Hart & Risley, 1968). Instructions (or mands) were often used by interventionists to increase the number of instructional opportunities for teaching communication skills in the natural environment (Rogers-Warren & Warren, 1980; Warren, McQuarter, & Rogers-Warren, 1984). As discriminative stimuli and instructional prompts, instructions or mands for communicative behavior offered numerous advantages. Instructions are relatively easy to deliver, can be repeated, and often proved reliable in getting the learner to produce the desired communicative act. In addition, instructions and questions by others frequently serve to set the occasion for communicative behavior in many exchanges (e.g. ordering a meal, interviewing for a job, talking with a peer). However, for learners with developmental disabilities, the potential exists for such instructions to gain exclusive control over one's communicative repertoire. The learner may only come to request a drink or food when told, 'Tell me what you want', or asked, 'What do you want?' Labels for objects may occur only when the learner is asked a direct question (e.g. 'What is this?'). Obviously, such control is less useful than if requests for food or drink were controlled by hunger and thirst, respectively. Similarly it would be of more practical benefit in the learner labelled objects (e.g. 'water' [in the road ahead]) without having to be explicitly instructed to do so. Hence, communicative acts which occurred in the absence of explicit instructional cues were a highly sought after by- product of training, a by-product that when it did occur was defined as a type of spontaneity.

During communication intervention a variety of antecedents, in addition to instructional cues, were often arranged to serve as discriminative stimuli or to prompt correct responses. Objects were prominently displayed, features of the environment pointed out, learners were looked at expectantly, or more intrusive gestural or physical prompts were arranged to recruit correct responses. Communicative responses taught during such intervention sessions that later occurred in the absence of the arranged explicit stimuli have been defined as spontaneous (Lovaas, 1977). Lovaas also included in this definition extended responding to a single discriminative stimulus, for example, describing 3–4 features of a single photograph, and new response forms that had not been targeted for instruction.

Halle (1982) pointed out that in practice language intervention programs for learners with disabilities are typically recommended for implementation in one-to-one structured therapy sessions. Consistent with this, targeted communicative behaviors which occurred outside of therapy were often defined as spontaneous (Guess, Sailor, & Baer, 1974). When the communicative behaviors taught during structured intervention sessions did not appear outside of therapy, the problem was often considered as a lack of generalization (Harris, 1975; Stokes & Baer, 1977). Spontaneity and generalization were often treated as identical problems. And as discussed later, both can indeed be viewed as issues of stimulus control.

Kent (1974) offered perhaps the most variant definition of spontaneity. Specifically, a learner was said to produce spontaneous speech (or manual signs) when he or she corrected his or her own errors without assistance. Although, initially, a learner might label a displayed cup incorrectly, if this was followed by the correct 'cup' the learner was credited with a degree of spontaneity.

A variety of definitions have been offered for spontaneous communicative acts. Most are definitions by default: for example, as communicative acts occurring in the absence of imitative prompts, in the absence of instructional cues, in the absence of explicit discriminative stimuli, or as communicative acts occurring outside of any structured therapy session. In addition, spontaneity has included extended and novel responses (Lovaas, 1977) and self-corrected errors (Kent, 1974). While these various definitions may at first seem at odds with one another, a definition of spontaneity in terms of stimulus control helps to provide a common classification to each of the separate definitions.

STIMULUS CONTROL AND SPONTANEITY

The term 'spontaneous' is often given to verbal behavior that occurs in the absence of some explicit instructional prompt (e.g. imitative models, questions). But this does not imply that the resulting behavior is then not determined by environmental variables. Most likely it means that the controlling variables are unknown (Skinner, 1957), or that some other aspect of the environment has gained control of the behavior. One goal of some studies that have investigated procedures for facilitating spontaneity has been to transfer stimulus control of

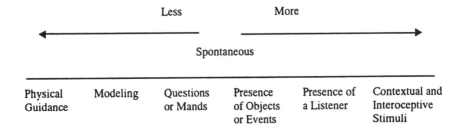

Figure 1: Continuum of spontaneity proposed by Halle (1987).

Source: Reprinted with permission of *The Journal of The Association for Persons with Severe Handicaps*

verbal behavior from explicit instructional prompts to more natural discriminative stimuli. For example, a learner whose repertoire of requests for water occurs
only when a glass of water is displayed and the learner is asked 'What do you
want?' is under the control of visual and vocal stimuli. A goal of intervention
in this case might be to bring requests for water under the control of more natural
variables, such as thirst brought on by deprivation with respect to water, physical
activity, or by eating salty foods. Issues involved in actually transferring control
to such establishing operations (Michael, 1982, 1988) will be taken up later. The
important point here is that spontaneity can best be viewed not as an absence of
stimulus control but rather as control by more natural discriminative stimuli.

Researchers (e.g. Charlop, Schreibman, & Thibodeau, 1985; Halle, 1987)
have suggested that the stimuli that control a repertoire of verbal behavior can
be arranged along a continuum of spontaneity. Generally, where a given class
of verbal behavior is controlled by physical prompts (e.g. molding a person's
hands and arms to produce a particular manual sign), imitative models (e.g. 'Say
water'), or questions (e.g. 'Tell me what you want'), the repertoire is considered
less spontaneous than if the same behaviors were controlled by contextual cues
(e.g. requesting help to open a stuck door) or interoceptive stimuli (e.g. requesting water when thirsty). Figure 1 displays the continuum proposed by Halle
(1987, p.29).

SPONTANEITY AND GENERALIZATION

Spontaneity is a relative term. It refers to the variables controlling a given class
of verbal behavior. Verbal behavior controlled by a spoken model, for example,
is often considered less spontaneous than if the same behavior were controlled
by more natural contextual cues. In teaching learners with developmental
disabilities, prompts such as providing models, physical assistance, or vocal
instructions are often needed to establish a repertoire of behavior. Once established, should the behavior occur in the absence of these instructional prompts,
the behavior would be considered more spontaneous. In this respect, spontaneity
and generalization share several common features.

Stimulus generalization has traditionally been described as a *process* involving the combination of two or more operations, with the outcome being an
extended range of stimulus conditions influencing the emission of a particular
utterance. For example, the learner being taught to greet person A (operation 1)
and person B (operation 2) may also greet persons C, D and E without additional
intervention (Stokes, Baer, & Jackson, 1974). In this example the greeting
response is said to have 'generalized' across persons. Stimulus generalization
may also occur across settings, tasks, materials, and so on. These types of
generalization occur because the stimulus conditions to which the behavior is
extended share common features with the stimulus conditions present when the

behavior was established. The persons in the above example may all have been familiar to the learner through prior histories of interaction or each may have approached the learner often enough and in a manner to occasion the greeting response. The important point is that behavior established under one set of conditions occurs in the presence of similar, yet novel stimulus arrays that were not included in prior instruction.

Several strategies have been described to promote generalization (Stokes & Baer, 1977). Some of these strategies involve the combination of operations to facilitate generalization. Strategies of this type include *general case programming* (Albin & Horner, 1988), *'loose' training*, and *programming common stimuli* (Stokes & Baer, 1977). With these strategies the emphasis is on establishing a common connection between two or more persons, settings, tasks, or sets of materials so that future situations that share these common features will also come, through the process of generalization, to occasion the appropriate behavior.

Other generalization strategies, such as *sequential modification* (Stokes & Baer, 1977, p.352), do not combine operations to achieve generalization but rather introduce explicit interventions to extend stimulus control to each new person, setting, task, or set of materials. These types of strategies are implemented typically post-hoc only after a particular discrimination has been established. In this respect the implementation of additional interventions to achieve generalized performance is similar to the implementation of transfer of stimulus control procedures to facilitate spontaneity. More will be said concerning transfer of stimulus control later. It is presently unclear if spontaneity is a process, similar to generalization, that can be achieved by the combination of two or more operations. Most efforts to achieve spontaneity have consisted of introducing explicit interventions to bring behavior under the control of more natural discriminative stimuli.

To demonstrate that spontaneity could emerge from the combination of operations it would be necessary to show that two operations would be necessary. For example, a learner would come to request a spoon when one was needed to eat applesauce (i.e. in the presence of contextual cues) having only been taught to request spoons when prompted to 'Say spoon' (operation 1) and when shown or offered a spoon (operation 2). While spontaneous requesting seems to emerge readily among most speakers, there are no empirical demonstrations of such emergent spontaneity. Therefore, it is unclear if spontaneity can be described as a process similar to generalization, if spontaneity is best viewed as a type of generalization, or if the two are best treated as separate issues.

Halle (1987) has carefully described several important differences between generalization and spontaneity. He illustrated how a communicative act could generalize yet remain less than spontaneous and vice versa. For example, consider a learner taught to label a book by saying 'book' each time trainer A holds up a copy of a small red book and asks, 'What is this?' It is conceivable that the learner would accurately say 'book' when also shown green books, blue books, white books, large, thick and thin books. If so, the response has 'generalized' to untrained or multiple exemplars. In addition, the learner may respond correctly for trainer B, C and D (generalize to persons) and in the classroom, hallway, kitchen, or den (generalize to settings). This generalized performance would not, however, imply that the response 'book' would occur spontaneously, that is, in the absence of being shown a book and asked, 'What is this?' Similarly, a class of verbal behavior may be quite spontaneous – the learner labels a book without having to be asked, 'What is this?' – but not generalized. The learner may label only small red books in the classroom with trainer A.

Generalization and spontaneity are both concerned with issues of stimulus control. Generalization involves bringing behavior under the control of variables different from those used during intervention. Spontaneity involves the display of behavior in the absence of the prompts that may have been required to establish the behavior. On the other hand, because the strategies implemented to promote generalization (e.g. general case instruction, programming common stimuli) are typically different from the procedures implemented to facilitate spontaneity, the two issues can at present be viewed as operationally distinct. Procedures used to facilitate spontaneity will be discussed later.

EXPLAINING THE LACK OF SPONTANEITY

Operant procedures have proved successful in teaching a variety of communicative behavior to persons with severe disabilities. Communicative behaviors have been taught in vocal, gestural, and graphic modes. Despite these successes, communicative repertoires established through operant techniques have often been characterized by a lack of spontaneity. Communicative behavior can be considered more spontaneous when it occurs without having to be explicitly prompted with physical assistance, models, vocal instructions, and so forth. Why is there this lack of spontaneity? Several explanations have been offered and are reviewed below.

Early interventions designed to teach verbal behavior to persons with developmental disabilities have been implemented in a rather regimented style. A single trainer taught a single learner in a distraction-free room. Intervention trials were implemented in a discrete-trial format (Carr & Kologinsky, 1983). Each intervention opportunity was initiated by the presentation of a distinct discriminative stimulus (e.g. the display of an object, the command 'Say ball'). Only responses that occurred immediately after the discriminative stimulus had been presented were reinforced and usually with some arbitrary edible (Ferster, 1967, 1972).

Investigators were careful to implement systematically teaching procedures under well controlled conditions. Had such control been sacrificed, the effectiveness of these procedures may have never been demonstrated. In addition, these controlled conditions allowed researchers to isolate important relations among controlling variables, ultimately leading to an improved technology for teaching verbal behavior.

Ironically, it now seems likely that the same tight experimental control that figured so effectively in the craft of teaching verbal behavior to persons with developmental disabilities, may be at least partially responsible for the resulting lack of spontaneity.

Several researchers (Carr & Kologinsky, 1983, p.310; Gobbi, Cipani, Hudson, & Lapenta-Neudeck, 1986, p.357; McCook, Cipani, Madigan, & LaCampagne, 1988, p.137; Oliver & Halle, 1982, p.50) attribute the lack of spontaneity to these characteristics of intervention. When a communicative response is reinforced only in the presence of a particular item or prompt and extinguished or punished at other times, it is not surprising that a rather precise and 'narrow' (Carr, 1982, p.153) stimulus control is achieved, with a resulting lack of spontaneity. Established repertoires were rarely displayed under more natural conditions when those precise stimuli were absent. Therefore, the logical solution involved bringing the repertoire under the control of a broader range of stimuli or under the control of more 'natural' stimuli.

PROCEDURES FOR OBTAINING SPONTANEOUS USE

Two basic strategies have been developed for bringing verbal behavior under the control of more natural stimuli. This dichotomy is somewhat arbitrary – the two strategies are distinguished in terms of whether implementation occurs *during* or *after* the initial verbal topographies have been established. Incidental teaching and a related mand-model procedure represent strategies of the first type. Transfer of stimulus control procedures represent strategies of the second type.

Incidental Teaching

In the incidental teaching paradigm, intervention opportunities are learner initiated as opposed to trainer initiated. Once a learner has indicated some interest in a particular object or activity, the interventionist approaches and requires a request from the learner. Should the learner not appropriately ask for the item, some type of prompt is given. Within this basic paradigm several variations are possible (Hart, 1985).

The procedures rely on arranging the environment principally by restricting access to preferred materials in order to create the need for learners to request materials from others. Those fulfilling a request use the learner's prior initiation toward objects or activities as a cue for the implementation of an incidental teaching opportunity. For example, when the learner has initiated reaching for an object placed out of reach, the interventionist approaches, directs his/her attention to the learner and waits for the targeted request. If a poor example of a request is initiated, the interventionist can prompt (using questions or models) a better response. When the learner emits the targeted request, the object of interest is provided. Across successive intervention opportunities, prompts are faded, bringing requests under the control of contextual cues arranged by restricting access to preferred items and the presence of an adult with a history of providing requested objects. Thus from the very early stages of intervention a degree of spontaneity is incorporated into the verbal repertoire established by incidental teaching procedures.

Incidental teaching has been used primarily and successfully to increase the complexity of speech in preschoolers (Hart, & Risley, 1968, 1974, 1975). The basic techniques of arranging opportunities for communication, such as restricting access to preferred materials, have also been implemented with success by teachers serving learners with severe disabilities (Haring, Neetz, Lovinger, Peck, & Semmel, 1987; McGee, Krantz, Mason, & McClannahan, 1983; McGee, Krantz, & McClannahan, 1985).

One potential limitation of the incidental paradigm is that it requires learners to initiate instructional opportunities. Yet many learners may not initiate or do so at very low rates. As a result there may be few instructional opportunities and hence little chance for establishing verbal topographies. To overcome this limitation, the mand-model paradigm is frequently offered.

Mand-Model

Instead of waiting for learners to initiate instructional opportunities, the mand-model uses teacher-initiated instructions for verbalizations to generate instructional opportunities in the natural environment. For example, a teacher may approach a child at snack time and say, 'Tell me what you want', or approach a child who is playing with a toy car and ask, 'What color is that car?' Communicative behaviors are thus brought under the control of the presence of a listener asking specific questions, representing an intermediate level of spontaneity.

The major difference between mand-model procedures and incidental teaching is in the arrangement or temporal sequencing of the verbal cues of instructions provided by the interventionist. Using a mand-model the teacher would instruct the learner to talk (e.g. 'Tell me what you want') to initiate an instructional opportunity. If the learner failed to answer the question correctly or in a timely fashion, additional prompts (e.g. imitative models) would be used to recruit the desired communicative behavior.

Mand-model techniques solve the problem of limited initiation by using teacher-initiated versus learner-initiated opportunities. This allows the teacher to determine the number of instructional opportunities available to the learner. However, because such opportunities arise during the course of everyday activities, as opposed to more traditional structured language training trials, the teacher needs to identify situations where mand-model opportunities are to be initiated. When exactly or during what activities should the teacher approach and ask, 'What is this?' or 'What do you want?' and how will the selection of activities influence the effectiveness of the procedure? Several studies have demonstrated the effectiveness of mand-model procedures for teaching communicative behavior in the context of less structured intervention opportunities. These studies clarify how the mand-model procedure can be and has been applied by interventionists to incorporate communication intervention opportunities into the everyday routines of the learner.

The mand-model procedures used by Rogers-Warren and Warren (1980) consisted of instructing children to request or describe materials (e.g. 'Tell me what you want', or 'Tell me what this is', p.367). Instructions to verbalize were provided by teachers when a child approached certain play materials. Appropriate replies from the child resulted in teacher mediated access to the materials and social praise. Further instructions (e.g. 'Give me a whole sentence') or models (e.g. 'Say red ball') were used if needed to obtain an appropriate response.

Teachers for three children with language delays quickly learned to implement the mand-model procedure in their classrooms during daily 30 minute freeplay periods. As a result of teachers systematically using mands and models to prompt vocalizations from children and then providing contingent access to materials or praise, all three children showed increased numbers of vocal responses, including a substantial number of untrained words and phrases. Warren, McQuarter, and Rogers-Warren (1984) systematically replicated the mand-model procedure and again found it effective in generating increased talking in three preschoolers with language delay.

Part of the success of the mand-model procedure is no doubt attributed to the increased opportunities to communicate. This increase is a direct result of teacher-initiated interactions using instructions to verbalize ('Tell me...'), questions ('What is this?'), and models ('Say car'). Both Rogers-Warren and Warren (1980) and Warren, et al. (1984) demonstrated that training teachers to use the mand-model procedure increased the systematic use of teacher-initiated teaching episodes. Therefore, it appears that incidental teaching and mand-model procedures are relatively easy-to-use techniques that work primarily to alter the behavior of interventionists; specifically to arrange communicative opportunities in the natural environment (Halle, 1988).

Limited initiations on the part of the learner may lead one to consider using mand-model procedures. Continued use of man- model techniques may, however, result in learners who communicate only when specifically instructed (manded) to do so. That is, communicative responses may come under the exclusive control of the verbal cues provided by the interventionist rather than some of the more natural cues present in the everyday environment. This is the same problem often noted following more traditional structured intervention; namely, the learner's communicative repertoire lacks spontaneity.

Given a verbal repertoire controlled by questions, mands, or other types of prompts, the question becomes how can control be transferred to variables reflecting more spontaneity, such as the presence of objects, contextual cues, or bodily states (e.g. hunger, thirst). Transfer of stimulus control procedures (Touchette, 1971) provides an answer that represents a second strategy for obtaining spontaneous use of communicative forms that have already been established as part of a learner's repertoire.

Transfer of Stimulus Control

Control of verbal behavior can be transferred from stimuli representing less spontaneity (e.g. physical guidance, modelling, questions) to stimuli representing more spontaneity (e.g. presence of objects, listeners, contextual or interoceptive states). Procedures used to effect such transfer involve the removal of prior controlling stimuli and the introduction of control by another class of stimuli (Smeets & Striefel, 1976; Striefel & Owens, 1980; Terrace, 1963; Touchette, 1971; Touchette & Howard, 1984). This process is accomplished by combining three operations: extinction, differential reinforcement, and stimulus fading. Spontaneity is the one feature of human language that is most compelling for an account by organocentric processes (Lee, 1988) and can be obtained in learners with severe disabilities through implementation of stimulus control procedures. Despite the seeming paradox, learners can be *taught* to 'be spontaneous' (Hubbell, 1977, p.217).

Two general types of procedures have been used to transfer control of verbal behavior from instructional prompts and cues to more natural discriminative stimuli. One procedure involves gradually reducing the amount of magnitude of the controlling stimulus while simultaneously presenting the stimulus that will eventually come to control the behavior. This procedure can be called 'prompt fading' (Carr & Kologinsky, 1983; Risley & Reynolds, 1970; Risley & Wolf, 1967). For example, to transfer control of the imitative response 'ball' to the presence of the object, the imitative model is gradually eliminated in a series of discrete steps (e.g. 'Say ball', 'Say ba', 'ba', etc...). Similar fading strategies are applicable in eliminating physical prompts or motor models often used to establish gestural or graphic mode repertoires.

The other basic procedure involves gradually separating the controlling prompt from the new discriminative stimulus along a temporal dimension. This procedure can be called 'time-delay' (Halle, Baer, & Spradlin, 1981; Halle,

Marshall & Spradlin, 1979) or 'delayed prompting' (Handen & Zane, 1987). For example, the model, 'Say ball' might be delayed a few seconds from the display of the ball. When correct responses occur prior to the delivery of the verbal prompt, control has been successfully transferred to the presence of the delayed object.

Both prompt fading and delayed prompting techniques have been used successfully to facilitate the display of spontaneous verbal behavior. Often the two techniques are combined. Prompts are faded as well as delayed (Gobbi et al., 1986; McCook et al., 1988; Reichle, Sigafoos, & Piche, 1989; Sigafoos, Doss, & Reichle, 1989; Sundberg, 1980). In addition, several variations exist on both of these strategies. Prompts have been successfully faded by reducing the *intensity* of the controlling stimulus and by eliminating the *prolongation* or *repetition* of the controlling stimulus (Striefel & Owens, 1980). This is particularly true in the case of vocal prompts. Empirical support can be found among several studies.

Carr and Kologinsky (1983) taught six boys with autistic behaviors to request ten preferred objects (e.g. food, toys, activities) using manual signs. Prompting, fading and differential reinforcement procedures were implemented to transfer control of the signing repertoires from imitative variables '...to the mere presence of an attending adult' (p.300). In their first experiment, an adult approached, looked at the child expectantly, and waited 5 seconds for any one of ten signs to occur. Signs emitted by the children were followed by delivery of the corresponding item, which the trainer kept concealed from the learner's sight. Prompts were provided at the end of 5 seconds if needed to recruit a sign. Over successive opportunities, prompts were faded in magnitude. Although these procedures were successful in facilitating the display of spontaneous signed requests for preferred items, it is not clear to what extent the repertoire consisted of discriminative operants (Catania, 1979, p.139). Because any sign produced was followed by a reinforcer, learners could perform well simply by emitting any or all available signs. Anecdotally, Carr and Kologinsky noted that signing appeared to be sensitive to establishing operations (e.g. Michael, 1982, 1987, 1988). For example, after a child had requested a number of salty foods, requests for liquids were highly probable. The ten 'spontaneous' signs may have been emitted, at least to some extent, in a discriminative manner. In addition, a second experiment included discrimination training that successfully established a discrimination between signed requests.

Fading models of the correct response was also successfully applied by Simic and Butcher (1980) to develop 'spontaneous' requests in five children with mental retardation. Verbalizations consisting of 'I want a' and 'out' were brought under the control of an adult with a tray of edibles and an adult with a tray of edibles standing behind a closed door with a window, respectively. It is possible that the closed door constituted an aversive stimulus for one predisposed to exit the room and thus gain access to the tray. If so the request 'out' may have been controlled by the contextual cue or conditioned establishing operations (Michael, 1987, 1988) created by this arrangement. However, displayed objects *and* an adult were also present, making it difficult to identify control exerted by any single variable in isolation.

Learners can be taught to speak or sign in the absence of prompts. Once a verbal repertoire has come under the control of models these prompts can be faded and control transferred to the presence of adults or the presence of objects. Several other studies have used these or similar fading procedures to develop more spontaneous verbal repertoires in learners with severe disabilities. Duker and Moonen (1985) transferred control of signed requests from physical guidance or models to the question, 'What do you want?' In this study, prompts were faded by delivery of different types of assistance beginning with physical guidance and then models, a strategy of most-to- least assistance. Duker and Moonen (1986) found prompts could be faded by using a reverse, least-to-most sequence. The question, 'What do you want?' was faded, and thus brought signed requests under the control of contextual cues arranged by withholding a needed item or a piece of a needed item (e.g. a piece of a jig-saw puzzle).

Using time-delay procedures, Halle, Marshall and Spradlin (1979) taught six children with severe to profound intellectual impairments to vocalize requests for trays at mealtimes in a state institution. By consistently delaying the presentation of food trays and prompts for 15 seconds upon a child's arrival at a food counter, as an adult held their trays in sight, 'spontaneous' requests for food trays emerged in five of the six children. Halle, Baer and Spradlin (1981) systematically replicated the use of time-delay procedures for teaching requests for displayed objects to children with developmental disabilities.

Similar to the constant 15-second delay procedure, Oliver and Halle (1982) transferred control of a moderately retarded boy's signed requests from physical prompts to the presence of objects. Establishing stimuli (Michael, 1982) were created by withholding a needed utensil, using a constant 10-second delay. A progressive time-delay procedure in which the interval advanced in 2-second increments after reach correct response was employed to bring requests under the control of the presence of an object (Charlop, Schreibman, & Thibodeau, 1985). Eventually, six of seven autistic boys came to request four preferred items as each was offered in the absence of any model (e.g. 'I want a *cookie*').

Gobbi, Cipani, Hudson and Lapenta-Neudeck (1986) combined prompting, fading, and time-delay tactics to teach two children with severe mental retardation to request food and beverage items at snack time. Control of vocalizations (child 1) and manual signs (child 2) was transferred from models to the presence of the teachers and the food (beverage) items. 'Spontaneous' requests for juice were similarly established in two adults with mental retardation (McCook, Cipani, Madigan, & LaCampagne, 1988). This combined technique has been termed the 'quick-transfer' procedure.

Transfer of stimulus control procedures consisting of prompt fading, delayed prompting, or their combinations have been widely used to bring verbal behavior under the control of specific discriminative stimuli that are thought to be more representative of the types of variables that control the repertoires of the intact speaker. These procedures are consistent with the explanation that a lack of spontaneity reflects narrow stimulus control resulting from precise discrimination training. These transfer of stimulus control procedures essentially represent an attempt to broaden this narrow stimulus control. Because the originally controlling stimuli are typically intrusive instructional prompts, these procedures also involve bringing the repertoire under the control of more 'natural' types of variables. It is helpful to think of distinct types of discriminative stimuli (e.g. physical guidance, models, questions etc.) arranged along a continuum. At one end of this continuum are the narrow, intrusive stimuli; at the other end are the more naturally controlling variables.

In the studies reviewed above, however, the validity of the continuum as a necessary training protocol is unclear. For example, some studies transferred control from models to the presence of objects, adults and/or contextual cues (e.g. Carr & Kologinsky, 1983; Charlop et al., 1985; Simic & Butcher, 1980), bypassing intermediate stimuli such as questions or mands. Halle (1987) proposed this continuum (see Figure 1) as a guideline for sequencing transfer of stimulus control procedures. He noted that some points along the continuum have been successfully bypassed. Just how many points can be excluded remains to be determined empirically. It may, for example, be possible to transfer control from physical guidance to interoceptive states, such as hunger, while bypassing every intermediate step.

Conceptualizing stimulus control along a continuum and then using the continuum as a guide for the transfer of stimulus control fits well with the more general practice of programmed instruction. In programmed instruction, the discrepancy between current performance and the expected criterion level of behavior is addressed by gradually shaping the presented repertoire into its final desired form through a series of discrete steps. Each successive step builds upon the behavioral outcome of the previous step. Gradually shifting from one source of stimulus control to another through a series of discrete steps represents a similar type of programmed instruction. Unlike response *shaping*, however, which by necessity must access the presenting repertoire of behavior, there is no compelling reason why stimulus control cannot be established initially at any point along the continuum. However, to establish the needed verbal topographies it would be necessary to develop control by physical guidance or models. Once a reliable prompt has been identified, the prompt can be faded as control by other discriminative stimuli is established.

Once a successful transfer of stimulus control has been achieved, are previous sources of control lost? A successful transfer of stimulus control is evidenced when the behavior occurs in the presence of the new and in the absence of the old controlling stimulus. For example, signing 'ball' when told to 'Sign ball' (new controlling stimulus) in the absence of a trainer modelling the sign for the learner to imitate (old controlling stimulus). In this case, it would be useful to determine if the learner's repertoire now under the control of the interventionist's command is still also controlled by trainer models. Imitative control would no doubt still be important, particularly when attempting to establish new topographies.

Further down the continuum control may be transferred from trainer questions (e.g. 'What is this?', 'What do you want?') to the presence of the object and later still to contextual cues. Arriving at this terminal locus would be a great success. However, there may still be times when the communicative act is needed in response to questions (e.g. 'What would you like to order?') or in the presence of the object. Much of verbal behavior is required not only under a single discriminative stimulus, however spontaneous it may the be, but under multiple sources of control (Skinner, 1957) as well.

An analysis of stimulus control following the transfer from one type of variable to another is needed. If previous sources of control are lost when a new discriminative stimulus is introduced, then it may be necessary at times to regain that lost control. Instead of enlarging the range of controlling variables, transfer of stimulus control procedures may instead simply shift control from one (narrow) stimulus to another.

At present, transfer of stimulus control procedures has proven successful in facilitating the display of spontaneous verbal behavior. The studies reviewed above brought children's requests under the control of displayed objects (e.g. Charlop et al., 1985; Gobbi et al., 1986; McCook et al., 1988; Simic & Butcher, 1980), the present of an attending adult (e.g. Carr, & Kologinsky, 1983) and less frequently contextual cues (Duker & Moonen, 1986; Oliver & Halle, 1982). However, motivational variables can be arranged to promote even more spontaneous requests, and multiple sources of control underlie a distinction between requests and other responses classes (e.g. providing information). Both of these issues need to be considered when attempting to obtain spontaneous verbal behavior in learners with developmental disabilities.

CREATING OPPORTUNITIES FOR SPONTANEOUS REQUESTING

Control by contextual cues or interoceptive states must be addressed carefully in creating opportunities for spontaneous requesting. We have already noted that incidental and mand-model procedures incorporate environmental arrangements (e.g. placing materials out of reach) to promote control by contextual cues. In addition, several studies have employed similar arrangements (e.g. withholding needed or preferred items) to create motivational conditions for teaching learners to request (Duker & Moonen, 1986; Oliver & Halle, 1982). Bringing verbal behavior under the control of these more spontaneous discriminative stimuli presents some unique challenges that are worth considering in detail. These challenges are particularly unique in attempts to establish control by interoceptive states, such as hunger or thirst.

Contextual cues and interoceptive states can themselves be viewed as distinct. Michael (1982, 1987, 1988) distinguished these two types of motivational variables and referred to the former as 'conditioned', the latter as 'unconditioned', and both as establishing operations. An establishing operation is '...any change in the environment which alters the effectiveness of some object or event as reinforcement and simultaneously alters the momentary frequency of the behavior that has been followed by that reinforcement' (Michael, 1982, pp.150–151). For example, deprivation with respect to food can be viewed as a *change in the environment*. This change *alters* the effectiveness of food as reinforcement, specifically by making food an effective and powerful type of reinforcement. Because of this change, behaviors that have resulted previously in access to food (i.e. such as making a sandwich or requesting an apple) are more likely to occur.

Some established operations do not depend on a past learning history and hence the term 'unconditioned'. No one has to learn to be hungry following food deprivation or thirsty after heavy exercise. In addition, it does not appear that a hungry or thirsty person needs to learn the reinforcing effects of food or water.

'Conditioned' establishing operations depend upon a favorable learning history for their repertoire altering effects. For example, a person must 'learn' the reinforcing effects of spoons, knives and forks when confronted respectively with applesauce, steak and salad. Therefore, a change in the environment that renders spoons an effective type of reinforcement may be the recipe of applesauce. The momentary frequency of any behavior that has in the past resulted in obtaining a spoon (e.g. searching the kitchen, asking for a spoon) would likely increase.

Bringing requesting behavior under the control of such conditioned establishing operations is, in principle, no different from the procedure used to develop control by questions, objects, or persons. To this end, transfer of stimulus control procedures have been successfully used. The unique challenge is in the determination of the motivative conditions under which requesting is to occur. Hall and Sundberg (1987) taught two adolescents with severe intellectual and profound hearing impairments to produce the signs representing items such as 'can opener' and 'cup' to provide information. Subsequently, using time delay and other prompt fading procedures, they transferred instructional control from the displayed objects to the conditioned established operations of having a can of fruit or soup and needing to produce a signed request in order to obtain the relevant utensil so that the item's contents could be accessed. Similar conditioned establishing operations were investigated by withholding utensils (e.g.

208 JEFF SIGAFOOS and JOE REICHLE

spoon, bottle opener) required to access previously requested foods and beverages. Spontaneous requests for these utensils were established by fading control by the present of the objects (Sigafoos, Doss, & Reichle, 1989).

Table 1: Examples of Procedures for Manipulating Establishing Operations to Provide Opportunities for Requesting.

Type of Manipulation	Examples
Natural schedules of deprivation/ satiation	Teach requests for food/drinks at mealtimes (Gobbi et al., 1986; Halle et al., 1979).
	Teach requests for drinks after eating salty foods (Carr & Kologinsky, 1983).
	Teach learners to reject offered food after becoming satiated (Sigafoos, Mustonen, & Reichle, 1989).
Withhold needed objects/actions	Teach requests for utensils needed to prepare or consume foods/beverages (Hall & Sundberg, 1987; Sigafoos et al ,. 1989).
	Teach requests for assistance with difficult tasks (Reichle, Anderson & Scherman, 1988).
	Teach requests for materials placed out of reach (Hart & Risley, 1968; 1974).
Interrupted- Chain Strategy	Teach learners to request continuation of in progress task (Goetz, Gee, & Sailor, 1985; Hunt, Goetz, Alwell, & Sailor 1986).
	Teach requests for missing objects at point in task when object is needed (Hall & Sundberg, 1987).

Reichle, Anderson and Schermer (1986) manipulated the difficulty of unwrapping a twist tie on a bread package to establish spontaneous requests for assistance in an adult with autism. After the learner had requested bread in a sandwich making task, he was confronted with either a loosely wrapped or tightly wrapped package. In the presence of a loosely wrapped bread bag, the learner was capable of independently continuing with the task. However, in the presence of a tightly wrapped bag, the learner could not gain access to the bread and could not, therefore, make a sandwich. Under these latter conditions, the learner was taught to open a communication wallet, search the pages, and point to a 'help' symbol. At this point the interventionist unwrapped the package for the learner.

Each of these studies extended transfer of stimulus control procedures to bring requests under the control of conditioned establishing operations. These establishing operations were created by arranging the environment to provide opportunities for requests. Sosne, Handleman and Harris (1979) provide numerous examples of these types of manipulations. Table 1 provides examples of three widely used methods for creating requesting opportunities.

Goetz, Gee and Sailor (1985) investigated a slightly different method for creating motivational conditions. for two adolescents with severe retardation who participated, unprompted symbol selections were more frequent during trials in the midst of the activity in comparison to trials at the beginning of the activity. Hunt, Goetz, Alwel and Sailor (1986) later replicated the effectiveness of this 'interrupted behavior chain strategy'.

One explanation for the effectiveness of interrupted chaining instructional techniques may be negative reinforcement. That is, the learner escapes from the aversive stimulation created by task interruptions. Both Goetz et al. (1985) and Hunt et al. (1986) provided evidence that such interruptions were moderately upsetting to the learners. In addition, stimuli associated with completing later steps in a chain of behaviors often function as more powerful and conditioned reinforcers than do the changes resulting from completion of earlier steps (Kelleher & Gollub, 1972). Consequently, interrupted-chain strategies may work in part because more powerful reinforcers follow the communicative responses made in the midst of an interrupted task as opposed to those made at the beginning of the task. Interrupting a chain of behavior appears to be one method for bringing verbal behavior under the control of contextual cues. Some control may also be gained by the aversive stimulation created by the interruption procedure. This latter source of control seems similar to the unconditioned establishing operations considered next.

One rationale frequently offered for teaching verbal behavior to persons with developmental disabilities is the resulting ability to 'express wants and needs'. Essentially, this refers to requesting behavior (cf. Sundberg, 1983) under the control of interoceptive states. Requests for food or drink are most spontaneous when controlled respectively by hunger and thirst. Requests for a warm sweater or for the cooling effects of a fan are most spontaneous and most beneficial when the speaker is respectively too cold or too warm. However, these refer to private events (Schnaitter, 1978; Skinner, 1945, 1953) and often cannot be independently verified. Verification is a major problem. Bringing verbal behavior under stimulus control depends upon differential reinforcement in the presence of the relevant stimulus. If the presence of the relevant controlling variables (e.g.

hunger, thirst) cannot be independently verified, the interventionist cannot differentially reinforce precisely requests with respect to these variables.

When teaching verbal behavior to persons with severe disabilities, the problem created by the private nature of some relevant variables has not been adequately addressed. For example, in teaching requests for edibles, it has been assumed often that the learners were hungry. This was usually a safe assumption. Requests have been incorporated also into mealtime or snack routines (Gobbi et al., 1986; Halle et al., 1979, 1981; McCook et al., 1988). In addition, the subsequent consumption of requested edibles provided evidence that the relevant motivative condition (i.e. hunger) was in effect. Such assumptions could be bolstered by depriving learners of food or drink prior to requesting opportunities, but this solution raises ethical issues. Requests for food may not occur in the absence of displayed food items, not because the repertoire lacks spontaneity but because the learner is not hungry. However, a solution is possible. Should the learner readily request and consume foods when they are displayed, the failure of requests to occur when these items are not displayed could be attributed to narrow stimulus control as opposed to the lack of a relevant establishing operation.

The problem of bringing verbal behavior under the control of private events, such as hunger and thirst, remains. Skinner (1945) described several ways a verbal repertoire controlled by private establishing operations could be set up. First, the presence of interoceptive states can be inferred by certain 'public accompaniments'. Thus we may infer that a learner sitting in the sun on a 90 degree day is hot. Hunger might be inferred from the sound of a growling stomach. 'Goose flesh' frequently appears as a physiological and visual accompaniment when one is cold. These public accompaniments could then set the occasion for teaching learners to request a cold beverage, a balanced meal, or heat. This may facilitate control by the establishing operations.

Second, the appearance of collateral behavior may provide evidence for an existing interoceptive state. For example, a person fans him or herself, and it is inferred that he/she is hot, or shivers and therefore must be cold. The occurrence of these behaviors provides natural opportunities to implement procedures designed to facilitate control by the relevant establishing operation. For example, the interventionist may approach a shivering learner, ask 'What do you need?' and then prompt a request for a warm sweater. Over successive opportunities the prompts can be faded until the learner 'spontaneously' requested warm clothes when cold.

In addition to public accompaniments and collateral behaviors, information concerning a person's past history can be used to infer certain bodily states. For example, it may be assumed that a learner who has not eaten for a while may be hungry. Therefore, a natural opportunity to teach requests for food may arise each time the learner has not eaten for approximately 3–4 hours. While it is ethically questionable to deliberately withhold food to create a relevant motivational state, interventionists can make use of such naturally occurring periods of deprivation as intervention opportunities.

Another possibility is to establish control by some verifiable public stimulus (e.g. the presence of objects), maintain that control through intermittent reinforcement, and hope for generalization to private accompaniments. This is how much verbal behavior comes under the control of private events. For learners with sever disabilities, however, it may be too much to assume this will occur. It is also not clear, as previously noted, if spontaneity will emerge in a manner similar to generalization.

At present, few studies have demonstrated procedures for bringing verbal behavior under the control of private interoceptive states (cf. Carr & Kologinsky, 1983), although in principle such control should be possible. Skinner's (1945) analysis of how the verbal community ordinarily creates such control may provide a framework for developing effective intervention procedures. However, in this analysis, Skinner was not concerned only or primarily with requesting behaviors. At issue was how speakers learn to name private stimuli. For example, how does the verbal community teach a speaker to call a particular sensation a 'sharp pain' when the verbal community has no direct access to what is felt? A similar problem arises when the interventionist is concerned with teaching a learner to label internal states (e.g. toothache, fever). The problem of privacy is relevant to both, but the differences highlight an important distinction between requesting and other types of verbal behavior. A given verbal topography is often under multiple sources of stimulus control, and as a result a given verbal topography can enter into more than one functional relationship.

MULTIPLE SOURCES OF CONTROL

A given verbal behavior is rarely a function of a single set of controlling variables (Skinner, 1957, p.227). First, a single verbal *operant* can come under the control of a wide range of variables and usually is in the mature speaker. Second, a single verbal *topography* may enter into more than one functional relationship and usually does so. Both of these issues have important implications for facilitating the display of spontaneous verbal behavior and will be taken up separately below.

An operant response class is typically defined in terms of its controlling variables, rather than in terms of topography. Thus 'requests for food' may be singled out by function, that is, the resulting access to food. Efforts to establish spontaneous requests typically involve transfer of stimulus control from instructional prompts to the presence of objects, persons *or* contextual cues. Persons with developmental disabilities may need to speak, sign or select symbols when asked questions, in the presence of objects, when relevant establishing operations are in effect, and in numerous other circumstances.

Often procedures are implemented which on the face seem to promote multiple stimulus control. A preferred object may be displayed and the learner instructed to 'Tell me what you want'. There are probable conditions for control by visual and auditory stimuli. Another example is prevalent among studies of the effects of 'total' or 'simultaneous communication' (Barrera & Sulzer-Aza-roff, 1983; Barrett & Sisson, 1987; Brady & Smouse, 1987; Sisson & Barrett, 1984). The interventionist signs and speaks simultaneously the name of an object. Again, the concurrent presentation of visual (sign) and auditory (speech) stimuli would be likely to promote multiple stimulus control.

An important issue involves the determination of control exerted by each stimulus when presented separately. For example, will the learner request when offered preferred items but not instructed to 'Tell me what you want', or when instructed but not shown the object? While some learners would continue to respond under these conditions, other learners would respond to one stimulus but not both. This tendency to respond to only one component of a compound stimulus is called 'stimulus overselectivity' and has been most often do-cumented in learners with autism (Koegel & Schreibman, 1977; Koegel & Wilhelm, 1973; Lovaas, & Schreibman, 1971; Lovaas, Schreibman, Koegel, & Rehm, 1971; Schreibman, Koegel, & Craig, 1977). If the compound stimulus consists of an auditory (e.g. spoken word) and visual component (e.g. signed word), overselectivity tends to favor the visual stimulus (Carr, Binkoff, Kolo-ginsky, & Eddy, 1978). Therefore, instructional objectives that include main-taining stimulus control of a verbal repertoire by each element of a compound stimulus, may prove difficult to achieve with learners who exhibit overselectiv-ity.

Procedures can be implemented to overcome selective responding. Schreib-man, et al. (1977), demonstrated that overselective responding was reduced when learners were given repeated testing in a two-choice visual discrimination task. Another solution with documented success (Koegel & Schreibman, 1977) consists of discrimination training in which learners are taught to respond first in the presence of a visual stimulus, and finally reinforcement is available only when both stimuli are present (i.e. conditional discrimination training). An interesting question is whether control by each stimulus in isolation would be lost following this final phase of discrimination training.

A third potential solution is to gradually introduce a second discriminative stimulus (Schreibman, 1975) after control has been established by one. Stimulus shaping and fading techniques can be applied to this end (Ault, Wolery, Doyle, & Gast, 1989; Etzel, LeBlanc, Schilmoeller, & Stella, 1981). For example, after a learner has been taught to name a displayed pen, the intraverbal counterpart may be set up by asking, 'What do you write with?' while fading control by the object (Sundberg, 1986). This is opposite to the direction of procedures usually taken in developing spontaneous verbal behavior through transfer of stimulus control procedures.

Increasing the spontaneity of a verbal repertoire is typically accomplished by eliminating control by one type of prompt (e.g. imitative models) while shifting control to another (e.g. the presence of an object). Equally important, however, is to ensure control by the range of discriminative stimuli that are appropriate to a given verbal operant. For some learners the establishment of such multiple stimulus control may necessitate implementation of procedures designed to overcome selective responding. Application of these procedures for the expressed purpose of bringing verbal behavior under the control of multiple discriminative stimuli has yet to be fully investigated. The previous example highlights the fact that a given verbal topography can enter into more than one functional relationship. This issue is discussed next.

A single topography is often a member of more than one response class (Skinner, 1957, pp.187–190). A given response form, for example, 'pen', may occur as a request for a writing implement, a label of a displayed object, and in intraverbal in reply to questions (e.g. 'What do you write with?', 'What did you purchase for your mother's birthday?'). A person may show also a tendency to say 'pen', sign 'pen', or select a 'pen' symbol simply because someone else has recently done so. In this case the person is said to imitate, and the response is called echoic (Skinner, 1957, pp.55–65). Other verbal operants involve textual (i.e. reading aloud) and transcriptive (i.e. writing from dictation). Within these rather broad classes, several writers have proposed distinct pragmatic classes based upon the physical characteristics of the controlling variables (i.e. the consequences which reinforce members of the response class) (Bates, 1976; Donellan, Mirenda, Mesaros, & Fassbender, 1984).

Empirical support for the classification of verbal behavior in terms of controlling variables, as opposed to in terms of topography, is just beginning to emerge. Organocentric accounts of language development frequently implied that the verbal topographies were acquired and hence available for use one the form could be comprehended or understood (Chomsky, 1965; Lennenberg, 1967). This latter assumption is supported somewhat by data from language development in normal children, in that children's non-verbal behavior comes under the control of comprehension prior to their actual production of these same words (Benedict, 1979; Goldin-Meadow, Seligman and Gelman, 1976; McCarthy, 1954).

However, Goldin-Meadow et al. (1976) reported that children sometimes produce a word (e.g. 'choochoo') different from that comprehended (e.g. 'train'). In addition, researchers demonstrated experimental evidence of limited generalization from receptive (comprehension) to expressive (production) language tasks among learners with developmental disabilities (Guess, 1969; Guess & Baer, 1973; Lee, 1981a; Siegel & Vogt, 1984). For example, having been taught to comprehend the word 'ball' by having the object pointed to when asked to 'Find the ball' will not automatically enable the learner to name the object when shown it and asked, 'What is this?'. Comprehension and production, in at least some instances, represent repertoires that are functionally independent. As a result, contingencies applied to one repertoire will not necessarily produce corresponding changes in the other.

In a similar vein, it has been assumed that once a learner had acquired a given verbal topography (i.e. a word, or a sign or symbol corresponding to a word), it could then be used to request, to name, and to serve as an intraverbal in conversation. A tact is defined '...as a verbal operant in which a response of a given form is evoked (or at least strengthened) by a particular object or event or property of an object or event' (Skinner, 1957, pp.82–83). For example, a speaker might say that 'Dinner is ready', because only then can he or she begin to eat. In this case, the apparent tact (i.e. 'Dinner is ready',) may prove to be controlled in part by mand variables, representing another example of multiple sources of control. Thus there is an emphasis in teaching learners to imitate words or tact objects, in the belief that this alone would enable learners to request spontaneously with the same vocabulary. When this outcome fails to occur it is viewed as a generalization problem.

However, Skinner (1957) argued that mands and tacts, as well as the other verbal behaviors (e.g. echoic, intraverbals, textual, transcriptive) were functionally independent even when incorporating identical response topographies. Several other writers have distinguished between 'knowing the meaning of the word' and 'use' of the word to request (Carr, & Kologinsky, 1983, p.300; Hart, & Risley, 1968, p.109). This distinction corresponds to that made by Skinner between tacts (knowledge) and mands (use).

Some early work on teaching speech to learners with autism (Risley, & Wolf, 1967) demonstrated that imitative responses did not readily occur as tacts. This suggests a degree of independence between the two repertoires. Tacts were eventually established by displaying an object (e.g. a ball), asking 'What is this?' and then prompting the correct response (e.g. 'Say *ball*'). Eventually, the imitative model was faded in magnitude (e.g. 'Say *ba*', 'Say *b*', 'Say __', etc.) until correct responses occurred in the presence of the object and the question, 'What is this?'. The repertoire had become more spontaneous, but another interpretation is that two repertoires (echoic and tact) had emerged from one (echoic). In either case, transfer of stimulus control procedures were used to shift control from imitative to tact variables.

There is also a growing literature supporting the description of mands and tacts as separate response classes. For example, Lamarre and Holland (1985) investigated the functional independence of mands and tacts in preschool children. Some participants initially learned to mand the experimenter's placement of objects with the prepositional phrases 'on the left' and 'on the right'. Probes were implemented, at regular intervals during acquisition, to determine collateral acquisition of a corresponding tact repertoire. The remaining children learned to tact the location of objects with the same phrases while receiving mand probes. Results demonstrated that acquisition of the phrases as mands did not result in collateral acquisition of a corresponding tact repertoire and vice versa. For six of the nine children, tacts and mands remained functionally independent after acquisition. Hart and Risley (1968) also provided evidence that color adjectives acquired as tacts did not readily occur in the mands of disadvantaged preschoolers.

In addition, several studies have confirmed that acquisition of a tacting repertoire in learners with developmental disabilities is not sufficient to instill a corresponding mand repertoire (Glennen & Calculator, 1985; Hall & Sundberg, 1987; McCook et al., 1988; Reichle & Yoder, 1985). Limited generalization has also been noted when progressing from mand to tact intervention (Romski, Sevcik, & Pate, 1988). Given these results, it is doubtful that responses acquired as intraverbals would be automatically available as mands or tacts. One implication of these findings is that each functional relationship (e.g. mand, tact, intraverbal) may require a separate intervention involving the transfer of stimulus control from one response class to another. For example, from echoic to tact (e.g. Risley, & Wolf, 1967), from tact to mand (e.g. Hall & Sundberg, 1987), or from tact to intraverbal (Braam & Poling, 1983; Luciano, 1986).

Spontaneity, as an intervention goal, has been most often addressed in the context of requesting. The issue is complicated, because interventionists often did not maintain a clear distinction between mands and tacts. This reflects the practices of the verbal community. For example, correctly tacting a displayed object was often reinforced by that same object. After naming an apple the learner received a piece of the apple. After naming a displayed raisin the reinforcer was that same raisin. Providing information tasks were often, therefore, part tact and part mand (Hall & Sundberg, 1987). Requesting tasks were similarly part mand and part tact. Responses established under these conditions may fail to 'generalize', therefore, because either the object is not displayed, or because the relevant establishing operation is not in effect. Often, verbal cues were added to the above teaching paradigm, creating a third potential source of control. Verbal cues represent a type of intraverbal control that is often relevant to mands (e.g. 'What do you want?') or tacts ('What is this?'). In retrospect, spontaneous verbal behavior has been conceptualized most closely with the response class of manding. As a result, efforts to facilitate the display of spontaneous verbal behavior have focused on eliminating the control exerted over this response class by external prompts, such as echoic (imitative models), intraverbal (questions), and tact (the presence of objects) variables.

THE INTERACTION OF SPONTANEITY WITH RESPONSE CLASS

What is most spontaneous for requesting is not necessarily the most spontaneous for other types of verbal operants. Most spontaneous for requesting behavior is control by establishing operations, whether they are conditioned (e.g. contextual cues) or unconditioned (e.g. interoceptive states). For other types of verbal operants (e.g. tact, intraverbal, echoic etc.), however, the discriminative stimuli corresponding to 'more spontaneity' fall at different points along the continuum (Figure 1).

Spontaneous Tacting

The context of people's verbalizations is controlled by objects or events in the physical world acting as discriminative stimuli. Interesting or important features of these objects or events are frequently 'named' or 'labelled' by a speaker primarily for the benefit of the listener. The tacts 'Dinner is ready', 'It's raining', or simply 'Telephone' set the occasion for effective action on the part of the listener. The listener may then come to dinner, grab an umbrella, or answer the telephone. The listener, in turn, maintains the speaker's tacts through generalized conditioned reinforcement (e.g. 'Thank you').

A well developed tact repertoire is obviously important to the verbal community in general. Only with such a repertoire will speakers be able to tell others what they see, hear and feel: information that will then enable listeners to act accordingly. For learners with severe disabilities, tacting has been a frequent goal of intervention and education. The typical paradigm has consisted of an interventionist holding up an object (e.g. a ball, an apple, a cup), asking 'What is this?' and reinforcing correct responses. As pointed out before, this task contains elements of a request in that the reinforcer is often the object named. In fact, one rationale for teaching object labels (tacts) was the assumption that the learner could then 'use' the label to spontaneously request those same objects. Unfortunately, spontaneity under these circumstances cannot be assumed.

In naming an object or activity displayed or demonstrated by the interventionist, the speaker is indeed tacting the object. This would ordinarily benefit the listener. Yet in this case, the interventionist knows the name of the object, and there is little practical benefit to the listener. This, of course, must be expected when initially setting up the tact repertoire. Contingencies required to establish the repertoire must necessarily be different from those under which the behavior is expected to be of practical benefit. Tacts established through educational practices such as these may or may not be defined as spontaneous. This is not to imply that tact intervention cannot incorporate functional activities. Once acquired, a learner's spontaneous tacts would provide important [verbal] discriminative stimuli to listeners. For example, intervention could focus on teaching learners to tell others 'It's raining', 'The phone is ringing', or 'The car headlights are on', as well as other tacts that would be functional for the listener.

Tact intervention might also be used to overcome the difficulty learners with severe disabilities may have with initiating conversational exchanges (Gaylord-

Ross, Haring, Breen, & Pitts-Conway, 1984. For example, children typically exhibited some discrete action in the presence of novel changes in the environment (Snyder, 1975). Adults may interpret such actions as an indication that the child is commenting upon the changed environment (McLean & Snyder-McLean, 1988). The child's action is reinforced as a tact and also sets the occasion for the adult to maintain, elaborate, or expand upon the 'conversation' initiated by the child's response to novelty. Similarly, learners with severe disabilities could be taught to tact novel aspects of the environment, setting the occasion for others to maintain, elaborate or otherwise extend the conversation. For example, the learner might be taught to tact or comment upon a peer's new hair style, clothing or automobile. These and similar tacts may provide the learner with an appropriate means of 'initiating a conversation'. To initiate a conversation by tacting novel aspects of the environment, it is important for the tacts to occur spontaneously.

Spontaneous tacts would be those tacts that are controlled by the presence of an object or event that occurred in the absence of other instructional prompts. The learner might name an object without being asked 'What is this?' or in the absence of a model. Or the learner might tact the new clothes worn by a peer without that peer having to prompt the learner by asking, 'Do you like my new shirt?'. Spontaneity may seem simple and unimportant. An object or event is present, and the learner names it. However, there are several different ways an object or event may be presented. In addition, a tact may be spontaneous but less than practical. Yet for a tact to be of any practical benefit it must be spontaneous. These two issues are clarified in the remainder of this section.

The presence of an object or event is presented as a single point along the continuum of spontaneity for requesting behavior (Figure 1). In reference to tacting, that single point can be defined more clearly. For example, naming an object prominently displayed by another seems less spontaneous than naming the object when it is placed inconspicuously about the room. Naming an object pointed out by another seems less spontaneous than if the same tact occurred before the listener had actually seen or heard, touched or smelled the object. There are many ways objects or events can be presented to establish them as controlling stimuli for tacts. Some modes of presenting objects or events may facilitate spontaneity more than others. For example, Woods (1984) compared two methods for teaching tacts. In one task, two boys with autism were instructed to speak the names of items depicted on the pages of a picture-story book (e.g. 'What do you see there?'). This was compared to a 7 second time-delay procedure implemented as the boys encountered objects and locations (e.g. the boiler room, an office) in their elementary school. During the time- delay procedure instructions to tact were not provided. During intervention tacts were modeled in both conditions when learners failed to respond correctly within 7 seconds. Unprompted tacts increased during both tasks when intervention was implemented. Generalization to untrained objects was greater in a later walking task that did not involve the use of instructions to tact. However, the instruction method was always paired with the story-book task, and the time-delay was always implemented during walks. The greater generalization could, therefore, be attributed to task (book versus walk) rather than intervention (instruction versus time-delay). Despite this limitation, the researchers demonstrated that learners with autism could be taught to tact objects spontaneously in the natural environment that were not overtly displayed and in the absence of explicit instructions to speak.

Tacts benefit primarily the listener (Skinner, 1957, p.36). The tact 'Dinner is ready' benefits the listener, who may then come to dinner. The tact 'It is raining' or simply 'Rain' is of benefit to the listener about to go outside without an umbrella. And the tact 'Telephone' sets the occasion for the listener to answer the phone. For maximum benefit the listener must be naive to the presence of the objects or events tacted by the speaker. If not, the tact is redundant. It is less beneficial to be told that 'Dinner is ready' when one has already seen the prepared meal set on the table. It is less beneficial to be told 'It's raining', when drops of rain have already fallen upon one's head. And it is less beneficial to be told 'Telephone' when the sound of this utility has been heard. Tacts must occur spontaneously to be of practical benefit. If the listener is required to prompt tacts through models, questions, or by displaying the object or event, direct contact with the stimulus has already been made, and no new information is provided.

In teaching learners with severe disabilities to tact or to engage in any type of verbal behavior, interventionists make extensive use often of spontaneous tacts that yield practical benefits to listeners. Extrapolating from investigations of spontaneous requests and transfer of stimulus control procedures appears applicable for teaching spontaneous tacts. No studies demonstrating this were found. An example might involve teaching a learner to tell another person that the telephone is ringing. Initially, both the learner and interventionist would be seated next to one another and near the telephone. When the telephone rings the listener would be prompted to say 'Telephone', sign 'Telephone', or point to a line drawing of a telephone. Upon hearing or seeing this tact, the interventionist would provide reinforcement (e.g. 'Thank you') and then would answer the phone. Prompts would be faded until tacts occurred solely in the presence of a ringing telephone. The next step would be to fade the presence of the listener. The listener would move gradually away from the speaker and the telephone, until eventually the listener would be completely out of the room. Now, when the telephone rings, the speaker would have to seek out the listener before tacting. Doss (1988) used a similar 'proximity fade' to teach adults with severe retardation to seek out listeners before making requests. Once a suitable rein-forcer can be found to strengthen the speaker's behavior, there appears to be no reason why the technique outlined above would not facilitate the display of spontaneous tacting in learners with severe disabilities.

One problem in attempting to establish spontaneous tacts in learners with severe disabilities may be in finding a suitable reinforcer. To maintain tacting behavior, listeners generally provide the speaker with social amities. For some learners, such consequences may not represent an effective type of reinforcement. As a result, it may be difficult to establish and maintain tacting behavior until the value of social reinforcers can be conditioned.

In order for social praise to acquire reinforcement value, the pairing of praise (e.g. 'Thank you', 'Good', 'That's right') with some arbitrary yet effective reinforcer is necessary. However, the use of arbitrary reinforcement in comparison to the specific reinforcement characteristic of the mand (i.e., if you request an apple you receive one) may impede the initial acquisition of a verbal topography (Reichle, Lindamood, & Sigafoos, 1986; Rogers & Seigel, 1984; Saunders & Sailor, 1979). This impediment may be partially offset by using a variety of reinforcers (e.g. three items instead of one) when establishing tact repertoires (Egel, 1980, 1981).

Teaching learners to tact not only provides a basic repertoire consisting of the 'names' for objects and events in the real world, but it may also provide a means for benefitting others. Too often learners with severe disabilities are characterized as people who have things done for them or to them with little potential to 'do for others' (Guess, Benson, & Siegel-Causey, 1985). A well developed repertoire of spontaneous tacts may enable learners with severe disabilities to benefit others. Further participation as a member of the verbal community may also occur from strengthening other forms of social verbal behavior; in particular, the intraverbal response class.

Spontaneous Intraverbals

In an intraverbal relationship, the stimulus is verbal (e.g. 'Where do you live?'), the response is verbal ('Elm Street'), and there is no point-to-point correspondence between the form of the stimulus and the form of the response. Intraverbals often occur to one's own verbal behavior, such as when one completes the common sense 'a stitch in time saves...' or 'a penny saved is a penny...'. Intraverbals also include replies to the verbal stimuli supplied by others, as in answering questions.

The controlling stimuli for intraverbals are spoken, signed, or selected graphic symbols, and the responses are in vocal, gestural, or graphic modes. A graphic mode intraverbal is exemplified by a learner who points to symbols depicting an apple, orange, and banana either when asked to 'Name some fruits' or when the interventionist pointed to a symbol of fruit. In the first case, the stimulus and response are in different modes (i.e. vocal and graphic, respectively); in the latter case, both stimulus and response are in the graphic mode. The modality of sample and choice stimuli along with their relationship is an important variable in match-to-sample tasks (Dixon, 1981; McIlvane, Withstandley, & Stoddard, 1984; Sidman, 1971; Sidman & Cresson, 1973; Sidman, Cresson, & Willson-Morris, 1974; Sidman & Tailby, 1982; Spradlin, Cotter, & Bagley, 1973; Spradlin & Dixon, 1976).

While few language intervention programs for persons with severe disabilities explicitly teach intraverbal behavior (cf. Cipani, 1988; Lovaas, 1977; Sundberg, 1980, 1983), procedures used to teach other types of verbal operants often contain elements of the intraverbal relationship. For example, in teaching requests for food, learners are often asked, 'What do you want?'. In teaching object labels learners are frequently asked, 'What is this?'. Both of these questions are verbal stimuli that may potentially exert some control (resulting in a part mad-part intraverbal in the first case and part tact- part intraverbal in the second). However, it is unclear to what extent the verbal stimuli actually come to control appropriate responses. It is possible that the learner would continue to request foods or name displayed objects in the absence of a question (i.e. spontaneously) or even when irrelevant questions were asked (e.g. 'What day is it?' 'What is your name?').

A spontaneous intraverbal is therefore controlled simply and solely by a prior (and topographically distinct) verbal stimulus. The intraverbals 'coffee', 'tea', or 'milk' are spontaneous when controlled by the verbal stimulus BEVERAGES, for example, without having to be prompted by models (e.g. 'Say coffee...') or by the actual presence of a beverage.

Intraverbal repertoires have been developed in learners with severe disabilities through transfer of stimulus control procedures. In a series of experiments, Braam and Poling (1983) transferred control of many signs from pictures (i.e. tact variables) to verbal stimuli consisting of the manual signs for various object categories (e.g. FOOD, CLOTHES, SCHOOL). Both a constant 10-second and progressive time-delay procedures were used with success to establish intraverbals in three adolescents with mental retardation, two of whom were also hearing impaired. Final performance was characterized by learners responding with the signs for apple, sandwich, green beans, or orange, when presented with the signed verbal stimulus FOOD. Luciano (1986) systematically replicated the use of a progressive time-delay to transfer control of spoken words from pictures or objects (e.g. a picture of or a real apple) to the spoken stimulus, 'Tell me names of foods (drinks, clothes)'. The subjects of this study were three adolescents with severe mental retardation.

In both of these studies the subjects had initially rather sizeable verbal repertoires. One of the learners described by Braam and Poling (1983), for example, could name 'approximately 200 different objects, actions, and events...[and] would emit a sign gloss for [about 100 English words]...' (p.283). Success in developing intraverbal behavior may depend upon or be improved by the availability of a sizeable repertoire of other verbal operants (e.g. tacts). Both studies transferred stimulus control from objects or pictures of objects to spoken or signed verbal stimuli, that is, from tacts to intraverbals. The feasibility of transferring stimulus control from models to verbal stimuli (i.e. from echoic to intraverbal), or from the intraverbal to the mand, has yet to be demonstrated. The investigation of graphic-mode intraverbal behavior using transfer of stimulus control procedures is a much needed systematic replication to Braam and Poling (1983) and Luciano (1986).

Procedures to transfer stimulus control of a given verbal topography from one functional relationship (e.g. tact) to another (e.g. mand) are based in part on the assumption that every vocabulary element selected will be useful as both mand and tact or intraverbal. In practice, a given response may simply be taught as either a mand or tact, not both. for some mands (e.g. Listen! Look!) there do not appear to be any corresponding tacts (Skinner, 1957, p.188). In addition, there may be little reason to teach learners mands for certain events or properties of objects (e.g. 'Toothache', 'Rain', 'Beautiful'), but much reason to teach the same forms as facts.

There are logistical reasons for developing procedures to transfer stimulus control from intraverbal or tact variables to the establishing operation for topographies required primarily or exclusively as mands. For example, in teaching a learner to prepare soup, it may be necessary to teach mands for required utensils (e.g. can opener, pan, spoon). Teaching the appropriate mands in the context of the activity is beneficial, but to rely exclusively on this context may limit the number of available teaching opportunities. Intervention at a purely verbal level (e.g. 'What do you need to make soup?') would provide massed opportunities to develop, initially as intraverbals, the required topographies. The intraverbals could be established then as mands in the context of the soup making task through transfer of stimulus control procedures. Similar massed opportunities could be arranged in an object labelling or tact intervention.

Few intervention programs include procedures to teach intraverbal behavior either as a useful part of an overall verbal repertoire or as an instructional phase in teaching spontaneous mands. Although it is difficult to gauge the relative importance of each of the major classes of communicative behavior, the intraverbal includes many of the behaviors involved in conversation, answering questions, telling stories, and other more social aspects of verbal interaction. This class of verbal behavior represents an important and socially valid instructional goal for person with severe disabilities (Sundberg, 1986). However, most recent efforts directed toward teaching an intraverbal repertoire to persons with severe disabilities have used relatively basic tasks, such as reciting lists of colors, foods, or beverages (Kent-Udolf, 1989). This situation will no doubt change as the technology for and importance of teaching intraverbals are more widely emphasized.

Spontaneous Echoic Behavior

Vocal or motor imitation is presented often as a prerequisite to the development of functional speech or manual signs respectively (Kent, 1974; Lovaas, 1977, Stremel & Waryas, 1974). A generalized imitative repertoire greatly facilitates acquisition of speech. In graphic mode systems, imitated behavior is exemplified when the learner imitates pointing to the same symbol as the interventionist. Therefore, control by such 'gestural prompts' may facilitate acquisition of symbol selection responses.

Once acquired through imitation training, transfer of stimulus control procedures can be implemented to bring established topographies under the control of tact or mand variables (e.g. Hall & Sundberg, 1987; Risley & Wolf, 1967). Imitative repertoires have been strengthened in learners with severe disabilities to reliably prompt an approximation of the desired communicative form.

In addition to representing a useful instruction tool, a well developed imitative repertoire is singly important. For example, when calling directory assistance, it is helpful to repeat the telephone number as the operator presents each digit. The imitated response enables the speaker to 'rehearse' and/or 'remember' the number. Repeating what another has said or signed or selected from a communication board helps also to clarify the message. Calculator and Delaney (1986) found exact repetition was the most frequently used clarification strategy among a group of adults without mental retardation using communication boards. In this case, the adults were imitating their own verbal behavior when the listener requested clarification (e.g. 'What?'). Imitation of at least part of another's verbal behavior is also used to sustain a conversation (e.g. 'Nice weather', 'Yes, it is nice weather'). The benefits resulting from rehearsal, clarification, and sustaining a conversation would tend to occur for spontaneity imitative behavior.

At first glance, 'spontaneous imitation' may seem an oxymoron. But when a learner imitates another's speech, signs, or symbol selections without having to be explicitly instructed to do so (e.g. 'Say ball', 'Do this', 'Point to…'), the response is properly termed 'spontaneous'. The establishment of spontaneous imitation involves transfer of stimulus control from instructional cues (e.g. 'Say ball', 'Do…',) to the prior verbal stimulus, with reinforcement contingent upon the topographical match between stimulus and response. As with establishing spontaneous tacts, there are many ways for the interventionist to present verbal stimuli for imitation. For example, approaching a learner, looking directly at him or her, and then saying slowly and clearly, 'Hello', is very different than presenting a learner with a quick emitted head nod. Within the class of imitative behavior, spontaneity, imitating in the absence of models, may occur at various levels. While related studies supported transfer of stimulus control procedures for obtaining spontaneous imitative behavior, there are no demonstrations of acquisition of such verbal behavior.

SUMMARY

Instructional efforts to teach verbal behavior to persons with severe disabilities have met with tremendous success over the past 25 years. Systematic interventions based upon operant principles have proven effective in teaching a variety of verbal forms and functions in vocal, gestural, and graphic modes. Through these efforts much has been learned about how to teach verbal behavior as well as the nature of verbal behavior itself.

The growing skills in effectively teaching verbal behavior are reflected in a growing concern for facilitating spontaneous verbal behavior. Spontaneity is often lacking in the verbal repertoires taught to learners. This lack of spontaneity may stem from the narrow stimulus control established during intervention. Bringing verbal behavior under the control of more natural types of variables and fading control by instructional prompts are two interrelated and compatible methods. Transfer of stimulus control procedures is one mechanism through which this goal of spontaneity can be and has been achieved. Naturalistic training procedures (e.g. incidental teaching, mand-model) are additional mechanisms.

Most efforts to establish spontaneous verbal behaviour have focused on bringing requests under the control of the presence of objects. Contextual or motivative variables can be arranged to promote even more spontaneous forms of requests. Requests can be appropriate in a variety of circumstances, and hence multiple sources of control may need to be established for a given verbal operant.

Multiple stimulus control involves a given verbal topography participating in more than one functional relationship. When the same topography occurs as a mand (request), tact (label), echoic (imitation), intraverbal, textual or transcriptive response, it is no longer the same response. Therefore, each functional relationship may need to be taught. In teaching a response in the context of different functional relationships, spontaneity becomes an issue. The definitions of spontaneity in different verbal response classes and how this spontaneity can best be achieved are issues that need to be addressed empirically.

Much of the needed empirical work in facilitating the display of spontaneous verbal behavior will depend upon the classification of response classes and the definition of spontaneity within those response classes. Classification of verbal behavior is based upon the reinforcing practices of the verbal community. Skinner's (1957) analysis of these practices may have much to offer researchers and teachers who investigate and teach verbal behavior to persons with developmental disabilities.

Preparation of this chapter was supported, in part, by Cooperative Agreement No. H133B80048 funded by the National Institute on Disability and Rehabilitation Research, US Department of Education. The opinions expressed herein do not necessarily reflect the opinion of the US Department of Education, and no official endorsement should be inferred. Our appreciation is extended to James W. Halle, PhD., for his commenting on earlier versions of this chapter.

REFERENCES

Albin, R. W., & Horner, R. H. (1988). Generalization with precision. In R. H. Horner, G. Dunlap, & R. L. Koegel (Eds.), *Generalization and maintenance* (pp.99–120). Baltimore: Paul H. Brookes Publishing Co.

Ault, M. J., Wolery, M., Doyle, P. M., & Gast, D. L. (1989). Review of comparative studies in the instruction of students with moderate and severe handicaps. *Exceptional Children, 55*, 346–356.

Barrera, R. D., & Sulzer-Azaroff, B. (1983). An alternating treatments comparison of oral and total communication training programs with echolalic autistic children. *Journal of Applied Behavior Analysis, 16*, 379–394.

Barrett, R. P., & Sisson, L. A. (1987). Use of the alternating treatments design as a strategy for empirically determining language training approaches with mentally retarded children. *Research in Developmental Disabilities, 8*, 401–412.

Bates, E. (1976). *Language and context: The acquisition of pragmatics*. New York: Academic Press.

Beisler, J. M., & Tsai, L. Y. (1983). A pragmatic approach to increase expressive language in young autistic children. *Journal of Autism and Developmental Disorders, 13*, 287–303.

Benedict, H. (1979). Early lexical development: Comprehension and production. *Journal of Child Language, 6*, 183–200.

Braam, S. J., & Poling, A. (1983). Development of intraverbal behavior in mentally retarded individuals through transfer of stimulus control procedures: Classification of verbal responses. *Applied Research in Mental Retardation, 4*, 279–302.

Brady, D. O., & Smouse, A .D. (1987). A simultaneous comparison of three methods for language training with an autistic child: An experimental single case analysis. *Journal of Autism and Childhood Schizophrenia, 8*, 271–279.

Bricker, W. A., & Bricker, D. D. (1970). A program of language training for the severely handicapped child. *Exceptional Child, 37*, 101–111.

Bricker, W. A., & Bricker D. D. (1974). An early language training strategy. In R.L. Schiefelbusch, & L. L. Lloyd (Eds.), *Language perspectives: Acquisition, retardation, and intervention* (pp.431–468). Baltimore: University Park Press.

Calculator, S., & D'Altilio-Luchko, C. (1983). Evaluating the effectiveness of a communication board training program. *Journal of Speech and Hearing Disorders, 48(2)*, 185–191.

Calculator, S. M., & Delaney, D. (1986). Comparison of non-speaking and speaking mentally retarded adults' clarification strategies. *Journal of Speech and Hearing Disorders, 51*, 252–259.

Carr, E. G. (1982). Sign language. In R. Koegel, A. Rincover and A. Egel (Eds.), *Educating and understanding autistic children* (pp.142–157). San Diego: College Hill Press.

Carr, E. G. (1988). Functional equivalence as a mechanism of response generalization. In R. H. Horner, G. Dunlap, & R. L. Koegel (Eds.), *Generalization and maintenance: Lifestyle changes in applied settings.* (pp.99–120). Baltimore: Paul H. Brooks Publishing Co.

Carr, E. G., Binkoff, J. A., Kologinsky, E., & Eddy, M. (1978). Acquisition of sign language by autistic children I: Expressive labeling. *Journal of Applied Behavior Analysis, 11*, 489–501.

Carr, E. G., & Kologinsky, D. (1983). Acquisition of sign language by autistic children II: Spontaneity and generalization effects. *Journal of Applied Behavior Analysis, 16*, 297–314.

Catania, A. C. (1979). *Learning.* Englewood Cliffs, NJ: Prentice-Hall, Inc.

Charlop, M. H. Schreibman, L., & Thibodeau, M. G. (1985). Increasing spontaneous verbal responding in autistic children using a time delay procedure. *Journal of Applied Behavior Analysis, 18*, 155–166.

Chomsky, N. (1965). *Aspects of the theory of syntax*. Cambridge, MA: MIT Press.

Cipani, E. (1988). *Behavior analysis language program (BALP): Theory, assessment and training practices for personnel working with people with severe handicaps*. Bellevue, WA: Edmark Corporation.

Dixon, L. S. (1981). A Functional analysis of photo-objet matching skills of severely retarded adolescents. *Journal of Applied Behavior Analysis, 14*, 465–478.

Donellan, A., Mirenda, P., Mesaros, R., & Fassbender, L. (1984). Analyzing the communicative functions of aberrant behavior. *Journal of the Association for Persons with Severe Handicaps, 9*, 210–212.

Doss, S. (1988). *The effects of communication instruction on food stealing in adults with developmental disabilities*. Unpublished doctoral dissertation, university of Minnesota, Minneapolis.

Duker, P. C. & Moonen, X. M. (1986). The effects of two procedures on spontaneous signing with Down's Syndrome children. *Journal of Mental Deficiency Research, 30*, 355–364.

Duker, P. C. & Moonen, X. M. (1985). A program to increase manual signs with severely/profoundly mentally retarded students in natural environments. *Applied Research in Mental Retardation, 6*, 147–158.

Egel, A. L. (1980). The effects of constant vs. varied reinforcer presentation on responding by autistic children. *Journal of Experimental Child Psychology, 30*, 455–463.

Egel, A. L. (1981). Reinforcer variation: Implications for motivating developmentally disabled children. *Journal of Applied Behavior Analysis, 14*, 345–350.

Etzel, B., LeBlanc, J., Schilmoeller, K., & Stella, M. (1981). Stimulus control procedures in the education of young children. In S.W. Bijou, & R. Ruiz (Eds.), *Contributions of behavior modification to education* (pp.3–37). Hillsdale, NJ: Lawrence Erlbaum Associates.

Ferster, C. B. (1967). Arbitrary and natural reinforcement. *The Psychological Record, 17*, 341–347.

Ferster, C. B. (1972). Clinical reinforcement. *Seminars in Psychiatry, 4*, 101–111.

Gaylord-ross, R. J., Haring, T. G., Breen, C., & Pitts-Conway, V. (1984). The training and generalization of social interaction skills with autistic youth. *Journal of Applied Behavior Analysis, 17*, 229–247.

Glennen, S. L., & Calculator, S. M. (1985). Training functional communication board use: A pragmatic approach. *Augmentative and Alternative Communication, 1*, 134–142.

Gobbi, L., Cipani, E., Hudson, C., & Lapenta-Neudeck, R. (1986). Developing spontaneous requesting among children with severe mental retardation. *Mental Retardation, 24*, 357–363.

Goetz, L., Gee, R., & Sailor, W. (1985) Using a behavior chain interruption strategy to teach communication skills to students with severe disabilities. *Journal of the Association of Persons with Severe Disabilities, 10*, 21–30.

Goetz, L., Schuler, A., & Sailor, W. (1979). Teaching functional speech to the severely handicapped: Current issues. *Journal of Autism and Developmental Disorders, 9*, 325–343.

Goldin-Meadow, S., Seligman, M. E. P., & Gelman, R. (1976). Language in the two year old. *Cognition, 4*, 189–202.

Gray, B., & Ryan, B. (1973). *A language program for the non-language child*. Champaign, IL: Research Press.

Guess, D. (1969). A functional analysis of receptive language and productive speech: Acquisition of the plural morpheme. *Journal of Applied Behavior Analysis, 2,* 55–64.

Guess, D. (1980). Methods in communication instruction for severely handicapped persons. In W. Sailor, B. Wilcox, & L. Brown (Eds.), *Methods of instruction for severely handicapped students* (pp.195–225). Baltimore: Paul H. Brooks.

Guess, D., & Baer, D. M. (1973). An analysis of individual differences in generalization between receptive and productive language in retarded children. *Journal of Applied Behavior Analysis, 6,* 311–329.

Guess, D., Benson, H. A., & Siegel-Causey, E. (1985). Concepts and issues related to choice-making and autonomy among persons with severe disabilities. *Journal of the Association for Persons with Severe Handicaps, 10,* 79–86.

Guess, D., Sailor, W., & Baer, D. M. (1974). To teach language to retarded children. In R. L. Schiefelbusch, & L. Lloyd (Eds.), *Language perspectives: Acquisition, retardation, and intervention* (pp.529–563). Baltimore: University Park Press.

Guess, D., Sailor, W., Keogh, W. J., & Baer, D. M. (1976). Language development programs for severely handicapped children. In N.G. Haring, & L. Brown (Eds.), *Teaching the severely handicapped* (pp.301–324). New York: Grune and Stratten.

Hall, G., & Sundberg, M. L. (1987). Teaching mands by manipulating conditioned establishing operations. *The Analysis of Verbal Behavior, 5,* 41–53.

Halle, J. W. (1982). Teaching functional language to the handicapped: An integrative model of natural environment teaching techniques. *Journal of the Association for Persons with Severe Handicaps, 7,* 29–37.

Halle, J. W. (1987). Teaching language in the natural environment: An analysis of spontaneity. *Journal of the Association for Persons with Severe Handicaps, 12,* 28–37.

Halle, J. W. (1988). Adapting the natural environment as the context of training. In S. N. Calculator, & J. L. Bedrosian (Eds.), *Communication assessment and intervention for adults with mental retardation* (pp.155–185). San Diego: College-Hill.

Halle, J. W., Baer, D. M., & Spradlin, J. E. (1981). Teachers' generalized use of delay as a stimulus control procedure to increase language use in handicapped children. *Journal of Applied Behavior Analysis, 14,* 389–409.

Halle, J. W., Marshall, A. M., & Spradlin, J. E. (1979). Time delay: A technique to increase language use and facilitate generalization in retarded children. *Journal of Applied Behavior Analysis, 12,* 431–439.

Handen, B. L., & Zane, T. (1987). Delayed prompting: A review of procedural variations and results. *Research in Developmental Disabilities, 8,* 307–330.

Haring, T. G., Neetz, J. A., Lovinger, L., Peck, C., & Semmel, M. I. (1987). Effects of four modified incidental teaching procedures to create opportunities for communication. *Journal of the Association for Persons with Severe Handicaps, 12,* 218–226.

Harris, S. L. (1975). Teaching language to non-verbal children with emphasis on problems of generalizations. *Psychological Bulletin, 82,* 565–580.

Hart, B. (1985). Naturalistic language training techniques. In S. F. Warren and A. K. Rogers-Warren (Eds.), *Teaching functional language,* (pp.63–88). Austin, TX: Pro-Ed, Inc.

Hart, B., & Risley, T. R. (1968). Establishing use of descriptive adjectives in the spontaneous speech of disadvantaged preschool children. *Journal of Applied Behavior Analysis, 1,* 109–120.

Hart, B., & Risley, T. R. (1974). Using preschool materials to modify the language of disadvantaged children. *Journal of Applied Behavior Analysis, 7,* 243–256.

Hockett, C. F. (1960). The origin of speech. *Scientific American, 203*, 89–96.

Hubbell, R. D. (1977). On facilitating spontaneous talking in young children. *Journal of Speech and Hearing Disorders, 42*, 216–231.

Hunt, P., Goetz, L., Alwell, M., & Sailor, W. (1986). Using an interrupted behavior chain strategy to teach generalized communication responses. *The Journal of The Association for Persons with Severe Handicaps, 11,*, 196–204.

Kelleher, R. T., & Gollub, L. R. (1972). A review of positive conditioned reinforcement. *Journal of Applied Behavior Analysis, 5*, 543–597.

Kent, L. (1974). *Language acquisition program for the retarded or multiply impaired.* Champaign, IL:Research Press.

Kent-Udolf, L. (1989). Behavior Analysis Language Instrument and Behavior Analysis Language Program: A short review. *The Behavior Analyst, 12*, 79–80.

Koegel, R. L., O'Dell, M. C., & Koegel, L. K. (1987). A natural language teaching paradigm for non-verbal autistic children. *Journal of Autism and Developmental Disorders, 17*, 187–200.

Koegel, R. L., & Schreibman, L. (1977). Teaching autistic children to respond to simultaneous multiple cues. *Journal Experimental Child Psychology, 24,*, 199–311.

Koegel, R. L., & Wilhelm, H. (1973). Selective responding to the components of multiple visual cues by autistic children. *Journal of Experimental Child Psychology, 15*, 442–453.

Lamarre, J., & Holland, J. G. (1985). The functional independence of mands and tacts. *Journal of the Experimental Analysis of Behavior, 43*, 5–19.

Lee, V. L. (1981a). Prepositional phrases spoken and heard. *Journal of the Experimental Analysis of Behavior, 35*, 227–242.

Lee, V. L. (1981b). Terminological and conceptual revisions in the experimental analysis of language development: Why. *Behaviorism, 9*, 25–53.

Lee, V. L. (1988). *Beyond behaviorism.* Hillsdale, NJ: Lawrence Erlbaum.

Lennenberg, E. H. (1967). *Biological foundations of language.* New York: John Wiley and Sons, Inc.

Lovaas, O. I. (1977). *The autistic child: Language development through behavior modification.* New York: Irvington Publishers.

Lovaas, O. I., Berberich, J. P., Perloff, B. F., & Schaeffer, B. (1966). Acquisition of imitative speech by schizophrenic children. *Science, 151*, 705–707.

Lovaas, O. I., Koegel, R., Simmons, J. Q., & Long, J. S. (1973). Some generalization and follow-up measures on autistic children in behavior therapy. *Journal of Applied Behavior Analysis, 6*, 131–166.

Lovaas, O. I., & Schreibman, L. (1971). Stimulus overselectivity of autistic children in a two stimulus situation. *Behavior Research and Therapy, 9*, 305–10.

Lovaas, O. I., Schreibman, L., Koegel, R., & Rehm, R. (1971). Selective responding by autistic children to multiple sensory input. *Journal of Abnormal Psychology, 77*, 211–222.

Luciano, M. C. (1986). Acquisition, maintenance, and generalization of productive intraverbal behavior through transfer of stimulus control procedures. *Applied Research in Mental Retardation, 7*, 1–20.

MacDonald, J. D. (1976). Environmental language intervention. In F. B. Withrow, & C. J. Nygren (Eds.), *Language, materials and curriculum management for the handicapped learner.* Columbus, OH: Charles E. Merrill.

MacDonald, J. D., & Blott, J. P. (1974). Environmental language intervention: The rationale for a diagnostic and training strategy through rules, context, and generalization. *Journal of Speech and Hearing Disorders, 39,* 244196256.

McCarthy, D. (1954). Language development in children. In L. Carmichael (Ed), *Manual of child psychology* (2nd ed.), (pp.492–630). New York: John Wiley, & Sons Inc.

McCook, B., Cipani, E., Madigan, K., & LaCampagne (1988). Developing requesting behavior: Acquisition, fluency, and generality. *Mental Retardation, 26,* 137–143.

McCoy, J. F., & Buckholt, J. A. (1981). Language acquisition. In J.L. Matson, & J.R. McCartney (Eds.), *Handbook of behavior modification with the mentally retarded* (pp.281–330). New York: Plenum Press.

McGee, G. G., Krantz, P. J., Mason, D., & McClannahan, L. E. (1983). A modified incidental-teaching procedure for autistic youth: Acquisition and generalization of receptive object labels. *Journal of Applied Research Analysis, 16,* 329–338.

McGee, G. G., Krantz, P. J., & McClannahan, L. E. (1985). The facilitative effects of incidental teaching on preposition use by autistic children. *Journal of Applied Behavior Analysis, 18,* 17–31.

McIlvane, W. J., Withstandley, J. K., & Stoddard, L. T. (1984). Positive and negative stimulus relations in severely retarded individuals' conditional discrimination. *Analysis and Intervention in Developmental Disabilities, 4,* 235–251.

McLean, J. E., & Snyder-McLean, L. (1988). Application of pragmatics to severely mentally retarded children and youth. In R.L. Schiefelbusch, & L. L. Lloyd (Eds.), *Language perspectives: Acquisition, retardation, and intervention* (2nd ed.), (pp.255–288). Baltimore: University Park Press. Austin, Texas: Pro-ed.

Michael, J. (1982). Distinguishing between discriminative and motivational functions of stimuli. *Journal of Experimental Analysis Behavior, 37,* 149–155.

Michael, J. (1985). Two kinds of verbal behavior plus a possible third. *The Analysis of Verbal Behavior, 3,* 2–5.

Michael, J. (1987). *Advanced topics in behavior analysis.* Unpublished manuscript, Western Michigan University.

Michael, J. (1988). Establishing operations and the mand. *The Analysis of Verbal Behavior, 6,* 3–9.

Miller, J. F., & Yoder, D. E. (1974). An ontogenetic language teaching strategy for retarded children. In R. L. Schiefelbusch, & L. L. Lloyd (Eds.), *Language perspectives: Acquisition, retardation, and intervention,* (pp.505–528). Baltimore: University Park Press.

Oliver, C. B., & Halle, J. W. (1982). Language training in the everyday environment: Teaching functional sign use to a retarded child. *Journal of The Association for Persons with Severe Handicaps, 8,* 50–62.

Reichle, J., Anderson, H., & Schermer, G. (1986). Establishing the discrimination between requesting objects, requesting assistance and 'helping yourself'. Unpublished manuscript, University of Minnesota, Minneapolis.

Reichle, J., Lindamood, L., & Sigafoos, J. (1986). The match between reinforcer class and response class: Its influence on communication intervention strategies. *Journal of The Association for Persons with Severe Handicaps, 11,* 131–135.

Reichle, J., Rogers, N., & Barrett, C. (1984). Establishing pragmatic distinctions among the communicative functions of requesting, rejecting, and commenting in a severely retarded adolescent. *Journal of The Association for Persons with Severe Handicaps, 9,* 31–36.

Reichle, J., Sigafoos, J., & Piche, L. (1989). Teaching an adolescent with blindness and severe disabilities: A correspondence between requesting and selected preferred objects. *Journal of The Association for Persons with Severe Handicaps, 14,* 75–80.

Reichle, J., & Yoder, D. E. (1985). Communication board use in severely handicapped learners. *Language, Speech, and Hearing Services in Schools, 16,* 146–157.

Risley, T. R., & Reynolds, N. J. (1970). Emphasis as a prompt for verbal imitation. *Journal of Applied Behavior Analysis, 3,* 185–190.

Risley, T. R., & Wolf, M. (1967). Establishing functional speech in echolalic children. *Behavior Research and Therapy, 5,* 73–88.

Rogers, N., & Seigel, G. (1984). *Reinforcement strategies with a language disordered child.* Unpublished master's thesis, University of Minnesota, Minneapolis.

Rogers-Warren, A. K., & Warren, S. F. (1980). Mands for verbalization: Facilitating the display of newly trained language in children. *Behavior Modification, 4,* 361–382.

Romski, M. A., Sevcik, R. A., & Pate, J. L. (1988). Establishment of symbolic communication in persons with severe mental retardation. *Journal of Speech and Hearing Disorders, 53,* 94–107.

Saunders, R., & Sailor, W. (1979). A comparison of three strategies of reinforcement on two choice learning problems with severely retarded children. *AAESPH Review, 4,* 323–333.

Schaeffer, B. (1978). Teaching spontaneous sign language to non-verbal children: Theory and method. *Sign Language Studies, 21,* 317–352.

Schnaiter, R. (1978). Private causes. *Behaviorism, 6,* 1–12.

Schreibman, L. (1975). Effects of within-stimulus and extra- stimulus prompting on discrimination learning in autistic children. *Journal of Applied Behavior Analysis, 8,* 91–112.

Schreibman, L., Koegel, R. L., & Craig, M. S. (1977). Reducing stimulus overselectivity in autistic children. *Journal of Abnormal Child Psychology, 5,* 425–436.

Sidman, M. (1971). Reading and auditory-visual equivalence. *Journal of Speech and Hearing Research, 14,* 5–13.

Sidman, M., & Cresson, O. (1973). Reading and crossmodal transfer of stimulus equivalences in severe retardation. *American Journal of Mental Deficiency, 77,* 515–523.

Sidman, M., Cresson, O., & Willson-Morris, M. (1974). Acquisition of matching to sample via mediated transfer. *Journal of the Experimental Analysis of Behavior, 22,* 261–273.

Sidman, M., & Tailby, W. (1982). Conditional discrimination vs. matching to sample: An expansion of the testing paradigm. *Journal of the Experimental Analysis of Behavior, 37,* 5–22.

Siegel, G. M., & Vogt, M. C. (1984). Pluralization instruction in comprehension and production. *Journal of Speech and Hearing Disorders, 49,* 128–135.

Sigafoos, J., Doss, S., & Reichle, J. (1989). Developing mand and tact repertoires in persons with severe developmental disabilities using graphic symbols. *Research in Developmental Disabilities, 10,* 183–200.

Sigafoos, J., Mustonen, T., & Reichle, J. (1989). *Education and training initiative staff development module: Augmentative and alternative communication systems.* Minnesota Governor's Planning Council on Developmental Disabilities, Minneapolis, MN.

Simic, J., & Butcher, B. (1980). Development of spontaneous manding in language deficient children. *Journal of Applied Behavior Analysis, 13,* 523–528.

Sisson, L. A., & Barrett, R. P. (1984). An alternating treatments comparison of oral and total communication training with minimally verbal, mentally retarded children. *Journal of Applied Behavior Analysis, 17,* 559–566.

Skinner, B. F. (1945). The operational analysis of psychological terms. *Psychological Review, 52,* 270–277.

Skinner, B. F. (1953). *Science and human behavior.* New York: Macmillan.

Skinner, B. F. (1957). *Verbal behavior.* Englewood Cliffs, NJ: Prentice-Hall, Inc.

Smeets, P. M., & Striefel, S. (1976). Acquisition of sign reading by transfer of stimulus control in a retarded deaf girl. *Journal of Mental Deficiency Research, 20,,* 197–205.

Snyder, L. S. (1975). *Pragmatics in language disabled children: Their prelinguistic and early verbal performatives and presuppositions.* Unpublished doctoral dissertation, University of Colorado.

Sosne, J. B., Handleman, J. S., & Harris, S. L. (1979). Teaching spontaneous-functional speech to autistic type children. *Mental Retardation, 17,* 241–245.

Spradlin, J. E., Cotter, V. W., & Bagley, N. (1973). Establishing a conditional discrimination without direct training: A study of transfer with retarded adolescents. *American Journal of Mental Deficiency, 77,* 556–566.

Spradlin, J. E., & Dixon, M. H. (1976). Establishing conditional discriminations without direct training: Stimulus classes and labels. *American Journal of Mental Deficiency, 80,* 555–561.

Stokes, T. F., & Baer, D. M. (1977). An implicit technology of generalization. *Journal of Applied Behavior Analysis, 10,* 349–367.

Stokes, T. F., Baer, D. M., & Jackson, R. L. (1974). Programming the generalization of a greeting response in four retarded children. *Journal of Applied Behavior Analysis, 7,* 599–610.

Stremel, K., & Waryas, C. (1974). A behavioral psycholinguistic approach to language training. In L. McReynolds (Ed.), *Developing systematic procedures for training children's language.* American Speech and Hearing Monographs, No. 18.

Striefel, S., & Owens, C. R. (1980). Transfer of stimulus control procedures: Applications to language acquisition training with the developmentally handicapped. *Behavior Research of Severe Developmental Disabilities, 1,* 307–331.

Sundberg, M. L. (1980). *Developing a verbal repertoire using sign language and Skinner's analysis of verbal behavior.* Unpublished doctoral dissertation, Western Michigan University.

Sundberg, M. L. (1983). Language. In J. L. Matson, & S. E. Breuning (Eds.), *Assessing the mentally retarded* (pp.285–310). New York: Grune and Stratton.

Sundberg, M. L. (1986). *Procedures for establishing an intraverbal repertoire.* Paper presented at the twelfth annual convention, Association for Behavior Analysis, Milwaukee, WI.

Terrace, H. S. (1963). Discrimination learning with, & without 'errors'. *Journal of the Experimental Analysis of Behavior, 6,* 1–27.

Touchette, P. E. (1971). Transfer of stimulus control: Measuring the moment of transfer. *Journal of the Experimental Analysis of Behavior, 165,* 347–354.

Touchette, P. E., & Howard, J. S. (1984). Errorless learning: Reinforcement contingencies and stimulus control transfer in delayed prompting. *Journal of Applied Behavior Analysis, 17,* 175–188.

Warren, S. F., McQuarter, R. J., & Rogers-Warren, A. K. (1984). The effects of mands and models on the speech of unresponsive language-delayed preschool children. *Journal of Speech, & Hearing Disorders, 49,* 43–52.

Woods, T. S. (1984). Generality in the verbal tacting of autistic children as a function of 'naturalness' in antecedent control. *Journal of Behavior Therapy and Experimental Psychiatry, 15,* 27–32.

APPLYING CONTEXTUAL FEATURES OF GENERAL CASE INSTRUCTION AND INTERACTIVE ROUTINES TO ENHANCE COMMUNICATION SKILLS

James W. Halle, Janis Chadsey-Rusch and Lana Collet-Klingenberg

---

For a long time behavioral and social scientists have looked beyond the individual to include interaction with the environment for explanations of behavior (Peck, 1984; Rogers-Warren & Warren, 1977). The difficulty of conceptualizing individual-environment interaction as the determinant of behavior is the complexity that is introduced by the three terms: individual, environment, and interaction. As educators or behavioral scientists, we know relatively little about the internal functioning of the human organism. We also are in our infancy in terms of describing environments (refer to Morris & Midgley, 1990 and Peck, 1989 for varying taxonomies of potentially influential environmental variables) and understanding their influence on behavior. We have learned something about structuring environments in specific ways to produce specific changes in learners' responses (see Twardosz, 1984), but again our comprehension of person-environment interaction is crude relative to the subtlety and complexity that characterizes human behavior.

Throughout this chapter we are making the assumption that environment influences behavior. We are not denying that global or macro-level environmental variables may influence learning and behavior (Bronfenbrenner, 1977), however, we will focus attention on a micro, stimulus-level analysis. It is due to our belief that macro-level variables comprise many stimuli acting in concert to produce a particular effect that we are pursuing this focus of inquiry. Furthermore, the paradigm from which we will be drawing most heavily is behavioral, thus antecedent and stimulus control are labels we ascribe to phenomena of environmental influence. We are attempting to bring together recent applications related to stimulus control – some which have been so labeled and others which have not – that have relevance for the language instruction of learners with severe mental retardation or developmental disabilities.

A few additional assumptions are implicit in a discussion of the influence of stimulus control on instruction. First, behavior is not a random event; it occurs under the control of some stimuli regardless of our ability to identify such control. This assumption is similar to the earlier statement that context influences behavior. Related to this assumption is an often overlooked aspect of the contingencies of reinforcement – we often speak of consequences 'reinforcing or strengthening behavior' and neglect the fact that the unit reinforced is not behavior in isolation, but rather behavior-under-a-particular-set-of-conditions. When the probability of a response increases due to reinforcement, the frequency of the response does not increase at random times throughout the day; rather it occurs more frequently under a specific set of circumstances (i.e., those present when the response was reinforced).

One final assumption pertains to the dynamic nature of stimulus control. At any moment in time, a stimulus-response (S-R) relationship may be identifiable and measurable, but immediately upon the emission of the response, it meets with a consequence that will modify the S-R relationship (e.g., weaken, strengthen, or change controlling variables). Thus, stimulus control is ethereal and ever-shifting – characteristics that defy simple identification and measurement.

In the first section of the chapter, we will define stimulus control and describe how it is established experimentally as well as how it comes to influence behavior regardless of a teacher's intention. We will elaborate its beneficial as well as untoward effects. Two major sections will elaborate two relatively recent and promising procedures, based in part on the principle of stimulus control, and their potential contribution to the assessment and intervention of communicative performance by learners with severe disabilities.

DEFINITION AND DESCRIPTION OF STIMULUS CONTROL

Stimulus control is the influence on the probability of behavior exercised by variables in place before or during the emission of the behavior. The presence of a stimulus (that controls a response) signals that reinforcement is available if that particular response occurs. Such stimuli are said to 'set the occasion' for the response. To establish stimulus control intentionally, a teacher might use discrimination training that involves differential reinforcement. For example, to teach a learner to walk at a crosswalk when the light is green and to refrain from walking when the light is red, the teacher would reinforce (differentially) walking when the light is green and would withhold reinforcement for walking when the light is red. Across trials, the learner would acquire the discrimination and walk under appropriate stimulus conditions.

Some interesting issues arise in this example. First, has the teacher taught a new behavior? Probably not – the learner already was walking. Rather the teacher brought the behavior under a new form of stimulus control. We often speak of 'bringing a behavior under appropriate control' when we conduct discrimination training. This is not quite accurate because walking already was occurring at appropriate times and under appropriate conditions (e.g., walking to obtain desired items or to get to places). This teacher brought the behavior under the control of one more set of conditions (i.e., walking at a crosswalk when the light is green and not walking when the light is red).

Another interesting issue gleaned from this example is the function of, or motivation for the behavior. In the example, motivation for walking when the light is green is sustained by an extrinsic positive reinforcer offered by the teacher contingent upon correct responding. Is this the same motivation operating for the rest of us when we cross streets? Probably not – a combination of variables may be involved. For example, we probably have somewhere to go and to get there we need to cross streets; in addition to distal variables related to our destination, each street-crossing episode represents proximal motivational variables that in all likelihood are related to avoiding injury primarily and, perhaps, a fine for jay-walking secondarily. An important question arises from this analysis of function or motivation – will street-crossing occur safely, functionally, and in a generalized manner when the motivation sustaining it is at variance with that sustaining the behavior for most of us?

Much of this chapter will be devoted to methods for establishing stimulus control to produce desired communicative outcomes for learners with severe disabilities. It is important, however, to realize the ubiquitous nature of stimulus control – it operates whether we attend to it or not. Like reinforcement, it is a principle of behavior (Skinner, 1953). A few simple examples may be instructive. When you close a door to reduce the noise level or open a window to dissipate heat, stimulus control is at work. You are responding in ways that have produced reinforcement in the past when noise was interfering with your concentration or when you were too warm. These antecedent conditions are discriminative for particular responses that have a high probability of producing reinforcement.

Both of these examples are restricted to interaction with the physical environment and therefore do not involve some of the potential complexity introduced when interactions occur between people. However, even in these rather simple examples, complexity of analysis enters when one considers alternative or competing responses and their determinants. For example, under conditions identical to those described above, placing your hands over your ears or removing a layer of clothing constitute alternative responses that may produce the same environmental effects (by definition such responses comprise a response class). Efficiency may be the key to determining which response of a class of equivalent responses may occur in a particular situation (Horner & Billingsley, 1988; Horner, Sprague, O'Brian, & Heathfield, 1990).

The examples above represent unprogrammed or 'natural' establishment of stimulus control that is appropriate and adaptive (i.e., under conditions of discomfort, socially acceptable responses occur that meet with desired environmental effects). The next example is illustrative of formal instruction that produced intended stimulus control that was desirable in obtaining short-term objectives, but had unintended effects on long-term objectives.

In the 1970s, language training programs for learners with moderate and severe disabilities proliferated (e.g., Bricker & Bricker, 1974; Gray & Ryan, 1973; Guess, Sailor, & Baer, 1978; Kent, 1974; Stremel & Waryas, 1974). These programs were characterized by: one-to-one training; a physical locale that was isolated from natural settings and minimized the number of distracting stimuli; direct training of attention to the teacher and to the task; tight control of how, which, and when stimuli were introduced; systematic use of prompting hierarchies and correction procedures; and careful programming and scheduling of consequences determined by the accuracy of the response and the level of mastery. These highly controlled training situations constituted optimal conditions for teaching new language forms and structures (i.e., short-term objectives) and their efficacy was demonstrated.

Corresponding display of these forms on occasions that arise naturally in ordinary everyday encounters (i.e., long-term objective) did not occur. This problem has been referred to variously as a failure to generalize or to use language functionally and spontaneously (Goetz & Sailor, 1988; Halle, 1984, 1988; Reichle & Keogh, 1985; Warren, Baxter, Anderson, Marshall, & Baer, 1981). From a stimulus control perspective, however, there was no failure; language responses were acquired under highly restricted conditions (Carr & Kologinsky, 1983) – conditions that did not exist in the natural settings in which the learners lived. Thus, it could have been predicted that such responses would not be emitted on occasions that varied in numerous stimulus dimensions from those extant during acquisition. In a sense, learners were making a discrimination between the conditions under which they were trained and those present in their natural environments. We, unintentionally taught them to behave this way.

The stimulus control literature is rife with terminology and jargon that has been employed to enhance clarity and accuracy of the phenomena described. The two most common terms are discriminative stimulus (S^D) and S-delta (S^Δ). Discriminative stimuli are those stimuli which signal that reinforcement is available for a particular response. The presence of stimuli that have not been associated with reinforcement (or the absence of S^Ds) are referred to as S^Δ and are stimulus conditions which signal that reinforcement for a particular response is *not* available. Both S^Ds and S^Δs achieve their function through their association (or lack of) with reinforcement in the social and physical environment.

For example, green lights are discriminative for walking because pedestrians can cross the street safely, they avoid a ticket for jay-walking, and they make progress toward their destination. Red lights are S^Δ for walking (although they may be S^Ds for other responses such as pushing a button to activate a change from a red to a green light) because pedestrians may be struck by a moving vehicle or they may receive a ticket – neither constituting a reinforcing outcome. Similarly, when you arrive at work in the morning, you are more likely to greet a colleague when she establishes eye contact and smiles (S^D) than when she is typing at her computer (S^Δ). Your discriminating behavior occurs because you have learned that in the former instance you receive a reciprocal greeting and attention, whereas in the latter instance you receive little, if any, attention.

Stimulus control is fundamental to two relatively new and exciting procedures that have begun to appear in the literature relevant to those working with persons who have severe disabilities. These two procedures are *general case instruction* and *interaction routines*. Our purpose is to elaborate each of these procedures in the context of communicative competence of learners with severe disabilities. *Interaction routines* have been associated with the assessment and/or intervention of communicative skills, but their pervasive influence on communicative performance has not been recognized. Empirical demonstrations of general case instruction with communication targets are virtually nonexistent, although such an extension has been recommended (O'Neill, Horner, Albin, Storey & Sprague, 1990).

For each procedure, we will offer a definition, describe its stimulus control features, review a sample of its applications in the literature, and finally elaborate on its potential contribution to the assessment and intervention of language with learners who have severe disabilities.

STIMULUS CONTROL FEATURES OF GENERAL CASE INSTRUCTION

One of the important features of stimulus control that affects the analysis of communicative behavior at any level is that responses frequently occur as a function of multiple stimuli. For example, learners may be more likely to request a candy bar when they are hungry, when they are at a grocery store, or when they see someone eating a candy bar. The presence of all three of these stimuli together might set the occasion for a learner to request candy, or the presence of just one of these stimuli might function as a controlling stimulus.

Although single or multiple stimuli may set the occasion for a specific communicative behavior to occur, these same stimuli may also occasion any one of a number of responses that result in the same reinforcer (i.e., they have the same function or effect on the environment). For example, when a learner sees a candy bar, the learner may request the candy by pointing, by saying, 'May I have a candy bar?', or by exclaiming, 'Boy, that candy bar looks good'.

When individuals have learned to make requests for food (e.g., candy) under specific stimulus conditions (e.g., seeing someone eat a candy bar), and have also learned to make requests when any members of the stimulus class are present (e.g., hunger, grocery store), then individuals have learned the 'general case' (Becker & Engelmann, 1978; Horner, Sprague, & Wilcox, 1982). General case instruction is inextricably related to the principles of stimulus control and has contributed significantly to the improvement of generalized responding for learners with severe disabilities. In this section of the chapter, general case procedures are described and representative studies discussed. These procedures have been used with success across a wide variety of behaviors (e.g., street crossing, grocery store purchasing, dressing) but their application has not been extended to communicative behaviors. Consequently, the application of the general case model to teach communicative behavior to learners with severe disabilities is proposed.

A Description of General Case Programming

General case programming for learners with severe disabilities has been described and elaborated by Horner and his colleagues (Albin & Horner, 1988; Horner, Bellamy, & Colvin, 1984; Horner, McDonnell, & Bellamy, 1986; Horner et al., 1982). As Horner et al. (1982) indicate, stimulus control is central to the general case approach. When particular responses repeatedly produce specific outcomes in the presence of certain environmental events, or discriminative stimuli, then stimulus control has occurred. Although stimulus control is generally thought of as unidimensional (i.e., discriminative stimulus (S^D) → response (R)), in general case, stimuli are conceptualized as being multi-dimensional and involve a stimulus class rather than a single stimulus. 'The general case has been learned when any member from a group of stimuli is able to produce the same effect as the single $S^{D'}$ (Horner et al., 1982, p.66). The stimulus class contains stimuli that all share a common and specific set of characteristics; stimuli that contain only a few or none of those characteristics are not members of the stimulus class.

Thinking of stimulus control in relationship to stimulus classes rather than in relationship to a single stimulus has intuitive appeal for work in applied settings. Early operant work was instrumental in demonstrating the principles of discrimination and stimulus control, but most of this research was carried out in analogue settings and generally involved discriminations between only two stimuli. Because it is highly likely that multiple stimuli set the occasion for the majority of our responding in natural settings, it may be more prudent to think of stimulus control in relationship to stimulus classes rather than single stimuli.

Although the general case approach rests on the assumption that all members of a stimulus class occasion the same response, it is just as important to recognize that stimuli which are *not* members of the stimulus class (i.e., s-deltas) should *not* set the occasion for responding. If responses occur in the presence of s-deltas, they would be regarded as inappropriate. For example, if learners with severe disabilities were taught to say 'Hi, how are you?' to a variety of people that they knew (e.g., female and male individuals of varying ages across a variety of settings), but were never taught *not* to say 'Hi, how are you?' to strangers, then in some contexts, or under some stimulus conditions, learners might be violating social rules.

Horner and his colleagues (Albin & Horner, 1988; Horner et al., 1982, 1984, 1986) stress the importance of avoiding errors, or inappropriate responding, through general case programming. In particular, when examples are selected for teaching, they must be of two types – positive and negative. Positive examples are used to teach the learner how to respond under a specific set of conditions and negative examples are used to teach the learner the conditions under which responding should not occur or when some other alternative response should be made (Albin & Horner, 1988). As Albin and Horner suggest, negative teaching examples can vary on a continuum depending on whether they contain stimulus features that are maximally or minimally different from the positive examples (e.g., they contain all of the critical features of the stimulus class but one).

As an example, let's consider the scenario presented above involving teaching a learner with severe disabilities to initiate the greeting, 'Hi, how are you?' A minimally different negative teaching example would be to take the learner to a shopping mall where he or she would be likely to encounter strangers. Strangers contain all but one of the critical features that define the stimulus class of positive examples. For example, strangers can engage in the same behaviors that set the occasion for greetings (e.g., establish proximity and eye contact) as those individuals who would be included in the stimulus class of people to greet. Strangers and known individuals differ only on the critical feature of familiarity.

An example of a maximally different negative teaching example would be to place the learner in a social context where greetings clearly would be viewed as socially unacceptable. For example, if a learner were attending a play, it would be inappropriate for the learner to greet the actors and actresses on the stage. Actors and actresses performing live share few of the relevant features of the stimuli in the class (e.g., proximity, smile, eye contact) that the learner should learn to greet.

The idea of positive and negative teaching examples brings up another important point related to general case programming. Horner and his colleagues (e.g., Horner et al., 1982) also stress how important it is for learners to ignore variation in irrelevant stimulus characteristics. Consider again, the example presented above. It should not matter to the learner if the people he or she knows are male or female, black or white, short or tall, young or old, at school or at work, and so on. Variation in these stimulus characteristics does not affect their membership in the stimulus class of people who should be greeted, and the learner must be able to respond the same way when encountering any of these individuals.

The Process of General Case Instruction

The process for teaching the general case has been carefully described by Engelmann and Carnine (1982) and Horner et al. (1982); the reader is referred to these sources for an in-depth analysis. Essentially, the process includes the following series of steps:

1. Define the instructional universe by specifying the range of relevant stimulus and response variations within that universe.
2. Select teaching and test examples from the instructional universe.
3. Sequence the teaching examples.
4. Teach the examples and test for generalization.

Defining the instructional universe

The first step in the general case approach is to define operationally the set of stimulus conditions and response variations across which the learner should perform the targeted skill. As Horner et al. (1986) point out, the instructional universe of the learner will change depending upon the behavior being trained, the abilities of the learner, and the characteristics of the performance environment. Instructional universes can vary – for example, a student could be taught to purchase a soft drink at all of the movie theaters in town (Instructional universe #1) or at all of the movie theaters and sporting facilities in town

(Instructional universe #2). Identifying the instructional universe assures that a specific outcome has been selected to judge the effects of teaching.

After the instructional universe has been defined, then the variations associated with the stimuli and responses required in that universe have to be specified. As Horner et al. (1982) indicate, this information is critical for selecting the examples used during instruction. Within this task, the generic responses associated with competent performance are first identified. Then, the generic discriminative stimuli that set the occasion for the generic responses to occur are noted. Variation across generic stimuli and responses are documented, and exceptions and potential errors that may make it difficult for the learner to discriminate relevant from irrelevant stimuli are identified.

Selecting teaching and test examples

After all the variations associated with the stimuli and responses present in the instructional universe have been identified, examples are selected from this group for teaching and testing. Since one example cannot provide all the variations present, representative examples must be selected that sample the range of variation (positive examples) as well as exceptions and errors (negative examples). Guidelines for selecting examples have been proposed by Becker, Engelmann, and their colleagues (Becker & Engelmann, 1978; Becker, Engelmann, & Thomas, 1975; Engelmann & Carnine, 1982) and Horner et al. (1982) and are presented in Table 1.

Table 1: Guidelines for Selecting Teaching and Testing Examples (Adapted from Horner et al., 1982)

---

1. Select the minimum number of training examples that sample the full range of stimulus and response variation in the instructional universe.

2. Select examples that contain equal amounts of new information.

3. Select examples that vary irrelevant stimuli.

4. Select examples that teach the student what not to do as well as what to do.

5. Select examples that include significant exceptions.

6. Select examples that are logistically feasible.

Sequence teaching examples

Horner et al. (1982) recommend that examples be taught in a particular sequence in order to save time and minimize errors. First, it is recommended that all components of an activity or skill be taught within each training session. Thus, if a task analysis has been conducted for a particular activity (e.g., handwashing) all the components associated with handwashing would be taught, rather than only teaching one or two components at a time (e.g., turning on the water, applying soap).

Second, multiple examples are taught within each session (i.e., no example is taught to criterion before another example is presented). Maximally and minimally different positive and negative examples are presented one right after the other within each session so that the individual learns under which conditions responses should and should not occur. Previously mastered or learned examples are reviewed during each session, and the general case is taught before significant exceptions are introduced.

Teaching examples and testing for generalization

After examples have been sequenced, they are taught. Traditional teaching strategies, such as those associated with systematic instruction (Snell, 1988) prompting, fading, shaping, and reinforcement are used. Once the examples have been taught, the student is tested on a new set of examples to see if generalized responding has been acquired.

Effectiveness of General Case Instruction

General case instruction has been used effectively to teach learners with severe disabilities a variety of behaviors. These learners have demonstrated generalized responding across a range of nontrained conditions or settings for such tasks as street crossing (Horner, Jones, & Williams, 1985), vending machine use (Sprague & Horner, 1984), telephone use (Horner, Williams, & Steveley, 1987), grocery-item selection (Horner, Albin, & Ralph, 1986), soap dispenser use (Pancsofar & Bates, 1985), dressing (Day & Horner, 1986) and pouring (Day & Horner, 1989).

Horner et al. (1987) examined the effects of general case instruction for selecting teaching examples for making and receiving telephone calls. Four high school students with moderate and severe mental retardation were taught to use the telephone; their generalized use of the telephone was assessed across three nontraining settings (i.e., home, school, and community) via a counterbalanced multiple-baseline design.

In order to select the teaching and probe examples, Horner et al. (1987) followed the guidelines provided by Horner et al. in 1982. The instructional universe was defined as telephone usage at home, at school, and in the community. The responses associated with 'receiving telephone calls' and 'making telephone calls' were defined and their discriminative stimuli were identified. For example, the generic responses associated with 'making calls' consisted of:

picking up the receiver, dialing the number, saying 'Hello', identifying self, requesting to speak to the desired person, initiating a conversation or leaving a message; and saying 'Good-bye' and hanging up. Within each of these generic responses, relevant stimuli and training variations were specified. For example, one of the relevant stimuli associated with picking up the receiver was the type of phone: the training variations present included a standard (rotary) telephone, pay telephone (push button), and trimline (rotary). Ten training trials each were selected for making and receiving telephone calls. Within each set of training trials, the stimulus and response conditions sampled the range of variation of relevant stimuli experienced in regular telephone use.

The results reported by Horner et al. (1987) demonstrated that general case instruction was efficient and effective for teaching generalized telephone use to learners with moderate and severe disabilities. In addition, parent reports regarding telephone use 18 months after training revealed that all four participants were receiving an average of at least two calls per week and two of the four were making calls daily.

In another study conducted by Day and Horner (1986), general case instruction was compared to single-instance training. Six individuals with mental retardation first were taught to put on pullover shirts with single-instance training and then with general case training. Following training with a single shirt, all of the subjects displayed limited success with eight nontraining shirts. It was not until two other shirts that sampled the range of stimulus and response variations for pullover shirts were added to training that generalization occurred across nontraining shirts. Although the design of this study made it difficult to separate the individual effects of single-instance training from general case training, because of a sequence confound, other research suggests the effectiveness of general case instruction (e.g., Horner & Budd, 1985; Horner et al., 1987).

In summary, Horner and his colleagues have described a series of steps used to implement general case instruction. These steps consist of defining the instructional universe by specifying the range of relevant stimulus and response variation, selecting teaching and test examples from the universe, sequencing the examples, and teaching and testing for generalization.

Past research has demonstrated the effectiveness of general case instruction. Individuals with severe disabilities have learned a variety of generalized behaviors such as street crossing, telephone use, and grocery-item selection. Within each of these skill areas, it has been relatively easy to define the instructional universe and specify the relevant stimulus and response dimensions. However, when one considers using the general case approach with more complex behavior such as language, the task becomes more difficult. Certainly, the goal of language acquisition is the same as those for which general case instruction has been applied: for learners to emit generalized responding across multiple stimulus conditions. It is an empirical question whether or to what degree this stimulus control approach can be used to facilitate language learning.

A Relationship Between Language and Stimulus Control

Language is extremely complex, consisting of such diverse areas of study as phonology, semantics, pragmatics, and syntax. Of all of these areas, the study of pragmatics has most significantly influenced language programming for learners with severe disabilities (Hart, 1981; Kaiser & Warren, 1988; Keogh & Reichle, 1985; Warren & Rogers-Warren, 1985). Pragmatics refers to the use of language in social contexts, and although it has been studied and described by linguists and sociolinguists (e.g., Bates, 1976; Dore, 1974; Searle, 1969), it is also possible to interpret it within the context of stimulus control.

Pragmatic knowledge and skills encompass three broad areas (McCormick & Schiefelbusch, 1984). One of these areas concerns the intentional meaning of the communicative act. That is, when individuals communicate, they intend for their utterances to have specific effects on listener behavior. If the speaker asks the listener to close the door, and the listener does so, then the intended effect of the speaker's utterance has occurred. It is not always possible to determine the intent of an utterance from its topographical form because the same form of the utterance can have a variety of meanings; it is also not always possible to determine the intent of the utterance *a priori*. Kaiser and Warren (1988) suggest that it is more useful to look at the function of the utterance, where the function is determined by observing the actual consequences associated with the communicative exchange (Skinner, 1957).

Another pragmatic area discussed by McCormick and Schiefelbusch (1984) concerns the rules associated with language use and how these rules are dependent on listener and contextual variables. Knowledge and skillful use of these rules enable an individual to know 'when to speak, when not to, and as to what to talk about, with whom, when where, in what manner' (Hymes, 1972; p.277). Speakers must be able to select the best possible forms for their communication to serve the function they intend based on such things as age and prior relationship with the listener, what the listener already knows about the topic, and contextual variables, such as physical setting, presence of other people, and so forth. For example, the way in which speakers would ask their friends for directions to a bathroom at a football game might be very different from the way in which they would ask a librarian for directions to a bathroom at the library. Even though they may be hard to identify and define, rules for our social use of language do exist and most people can recognize and agree on instances when they are broken (McFall, 1982).

The last pragmatic area discussed by McCormick and Schiefelbusch (1984) concerns the rules used in dialogue – that is, the rules associated with conversational exchanges. Successful speakers know how to successfully enter and initiate conversations, leave or terminate conversations, and maintain conversations by taking turns, shifting topics, handling digressions, and asking questions.

Can an analysis of stimulus control within the context of the general case approach be applied to the three areas of pragmatics discussed above? Perhaps only in a simplistic fashion due to the complexity of the stimuli that set the occasion for communication and the difficulty inherent in identifying them as well as the *a priori* reinforcers associated with the communicative act. Implied within these areas of pragmatics is the assumption that particular stimulus classes (i.e., listener, contextual, and discourse variables) set the occasion for particular responses to occur (i.e., the communicative act) and if that communicative act functions in the way the speaker intends (or is reinforcing), then the likelihood of that same communicative act occurring again under similar stimulus conditions is enhanced. Consider the following example. Under certain conditions (e.g., a child is thirsty and in the presence of his mother who is drinking orange juice at home), a child makes a request for a drink (intent), and his mother gives him a sip of the juice. There is a high likelihood that under similar stimulus conditions, the child will make the same request again. Now let's assume a female guest is visiting the mother and they are both drinking orange juice. If the child requests a drink from the female guest, the mother will likely admonish the child and tell him it is not polite to request a drink from guests. After the child requests the drink from the mother, she gives him a drink. Within this paradigm, the child has learned to request a drink in the presence of the mother and the juice (discriminative stimuli), but not to request the drink in the presence of a female other than mom (s-delta) but who is also drinking juice.

The discriminations that must be made in order to know when, where, and how to respond to affect the listener in intended ways seems almost infinite (at least from a teaching perspective). Certainly, over time, children without disabilities learn to use language effectively across a variety of contexts without much systematic intervention – they learn how to communicate effectively, in part, because of stimulus control relationships formed by their interactions and experiences with others. Unfortunately, this seemingly effortless learning does not occur in the same way for persons with severe disabilities.

Learners with severe disabilities must be taught that their communication can affect the environment through the mediation of others under certain stimulus conditions. Ideally, they need to learn under which 'natural' conditions their communicative efforts will and will not be reinforced.

Applying the Process of General Case Instruction to Language

As Horner et al. (1982) suggest, there are several steps in the general case approach. Of all of these steps, the first one which consists of defining the instructional universe by specifying the range of relevant stimulus and response variations within that universe seems the most directly related to stimulus control and the most problematic in relation to language intervention procedures. The other steps (selecting and sequencing examples, and teaching and testing for generalization) seem less complicated. This should not imply, however, that these steps would have little impact on language instruction. On the contrary, certain procedures advocated within the general case approach (e.g., part versus whole training) merit discussion in their own right (Weld & Evans, 1990), but are beyond the scope of this chapter.

The first step in the general case approach is to define the instructional universe by specifying the range of relevant stimulus and response variations within that universe. In many studies seeking to teach learners with severe disabilities pragmatic classes of behavior such as requesting, language responses have been taught under restricted stimulus conditions (e.g. Reichle, Barrett, Tetlie, & McQuarter, 1987; Reichle, Rogers, & Barrett, 1984). Although generalized responding has occurred, it has been narrowly defined, and one could not claim that learners were taught to make requests across a range of relevant stimulus and response variation.

It would seem that the number of stimulus and response variations associated with the behavior of requesting would be numerous. As Kaiser and Warren (1988) have stated 'Language use is more than learning which specific stimuli control particular responses and then (forever) acting upon this information. It is learning increasingly complex conditional discriminations for controlling relationships and integrating and reorganizing response classes on the basis of newly learned information and/or environmental contingencies. In short, the process is never static' (p.411). This statement may seem to imply that the task of specifying the stimulus and response variation of language within the instructional universe is insurmountable. Depending on how one wants to define the instructional universe, however, the task may be feasible.

As Horner et al. (1982) suggest, the instructional universe of the learner will vary depending upon the behavior trained, the abilities of the learner, and the characteristics of the performance environment. Considering these variables, the instructional universe for language training needs to be chunked into some manageable yet comprehensive unit.

As an example, let's consider the communicative act of making requests for objects and food. Let's also assume that we want to teach this behavior to a female adolescent who is verbal, echolalic, and rarely initiates requests but who has the vocabulary in her repertoire to make such requests. The instructional universe for this learner has been defined as 'making requests for objects and food under appropriate stimulus conditions at school and work'. Specifically, these requests consist of (a) requesting a coke during lunch at school (Request 1), (b) requesting a hamburger at school (Request 2), (c) requesting a radio during free time at school (Request 3), (d) requesting more condiment supplies when she runs out of them at work (Request 4), (e) requesting lotion for her hands at school (Request 5) and (f) requesting the key to unlock the bathroom at work (Request 6). Certainly, this instructional universe could be expanded or

Table 2: Stimulus Variation Matrix

General Responses	Generic Stimuli	Request 1	Request 2	Request 3	Request 4	Request 5	Request 6
				Specific Antecedent Stimuli			
	Activity: Initiated Requests for Objects and Food			Instructional Universe: Requests in school & work settings			
1. Get the listener's attention	Listeners who have the potential for honoring the request	Presence of coke (and listeners); Thirst; Different servers working in cafeteria line; Servers look expectantly at speaker; Servers say 'May I help you?', 'What do you want?'	Presence of hamburger (and listeners); Hunger; Same as Request 1, but different server	presence of radio (and listeners); 10:15-11:00 a.m.; Teacher or aids say 'It's free time.'; Teachers or aids look expectantly at speaker	Different times throughout day; Absence of condiments; Supervisor and co-worker working in different sections of work setting, but nearby; Supervisor or co-worker says, 'Do you need something?' 'Whats up?'	After washing hands; Presence of lotion (and listeners); Teacher/aid says 'Do you want something?'; Teacher/aid looks expectantly at speaker	Urge to go to the bathroom; Supervisor is working in different section at worksite, but nearby; Supervisor looks expectantly or says, 'yes?', or 'do you need something?'
2. Make the request	Eye contact with listener	Servers look at speaker	← Same	Teacher/aids look at speaker	Supervisor/ co-workers look at speaker	Teacher/aid looks at speaker	Supervisor looks at speaker
3. Thank the listener	Listener gives requested food, object	Coke	Hamburger	Radio	Condiments	Lotion	Key
4. Thanks anyway	Listener indicates speaker can't have the item requested	No It's gone We don't have any	← Same	← Same	← Same	← Same	← Same

Table 3: Response Variation Matrix

Activity: *Initiated requests for objects and food*						
Generic Responses	Instructional Universe: *Six requests in school & work settings*					
	Request 1	Request 2	Request 3	Request 4	Request 5	Request 6
1. Get the listener's attention	Say 'Excuse me' Touch listener's arm	← Same	← Same	← Same	← Same	← Same
2. Make the request	'I want coke, please'	'I want hamburger, please'	'I want radio, please'	'I want more condiments, please'	'I want lotion, please'	'I want the key, please'
3. Thank the listener	'Thank you' 'Thanks anyway'	↑ ← Same ↑ ← Same	↑ ← Same ↑ ← Same	↑ ← Same ↑ ← Same	↑ ← Same ↑ ← Same	↑ ← Same ↑ ← Same

Table 4: General Case Analysis Form

Activity: *Initiated Requests for Objects and Food*		Instructional Universe: *Six Requests In School & Work Settings*		
Generic Responses	*Generic Stimuli*	*Relevant Stimulus Variation*	*Relevant Response Variation*	*Exceptions/Potential Errors*
1. Get the listener's attention	Listeners who have the potential for honoring the requests	More than one server in cafeteria line	'Excuse me'	Listeners are helping, talking to, or serving someone else
		At least two different listeners look expectantly or are present at work and school	Touch listener's arm	
		At least two different listeners ask 'What do you want? What's up?'		
		Absence of condiments		
		Different times of day after break, after washing hands		
		Urge to go to the bathroom		
		Presence of at least two objects (e.g., radio, coke)		
2. Make the Request	Eye contact with listener	Listeners look at speaker	'I want coke (hamburger, radio, condiments, lotion, key) please'	
3. Thank the listener	Listener gives the object or food	Coke, hamburger, radio condiments, lotion, key	'Thank you'	
	Listener indicates speaker can't have item requested	'No'	'Thanks anyway'	
		'It's gone'		
		'We don't have any'		

reduced, but for this learner (and this example), these requests will represent the instructional universe.

After the instructional universe has been defined, then the variations associated with the stimuli and responses present in that universe need to be specified. The stimulus control and response variation matrices for requesting objects and foods at school and work are presented in Tables 2 and 3. The final general case analysis form is shown in Table 4.

Analysis of the General Case Language Matrix

After conducting this analysis, several things become obvious. First, the range of stimuli associated with this instructional universe are quite diverse. Requesting would need to vary across people (e.g., servers, co-workers); physical settings (e.g., work, cafeteria); time (e.g., after break, 10:15 a.m.) verbalizations from others (e.g., 'What's up?', 'It's free time'.); interoceptive stimuli (e.g., urge to void); presence and absence of objects (e.g., radio, condiments); and nonverbal behavior (e.g., expectant looks).

In contrast, the responses needed to make requests are far less varied, consisting primarily of verbalizations that differ in terms of the label of the object or food being requested. Certainly, the forms that could be used to make requests could be quite diverse, ranging from gestures to varying verbal forms (e.g., 'I want coke, please' or 'Coke, please'.). Response requirements would need to be matched to each learner's current level of expressive language functioning and therefore would probably not vary a great deal. Even though a gesture could function as a request, intervention programs would likely strive to teach the most conventional form of communication because the most conventional form would probably be the most useful and efficient for the learner.

A second issue that becomes apparent from the analysis of the matrix is that one would need to teach nearly all the stimulus and response variations associated with each example. That is, each request in this universe presents new information that would need to be included in both the probe and teaching examples. Therefore, it becomes difficult to pick a subset for teaching and a subset for generalization probes. Perhaps this occurred as an artifact of this example. Had the instructional universe been defined to include only requests for food across a variety of restaurant settings (e.g., several different fast food restaurants, cafes, soda fountains, and elegant restaurants), it would have been easier to select teaching and generalization probes because the stimulus variation, although diverse, would have been more restricted because all of the settings and responses were of one general type (i.e., requests for food in restaurants). In the present example, the types of requests focused on food and objects across a wide range of settings and people. It is an empirical question whether the instructional universe for requests should be restricted to one pragmatic class (i.e., food) or should be considered across pragmatic classes (e.g., food, objects, assistance, affection). An equally interesting question arises: if requesting were taught within one class (e.g., food) or within several classes (e.g. food, assistance), would generalization occur to other classes of requests (e.g., objects, affection) (Haring, 1985).

Conclusion

The principle of stimulus control inherent in general case programming would seem to have relevance for language instruction in the area of pragmatics for learners with severe disabilities. The desirability of this approach emphasizes an analysis of multiple stimuli that may set the occasion for communicative responding, and clearly, these can be numerous. Except for milieu teaching (e.g., Halle, Marshall, & Spradlin, 1979; Hart, 1985), past language programs have taught learners to respond under restricted stimulus conditions that have not resulted in generative responding (Bryan & Joyce, 1985). Even with milieu strategies, a systematic analysis of the stimuli that set the occasion for responding is not conducted; however, communicative responses are generally solicited under varying stimulus conditions (e.g., across a variety of toys or a variety of adult cues).

It remains to be seen whether generative responding will occur if general case instruction is applied to language intervention programs. An analysis of the stimulus variables that could potentially control communicative responding has great intuitive appeal, thus the strategy seems worthy of consideration.

STIMULUS CONTROL FEATURES OF INTERACTIVE ROUTINES

A pervasive phenomenon in both the child language literature and the language literature pertaining to learners with disabilities is that of routines or rituals (Bruner, 1975; Ratner & Bruner, 1978; Snyder-McLean, Solomonson, McLean, & Sack, 1984). Routines have been used in a multitude of ways to assess and teach a variety of language forms and functions, but their role in social communication has been hypothesized to be much more basic than a tool for assessment and intervention. Bruner and his colleagues have speculated that routines are central to the acquisition of language because they are the context within which the earliest communicative acts occur. Rules about when and how to interact are learned in the context of caregiving and play routines between mother and infant.

Abelson (1981) elaborated another basic interpretation of the influence of routines, but his interpretation was not confined to language. He used the term 'script' and attempted to reveal its unifying role within cognitive, social, developmental, and clinical psychology. Abelson believes the script concept has heuristic value in understanding the schematic nature of mental representations of real-world objects and events. He cites an example of the psychological reality of scripts in the following story: 'John was feeling very hungry as he entered the restaurant. He settled himself at a table and noticed that the waiter was nearby. Suddenly, however, he realized that he'd forgotten his reading glasses' (p.715). The realization that he'd forgotten his glasses makes sense to the reader only when an implied fact is considered: John needed his glasses to read the menu. But a menu was never mentioned, thus the question arises about the origin of this implication or expectation. Schank and Abelson (1977) invoke the 'restaurant' script as explanatory. That is, the reader is familiar with a standard sequence of events that characterize typical activities at a restaurant and thus 'fills in' the missing information.

Abelson (1981) discussed eight factors that define script variation. Three examples are described here. *Equifinal actions* are very similar to the notion of response classes; different forms of behavior produce the same result. In a restaurant, a customer can order by naming the food, providing a number for the item, or pointing to the item on the menu. *Scene selection* is another factor that applies to routines that do not impose a sequential constraint. The greater the requirement for sequence the less *scene selection* allowed. The learners to whom this chapter is devoted may have more difficulty acquiring routines in which sequential properties are minimal because for them consistent sequencing of events is the 'glue' that holds routines together.

The two variations described above can be anticipated; others represent unexpected sources of variation. One example of these is *interference* which assumes two forms: *obstacles* and *errors*. *Obstacles* remove a precondition for a given event (e.g., menus are on the table when customers arrive, pre-empting menu requests). *Errors* are incorrect execution of an event within the routine (e.g., french fries were served instead of a baked potato). *Interference* is very similar to methods that currently are employed intentionally to evoke communicative acts by learners with severe disabilities (discussed more fully in the latter part of this section).

A third rather basic perspective on the concept of routines is their pervasive influence on the organization of our lives. Our daily schedule of events is organized around a multiplicity of routines and subroutines of our own design. For example, when I (the first author) wake up in the morning, I reach for my glasses, then put on my watch, then get dressed, and finally go downstairs to begin preparations for breakfast. Within each of these steps of my 'wake-up' routine, I engage in subroutines (e.g., each piece of clothing is donned in a particular order; I grind coffee beans before I prepare the frozen juice). Although every day is different to some degree, I organize daily events around a number of these familiar, frequently practiced routines.

Engaging in routines is such a ubiquitous phenomenon that one might assume such engagement is functional for the completion of daily tasks.

Invoking the concept of an operant chain may provide a context for understanding the function of routines. Performing each step is discriminative for the next; to the extent that a chain is established, the completion of each step becomes a conditioned reinforcer for performance of that step because of its association with completion of the chain (terminal reinforcer). If daily routines operate as operant chains, then their function might be related to simplification and organization of daily responsibilities. To the extent that tasks that need to be accomplished can be organized into well practiced chains, time and effort are minimized.

For the purposes of this chapter, an important distinction among routines is warranted: some routines are very similar to behavior chains and do not require the presence of others; other routines are not so clearly prescribed and do depend on the presence and participation of communicative partners. These latter *interactive* routines are the focus of this section and because they require interaction between and among people, they are necessarily *communicative*. The former type of routine, that does not require the presence of others, can be transformed through varied sources of 'sabotage' into an interactive routine.

In the remainder of this section, literature pertaining to the application of routines to enhance the communicative functioning of learners with severe disabilities will be reviewed. This review will emphasize the conceptual underpinnings as well as the practical applications of interactive routines. Their implications for understanding the context of communication as well as potential avenues for communication assessment and intervention will be explored. Finally, we will delineate four bases on which routines can be distinguished that have implications for the assessment and teaching of communication skills to learners with severe disabilities.

Conceptual Perspectives and Practical Applications

In their discussion of the influence of routines on normal language development, Snyder-McLean et al. (1984) pointed to three relevant lines of inquiry. First, Ratner and Bruner (1978) hypothesized that play routines may encourage the acquisition of language because they are highly familiar, sequential, and predictable. These characteristics enable the young learner to assume roles that are clearly prescribed and to make responses that are appropriate in terms of turn-taking and content. Second, Piaget's constructs of assimilation and accommodation reflect a similar analysis – young children acquire new information (i.e., language) most readily in the context of familiar well established routines. Finally, routines may be an especially appropriate context for teaching the pragmatic properties of conversation (e.g., turn-taking, joint attention) because language is an act performed in a dynamic social context (Bruner, 1975; Mahoney, 1975). Familiar and predictable routines may provide the setting factors needed to acquire the pragmatic properties of language while simultaneously enabling attention to meaning (semantics) and grammar (syntax).

Snyder-McLean et al. (1984) argue that although the child development and child language literatures focus on young, normally developing children, the facilitative features of routines extend to older learners with more severe disabilities who are functioning at prelanguage and emerging language levels. They believe that the structure of routines provide a 'scaffold' that enables learners with restricted communicative repertoires to respond appropriately whereas other contexts may be too novel or too complex to occasion appropriate responding.

These authors have coined the name 'joint action routines' (JAR) to describe routines that involve interdependent actions between people. Eight elements are critical in defining a JAR:

1. an obvious unifying theme (e.g., snack routine)

2. joint focus and interaction – establish a reason to communicate

3. clearly delineated roles – each is definable and predictable

4. exchangeable roles – maximize the number of learning opportunities

5. a logical, nonarbitrary sequence – allows for predictability and simplifies task by narrowing response options

6. a predictable structure for turn-taking – clear expectations for when to wait and when to speak

7. planned repetition (both within and across days) – establishes role expectancy and sequence predictability

8. plan for controlled variation – elements above provide a predictable context into which novel elements can be introduced with success. According to Snyder-McLean et al. (1984), two overarching criteria are basic for successful application of JARs; they must facilitate communication and language development and they must be motivating (i.e., learners willingly engage in the JARs).

An issue that arises from this description of JARs is their degree of contrivance. To the extent that one needs to teach the routine to later exploit it for communicative purposes, its feasibility for learners with severe disabilities may be restricted to simple interactive routines. Exploiting already existing routines that meet many of the eight elements and the two criteria may be a fruitful approach.

Hall and Sundberg (1987) provide a very different theoretical rationale for the use of routines in teaching language to learners with severe disabilities. They relied on Skinner's (1957) analysis of verbal behavior to explain their teaching of mands (similar to requests). At least two types of manding instruction are represented in the literature. The first involves an already established reinforcer in whose presence requests are made. Examples of this type of training are included in studies using delayed prompting (Charlop, Schreibman, & Thibodeau, 1985; Halle, et al., 1979; Simic & Bucher, 1980) and incidental teaching (Hart & Risley, 1968, 1974, 1975, 1980).

In these studies, manding was freed from control by verbal discriminative stimuli such as 'What do you want?' It was, however, under the control of nonverbal discriminative stimuli (i.e., presence of reinforcing items or events). The second type of mand instruction depends neither on already established reinforcers nor on the presence of the to-be-requested item or event. Three studies are exemplary. First, Hall and Sundberg (1987) taught learners to complete short chains of behavior (routines) leading to reinforcers. These routines included, among others, making instant soup, opening a can of fruit, and operating a vending machine to obtain candy. Once the routines were acquired and practiced, needed items could be omitted from those presented (e.g., no spoon in the soup routine) to occasion requests by the participants. Two points are germane: one, the spoon in and of itself was not a reinforcing object, only in the context of soup-making did the spoon become a conditioned reinforcer; two, history with the soup-making routine provided a context within which missing items could be distinguished and their absence in the routine became discriminative for a request.

In the second example, Carr and Durand (1985) investigated communicative functions of excess behavior among learners labeled autistic. They manipulated the reinforcing value of a previously neutral stimulus in a way similar to Hall and Sundberg's manipulation of the spoon. By introducing difficult tasks to the learners, Carr and Durand enhanced the reinforcing value of the trainer as a source of assistance. Unlike the example of the spoon that followed a positive reinforcement paradigm, however, trainer assistance became a negative reinforcer because it allowed escape from an unpleasant situation (a difficult task).

In a third example, Sigafoos, Reichle, and Doss (in press) displayed food and beverage items on a table. For each, a utensil was required to access the item (e.g., soft drink bottle opener, juice straw). Displayed items were delivered contingent on a point response to a 'want' symbol. Accessing the displayed item rendered the required utensil as an effective reinforcer. Sigafoos, Doss, and Reichle (1989) exploited routines in a similar fashion to teach manding to three adults with severe disabilities.

The theoretical contribution of these works was captured by Michael (1982, 1988) who re-introduced and defined the concept of 'establishing operation' (Keller & Schoenfeld, 1950 coined the term). An establishing operation is similar to a setting factor (Kantor, 1959) or a setting event (Bijou & Baer, 1961; Wahler & Fox, 1981) in that it influences the probability of behavior, but is distinct from stimulus events that are simple, discrete, and immediately precede behavior. Setting events or establishing operations are more complex, more distant temporally, and either facilitate or inhibit the occurrence of subsequent stimulus-response relationships. Examples are deprivation, satiation, aversive conditions (that potentiate escape responses), and the presence or absence of certain events or objects. This concept that includes consideration of prior events in the analysis of behavior is central to a discussion of routines because it is a time-based concept (i.e., one whose definition depends on a sequence of temporally ordered events).

The applied relevance of considering setting events in our analysis of routines is that their manipulation facilitates the teaching of requesting *any* objects or actions; target requests do not need to specify reinforcers because the items requested can be embedded in a context of a reinforcing routine. 'With such procedures, the experimenter might not have to "capitalize on opportunities, when they arose" to train manding; these opportunities would be created' (Hall & Sundberg, 1987; p.44). In the three examples cited above, the spoon, trainer assistance, and the utensil were not reinforcing stimuli in an absolute sense; rather they were established as conditioned reinforcers because of their relationship to other events in the context of the routine. The potential for generating additional routines that establish objects or events as reinforcers for requesting or commenting is infinite.

From a similar theoretical perspective, Schussler and Spradlin (1990) conceptualized routines as crucial prerequisites for much of the spontaneous requesting that occurs in the absence of a referent. They argue that symbolic communication (i.e., speech, sign) is most relevant in those situations when the referent is absent; when present, one can simply gesture or retrieve it. The mechanism by which specific requests are occasioned (in the absence of their referent) is their historical relationship to particular contextual stimuli established in routines that are repeatedly practiced. Thus, when the contextual stimuli associated with the to-be-requested item are present, they cue the request.

Schussler and Spradlin (1990) provided three examples. The requester may have a history of requesting certain things from certain people (e.g., cookies from grandma); certain places or locales may enhance the probability of a particular class of requests (e.g., a hamburger might be requested in a restaurant, but not in an appliance store); and finally, certain materials or events may occasion requests for other items typically associated with them (e.g., people given bacon and toast may be more likely to request an egg than had they been given fruit and a pastry). The experiences that cluster within routines may be unique to an individual (when awakening in the morning, I put on my glasses and my watch before I get out of bed), or may be shared by a family (cookies from grandma), or by a culture (bacon and eggs for breakfast).

In their investigation, Schussler and Spradlin (1990) employed a snack routine to identify the variables that influenced 'spontaneous' requests. They examined requests for snack under three conditions by three adolescents who were mentally retarded. The three conditions included *all items visible* (all items and utensils were in sight), *nothing visible* (teacher and students were seated at table), and *one-item missing* (two of a set of three snack items were present).

Prior to beginning the study, a snack routine was established whereby a teacher and the three participants sat around a table. The teacher placed utensils in front of the students, then snack items were placed in the middle of the table in full view but out of reach of the students, and finally the teacher introduced a sequence of prompts to evoke requests. At each juncture described above, a delay was inserted to provide clear opportunities for the targeted response. In addition to assessing the influence of the three contextual variations, the effect of peer modeling was included in the analysis because the snack sessions were conducted with the group. To assess the influence of peer modeling, the one student who dominated (frequently this was the first student to request) was omitted from one third of the sessions.

The results revealed a variation among the contextual variables that controlled each participants' requests. One student requested snack items under audience control (i.e., he responded to the presence of the trainer within the snack context). Such requests, occurring in the presence of the audience but in the absence of the requested item, would seem to represent the purest form of 'spontaneous' language. For this student, *less spontaneous* language appeared to be controlled by the presence of the to-be-requested items and by other members of a food group. This latter type of stimulus control was established by presenting repeatedly the same three foods together in a group; one of three such groups were offered during any given snack. Control exerted by food groups was assessed by introducing two items to determine if the third member of the group (i.e., the missing item) would be requested.

The requests of a second participant appeared to be controlled predominantly by a peer's model or by a teacher prompt. For this student, the missing-item condition occasionally evoked a request. The majority of the third students' requests occurred after a peer's model, however when that peer was absent, the missing-item condition consistently occasioned requests. Schussler and Spradlin (1990) noted not only wide variation in stimulus control of requests across participants but also within a student over time (e.g., missing items came to control requests with greater frequency later in the study).

Goetz and her colleagues (Alwell, Hunt, Goetz, & Sailor, 1989; Goetz, Gee, & Sailor, 1985; Hunt, Goetz, Alwell, & Sailor, 1986) have explored the interruption of behavior chains as a strategy for teaching initial communication skills to learners with severe disabilities. Although the actual procedures used are very similar to Hall and Sundberg (1987), the theoretical underpinnings of the approach are quite different. Goetz et al. (1985) draw on two sources of literature pertaining to motivation to explain the effectiveness of the chain-interruption strategy. The first source suggests that responses that function as requests and produce the object or event specified (i.e., response specificity) are learned more rapidly than responses that function as labels and produce access to 'arbitrary' reinforcers. For example, a request for a book is acquired more quickly than the label 'book' when the request produces the book and a label produces an unrelated reinforcer. 'Evidently, teaching an instrumental response provided a motivational 'boost' to the learning process' (p.21).

The second literature source reveals that active, motoric interactions with objects or events associated with instruction may provide another type of motivational boost. For example, Koegel and Williams (1980) found that students acquired responses more quickly when they acted upon the instructional stimulus (e.g., when verbally cued, they picked up a book that exposed a reinforcer hidden beneath) than when they simply pointed to it (e.g., when verbally cued, they pointed to a book and then were handed the identical reinforcer). Both motivational hypotheses, response specificity and motor manipulation, are intuitively appealing and have face validity but the data supporting their efficacy are not yet compelling.

The findings of the studies by Goetz and her colleagues demonstrate the potential role of interactive routines for teaching communication skills to learners with severe disabilities. The authors suggest that a key to the success of the chain interruption strategy is that routines are *interrupted* while ongoing rather than at the beginning before the chain is initiated. They also discuss the merits of motivationally powerful single (vs massed) trials in terms of normalization and teaching in functional, age-appropriate, community-based contexts.

Using Routines for Assessment and Intervention

Routines may be exploited for purposes of assessment and intervention. For example, to assess various pragmatic functions used by learners with severe disabilities, investigators have created routines as the context for such assessments (e.g., Cirrin & Rowland, 1985; Halle, Chadsey-Rusch, Collet-Klingenberg, & Reinoehl, 1989; Snyder-McLean, McLean, & Etter, 1987). The distinction between assessment and intervention is blurred in these examples because intervention is determined by performance during assessment (i.e., those functions that are not in place are taught). If, however, the assessment is comprehensive, then teaching targets necessarily should be prioritized such that only a subset will constitute the focus of treatment at any one time.

Our discussion of intervention in the context of routines will center on strategies of environmental arrangement (Fey, 1986; Halle, 1984, 1988; Hart, 1985; Hart & Rogers-Warren, 1978). Ostrosky and Kaiser (1991) named and described seven strategies that are based on routine or scripted situations. They include: (a) interesting materials and activities, (b) materials in view but out of reach, (c) inadequate portions, (d) choice-making, (e) assistance, (f) sabotage, and (g) silly situations. We will discuss the stimulus control inherent in as well as the target form that is appropriate (obligatory) for these strategies.

Interesting materials and activities are prerequisite to any effort to set the occasion for language by arranging the environment. They create the motivation for and reinforcement of communicative acts. They do not, however, need to be based in the context of a routine to be discriminative for a communicative response. *In view but out of reach* is a strategy that assumes interesting materials and simply specifies the conditions under which the materials are made available. This strategy, however, presumes a history with the materials or there would be no basis for determining that they were interesting or 'reinforcing'. *In view but out of reach* could be exploited to occasion either requests (if the material or activity is familiar) or comments (if the material or activity is novel).

Inadequate portions again presumes that materials (e.g., blocks, crayons, food) are reinforcing and requires a history of experience with the items (perhaps with the exception of unconditioned reinforcers). That is, if a learner is never given the opportunity to play with more than one block at a time, then the provision of one block will not be discriminative for a request 'More'. If, however, the learner's history with blocks includes play with tens of blocks, the presentation of only one may enhance the probability of the target request. This latter situation might be conceptualized as sabotage that may occasion a protest or a comment.

Choice-making may be embedded in many on-going routines, but does not require a context of routine for its effectiveness. Occasions for *choice-making* are discriminative for requests. The success of such an occasion depends on the reinforcing properties of the items offered. An effective means of introducing choice might include the concept of establishing operations. That is, many items that do not possess reinforcing properties out of context can become reinforcers by making them necessary for the completion of a reinforcing routine (e.g., a spoon for eating hot cereal).

Another environmental strategy that might be considered in terms of establishing operations is *assistance*. This strategy depends on creating a situation in which assistance is needed to access a reinforcer. Because the request for assistance does not produce the reinforcer directly, but rather produces an action that allows direct access to the reinforcer, this set of circumstances defines establishing operation. Examples include asking for help to get into a swing to access a reinforcing motion or to open a tightly screwed lid to a jar of apple-butter that is a preferred snack food.

Sabotage may be the most frequently mentioned environmental strategy. Intentionally omitting needed items to complete a task or allowing only a tantalizing sample of a favorite activity (e.g., swinging) are examples of *sabotage*, but the essence of sabotage is tapped within frequently practiced everyday routines. By introducing unexpected change into highly consistent, rarely altered routines, communicative acts are prompted. Ostrosky and Kaiser (1991) suggest that this strategy requires problem-solving by the learner to determine what is missing or wrong and thus it may not be appropriate for those with more severe intellectual disabilities. To the extent that the routine is practiced daily and the steps occur in an unaltered sequence (little variation is tolerated in its execution), the strategy ought to be effective with learners of all levels. The three most probable outcomes of a successful *sabotage* are requests that enable the routine to be continued (e.g., for a missing item or for permission to complete a task), protests about the unexpected event, or comments that describe what was anticipated.

The final environmental strategy employed to create communicative opportunities is *silly situations*. Typically, environmental arrangements that violate expectations define this strategy. Examples include providing a child with an empty box of crayons (that were requested) or attempting to place an adult's shoe on a young child. *Silly situations* may produce either requests, protests, or comments with the latter being more probable. Clear expectations are a prerequisite to the success of this strategy. Learners must have expectations before they can be violated. Such expectations can be established only in the context of familiar routines. Thus, in the examples above, a history of frequent crayon play that is initiated by accessing a box of crayons and a history of daily assistance with putting on shoes must be assumed.

Three comments are warranted in summarizing the seven environmental strategies described and discussed by Ostrosky and Kaiser (1991). First, with perhaps the exception of *interesting materials*, the strategies depend on prior experiences with materials or activities that to varying extents define routines. *Inadequate portions, assistance, sabotage,* and *silly situations* require consistent and repeatedly practiced routines; whereas *in view out of reach* and *choice-making* place fewer demands on prior experience for their effect. Second, the strategies are not mutually exclusive. For example, *inadequate portions, assistance,* or *silly situations* may possess properties of *sabotage*. Third, the communicative functions that are occasioned by these seven strategies are restricted to requests, comments, and protests. Although these functions are the ones most frequently used by learners with severe disabilities, they are restrictive and diversity of communicative function and context ought to be goals.

Four Bases for Distinguishing Among Routines

To conclude this section, we have gleaned from the literature four bases on which routines may vary: (a) their relationship to verbal behavior; (b) level of contrivance; (c) level of demand for interactive responding; and (d) level of predictability. Each of these is described and their implications for communication instruction of learners with severe disabilities are elaborated.

Routines constitute an aggregate of stimuli that may control verbal behavior in varying relationships (Spradlin, personal communication, 1990) For example, by interrupting a known reinforcing routine, a *mand* or a request is made more probable. By introducing a departure from a known routine (e.g., after requesting juice, an empty cup is delivered), a *tact* or comment becomes more likely. In compliance training or instruction-following, the control exercised by the instruction might be enhanced if completing a well practiced routine constitutes compliance. Some of the stimulus features required to comply with the instructions include the stimulus control developed within the routine (i.e., each step functions as a conditioned reinforcer for the previous step and a discriminative stimulus for the next step). Thus, the control established by the instruction is combined with the stimuli controlling the motor responses of the routine.

One additional relationship between verbal behavior and routines is related to the *tact* relationship, but differs from the one described above – a routine, interactive or not, might function as a stimulus complex that enters into a conjoint relationship with a question like 'What did you do yesterday?' 'What are you doing?' or 'What will you do this evening?' The routine becomes a referent and in combination with the question sets the occasion for a *tact*.

A second basis on which routines may be distinguished is by *level of contrivance*. Routines are often described as natural or contrived. Such a dichotomy may be counterproductive unless a continuum is invoked in which *natural* and *contrived* define the two extremes. To the extent that the routine is contrived and therefore new, feasibility becomes an issue for learners with severe intellectual disabilities. Using naturalistic routines prevents unnecessary additional teaching (of the steps in the routine) and allows for repeated practice naturally: the routine is already part of the everyday environment. The type of contrived routine that involves pretend play and exchangeable roles (e.g., Culatta, 1984; Snyder-McLean et al. 1984) has been employed with learners who are functioning at higher levels.

Regardless of the level of contrivance, another basis on which a routine might be distinguished is the *level of demand for interactive responding*. For example, the interactive demands represented by a missing, but needed, object are less than those represented by a customer at a restaurant who needs to order a meal with a waiter. The former level of demand may be more appropriate when beginning communication intervention with learners who have severe disabilities. Chaining together communicative responses in social interaction becomes extremely complex very quickly because at each juncture (i.e., turn) more than one response must be acquired. Some of the stimuli that control responses in interaction are highly dependent on what was said previously by the communicative partner. Depending on the extent to which the partner's responses can be predicted, a few or many responses must be taught to anticipate the many potential responses of the communicative partner.

In the literature related to communication intervention with learners who have severe disabilities, the routines most often employed are characterized by a low level of demand. In fact, such routines typically are not interactive routines (e.g., making instant coffee or soup, accessing a soft drink from a vending machine, going out to recess); however, they are manipulated intentionally in such a way (e.g., sabotage, interrupting, blocking) as to require the mediation of another person.

Routines also may be examined in light of *predictability* produced when they are manipulated. The seven strategies delineated by Ostrosky and Kaiser (1991) can be divided into two categories: (a) those that produce requests for the anticipated next step, and (b) those that produce protests or comments because they violate the anticipated next step. Both possibilities depend on repeatedly practiced and consistently executed routines that produce expectations of what happens next. The distinction lies in the confirmation or disconfirmation of anticipated events. Examples illustrating each category are provided below.

In Hall and Sundberg (1987), making instant soup including use of a spoon was repeatedly practiced. When learners were instructed to make soup and the spoon was not available (as it had been in all previous executions of the routine), learners requested it. Similarly, Goetz et al. (1985) blocked a learner from pushing down the lever of a toaster in a well practiced toast-making routine and set the occasion for a request. In contrast to confirming expectations, we have used sabotage to occasion comments by placing a sponge in a MacDonald's hamburger styrofoam package or by substituting a plastic apple for a real apple (Halle et al., 1989). At home, the first author's 3-year-old twins have their own cups with Mickey Mouse on one and Minnie Mouse on the other. Whenever he accidently or intentionally offers the 'wrong' cup to them, they are quick to protest or comment about the mistake.

An aspect of the controlling stimuli for these requests and comments is a notable change in a familiar routine, either the omission of a needed item (blocking of a required event) or the violation of an anticipated event (receipt of personal cup). The former is likely to occasion requests while the latter is likely to produce protests or comments. These outcomes, however, are not totally predictable. The learner involved in making soup may *protest* or *comment* about the missing spoon or my twins might *request* their own cup. Particular environmental arrangements may render specific pragmatic functions more probable, but their probability is not entirely predictable.

That the seven strategies provide opportunities for only three pragmatic functions (request, protest, and comment) represents a limitation in terms of pragmatic functions sampled. For example, greetings, leave-taking, and functions related to interactive conversation are omitted. One reason for this omission may be that all seven strategies depend on materials and events that are interesting or reinforcing. The accessing of materials or events fulfills an instrumental function (Cirrin & Rowland, 1985; Goetz, Schuler & Sailor, 1981). Greetings and leave-taking are social occasions that depend on social consequences for their support. If the consequences for a response are not adequate to support the response, the conditions under which the response occurs will not acquire controlling properties. Thus, if a listener's attention is not reinforcing, then a greeting response acquired in the presence of that listener may not maintain without some additional and artificial reinforcement. The distinction between social and nonsocial reinforcers may have important implications for the acquisition of varying pragmatic functions by learners with severe disabil-ities.

Conclusion

Interactive routines have been touted as the fundamental context within which the earliest communicative acts occur. In recent years, this observation has not been overlooked by those working with learners who have severe communication deficits. Perhaps due to concerns about functional and gener-alized use of learners' communicative repertoires, researchers have adopted and adapted naturally occurring interactive routines as contexts for communication assessment and intervention. By acquiring communicative skills under condi-tions that naturally occur, learners' repertoires have a greater probability of coming under the control of 'relevant and appropriate' stimuli. Furthermore, the support or reinforcement for responses acquired in this way has a greater probability of emanating from naturally available stimuli, and thus response maintenance may be enhanced.

SUMMARY

As Yoder (1988) recently concluded, 'Without doubt the most pervasive prob-lem confronting the person with mental retardation lies in the area of communi-cation' (p.ix). As the severity of the intellectual disability increases, this conclusion assumes even greater relevance. Without communication skills, people are isolated from their social environment. The major means of affecting the behavior of those with whom one lives and works is compromised. The centrality of communication for learners with severe disabilities cannot be overstated.

Our past endeavors to teach communicative skills to this group have yielded only small gains; we know how to teach specific language forms but functional and generalized communication have eluded us. One explanation for this failure is related to the manner in which the social and physical environment are arranged. In our efforts to structure the learning environment to optimize the acquisition of communicative forms, we unintentionally have brought these forms under such narrow and restricted stimulus control that they are not produced in natural everyday settings that are at variance with settings we have contrived.

This explanation for past failures has produced a spate of research on language generalization. In this chapter, our approach to generalization focuses on stimulus control. What are the stimulus variables that currently set the occasion for communication? What stimuli ought to occasion communicative responses? And how can we bring the communicative repertoires of learners with severe disabilities under the control of these stimuli? We believe that the answers to these questions and others might be forthcoming if current technologies are applied strategically to the language arena.

Two promising instructional procedures, general case and interaction routines, based on the principle of stimulus control are described and elaborated. Although general case instruction has not yet been extended to the acquisition of language in an empirical way, this procedure is ripe for exploration. Such an extension would include the specification of the range of relevant stimulus and response variations within the instructional universe (e.g., teaching requests for help). This implies that the conditions under which requests for help occur, as well as the many equivalent forms of such requests, must be delineated. Then training and generalization examples are selected and sequenced. Finally, training examples are taught and generalization examples are assessed. A hallmark of general case instruction is the establishment of stimulus and response classes that approximate those that exist naturally.

The strategic deployment of naturally occurring routines can set the occasion for a variety of communicative behaviors. Furthermore, the multiple ways in which routines may be arranged and manipulated produce multiple possibilities for assessment and intervention. We have the potential to pinpoint specific functions of language (e.g., request, protest, comment) by manipulating routines in particular ways (e.g., sabotage, in view but out of reach).

From our perspective, the most exciting and promising aspect of these two procedures is that language is naturally acquired in the context of interaction routines and by means very similar to those at work in general case instruction. The acquisition of language among individuals who are nondisabled occurs so rapidly and so effortlessly that examination of the stimulus control established may not be possible. Perhaps we can observe this principle at work by studying it in the context of general case instruction and interaction routines with learners who have more severe intellectual disabilities. Clearly, the analysis of stimulus or contextual variables and their influence on the communicative competence of persons with severe disabilities appears to be a promising area for future research and practice.

Preparation of this chapter was supported, in part, by a grant from the US Department of Education (Project #H086P900240).

REFERENCES

Abelson, R.P. (1981). Psychological status of the script concept. *American Psychologist, 36,* 715–729.

Albin, R. W., & Horner, R. H. (1988). Generalization with precision. In R. H. Horner, G. Dunlap, & R. L. Koegel (Eds.), *Generalization and maintenance: Life-style changes in applied settings* (pp.99–120). Baltimore: Paul H. Brookes Publishing Co.

Alwell, M., Hunt, P., Goetz, L., & Sailor, W. (1989). Teaching generalized communicative behaviors within interrupted behavior chain contexts. *Journal of The Association for Persons with Severe Handicaps,* 14, 91–100.

Bates, E. (1976). *Language and context: The acquisition of pragmatics.* New York: Academic Press.

Becker, W. C., & Englemann, S. (1978). Systems for basic instruction: Theory and applications. In A. C. Catania & Brigham (Eds.), *Handbook of applied behavior analysis: Social and instructional processes* (pp.325–378). New York: Irvington Publishers.

Becker, W. C., Englemann, S., & Thomas, D. R. (1975). *Teaching 2: Cognitive learning and instruction.* Chicago: Science Research Associates.

Bijou, S. W., & Baer, D. M. (1961). *Child Development. Vol. I.* New York: Appleton-Century-Crofts.

Bricker, W. A., & Bricker, D. (1974). An early language training strategy. In R. L. Schiefelbusch & L. L. Lloyd (Eds.), *Language perspectives: Acquisition, retardation, and intervention* (pp.431–468). Baltimore: University Park Press.

Bronfenbrenner, U. (1977). Toward an experimental ecology of human development. *American Psychologist, 32,* 513–531.

Bruner, J. S. (1975). The ontgenesis of speech acts. *Journal of Child Language,* 2, 1–19.

Bryan, D. N., & Joyce, D. G. (1985). Language intervention with the severely handicapped: A decade of research. *The Journal of Special Education,* 19, 7–39.

Carr, E. G., & Kologinsky, E. (1983). Acquisition of sign language by autistic children II: Spontaneity and generalization effects. *Journal of Applied Behavior Analysis,* 16, 297–314.

Carr, E. G., & Durand, V. M. (1985). Reducing behavior problems through functional communication training. *Journal of Applied Behavior Analysis,* 18, 111–126.

Charlop, M. H., Schreibman, L., & Thibodeau, M. G. (1985). Increasing spontaneous verbal responding in autistic children using a time delay procedure. *Journal of Applied Behavior Analysis,* 18, 155–166.

Cirrin, F. M., & Rowland, C. M. (1985). Communicative assessment of nonverbal youths with severe/profound mental retardation. *Mental Retardation,* 23, 52–62.

Culatta, B. (1984). A discourse-based approach to training grammatical rules. *Seminars in Speech and Hearing,* 5, 253–263.

Day, H. M., & Horner, R. H. (1989). Building response classes: A comparison of two procedures for teaching generalized pairing to learners with severe disabilities. *Journal of Applied Behavior Analysis,* 22, 223–229.

Day, H. M., & Horner, R. H. (1986). Response variation and the generalization of a dressing skill: Comparison of single instance and general case instruction. *Applied Research in Mental Retardation,* 7, 189–202.

Dore, J. A. (1974). Pragmatic description of early language development. *Journal of Psycholinguistic Research,* 4, 343–350.

Engelmann, S., & Carnine, D. (1982). *Theory of instruction: Principles and applications.* New York: Irvington Publishers.

Fey, M. E. (1986). *Language intervention with young children.* Boston: Little, Brown & Co.

Goetz, L., Gee, K., & Sailor, W. (1985). Using a behavior chain interruption strategy to teach communication skills to students with severe disabilities. *Journal of The Association for Persons with Severe Handicaps, 10,* 21–31.

Goetz, L., & Sailor, W. (1988). New directions: Communication development in persons with severe disabilities. *Topics in Language Disorders, 8,* 41–54.

Goetz, L., Schuler, A. L., & Sailor, W. (1981). Functional competence as a factor in communication instruction. *Exceptional Education Quarterly, 2,* 51–61.

Gray, B., & Ryan, B. (1973). *A language program for the nonlanguage child.* Champaign, IL: Research Press.

Guess, D., Sailor, W., & Baer, D. (1978). Children with limited language. In R. L. Schiefelbusch (Ed.), *Language intervention strategies* (pp.101–143). Baltimore: University Park Press.

Hall, G., & Sundberg, M. (1987). Teaching mands by manipulating conditioned establishing operations. *The Analysis of Verbal Behavior, 5,* 41–53.

Halle, J. W. (1984). Arranging the natural environment to occasion language: Giving severely language-delayed children reasons to communicate. *Seminars in Speech and Language, 5,* 185–197.

Halle, J. W. (1988). Adopting the natural environment as the context of training. In S. N. Calculator & J. L. Bedrosian (Eds.), *Communication assessment and intervention for adults with mental retardation* (pp.155–185). Boston: Little, Brown & Co.

Halle, J. W., Chadsey-Rusch, J., Collet-Klingenberg, L., & Reinoehl, R. B. (1989). Communication Strategies Project (Annual Report). Champaign, IL: University of Illinois, Department of Special Education.

Halle, J. W., Marshall, A., & Spradlin, J. E. (1979). Time delay: A technique to increase language use and facilitate generalization in retarded children. *Journal of Applied Behavior Analysis, 12,* 431–439.

Haring, T. (1985). Teaching between-class generalization of toy play behavior to handicapped children. *Journal of Applied Behavior Analysis, 18,* 127–139.

Hart, B. (1981). Pragmatics: How language is used. *Analysis and Intervention in Developmental Disabilities, 1,* 299–313.

Hart, B. (1985). Naturalistic language training techniques. In S. F. Warren & A. K. Rogers-Warren (Eds.), *Teaching functional language* (pp.63–88). Baltimore: University Park Press.

Hart, B., & Risley, T. R. (1968). Establishing use of descriptive adjectives in the spontaneous speech of disadvantaged preschool children. *Journal of Applied Behavior Analysis, 1,* 109–120.

Hart, B., & Risley, T. R. (1974). Using preschool materials to modify the language of disadvantaged children. *Journal of Applied Behavior Analysis, 7,* 243–256.

Hart, B., & Risley, T. R. (1975). Incidental teaching of language in the preschool. *Journal of Applied Behavior Analysis, 8,* 411–420.

Hart, B., & Risley, T. R. (1980). In vivo language intervention: Unanticipated general effects. *Journal of Applied Behavior Analysis, 12,* 407–429.

Hart, B., & Rogers-Warren, A. K. (1978). A milieu approach to teaching language. In R. L. Schielbusch (Ed.), *Language intervention strategies.* Baltimore: University Park Press.

Horner, R. H., Albin, R. W., & Ralph, G. (1986). Generalization with precision: The role of negative teaching examples in the instruction of generalized grocery item selection. *Journal of The Association for Persons With Severe Handicaps, 11,* 300–308.

Horner, R. H., Bellamy, G. T., & Colvin, G. T. (1984). Responding in the presence of nontrained stimuli: Implications of generalization error patterns. *Journal of The Association for Persons With Severe Handicaps, 9,* 287–295.

Horner, R. H., & Billingsley, F. F. (1988). The effect of competing behavior on the generalization and maintenance of adaptive behavior in applied settings. In R. H. Horner, G. Dunlap & R. L. Koegel (Eds.), *Generalization and maintenance: Lifestyle changes in applied settings* (pp.197–220). Baltimore: Paul H. Brookes Publishing.

Horner, R. H., & Budd, C. M. (1985). Teaching manual sign language to a nonverbal student: Generalization of sign use and collateral reduction of maladaptive behavior. *Education and Training for the Mentally Retarded, 20,* 39–47.

Horner, R. H., Jones, D., & Williams, J. A. (1985). A functional approach to teaching generalized street crossing. *Journal of The Association for Persons With Severe Handicaps, 10,* 71–78.

Horner, R. H., McDonnell, J. J., & Bellamy, G. T. (1986). Teaching generalized skills: General-case instruction in simulation and community settings. In R. H. Horner, L. H. Meyer, & H. D. B. Fredericks (Eds.), *Education of learners with severe handicaps:* Exemplory service strategies (pp.289–315). Baltimore: Paul H. Brookes Publishing Co.

Horner, R. H., Sprague, J., O'Brien, M., & Heathfield, L. T. (1990). The role of response efficiency in the reduction of problem behaviors through functional equivalence training: A case study. *Journal of The Association for Persons with Severe Handicaps, 15,* 91–97.

Horner, R. H., Sprague, J., & Wilcox, B. (1982). General case programming for community activities. In B. Wilcox & G. T. Bellamy. *Design of high school programs for severely handicapped students* (pp.61–98). Baltimore: Paul H. Brookes Publishing Co.

Horner, R. H., Williams, J. A., & Stevely, J. D. (1987). Acquisition of generalized telephone use by students with moderate and severe disabilities. *Research in Developmental Disabilities, 8,* 229–247.

Hunt, P., Goetz, L., Alwell, M., & Sailor, W. (1986). Using an interrupted behavior chain strategy to teach generalized communication responses. *Journal of The Association for Persons with Severe Handicaps, 11,* 196–204.

Hymes, D. H. (1972). On communicative competence. In J. B. Pride, & J. Holmes (Eds.), *Sociolinguistics* (pp.269–293). Harmondsworth, UK: Penguin Books.

Kaiser, A. P., & Warren, S. F. (1988). Pragmatics and generalization. In R. L. Schiefelbusch & L. L. Lyod (Eds.), *Language perspectives: Acquisition, retardation, and intervention* (2nd ed.), (pp.393–442). Austin, TX: Pro-Ed.

Kantor, J. R. (1959). *Interbehavioral psychology.* Chicago: Principia Press.

Keller, F. S., & Schoenfeld, W. N. (1950). *Principles of psychology.* New York: Appleton-Century-Crofts.

Kent, L. (1974). *Language acquisition program for the retarded or multiply impaired.* Champaign, IL: Research Press.

Koegel, R. L., & Williams, J. (1980). Direct versus indirect response-reinforcer relationships in teaching autistic children. *Journal of Abnormal Child Psychology, 4,* 536–547.

Keogh, W. J., & Reichle, J. (1985). Communication intervention for the 'Difficult-to-Teach' severely handicapped. In S. F. Warren & A. K. Rogers-Warren (Eds.), *Teaching functional language,* (pp.157–194). Baltimore, MD: University Park Press.

Mahoney, G. (1975). An ethological approach to delayed language acquisition. *American Journal of Mental Deficiency, 80,* 139–148.

McCormick, L., & Schiefelbusch, R. L. (1984). An introduction to language intervention. In L. McCormick & R. Schiefelbusch (Eds.), *Early language intervention* (pp.2–33). Columbus: Charles E. Merrill.

McFall, R. M. (1982). A review and reformulation of the concept of social skills. *Behavioral Assessment, 4,* 1–33.

Michael, J. (1982). Distinguishing between discriminative and motivational functions of stimuli. *Journal of The Experimental Analysis of Behavior, 37,* 149–155.

Michael, J. (1988). Establishing operations and the mand. *The Analysis of Verbal Behavior, 6,* 3–9.

Morris, E. K., & Midgley, B. D. (1990). Some historical and conceptual foundations of ecobehavioral analysis. In S. R. Schroeder (Ed.), Ecobehavioral analysis and developmental disabilities: The twenty-first century (pp.1–32). New York: Springer-Verlag.

O'Neill, R. E., Horner, R. H., Albin, R. W., Storey, K., & Sprague, J. (1990). *Functional analysis: A practical assessment guide.* Sycamore, IL: Sycamore Publishing.

Ostrosky, M. M., & Kaiser, A. P. (1990). Arranging preschool classroom environments to promote communication. *Teaching Exceptional Children 23* (4), 6–10.

Pancsofar, E. L., & Bates, P. (1985). The impact of the acquisition of successive exemplars on generalization. *Journal of The Association for Persons With Severe Handicaps, 10,* 3–11.

Peck, C. A. (1984). *Student control in classrooms for children with severe handicaps: Effects on student behavior and perceived social climate.* Unpublished doctoral dissertation, University of California, Santa Barbara.

Peck, C. A. (1989). Assessment of social communicative competence: Evaluating environments. *Seminars in Speech and Language, 10,* 1–15.

Ratner, N., & Bruner, J. (1978). Games, social exchange and the acquisition of language. *Journal of Child Language, 5,* 391–401.

Reichle, J., Barrett, C., Tetlie, R., & McQuarter, R. (1987). Teaching direct select color encoding to an adolescent with multiple handicaps. *Augmentive and Alternative Communication, 3,* 3–11.

Reichle, J., Rogers, N., & Barrett, C. (1984). Establishing pragmatic discriminations among the communicative functions of requesting, rejecting, and commenting in a severely retarded adolescent. *Journal of The Association for Persons With Severe Handicaps, 9,* 31–36.

Reichle, J., & Keogh, W. J. (1985). Communication intervention: A selective review of what, when, and how to teach. In S. F. Warren & A. K. Rogers-Warren (Eds.), *Teaching functional language* (pp.25–59). Baltimore: University Park Press.

Rogers-Warren, A. K. & Warren, S. F. (1977). *Ecological perspectives in behavior analysis.* Baltimore: University Park Press.

Schank, R. C., & Abelson, R. P. (1977). *Scripts, plans, goals, and understanding.* Hillsdale, NJ: Erlbaum.

Schussler, N., & Spradlin, J. E. (1990). *Analysis of stimuli controlling the requests of severely retarded adolescents during snack periods.* Manuscript submitted for publication.

Searle, J. (1969). *Speech acts: An essay in the philosophy of language.* London: Cambridge University Press.

Sigafoos, J., Doss, S., & Reichle, J. (1989). Developing mand and tact repertoires in persons with severe developmental disabilities using graphic symbols. *Research in Developmental Disabilities, 10,* 183–200.

Sigafoos, J., Reichle, J., & Doss, S. (in press). Spontaneous transfer of stimulus control from tact to mand contingencies. *Research in Developmental Disabilities.*

Simic, J., & Bucher, B. (1980). Development of spontaneous manding in language deficient children. *Journal of Applied Behavior Analysis, 13,* 523–528.

Skinner, B. F. (1953). *Science and human behavior.* New York: Macmillan.

Skinner, B. F. (1957). *Verbal behavior.* New York: Appleton-Century-Crofts.

Snell, M. E. (1988). *Systematic instruction of persons with severe handicaps.* Columbus: Charles E. Merrill.

Snyder-McLean, L., McLean, R. N., & Etter, R. (1987). *A comparison of three sources of communication data.* Workshop presented at the annual meeting of The Association for Persons with Severe Handicaps.

Snyder-McLean, L., Solomonson, B., McLean, J., & Sack, S. (1984). Structuring joint action routines: A strategy for facilitating communication and language development in the classroom. *Seminars in Speech and Language, 5,* 213–228.

Sprague, J. R., & Horner, R. H. (1984). The effects of single instance, multiple instance and general case training on generalized vending machine use by moderately and severely handicapped students. *Journal of Applied Behavior Analysis, 17,* 273–278.

Stremel, K., & Waryas, C. (1974). A behavioral-psycholinguistic approach to language training. In L. McReynolds (Ed.), *Developing Systematic Procedures for Training Children's Language. ASHA monograph, 18,* 96–130.

Twardosz, S. (1984). Environmental organization: The physical, social, and programmatic context of behavior. In M. Hersen, R. M. Eisler, and P. M. Miller (Eds.) *Progress in behavior modification.* New York: Academic Press.

Wahler, R. G., & Fox, J. J. (1981). Setting events in applied behavior analysis: Toward a conceptual and methodological expansion. *Journal of Applied Behavior Analysis, 14,* 327–338.

Warren, S. F., Baxter, D. K., Anderson, S. R., Marshall, A. & Baer, D. M. (1981). Generalization of question-asking by severely retarded individuals. *Journal of The Association for Persons with Severe Handicaps, 6,* 15–22.

Warren, S. F., & Rogers-Warren, A. K. (1985). *Teaching functional language.* Baltimore, MD: University Park Press.

Weld, E. M., & Evans, I. M. (1990). Effects of part versus whole instructional strategies on skill acquisition and excess behavior. American Journal on Mental Retardation, 94, 377–386.

Yoder, D. (1988). Forward. In S. N. Calculator & J. L. Bedrosian (Eds.), *Communication assessment and intervention for adults with mental retardation.* Boston: Little, Brown & Co.

COMMENTARY:
POLICY AND PROCEDURE,
AS ALWAYS

Donald M. Baer

What are the most important issues for instructional research relevant to cases of severe disability? These timely, exceptionally competent four chapters in Part II offer the two eternally correct answers: policy and procedure. It is policy to decide what we will teach our students with severe mental retardation, and why, and to acknowledge that we must also teach our society to support that policy; it is effective procedure that will make those decisions real rather than idle verbal behavior. Interestingly, one class of policy decisions requires two types of procedures: the procedures that teach students the skills targeted by our policy, and the procedures that teach society to implement that policy everywhere.

These have always been the guiding issues of any research field that was not only applicable but also was about application. They are interactive issues, of course: without effective procedure for teaching its target skills, policy is likely to reflect only what is possible, or what its audience can be made to accept as possible. What an audience will accept is in turn determined in part by their knowledge of the current possibilities for teaching target skills. Given newly effective procedure that becomes known as effective, policy may expand to fill the potential suddenly revealed – or constrict to avoid the potential suddenly revealed. An expanded policy is likely to stimulate the development of even more new teaching procedure to serve its target skills. But whether policy expands or constricts will depend less on the new procedures for teaching target skills than on the procedures for teaching a society whether or not to espouse, fund, and implement a new policy. Thus, policy and procedure should never be discussed separately – except, of course, by those who have no intentions of improving either of them.

These four chapters are about some newly effective procedures for teaching any policy's target skills; some of those procedures are in hand, and more are in reach. Some of these four chapters are also about specific policies for which some of these procedures are especially useful. None of them is about newly effective procedures for teaching society to expand or constrict policy.

Thus, some of these authors are dreaming beyond the present technology, and perhaps beyond the present politics, aiming with great integrity at either the target skills or the stimulus controls they suppose necessary for a policy of broader integration – target skills and controls apparently not achieved by the present technology. Sometimes they argue that the future is being delayed by insufficient development of the present technology, sometimes by overdependence on it. Whether this delay is massive or slight is also unsettled: Halle, Chadsey-Rusch, and Collet-Klingenberg assert that 'Our past endeavors to teach communication skills to this group have yielded only small gains'; Sigafoos and Reichle argue that those same efforts '...have met with tremendous success over the past 25 years'. Yet both teams have the same complaint about what has not been achieved: Their problem is not the inability to teach the necessary target skills, but rather the failure to give those skills enough of the proper stimulus controls.

Indeed, stimulus control – which is perhaps only a more task-analytic way of labelling the key problem of the past two decades, generalization – seems to be the common problem under attack in all four chapters:

(1) Bambara and Warren seem only to be rescuing the reputation of massed-trials technique from its connotations of regimentation, artificiality, and restriction. True, those connotations are out of character for modern approaches driven by the logic of integration. The Bambara and Warren chapter successfully puts connotation in its place, which is with things like hem lines, tie widths, and whether or not shoe laces are tied – pseudo-policies that change not one other thing in the world. The functional point is that massed trials, like distributed trials, teach; therefore, they can teach the target skills seen as essential to integration, despite those (trivial) connotations; and for some of those skills, some of the time, they will in fact be the technique of choice.

Asserting that, which is clear from the literature and some apolitical, incisive, calm logic, is an excellent service, but it is the smaller service of their chapter. Its larger service is to begin sketching the proper stimulus controls over a teacher's behavior: not *whether*, but at least five categories of contextual controls that determine *when* to use massed and when to use distributed trials – and when to use a combination of both. Therein lies the functional reality of the issue, and the more effective service of policy – in their case, any policy.

(2) Haring is pursuing a better task analysis of the social skills that will integrate those with severe handicaps into the mainstream. He may indeed need a better task analysis of that outcome; as he writes, 'A major weakness in this literature is the lack of demonstrated relationships between the acquisition of specific skills and the attainment of the larger objectives for the training of these skills; that is, social acceptance'. On the other hand, Haring may need not a better set of target skills but a better set of stimulus controls over the currently targeted skills. Haring is wise to question them, but these skills may not be the wrong ones. Their lack may be only that they are not practiced when and where they would achieve enough real-life integration to be called 'social acceptance'. That is a much larger world than social-skill research settings have encompassed so far. Then we might restate the problem: to add to the current stimulus controls over those skills the stimuli of that larger real world.

Allied with that, Haring notes that students with severe disabilities constitute the wrong stimulus controls for the behavior of their mainstream peers, who, without steady prompting or extrinsic reinforcement, ignore students with severe disabilities and form social groups only among themselves. Haring declares a small timely policy around this issue: We have gone far enough in changing the students with severe disabilities so as to make them attractive to their mainstream peers; now we shall let them be what they are (after our social-skills training programs, which may improve as a result of Haring's argument), and look into changing the mainstream peers, so that the stimuli their disabled peers offer them control not their avoidance but their approach, with or without adult prompting. It is characteristic of a pragmatic stimulus-control approach to nominate the stimulus controls of *both* sides of an interaction for potential modification. (If it is not, then Haring shows us that it ought to be.)

(3) and (4) Halle, Chadsey-Rusch, and Collet-Klingenberg, as well as Sigafoos and Reichle, want communication skills to have the kind of spontaneity noted first in most dictionaries: communication arising from natural causes. (They do not want any of the other usual meanings: not impulsively sudden communications, nor communications arising only from internal sources, nor communications uncultivated by us, the audience. *Those* kinds of communication can get one institutionalized.) Their underlying argument seems to be that when communication is spontaneous in that one sense, developmental delay is less obvious, and integration goes better. Both teams explicitly and correctly analyse that as a problem in stimulus control, but unfortunately as a negatively defined one. They do not want communication skills to be controlled only by physical guidance, models, questions, mands, and the presence of the referents of communication; they want something more. To the extent that the 'something more' is not well defined in their chapters, spontaneous communication is defined only negatively. However, they do characterize it as 'natural', as what

the rest of us do, and that is enough of a challenge for researchers to go to work on the problem.

Thus, as a first tactic, we must become more analytic about those additional stimulus controls. We shall have to venture much further into a behavioral linguistics than we have so far ventured. Sigafoos and Reichle have begun the relevant literature survey, thus projecting the necessary future work. They were wise to cite Skinner's *Verbal Behavior* (1957). We will need a behavioral linguistics, because a nonbehavioral one is not likely to nominate teachable targets, and that would preclude an experimental validation of the numerous hypotheses that will be generated.

This kind of analysis is crucial, because a teaching program driven only by the need to program more stimulus controls than physical guidance, models, questions, mands, and the presence of the referent has an excellent chance of bringing communication skills under the control of events that are sometimes bizarre, sometimes wrong. For example: I once heard a beloved, very old man break a long silence while being driven through a new city's downtown; he said, 'They put those buttons down and leave them there'. My immediate reaction was bafflement; my second was heartbreak over this presumed first bit of senility. Fortunately, my third reaction was to look for a stimulus control, and find it in the just-passed lines of regularly spaced circular discs that city affixed to its streets as turn-lane markers at intersections – a new practice to him. Suddenly his comment was completely reasonable. Buttons indeed – I had no better term for them.

His utterance certainly met the analytic criteria for relative spontaneity these teams are recommending; but the probability that his audience would not understand why it occurred shows us that a prior analysis of conventional contextual control is crucial – as these teams recommend. When speaker and listener do not fully share context, some communications will be bizarre until they are explained or reclassified as poetry. If language skills are deficient, as is likely in those with severe disabilities, explanation skills may not be adequate, and we probably will not assume poetry. Indeed, in their case, if we are not very careful in extending stimulus control over communication from times when we know that we are correct to times when we can hardly be sure that we are, we risk creating stimulus controls that in the future we may never appreciate as such: We will not understand the explanation if it is given. Inevitably, we shall have to term the result bizarre. If that happens often, we will not have served our students well.

Meanwhile, we might well remember that an extraordinary amount of conventional, everyday mainstream language is question-driven, mand-driven, referent-driven, and echoic. It is not thereby wrong, deviant, stigmatizing, or isolating. In fact, it is quite wonderful, given the language capabilities of students with severe disabilities *prior* to our best language programming. (I recently listened to two people in an elevator discussing their mutual housekeeper: 1:

'She's wonderful!' 2: 'Yes, wonderful!' 1: 'Umm-hmm, wonderful'. 2: 'Yes, so good!' 1: 'So good! A wonderful woman!' 2: 'Don't you just love her?' 1: 'Yes, just love her!'. That is upper-middle-class communication in at least one region of this society, and it is hugely echoic. You can substitute for the housekeeper in that script the art museum's latest show, the President's latest speech, or one of their children's latest achievements at school, and have conventional mainstream communication each time, testifying respectively to high culture, political awareness, and family spirit. How much better than that are those with severe disabilities supposed to achieve, and how often?)

Perhaps one other consideration should be noted about the generalization of language skills to their desirable stimulus controls. Some years ago, I asked my new postdoctoral fellow, Ann Kaiser, to observe the residents of a state retardation institution in which the Guess-Sailor-Baer language-training program had just seen considerable application. My question was, what skills taught by the program were in frequent use among the residents tutored in it, and what skills taught by the program were rarely or never used? The answer might inform the design of a shorter yet more functional successor program.

Unhappily, Kaiser's fastidiously empirical answer was that virtually none of the programmed skills was in use by those residents. But she also offered a stimulus-control analysis of that lack: she remarked how thoroughly the institution environment made those residents' new language skills nonfunctional.

Years of mutual experience prior to the residents' language-training had taught the staff that the residents had no language, and had also taught them what the residents wanted, and when; thus many of those things were provided, benevolently, without request or comment, and worse yet, almost always *just prior* to the moment when a request or comment might well occur. On the other hand, many other things that the residents might want were never available, requested or not. And many other desirable things were thoughtfully provided several times every day, but in a rigid schedule absolutely resistant to change, no matter who asked (including the Superintendent). Perhaps our language-teaching program was a powerful one, she remarked, but the institution was running a much more powerful, much more comprehensive, 24-hour-per-day program with truly powerful reinforcers, aimed homogeneously most often at pre-empting, and next most often at extinguishing, new-language use.

Perhaps it is premature to conclude that such programs are characterized by a failure of generalization. Consider instead an anecdote from that program, and a formal study following from that anecdote. The anecdote: Years after the language-training program had ended at that institution, with its graduates silent, a staff member who always brought his lunch to work in a small paper bag arrived one day with a very large paper bag. When he had prepared lunch that morning, the only bag he could find was the largest size of grocery sack. So he walked to his office through an institution ward that morning, as always, but this time with a hugely oversized lunch bag, and heard from several language-program graduates in that ward one of their program's items: 'What's that?' they said, pointing to his sack – a perfect generalization from their years-earlier training, and also a response that no one had heard any of them utter for years. There had been nothing worthy of it for years.

A subsequent formal study (Warren, Baxter, Anderson, Marshall, & Baer, 1981) showed more of the same phenomena. The point is not that the language-training program had not produced remarkably durable results in at least some of its students; it had. The point is that their subsequent environment offered them no occasion for using those skills – except by rare accident. That is not properly labelled a failure of generalization; that is properly labelled counter-control. Generalization was never assessed; in the teeth of powerful counter-control, it hardly can be.

Thus we may well ask how often the literature is describing a failure of generalization, i.e., of extending stimulus control to where it ought to be, and how often a success of counter-control, i.e., of wiping out that extension of stimulus control as soon as it occurs. The counter-control is not Machiavellian, rebellious, or malicious counter-control, of course; it is the most natural of benevolent caretakings. (We may even consider it spontaneous.) Then we may re-examine the interactive routines and scripts described by Halle, Chadsey-Rusch, and Collet-Klingenberg, and by Sigafoos and Reichle. Very likely they are indeed good teaching techniques, and perhaps they are uniquely good, exactly because they incorporate examples of the kinds of stimulus controls desired for future use of the language skills being programmed. A subtly different alternative would be to see them as counter-control to the counter-control just described – as finally introducing into a blandly need-satisfying yet quite unmodifiable non-language routine an event that, quite the opposite, *requires* language to let the chain proceed and the reinforcer be acquired.

If only the institution would have not served meals, not scheduled free-time activities, and not made materials available *until the residents asked for them,* perhaps we would never have seen a failure of generalization in those early language-training programs. If that is correct, then even these ways of improving the program will not improve the program, in that they will not improve the program's long-term results. If that is correct, there is no serious flaw in the programs, only (only!) in the post-program environments. Improve *them.* (That will be truly difficult.) If *they* were improved, you would not need to teach by breaking chains in interactive routines that would continue only if the correct language skills were used. Indeed, if you need to teach in such routines, that probably signifies mainly that the post-program and extra-program environment has not been improved at all, and is still up to its old generalization-destructive benevolence of not requiring its beneficiaries to speak to it. That is, just as fast as you make its stimuli into controls for new language skills, it re-makes them into controls for nonlanguage. You are working briefly and indirectly; it is working all the rest of the time, and directly. If so, it will win. It uses the same techniques that you do, but better than you can.

Perhaps we know more about stimulus control than we know. What we may not know nearly so well is how to move post-training environments from their supposed benevolences to true benevolences. We probably should never suppose that we can teach so well in our brief training sessions (even with interactive routines) or that the indirect effects of that teaching will survive direct, massive, powerful counter-control everywhere and all the time outside of that teaching. Put the contest that way, and any behavior modifier will acknowledge defeat in advance.

So much for procedure. But since procedure and policy always interact and should never be discussed separately, then consider a final argument about policy. At least three of these chapters show a firm commitment to a common policy, that of full integration of students with severe disabilities into the same society in which the rest of us live. Haring makes clear that, at least for him, this is not a policy of gradualism – of incrementally fitting students with severe disabilities for correspondingly incremental integration. He prescribes instead a policy of immediate and full immersion into society of all with severe handicaps. That raises with corresponding immediacy the classic issue of policy evaluation.

Policy is evaluated in any or all of three ways: religio-politically, by fiat; morally, by careful derivation from undoubtable premises; and empirically, by measuring its consequences to see if we (the we who can decide) like it better than what will happen otherwise. Thus, (1) we can respond to Matthew (25:40) as religious instruction, learning there that how we treat 'the least of these my brethren' shows our respect for our god, note that in the past those with disabilities have been considered the least of us, and see that we are required to treat them instead with the same respect that we accord our god. Alternatively, but similarly, we can note that politics has produced a Public Law 94–142 in the United States and two amendments, which legally require a far less thorough but conceptually related pattern of behavior. In either case, we are supposed to proceed accordingly even if we do not like all the consequences; these policies either never did or no longer require evaluation. (2) We can affirm our moral preference for the principles of equal opportunity under the law for our society, see that severe disability ought not and does not disbar any of us from membership in that society, and conclude that to the extent that we have control over opportunities, we must provide all of us with equal access to them, thereby not ignoring disability but instead compensating for it in ways that functionally equalize opportunity despite handicap. If there is anything to evaluate in this policy, it is only how carefully, thoroughly, and logically we have analyzed how to equalize opportunity. (3) We can assume that integration is an option, if we do not subscribe that thoroughly to the New Testament or to the moral premise of equal opportunity, and because PL 94–142 and its amendments can always be repealed by political process. Then we can ask if we like the consequences of integration better than what would happen otherwise.

To ask that is a classic research problem: Because we do not have the resources to measure every differential consequence of a policy, we necessarily measure only a sample of them, and in only a sample of the policy's participants. How we choose the components of those two samples can powerfully control the evaluation that results. Personal choices lead to personal evaluations, political choices to political evaluations, conventional choices to conventional evaluations, and randomly sampled choices to arbitrary evaluations. Perhaps only repeated, ever-varying choices, done in large-scale samplings driven by a variety of logics about the dimensions relevant for sampling, and done over many years, can finally be taken together as a totality (no doubt by someone writing a review chapter), and can offer an evaluation with some generality, durability, and objectivity (should that ever be wanted).

These four chapters seem problematic in these terms. Some of them, sometimes, are written as if integration is an unquestionably good policy; while they do not subscribe explicitly to the first or second case above, neither do they suggest criteria for evaluating whether integration is good or bad. Instead, they evaluate *procedure* by asking how well it contributes to integration. But sometimes these chapters are written as if integration belonged to the third case above, and ought to be evaluated as good or bad by measuring its consequences. Haring is the most explicit in opening this third case for discussion, by suggesting some ultimately specifiable and measureable consequences of integration, and recommending their future study. Yet, apparently, he has not decided how he will proceed himself. But he does us all a service by invoking the question, even if only indirectly.

It is unfinished business to operate expensive, extensive research programs aimed at a goal that itself has either not been thought through, or to which commitment, and the process behind that commitment, has not been made explicit. Nothing in this point is designed to favor the first, second, or third of the cases sketched above. Its entire function is only to ask for explicit choice among them, and, more important, the rationales for that choice, so that the audience may choose also, and choose better than they would without that discussion before them. It is not that one choice is correct; it is that failure to consider the choice, merely implicit choice, and choice lacking an examinable rationale are incorrect for people designing procedure, policy, or research into their interaction.

Policy and procedure – as always.

REFERENCES

Skinner, B. F. (1957). *Verbal behavior.* New York: Appleton-Century-Crofts.

Warren, S. F., Baxter, D. K., Anderson, S. R., Marshall, A., & Baer, D. M. (1981). Generalization of question-asking by severely retraded individuals. *Journal of the Association for Persons with Severe Handicaps, 6,* 15–22.

SUBJECT INDEX

NAME INDEX

285

Howell *103*
Hoyson, M. 138, 148, 151
Hubbell, R.D. 192, 193, 202
Hudson, C. 175, 193, 199, 204
Hudson, P. 31
Hughes, C. 31, 137
Hughes, J.N. 100
Hughes, L.A. 144, 148
Hulse, S.H. 167
Hunt, P. 146, 165, *208*, 209, 255
Hutten, L.R. 49, 50
Hymes, D.H. 242

Ivancic, M.T. 175
Iwata, B. 40, 171, 175

Jackson, D.A. and N.F. 83, 84, 87, 89
Jackson, R.L. 145, 196
James, S.D. 137, 148
Jamieson, B. 138, 148, 151
Jason, L.A. 99
Jastak, F. and S. 52
Jaquish, C. 77, 80
Jensen, A. 118
Jensen, W.R. 79, 80, 85, 87, 89
Johnson 28, 30
Johnson 28
Johnson, D.W. 124
Johnson, M.R. *103*
Johnson, G.O. 132
Johnson, R.W. 124
Johnson, S.M. 79
Johnston, M.B. *103*, 108
Jones, D. 240
Jones, R.T. 110
Joyce, B. 16, 44
Joyce, D.G. 249
Judd, W.A. 59
Julyan, C.L. 119
Jurica, J. 53

Kaiser, A. 2, 145, 171, 183, 242, 244, 256, 257, 258, 260, 273
Kameenui, E. 13
Kantor, J.R. 253

Karlsen, B. 52
Karweit, N. 26
Kaskowitz, D. 12
Kauffmann, J.M. 99, 104
Kazdin, A.E. 55, 110, 135
Keetz, A. 2
Kehle, T.J. 74
Kelleher, R.T. 209
Keller, C.E. 107
Keller, F.S. 253
Kelly, A.C. 59
Kelly, W.J. 146
Kennedy, C.H. 134, 155
Kent, L. 191, 195, 222, 234
Kent-Udolf, L. 221
Keogh, B.K. 6
Keogh, D.A. *103*
Keogh, W.A. 166, 175, 176, 177, 191, 234, 242
Kerr, M.M. 80, 87, 89, 148
Kleefeld, J. 90
Klein, P. 82
Klein, R.D. *103*, 105
Knapczyk, D.R. *103*, 107
Koegel, L.K. 133, 149, 150, 171, 179, 182, 193
Koegel, R.L.
    chapter 7 133, 139, 149, 150
    chapter 8 166, 170, 171, 179, 181, 182, 183
    chapter 9 192, 193, 212
    chapter 10 256
Kohler, F.W. 26
Kologinsky, D. 192, 193, 198, 202, 203, 205, 206, *208*, 211, 214
Kologinsky, E. 212, 234
Komisar, S. 176
Konke, J.L. 175
Korinek, L. 72
Kosberg, B. 50, 51-2, 54, 55, 56, 57
Kosiewicz, M.M. 106
Krantz, P.J. 200
Kulgen 133
Kyle, W.C. 122

LaCampagne 199, 204
Lacy, L. 170
LaGreca, A. 87

Laitinen, R.E. 152
Lalli, J. 176
Lamarre, J. 214
Lancioni, G.E. 137, 148
Landrum, T.J. 101, 120
Langone, J. 81
Lapenta-Neudeck, R. 193, 199, 204
Larsen, S. 27
Leary, C. 158
LeBlanc, J. 212
Ledwidge, B. 100
Lee, J. 20
Lee, M. 146, 154
Lee, V.L. 202, 213
Lees, C. 106
Lennenberg, E.H. 192, 213
Lenz, B.K. 86
Leon, J.A. *103*, 107, 108, 111
Levin, J. 39
Levine, D.U. 60
Levitan, G.W. 76
Liberty, K. 89, 150, 179
Lieber, J. 58
Light, R.J. 51
Lindamood, L. 219
Lindeman, D. 137, 147
Linden, B.E. 77
Lindsley, O.R. 100
Lipinski, D.P. *103*, 105
Livingston, G. *103*, 107
Lloyd, J. 60, 101, 104, 107, 120, 121
Long, J.S. 192, 193
Lovaas, O.I. 191, 192, 193, 194, 195, 212, 220, 222
Lovinger, L. 135, 137, 145, 152, 200
Lovitt, T.C. 60, 109
Luciano, M.C. 215, 220, 221
Luebke, J. 75
Luftig, R.L. 74, 78

MacDonald, J.D. 191, 193
MacMillan, D.L. 72, 74, 77, 132, 155
Madden, N. 26
Madigan, K. 199, 204